EMOTIONAL INTELLIGENCE, OCCUPATIONAL STRESS AND JOB PERFORMANCE OF TEACHERS

EMOTIONAL INTELLIGENCE OCCUPATIONAL STRESS AND JOB PERFORMANCE OF TEACHERS

By

R.Vijaya Anuradha

Research Scholar

Department of Education

School of Education and HRD

Dravidian University

Kuppam – 517 426 (India)

DPH

DISCOVERY PUBLISHING HOUSE PVT. LTD.

NEW DELHI-110 002

Published by:
Tilak Wasan

DISCOVERY PUBLISHING HOUSE PVT. LTD.
4383/4B, Ansari Road, Darya Ganj
New Delhi-110 002 (India)
Phone : +91-11-23279245, 43596064-65
Fax : +91-11-23253475
E-mail : discoverypublishinghouse@gmail.com
sales@discoverypublishinggroup.com
parul.wasan@gmail.com
web : www.discoverypublishinggroup.com

First Edition: **2014**

ISBN: 978-93-5056-398-4

Emotional Intelligence, Occupational Stress and Job Performance of Teachers

Printed at:
Aditi Fine Art Press
Delhi

PREFACE

EDUCATION IS CONCEIVED as a powerful tool in bringing the desired behavioural changes in the social life of an individual to build a progressive nation. It is the only field where knowledge passes through all walks of life from person to person with varying degrees. It helps an individual to move towards the goal and it may be said that people reach their destination by having definite goals and by following clear cut paths. It has viewed as an instrument to develop the cognitive qualities, intelligence, tolerance and understanding of people. It should prepare the younger generation to understand and face the challenges of the world and teacher is the backbone to mould the future of these generations. They help the young generation to face the future with confidence but to build it with purpose and accountability. Teaching is the profession that shapes an individual. Well qualified, caring and committed teachers will improve the standard and quality of student life. It is a demanding job that requires in-depth knowledge of subject, content, developing good intra and interpersonal relationships, leadership qualities, thrust for acquiring new knowledge, creativity, administrative abilities, mastery in counseling etc.

Higher secondary stage is the stage of education, which helps students to become matured members of the complex modern society. It is the most crucial and delicate period in the life of adolescents with lots of academic pressure and confusions over their future, which they can overcome only with the support and guidance from the teachers. It is the stage where, students find it difficult to decide on their own on many occasions as well as on many issues without proper advice and suggestions. It enables the adolescents to enter the real life as a knowledgeable, active-minded and sociable individual only when they are influenced and motivated by their teachers. For this, the teacher has to play many roles and produce value oriented citizens to the society. Teachers help the physical, mental, emotional and intellectual growth and development of students and have to take care of affective domain of the students, besides stress on academic excellence. For academic excellence of students, first the teacher should possess the good attitude towards teaching, higher levels of emotional intelligence, optimum levels of stress and better performance abilities.

The primary aspect in the present book is to empirically identify the conceptualizations of the emotional intelligence, occupational stress and job performance of higher secondary teachers. For this, the theories of Mayer and Salovey's (1997), Bar-On's (1997) and, Goleman's (1998) on emotional intelligence; interactional and transactional models of work stress theories and; Campbell's (1990) Taxonomy of job performance, Borman and Motowidlo's (1993) theory of conceptual performance, Viswesvaran's (1993) and Murphy's (1994) theory of job performance were discussed briefly. To access the level of Emotional Intelligence, Occupational Stress and Job Performance of Higher Secondary teachers, ratings scales were developed. The survey method was adopted to find out the effect of personal and demographic variables such as gender, age, community, marital status, educational qualification, nature of the subjects teachers handling, type of schools the teachers working in, location of the school and the salary received by the teachers. Also the relationship between Emotional Intelligence and Occupational Stress, Occupational Stress and Job Performance, Emotional Intelligence and Job Performance of higher secondary teachers were established. Further, the study attempted to predict how far and to what extent the independent variables (gender, age…) influenced the dependent variables *i.e.,* EI, OS and JP of higher secondary teachers.

The conceptual framework of emotional intelligence, occupational stress and job performance of higher secondary teachers are dealt in detail in the first chapter along with the components of emotional intelligence, various models/theories, importance and need for emotional intelligence; symptoms and sources of stress, consequences of stress and, stress theories; determinants of job performance, perspectives of job performance and their relationship, task oriented and contextual oriented performance and their relationship; the relationship between emotional intelligence and occupational stress, occupational stress and job performance and, emotional intelligence and job performance.

The holistic and comprehensive review of literature on studies conducted both in India and abroad has been presented in the second chapter under different headings like emotional intelligence of teachers, students and other professionals; occupational stress of teachers, students, student teachers and other professional and; job performance of teachers and other professionals. The review of studies is done with a broad perspective keeping in mind the existing research gaps and the new knowledge that can be incorporated into the existing knowledge. An overview of the literature reviewed given at the end of the chapter clearly focuses on the various types of tools used, the sampling size and procedures, the methodologies adopted and, the statistical techniques that are incorporated both in India and abroad. This comparing and contrasting views of the studies in Indian and foreign context shows the research gaps that can be of an utmost interest for the future researchers to focus in different directions.

The third chapter clearly identifies the objectives, hypotheses, assumptions, scope, need, importance and delimitations of the study, whereas, the fourth chapter highlights the research tools that are developed and adopted, methodologies that are used, the data collection and the statistical techniques that are employed to analyze the collected data.

The results and discussion in the fifth chapter elaborately deals with the analysis of data, testing of hypotheses and presentation of results both in descriptive and differential methods. The discussion of results are highlighted in such a way that most of the results were substantiated with both supportive and contrasting results from the review of literature done, giving scope for critical and analytical way of reviewing the previous studies. The final chapter concludes with the empherical based educational implications for enhancing emotional intelligence, reducing occupational stress and improving the performance. It provides better insights into the positive aspects of emotional well being, strategies to combat stress at both the organizational and individual levels, strengthen intra and inter personal relationship and equip the teachers with components required for dealing with the adolescents to meet their emotional, behavioural and social needs.

I hope, this book will serve as a valuable resource guide for all the stakeholders of the society including students, research scholars, teachers at all levels, policy makers and planners to provide and to have a better organizational setup so as to upgrade the teaching learning process through appropriate and enhanced techniques and resources.

— Author

ACKNOWLEDGMENTS

I AM GREATLY INDEBTED to the Lord Almighty for giving me the opportunity to complete this research work. It is a great pleasure to put on record my heartfelt thanks to my revered guide Dr. G. Lokanadha Reddy, Professor, Department of Education, School of Education and HRD, Dravidian University, Kuppam, for his constant encouragement, immense patience, meticulous guidance, care and concern throughout the research work.

I express my deep gratitude to the Dravidian University Administration for providing the Ph.D. Registration and giving all infrastructural support to carryout the present study. I am also thankful to the Head and the Staff, both teaching and non-teaching of the Department of Education, Dravidian University, Kuppam, for their constant support.

I take this opportunity to sincerely thank the CEO of Vellore District for giving me the permission to collect data from the higher secondary schools, and the entire Principals' and Teachers of these schools for their cooperation in providing the data. Also, I am grateful to all the investigators whose findings are cited/substantially used for the present study. I acknowledge the help rendered by Ms. Geetha Stephen and also Dr. Harish for assisting in statistical analysis. I also express my appreciation to all my friends, relatives and well wishers for their timely support.

I sincerely acknowledge this entire research work to the eternal blessings of my parents, Smt. Pramila and Sri. G.M. Raghupathi Gowda, who are the source of inspiration in every stage of my life. Last but not the least, my heart goes with my husband, K. Murali Mohan and my two little gems, K. Tejus Vamshi and K. Hardik Vamshi for being my strength and backbone in fulfilling my ambition and without whose moral support and co-operation, this research would have been a dream for me.

R. Vijaya Anuradha

CONTENTS

Preface

Acknowledgments

Abbreviations

1. **Introduction** 1

Introduction; Concept, Meaning and Definitions of Emotional Intelligence; Concept, Meaning and Definitions of Occupational Stress; Occupational Stress; Concept, Meaning and Definitions of Job Performance; Relationship between Emotional Intelligence, Occupational Stress and Job Performance.

2. **Review of Related Literature** 55

Introduction; Studies Conducted in India; Studies Conducted Abroad; An Overview of the Research Reviewed.

3. **Statement of the Problem** 132

Introduction; Title of the Problem; Operational Definition of the Terms Used in the Study; Objectives of the Study; Assumptions; Hypotheses of the Study; Scope of the Study; Need and Importance of the Study; Delimitations of the Study.

4. **Methodology** 146

Introduction; Design of the Study; Construction of Research Tools Used in the Study; Development of the Research Tools; Pilot Study; Reliability of the Research Tools; Validity of the Research Tools; Locale and Sample of the Study; Rationale behind the Locale and Sample Selection; Data Collection; Statistical Techniques Used in the Study.

5. **Results and Discussion** 168

Introduction; Part — I: Descriptive Analysis; Descriptive Analysis of Emotional Intelligence (EI), Occupational Stress (OS) and Job Performance (JP) of Higher Secondary Teachers; Assessment of JP of Higher Secondary

Teachers by their Self-Ratings and the Ratings of their Respective Principal's /H.M's; Part — II: Differential Analysis; Effect of Gender, Marital Status, Educational Qualification, Type of School the Teachers are Working-in, Location of the School, Years of Experience, Age, Community, Subjects the Teachers Handling, and Salary they Receive on the Dimensions of EI, OS and JP of Higher Secondary Teachers; Correlation Studies; Step-wise Multiple Regression Analysis.

6. Summary and Suggestions **231**

Introduction; Title of the Problem; Operational Definition of the Terms Used in the Study; Objectives of the Study; Assumptions; Hypotheses of the Study; Scope of the Study; Need and Importance of the Study; Methodology Used in the Study; Findings of the Study; Implications of the Study; Delimitations of the Study; Suggestions for Further Research.

Bibliography ***257***

Index ***307***

ABBREVIATIONS

ANGRAU	Acharya NG Ranga Agricultural University
ANOVA	Analysis of Variance
ASSET	Organizational Stress Screening Tool
B.Ed.	Bachelor of Education
BC	Backward Community
BIA	Bureau of Indian Affairs
D.Ed	Diploma in Education
DASS	Depression Anxiety Stress Scale
ED	Emotional Dissonance
EE	Emotional Effort
EI	Emotional Intelligence
EI_1	Self-awareness
EI_2	Self-management
EI_3	Social awareness
EI_4	Social Skills
EIRS	Emotional Intelligence Rating Scale
EIS	Emotional Intelligence Scale
EISA	Emotional Intelligence Scale for Adolescents
EIW	Emotional Intelligence as a Whole
EL	Emotional Labour
EQ	Emotional Quotient
EQ-i	Emotional Quotient Inventory
ERI	Effort- Reward Imbalance
GHQ	General Health Questionnaire
H.M.	Head Master

HI	Hearing Impaired
HPLP	Health Promoting Lifestyle Profile
HRM	Human Resource Management
HUFLIT	Ho Chi Minh City University of Foreign Languages and Information Technology
IOP	Industrial and Organizational Psychology
IAS	Indian Administrative Service
ICDS	Integrated Child Development Scheme
IOB / JP_2	Interpersonally Oriented Behaviour
IQ	Intelligent Quotient
IT / ITES	Information Technology / Information Technology Enabled Services
JDC or DCS	Job Demand- Control/ Support Model
JP	Job Performance
JPRS	Job Performance Rating Scale
JPW	Job Performance as a Whole
JSS	Job Stress Survey
M.Ed.	Master of Education
MBC	Most Backward Community
MC / JP_3	Managerial Capabilities
MD	Mental Disorder
MEIS	Multifactor Emotional Intelligence Scale
MMEI	Multidimensional Measure of Emotional Intelligence
MR	Mental Retardation
MSCEIT	Mayer–Salovey–Caruso Emotional Intelligence Test
NMR	Negative Mood Regulation
NPAS	New Performance Appraisal System
OC	Open Category / Other Communities
OCB	Organizational Citizenship Behaviour
OCS	Organizational Commitment Scale
OCS	Organizational Climate Scale
OH	Orthopedically Handicapped
ORS	Organizational Role Stress
OS	Occupational Stress
OS_2	Personal and Professional Efficiency
OS_3	Intra and Interpersonal Interactions
OS_4	Home-Work Interface
OS_5	Environmental Factors
OSC / OS_1	Organizational Structure and Climate

OSI	Occupational Stress Index
OSI-R	Occupational Stress Inventory Revised edition
OSRS	Occupational Stress Rating Scale
OSW	Occupational Stress as a Whole
PDLQ / JP_4	Personal Discipline and Leadership Qualities
PIRS	Parental Involvement Rating Scale
PMI	Pressure Management Indicator
PSQ	Personal Strain Questionnaire
PUC	Pre-University Course
SC	Schedule Caste
SCAT	Sinha's Comprehensive Anxiety Test
SD	Standard Deviation
SEC	Socio-Emotional Competence
SEL	Social and Emotional Learning
SEM	Structural Equation Modeling
SEN	Special Education Needs
SF-36	Short-Form Health Survey
SPA	Self Performance Assessment
ST	Schedule Tribes
STEM	Situational Test of Emotional Management
STEU	Situational Test of Emotional Understanding
SUEIT	Multifactor Emotional Intelligence Scale
TEIQUE	Trait Emotional Intelligence Questionnaire
TOB / JP_1	Task Oriented Behaviour
TTD	Tirumala Tirupati Devasthanam's
UK	United Kingdom
US	United States
VI	Visually Impaired
WAI	Work Ability Index
WPQ-EI	Work Profile Questionnaire-Emotional Intelligence version

INTRODUCTION

INTRODUCTION

THE PROGRESS, welfare and prosperity of a nation mainly depend on rapid, planned and sustained growth in the quality and extent of education. It is conceived as a powerful agency that is instrumental in bringing about the desired behavioural changes in the social life of the people of the nation. It is the only field where knowledge passes through all walks of life from person to person with varying degrees. It has been identified as an essential investment for accelerating pace of development of any nation. The process and pace of development are determined by disciplined citizens who are suitably educated and properly trained. It helps an individual to move towards the goal and it may be said that people reach their goal by following clear cut paths. It has viewed as an instrument to develop the cognitive qualities, intelligence, tolerance and understanding of people. It should prepare the younger generation to understand and face the challenges of the world.

In this context, the teacher occupies a pivotal position in any progressive society. Whether viewed as a model, a supervisor, a guide or a leader, the task of a teacher is crucial in moulding the youth. The changing role from that of a dispenser of knowledge to that of innovator, stimulator, motivator, helper and agent of social change presumes that teachers possessing certain personality traits alone can perform any of those roles effectively. Teachers are the crucial elements in preparing the young people, not only to face the future with confidence but to build it with purpose and accountability. Their role as an agent of change has never been more obvious and critical than today.

The teacher today must be versatile, continuously learning with wide interests and looking at every problem as a challenge. The teacher must love his/her job, have a desire to grow professionally and thereby become a source of inspiration to the students and not just a source of information. Motivation, knowledge and creativity should be inculcated among students along with the scientific temper (Parameswaran, 2001). The National Policy on Education (1986) states that 'the status of the teacher reflects the socio-cultural ethos of a society'. It is said that no people can rise above the level of teachers. This statement makes clear the dignity, which teachers command from the society. The status which the teachers enjoy and the dignity of the profession are influenced to a great extent by the numerous roles which teachers play. Teaching is the profession that shapes an individual. Well qualified, caring and committed teachers will improve the standard and quality of student life. It will ensure that our children are prepared to face the challenges and utilise the opportunities. It is a demanding job that requires in-depth knowledge of subject, content and age specific pedagogy. It also requires many skills such as patience, leadership, creativity, administration, counseling etc.

Higher secondary stage is the stage of education, which helps students to become matured members of the complex modern society. It is the most crucial and delicate period in the life of adolescents with lots of academic pressure and confusions over their future, which they can overcome only with the support and guidance from the teachers. It is the stage where, students find it difficult to decide on their own on many occasions as well as on many issues without proper advice and suggestions. It enables the adolescents to enter the real life as a knowledgeable, active-minded and sociable individual only when they are influenced and motivated by their teachers. For this, the teacher has to play many roles and produce value oriented citizens to the society. Dash (2005) has classified these roles of teachers as efficient professional, manager, facilitator, counselor and community leader. The one single factor that enables a teacher to fulfill his/her responsibilities to the institution, to the society and to the nation is the commitment to the cause of education. The commitment is multi-dimensional. Some of the components of teachers' commitment are:

1. Commitment to students,
2. Commitment to the profession,
3. Commitment to the society, and
4. Commitment to the ethical value system (Azad, 2003).

Improvement in the quality, efficiency, and equity of education to a considerable extent, depends on the nexus of teaching and learning, which in turn is influenced by the quality of teachers. The teacher has been identified as the single most important factor influencing the quality of education by the National Policy on Education (1986). Consequently, the Government of India, like that of many other developing countries, has been trying to meet the challenge of improving the quality of education by improving teacher quality on several fronts — by raising pre service education requirements, improving the quality of teacher training, increasing the diversity of teaching force and promoting stronger participation by local government and community organizations.

The changing role of teachers and the changing definitions of teacher effectiveness have been increasingly studied and analyzed, with research undertaken and the outcomes being feedback into the system to facilitate the process of educational reform. The current focus of researchers, policy makers and practitioners with regard to teacher education is on the development of professional competencies, and on the most effective ways of achieving higher levels of commitment, motivation and higher-level performance on the part of teachers. In addition, important possibilities are arising with regard to current developments involving the new information and communication technologies. As a result, education in India is on the brink of a major transformation (Rajput and Walia, 2010). The teachers have more responsibilities in moulding the character of students. Teachers help the physical, mental, emotional and intellectual growth and development of students. They have to take care of affective domain of the students, besides stress on academic excellence. For academic excellence of students, first the teacher should possess the good attitude towards teaching and better emotional intelligence (Sahaya and Manorama, 2010).

CONCEPT, MEANING AND DEFINITIONS OF EMOTIONAL INTELLIGENCE

The roots of emotional intelligence theory go back to the beginning of the intelligence testing movement. When psychologists began to think about intelligence they focused attention on cognitive aspects such as memory and problem solving. Emotional intelligence has become a major topic of interest in scientific circles as well as in the lay public since the publication of 'Emotional Intelligence' by Goleman (1995). Despite this heightened level of interest in this new idea over the past decades, scholars have been studying this construct for the greater part of the twentieth century; and the historical roots of this wider area can actually be traced back to the 19th century.

Publications began appearing in the 20th century with the work of Edward Thorndike on social intelligence in 1920. Many of these early studies focused on describing, defining and assessing socially competent behaviour (Thorndike, 1920; Moss and Hunt, 1927; Moss *et. al.* 1927; Doll, 1935; Chapin, 1942). Edgar Doll (1935) published the first instrument designed to measure socially intelligent behaviour in young children. Possibly influenced by Thorndike and Doll, David Wechsler (1939) included two subscales (Comprehension and Picture Arrangement) in his well-known test of cognitive intelligence that appear to have been designed to measure aspects of social intelligence. A year after the first publication of his cognitive testing, Wechsler described the influence of non-intellective factors on intelligent behaviour which was yet another reference to this constructs. In the first of a number of publications following this early description, he argued that the models of intelligence would not be complete until factors are adequately described (1940).

Thorndike (1920), professor of educational psychology at Columbia University Teachers College, was one of the first to identify the aspect of emotional intelligence called social intelligence. In 1920 he included it in the broad spectrum of capacities that individuals posses, 'varying amount of different intelligence'. Social intelligence, wrote Thorndike, is 'the ability to understand and manage men and women, boys and girls to act wisely in human relations'. Although Thorndike did once propose a means of evaluating social intelligence in the laboratory, a simple process of matching pictures of emotive faces with descriptions of emotions, he also maintained that because social intelligence manifests in social interaction, 'genuine situations with real persons' would be necessary to accurately measure it. David Wechsler (1944) defined intelligence as the aggregate or global capacity of the individual to act purposefully, think rationally, and deal effectively with his/her environment. He submitted that non-intellective abilities are essential for predicting one's ability to succeed in life. Later, Howard Gardner (1983) wrote about multiple intelligence and proposed that intrapersonal and interpersonal intelligences are as important as the type of intelligence typically measured by intelligence quotient and related tests. Emotional intelligence draws from branches of behavioural, emotional, and communications theories. Reuven Bar-On (1988) developed perhaps the first attempt to assess emotional intelligence in terms of a measure of well-being. In his doctoral dissertation he used the term *Emotional Quotient* (EQ) as a counterpart to *Intelligence Quotient* (IQ), that is, to cognitive ability, long before it gained widespread popularity as a name for emotional intelligence and before Salovey and Mayer (1990) had published their first model of emotional intelligence. Bar-On thought of EQ as representing a set of social and emotional abilities that help individuals cope with the demands of daily life. Soon after, John Mayer and Peter Salovey (1990) described that as the ability to monitor one's own and others' feelings and emotions, to discriminate among them, and to use this information to guide one's thinking and actions. Mayer and Salovey (1997), in their revised four branch model, defined emotional intelligence as involving the abilities to perceive emotions accurately in one-self and others; use emotions to facilitate thinking; understand the meaning of emotions; and manage emotions. They also tried to develop a way to scientifically measure differences between people's abilities in the area of emotions. Finally, Goleman (1995a) saw emotional intelligence as an idea or theme that emerged from a large set of research findings on the role of the emotions in human life. These findings pointed to different ways in which competencies such as empathy, learned optimism, and self-control contributed to important outcomes in the family, the workplace, and other life arenas. Goleman (1995) illuminated theories about attachment, bonding, and the making and remaking of memory as he examined how our brains are wired for altruism, compassion, concern, and rapport. Good relationships nourish us and support our health, while toxic relationships can poison us. He proposed that social intelligence is made up of social awareness (including empathy, attunement, empathic accuracy, and social cognition) and social facility (including synchrony, self-presentation, influence, and concern).

Before elaborating 'emotional intelligence', it would be desirable to define the term emotion'. The word *emotion* comes from the Latin word 'emoveo', which means 'to move from'. According to Webster's Dictionary (1996), emotion is 'moving of the mind or soul' (Phin, 2009). Historically, the word emotion has been associated with a strong sense of feelings or drama. 'Emotion' is a complex state of the human mind involving wide range of bodily changes. Emotions originate from exposure to specific situations. Our responses are governed by our thoughts, by what we tell ourselves. We take responsibility for our thoughts, emotions and actions. Emotion includes the situation, the interpretation and the perception of a situation. In the most literal dictionary sense, emotion is defined as 'any agitation or disturbance of mind, passion, any vehement or excited mental state'. Emotion refers to a response with its distinctive thoughts, psychological and biological states and ranges of propensities to act.

Generally there are two dimensions of emotions: *Physiological Dimension* — emotion is a complex state of human mind, involving bodily changes of widespread nature such as breathing, pounding heart, flushed face, sweating palms, high pulse rate, glandular secretions, etc. *Psychological Dimension* - emotion is a state of excitement or perturbation marked by strong feelings. The 'feelings', are what one experiences as the result of having emotions. Some of the main emotions are anger, depression, anxiety, happiness, love, surprise, disgust, embarrassment, etc. Some of the negative emotions which require emotional management and regulation are anger, failure, fear, disappointment, frustration, obligation, guilt, resentment, emptiness, bitterness, dependence, depression, loneliness and lethargy. Similarly, positive emotions such as motivation, appreciation, friendship, self-control, satisfaction, freedom, fulfillment, autonomy, peace, desire, awareness, contentment, elation and happiness can be used effectively as and when the situation demands. Emotions are like an internal Gyroscope that helps keep us on the right track by ensuring that we are guided more by emotional quotient and less by intelligence quotient.

The expression 'Emotional Intelligence' (EI) indicates a kind of intelligence or skill that involves the ability to perceive, assess and positively influence one's own and other people's emotions. EI embraces two aspects of intelligence: understanding oneself, one's own goals, intentions, responses, behaviour etc., and understanding others and their feelings. Salovey and Mayer's original model (1990) identified emotional intelligence as the 'ability to monitor one's own and other's feelings and emotions, to discriminate among them, and to use this information to guide one's thinking and action'. In their modified model, Salovey and Mayer (1997) defined emotional intelligence as 'the ability to perceive emotions, to access and generate emotions so as to assist thought, to understand emotions and emotional knowledge, and to reflectively regulate emotions so as to promote emotional and intellectual growth'.

Daniel Goleman (1998) defined emotional intelligence as 'the capacity for recognizing our own feelings and those of others, for motivating ourselves, and for managing emotions well in us and in our relationships'. According to Freedman *et. al.* (1998), emotional intelligence is a way of recognizing, understanding and choosing how we think, feel and act. It shapes our interaction with others and our understanding of ourselves. It defines how and what we learn, it allows us to set priorities and determines the majority of our daily actions.

Bar-On (2000) defined emotional intelligence in terms of an array of emotional and social knowledge and abilities that influence our overall ability to effectively cope with environmental demands. This array includes the ability to be aware of, to understand, and to express oneself; the ability to be aware of, to understand, and to relate to others; the ability to deal with strong emotions and control one's impulses; and the ability to adapt to change and to solve problems of a personal or a social nature.

According to Dalip Singh (2003), emotional intelligence is the ability of an individual to appropriately and successfully respond to a vast variety of emotional stimuli being elicited from the inner self and immediate environment. Emotional intelligence constitutes three psychological dimensions: *1. Emotional sensitivity, 2. emotional maturitys and 3. emotional competency*, which motivate an individual to recognize truthfully, interpret honestly and handle tactfully the dynamics of human behaviour.

In simple terms, emotional intelligence can be defined as one's ability to deal with daily environment challenges and helps predict one's success in life, including professional and personal pursuits and also the ability of a person to control impulses and persist in the face of frustration. Emotional intelligence describes an ability, capacity, skill, or self-perceived ability to identify, assess, and manage the emotions of one's self, of others, and of groups. The theory is enjoying considerable support in the literature and has had successful applications in many domains. From Thorndike to the present, most descriptions, definitions and conceptualizations of emotional intelligence have included one or more of the following key components: the ability to recognize, understand and express emotions and feelings; the ability to understand how others feel and relate with them; the ability to manage and control emotions; the ability to manage change, adapt and solve problems of a personal and interpersonal nature; and the ability to generate positive affect and be self-motivated.

Relationship between EQ and IQ

It is very important to understand that Emotional Quotient (EQ) is not the opposite of Intelligence Quotient (IQ) - it is the unique interaction of both. Traditionally, psychologists measure intelligence through various intelligence quotient tests. The formula used for IQ tests is simple and elegant. It compares an individual's 'Chronological Age' with his/her 'Mental Age'. For ex., if a person's mental age is 30 and chronological age is 20, then

$$IQ=MA/CA \times 100$$

$$IQ=30/20 \times 100=150$$

The average intelligence of majority of people is 100, *i.e.,* their mental age equals to their chronological age. Some people have high EQ as well as high IQ, while others are low on either. Researchers have been making efforts to understand how they complement one another, how a person's ability to handle stress, for instance, affects his/her ability to concentrate and put his/her intelligence to use. Some people can handle anger well but cannot handle fear. Others are incapable of reacting to joy. Therefore, each emotion needs to be viewed differently. IQ is a measure of Intelligence Quotient whereas EQ is a measure of Emotional Quotient. It is now widely believed that emotions, rather than IQ, may be the true measure of human intelligence. Therefore, scientists are shifting their focus from the hardware of the brain to the software of the mind. We should keep in mind that cognitive (IQ) and non-cognitive (EQ) abilities are closely related. In fact, research suggests that emotional and social skills help improve cognitive functioning (Dalip Singh, 2006).

Emphasizing EQ does not mean de-emphasizing IQ. The latter is not less relevant for success in job performance or life than the former. The fact remains that one needs a relatively high level of IQ merely to get admitted to a science or engineering course. However, once admitted, comparing with peers has less to do with IQ differences and more to do with emotional factors, or EQ. It is more important to be able to persist in the face of difficulty and to get along well with colleagues and subordinates than it is to have an extra 10 or 15 points of IQ. However, this need not lead us to the erroneous conclusion that low academic scores with high EQ have a better chance of being successful. IQ, by itself, is not a very good predictor of job performance. There are other factors that add to overall personality development and satisfying performance at work. These 'other' factors relate to behaviour, moods and emotions, and are now broadly coined as emotional factors. This premise has led to the propagation of the concept of emotional quotient (Dalip Singh, 2006).

When discussing emotional intelligence in relation to work, psychologists often compare it with the effects of IQ. IQ and EQ are relatively independent from but complement each other. IQ is more stable than EQ but high EQ creates favorable conditions to develop IQ. In reality, all intellectual actions of people relate to emotion because emotion fosters cognitive activities which then implicate the causation of actions. The roles of IQ and EQ have been understood popularly by famous slogan 'IQ gets you hired, but emotional intelligence gets you promoted' (Gibbs, 1995). It is also stated that with a high IQ one can become a whiz at the daily routine, but with a high emotional intelligence he or she can thrive during times of change and uncertainty.

Psychologists do not deny the important role of IQ when combined with EQ. Studies have proved that both EQ and IQ significantly affect job performance. They suggested that data establishing the relative contribution of EQ and IQ should be balanced properly in hiring and promotion decisions. Goleman (2001) stated that IQ is a more powerful predictor than emotional intelligence of individuals' career success because it sorts people before they embark on career, determining which fields or professions they can enter. However, when studies looked within a job or profession to find out which individual become star performer, emotional intelligence was proved a more powerful predictor of success than IQ. Having enough cognitive intelligence to hold a given job does not by itself predict whether one will be a star performer or rise to management or leadership positions in her or his field. So, selection of employees solely based on academic intelligence and working expertise and ignoring emotional intelligence, often leads to poor choices that can be disastrous for an organization.

Goleman (1998) conducted research on EI-based competencies with the data collected from several hundred organizations and concluded that emotional competencies were twice as prevalent among distinguishing competencies as were technical skills and purely cognitive abilities combined. For leadership positions, 85 per cent of their competencies were in emotional intelligence domains. Dulewicz and Higgs (1999) compared the contribution of EQ and IQ to job performance by assessing 58 general managers in the United Kingdom and Ireland in three domains of ability: emotional skill, intellectual aptitude and managerial competency. They found that emotional intelligence accounted for 36 per cent of variance in organizational advancement whereas, IQ accounted for 27 per cent and the managerial quotient was 16 per cent. The findings could lead to a conclusion that emotional intelligence is slightly more important to career advancement than IQ.

Components of Emotional Intelligence

Individuals have different personalities, wants, needs, and ways of showing their emotions. Navigating through this requires tact and shrewdness — especially if one hopes to succeed in life. This is where emotional intelligence theory helps. Emotional

Intelligence, developed by Daniel Goleman (1998), identifies five components as essential to leadership success. In the most generic framework, five domains of emotional intelligence cover together personal (self-awareness, self-regulation, and self-motivation) and social (social awareness and social skills) competences. They are:

Self-Awareness

- *Emotional awareness:* recognizing one's emotions and their effects.
- *Accurate self-assessment*: knowing one's strengths and limits.
- *Self-confidence:* sureness about one's self-worth and capabilities.

Self-Regulation

- *Self-control:* managing disruptive emotions and impulses.
- *Trustworthiness*: maintaining standards of honesty and integrity.
- *Conscientiousness*: taking responsibility for personal performance.
- *Adaptability*: flexibility in handling change.
- *Innovativeness*: being comfortable with and open to novel ideas and new information.

Self-Motivation

- *Achievement drive*: striving to improve or meet a standard of excellence.
- *Commitment*: aligning with the goals of the group or organization.
- *Initiative*: readiness to act on opportunities.
- *Optimism*: persistence in pursuing goals despite obstacles and setbacks.

Social Awareness

- *Empathy*: sensing others' feelings and perspective, and taking an active interest in their concerns.
- *Service orientation*: anticipating, recognizing, and meeting customers' needs.
- *Developing others*: sensing what others need in order to develop, and bolstering their abilities.
- *Leveraging diversity*: cultivating opportunities through diverse people.
- *Political awareness*: reading a group's emotional currents and power relationships.

Social Skills

- *Influence*: wielding effective tactics for persuasion.
- *Communication*: sending clear and convincing messages.
- *Leadership*: inspiring and guiding groups and people.
- *Change catalyst:* initiating or managing change.
- *Conflict management*: negotiating and resolving disagreements.
- *Building bonds*: nurturing instrumental relationships.
- *Collaboration and cooperation*: working with others toward shared goals.
- *Team capabilities*: creating group synergy in pursuing collective goals.

In brief, the five domains relate to knowing one's emotions; managing one's emotions; motivating oneself; recognizing and understanding other people's emotions; and managing relationships, *i.e.,* managing the emotions of others.

Rahim and Minors (2003) tested the relationships of the three dimensions of emotional intelligence (self-awareness, self-regulation, and empathy) to managers' concern for the quality of products and services, and problem-solving behaviour of subordinates during conflict. The results of the study show that self-awareness and self-regulation are positively associated with problem solving, and self-regulation was positively associated with concern for quality. There was a significant effect of empathy on quality and interaction effect of self-regulation and empathy on concern for quality. The study implies that supervisors, who are deficient in EI, may be provided appropriate training to improve their concern for quality and problem solving.

In his theory of emotional intelligence, Bar-On (1997) outlines five components of emotional intelligence: intrapersonal, interpersonal, adaptability, stress management, and general mood. Within these components are sub-components which are given below:

- *Intrapersonal:* self-regard, emotional self-awareness, assertiveness, independence, and self-actualization.
- *Interpersonal:* empathy, social responsibility, and interpersonal relationship.
- *Adaptability*: reality testing, flexibility and problem solving.
- *Stress management:* stress tolerance and impulse control.
- *General mood:* optimism.

Emotional intelligence may subsume Gardner's (1983) inter and intrapersonal intelligences, and involves abilities that may be categorized into five domains (Salovey and Mayer, 1990):

- *Self-awareness*: observing oneself and recognizing a feeling as it happens.
- *Managing emotions:* handling feelings so that they are appropriate; realizing what is behind a feeling; finding ways to handle fears and anxieties, anger, and sadness.
- *Motivating oneself*: channeling emotions in the service of a goal; emotional self control; delaying gratification and stifling impulses.
- *Empathy:* sensitivity to others' feelings and concerns and taking their perspective; appreciating the differences in how people feel about things.
- *Handling relationships*: managing emotions in others; social competence and social skills.

Theories/Models of Emotional Intelligence

Since the time of Thorndike (1920), a number of different conceptualizations of emotional intelligence have appeared which have been creating an interesting mixture of confusion, controversy and opportunity regarding the best approach to defining and measuring this construct. In an effort to help clarify this situation, the *Encyclopedia of Applied Psychology* (Spielberger, 2004) suggested that there are currently three major conceptual models:

(i) The Salovey and Mayer model (1997) which defines this construct as the ability to perceive, understand, manage and use emotions to facilitate thinking, measured by an ability-based measure (Mayer *et. al*. 2002);

(ii) The Goleman model (1998) which views this construct as a wide array of competencies and skills that drive managerial performance, measured by multi-rater assessment (Boyatzis *et. al.* 2001); and

(iii) The Bar-On model (1997a, 1997b, 2000) which describes a cross-section of interrelated emotional and social competencies, skills and facilitators that impact intelligent behaviour, measured by self-report within a potentially expandable multi-modal approach including interview and multi-rater assessment (Bar-On and Handley, 2003a, 2003b).

Each theoretical paradigm conceptualizes emotional intelligence from one of two perspectives: ability or mixed model. Ability models regard emotional intelligence as a pure form of mental ability and thus as a pure intelligence. In contrast, mixed models of emotional intelligence combine mental ability with personality characteristics such as optimism and well-being (Mayer, 1999). Currently, ability model of emotional intelligence proposed by John Mayer and Peter Salovey and two mixed models of emotional intelligence, each within a somewhat different conception proposed by Reuven Bar-On and Daniel Goleman are presented here. Reuven Bar-On has put forth a model based within the context of personality theory, emphasizing the co-dependence of the ability aspects of emotional intelligence with personality traits and their application to personal well-being. In contrast, Daniel Goleman proposed a mixed model in terms of performance, integrating an individual's abilities and personality and applying their corresponding effects on performance in the workplace (Goleman, 2001).

Mayer and Salovey's (1997): Four Branch Ability Model of Emotional Intelligence

Peter Salovey and John Mayer coined the term 'emotional intelligence' in 1990 (Salovey and Mayer, 1990) and have since continued to conduct research on the significance of the construct. Their pure theory of emotional intelligence integrates key ideas from the fields of intelligence and emotion. From intelligence theory comes the idea that intelligence involves the capacity to carry out abstract reasoning. From emotion research, comes the notion that emotions are signals that convey regular and discernable meanings about relationships and that at a number of basic emotions are universal (Mayer, Salovey, and Caruso, 2002). They propose that individuals vary in their ability to process information of an emotional nature and in their ability to relate emotional processing to a wider cognition. They then posit that this ability is seen to manifest itself in certain adaptive behaviours.

Mayer and Salovey's conception of emotional intelligence is based within a model of intelligence, that is, it strives to define emotional intelligence within the confines of the standard criteria for a new intelligence (Mayer, Salovey, Caruso, and Sitarenios, 2003). It proposes that emotional intelligence is comprised of two areas: experiential (ability to perceive, respond, and manipulate emotional information without necessarily understanding it) and *strategic* (ability to understand and manage emotions without necessarily perceiving feelings well or fully experiencing them). Each area is further divided into two branches that range from basic psychological processes to more complex processes integrating emotion and cognition.

The first branch, *emotional perception*, is the ability to be self-aware of emotions and to express emotions and emotional needs accurately to others. Emotional perception also includes the ability to distinguish between honest and dishonest expressions of emotion. The second branch, *emotional assimilation*, is the ability to distinguish among the different emotions one is feeling and to identify those that are influencing their thought processes. The third branch, *emotional understanding*, is the ability to understand complex emotions (such as feeling two emotions at once) and the ability to recognize transitions from one to the other. Lastly, the fourth branch, *emotion management,* is the ability to connect or disconnect from an emotion depending on its usefulness in a given situation (Mayer and Salovey, 1997).

In their revised model, Mayer and Salovey (1997) suggested that the capacity to perceive and understand emotions defined a new intelligence. The Mayer-Salovey model defines emotional intelligence as 'the capacity to understand emotional information and to reason with emotions'. More specifically, they divide emotional intelligence abilities into four areas — in their four branch model:

1. The capacity to accurately perceive emotions,
2. The capacity to use emotions to facilitate thinking,
3. The capacity to understand emotional meanings, and
4. The capacity to manage emotions.

Citing a need to distinguish emotional intelligence abilities from social traits or talents, Mayer and Salovey evolved a model with a cognitive emphasis. It focused on specific mental aptitudes for recognizing and marshalling emotions (for example, knowing what someone is feeling is a mental aptitude, whereas being outgoing and warm is a behaviour). A comprehensive emotional intelligence model, they argued, must include some measure of 'thinking about feeling', an aptitude lacked by models that focus on simply perceiving and regulating feelings. In the revised model of Mayer and Salovey (1997), emotional intelligence comprises four tiers of abilities that range emotional intelligence: issues in paradigm building from basic psychological processes to more complex processes integrating emotion and cognition.

In the first tier of this 'mental ability model' is the complex of skills that allow an individual to perceive, appraise, and express emotions. Abilities here include identifying one's own and other's emotions, expressing one's own emotions, and discriminating the expressions of emotion in others. The second tier abilities involve using emotions to facilitate and prioritize thinking: employing the emotions to aid in judgement, recognizing that mood swings can lead to a consideration of alternative viewpoints, and understanding that a shift in emotional state and perspective can encourage different kinds of problem solving. In the third tier are skills such as labeling and distinguishing between emotions, understanding complex mixtures of feelings, and formulating rules about feelings: for example, the anger often gives way to shame and the loss is usually accompanied by sadness. The fourth tier of the model is the general ability to marshal the emotions in support of some social goal. In this more complex level of emotional intelligence are the skills that allow individuals to selectively engage in or detach from emotions and to monitor and manage emotions in themselves and in others.

Salovey and Mayer's (1997) model is developmental: thc complexity of emotional skill grows from the first tier to the fourth. However, all the mental aptitudes they describe fit within the general matrix of self-recognition or regulation.

Bar-On's (1997): Mixed Model of Emotional Intelligence

The Bar-On (1997) model of emotional-social intelligence describes EI as an array of interrelated emotional and social competencies, skills and facilitators that impact intelligent behaviour. The Bar-On model can be divided into two main parts. The first part is the *theory*, or conceptualization of emotional-social intelligence; and the second part is the psychometric aspect of the model which is, essentially, the *measure* of emotional-social intelligence which was based on the theory and designed to assess it. These two aspects of the model have also been referred to as: (a) *the Bar-On conceptual model of emotional-social intelligence* and (b) *the Bar-On psychometric model of emotional-social intelligence*, while (c) *the Bar-On model of emotional-social intelligence* refers to both the conceptual and the psychometric aspects of this model combined into one entity.

Reuven Bar-On developed one of the first measures of emotional intelligence that used the term 'Emotion Quotient'. Bar-On's model of emotional intelligence relates to the potential for performance and success, rather than performance or success itself, and is considered as process-oriented rather than outcome-oriented (Bar-On, 2003). It focuses on an array of emotional and social abilities, including the ability to be aware of, understand, and express oneself; the ability to be aware of, understand, and relate to others; the ability to deal with strong emotions; and the ability to adapt to change and solve problems of a social or personal nature (Bar-On, 1997). In his model, Bar-On outlines five components of emotional intelligence: *(i)* intrapersonal, *(ii)* interpersonal, *(iii)* adaptability, *(iv)* stress management, *(v)* and general mood. Bar-On posits that emotional intelligence develops over time and that it can be improved through training, programming, and therapy (Bar-On, 2003).

Darwin's work (1872-1965) on the importance of emotional expression for survival and adaptation influenced the development of the Bar-On model, which also stresses the importance of emotional expression and views the outcome of emotionally and socially intelligent behaviour in terms of effective and successful adaptation. Additional influence on the development of this model can be traced to Thorndike's (1920) description of social intelligence and its importance for human performance as well as Wechsler's (1940) observations related to the impact of non-intellective (non-cognitive) factors on what he referred to as intelligent behaviour. Sifneos' (1967) description of alexithymia on the pathological end of the EI continuum and Appelbaum's (1973) conceptualization of psychological mindedness on the healthy end of this continuum have also had an impact on the development of the Bar-On model as well. Additionally, Gardner's (1983) introduction of the concept of intrapersonal and interpersonal intelligence, within the context of multiple intelligences, had an impact on the development of the intrapersonal and interpersonal components of the Bar-On model of emotional-social intelligence.

The Bar-On model provides the theoretical basis for the EQ-i, which was originally developed to assess various aspects of this construct as well as to examine its conceptualization. According to this model, emotional-social intelligence is a cross-section of interrelated emotional and social competencies, skills and facilitators that determine how effectively we understand and express ourselves, understand others and relate with them, and cope with daily demands. The emotional and social competencies, skills and facilitators referred in this conceptualization include the five key components described above; and each of these components comprises a number of closely related competencies, skills and facilitators. Consistent with this model, to be emotionally and socially intelligent is to effectively understand and express oneself, to understand and relate well with others, and to successfully cope with daily demands, challenges and pressures. This is based, first and foremost, on one's *intrapersonal ability* to be aware of one-self, to understand one's strengths and weaknesses, and to express one's feelings and thoughts non-destructively. On the *interpersonal level*, being emotionally and socially intelligent encompasses the ability to be aware of others' emotions, feelings and needs, and to establish and maintain cooperative, constructive and mutually satisfying relationships. *Adaptability* is the verifying of feelings with external cues, being emotionally and socially intelligent to effectively manage personal, social and environmental change by realistically and flexibly coping with the immediate situation, solving problems and making-decisions. Finally, *stress management* is coping and controlling impulses to manage emotions so that they work for us and not against us, and general mood is being sufficiently optimistic, positive and self-motivated.

Bar-On hypothesizes that those individuals with higher than average E.Q.'s are in general more successful in meeting environmental demands and pressures. He also notes that a deficiency in emotional intelligence can mean a lack of success and the existence of emotional problems. Problems in coping with one's environment is thought, by Bar-On, to be especially common among those individuals lacking in the subscales of reality testing, problem solving, stress tolerance, and impulse control. In general, Bar-On considers emotional intelligence and cognitive intelligence to contribute equally to a person's general intelligence, which then offers an indication of one's potential to succeed in life (Bar-On, 2003).

Goleman's (1998): Mixed Model of Emotional Intelligence

Daniel Goleman, a psychologist and science writer who has previously written on brain and behaviour research for the New York Times, discovered the work of Salovey and Mayer in the 1990's. Inspired by their findings, he began to conduct his own research in the area and eventually wrote *Emotional Intelligence* (1995), the landmark book which familiarized both the public and private sectors with the idea of emotional intelligence. Goleman's (1998) model outlines four main emotional intelligence constructs. The first, *self-awareness*, is the ability to read one's emotions and recognize their impact while using feelings to guide decisions. *Self-management*, the second construct, involves controlling one's emotions and impulses and adapting to changing circumstances. The third construct, social awareness, includes the ability to sense, understand, and react to other's emotions while comprehending social networks.

Finally, *relationship management,* the fourth construct, entails the ability to inspire, influence, and develop others while managing conflict.

In Goleman's view, these emotional competencies build on each other in a hierarchy. One must identify one's emotions in order to manage them. One aspect of managing emotions involves entering into drive-to-achieve emotional states. These three abilities, when applied to other people, lead to the fourth one: to read and influence positively other people's emotions. All four competencies lead to increased ability to enter and sustain good relationships. Goleman has made a distinction between emotional intelligence and emotional competencies. According to this view, emotional intelligence provides the bedrock for the development of a large number of competencies that help people perform more effectively. For instance, managers who possess a high level of what Salovey and Mayer (1990) think of as EI will not necessarily be more effective than other managers in dealing with conflict among their employees. However, they will be able to learn and to use conflict management skills more readily than will individuals who bring less EI to the job (Cherniss and Goleman, 2001).

EI is composed of varied competencies, and it still is unclear exactly how they are related. Both Mayer *et. al.* (1999) and Goleman (1998) have developed models suggesting how different competencies may be related. For instance, Goleman proposes that Self-awareness is the foundation for two other EI abilities: Self-control and Social-awareness. Self-control and Social-awareness, in turn, are the foundations for Social-skills. The same conditions that make EI so vital for organizational effectiveness also make EI difficult to nurture in organizations. Goleman summarized this comprehensive approach and developed a framework of five elements that are at the core of emotional intelligence. These elements constitute the abilities that characterize and distinguish emotionally intelligent person:

Self-Awareness

People with high emotional intelligence are usually very self-aware. They understand their emotions, and because of this, they don't let their feelings rule them. They are confident because they trust their intuition and don't let their emotions get out of control. Also, they are willing to take an honest look at themselves. Many people believe that this self- awareness is the most important part of emotional intelligence. It is the ability to recognize and understand personal moods and emotions and drives, as well as their effect on others. Hallmarks of self-awareness include self-confidence, realistic self-assessment, and a self-deprecating sense of humor. Self-awareness depends on one's ability to monitor one's own emotion state and to correctly identify and name one's emotions.

Self-Regulation

This is the ability to control emotions and impulses. People who self-regulate typically don't allow themselves to become too angry or jealous, and they don't make impulsive, careless decisions. It is the ability to control or redirect disruptive impulses and moods, and the propensity to suspend judgement and to think before acting. Characteristics of self regulation are thoughtfulness, comfort with change, integrity, and the openness to change.

Motivation

People with a high degree of emotional intelligence are usually motivated. They are willing to defer immediate results for long-term success. They're highly productive, love a challenge, and are very effective in what they do. A passion to work for internal reasons that go beyond money and status – which are external rewards, such as an inner vision of what is important in life, a joy in doing something, curiosity in learning, a flow that comes with being immersed in an activity, a propensity to pursue goals with energy and persistence. Hallmarks include a strong drive to achieve, optimism even in the face of failure, and organizational commitment.

Empathy

This is perhaps the second-most important element of emotional intelligence. Empathy is the ability to identify with and understand the wants, needs, and viewpoints of those around us. People with empathy are good at recognizing the feelings of others, even when those feelings may not be obvious. As a result, empathetic people are usually excellent at managing relationships, listening, and relating to others. They avoid stereotyping and judging too quickly, and they live their lives in a very open, honest way. It is the ability to understand the emotional makeup of other people, a skill in treating people according to their emotional reactions. Hallmarks include expertise in building and retaining talent, cross-cultural sensitivity, and service to clients and customers. In an educational context, empathy is often thought to include or lead to, sympathy which implies concern, or care or a wish to soften negative emotions or experiences in others. It is important to note that empathy does not necessarily imply compassion. Empathy can be 'used' for compassionate or cruel behaviour.

Social Skills

It is usually easy to talk to and like people with good social skills, another sign of high emotional intelligence. Those with strong social skills are typically team players. Rather than focus on their own success first, they help others develop and shine. They can manage disputes, are excellent communicators, and are masters at building and maintaining relationships, proficiency in managing relationships and building networks, and an ability to find common ground and build rapport. Hallmarks of social skills include effectiveness in leading change, persuasiveness, and expertise building and leading teams.

Goleman includes a set of emotional competencies within each construct of emotional intelligence. Emotional competencies are not innate talents, but rather learned capabilities that must be worked on and developed to achieve outstanding performance. Goleman posits that individuals are born with a general emotional intelligence that determines their potential for learning emotional competencies. The organization of the competencies under the various constructs is not random; they appear in synergistic clusters or groupings that support and facilitate each other (Boyatzis, Goleman, and Rhee, 2000).

Salovey and Mayer (1997) first proposed their theory of emotional intelligence in 1990. Over the intervening decade, theorists have generated several distinctive EI models, including the elaborations by Salovey and Mayer on their own theory. The theory as formulated by Salovey and Mayer (1990); Mayer, Salovey, and Caruso (2002) framed EI within a *model of intelligence*. Reuven Bar-On (1997) has placed EI in the context of *personality theory*, specifically a model of well-being. Goleman's (1998) model formulates EI in terms of a *theory of performance.* An EI-based theory of performance has direct applicability to the domain of work and organizational effectiveness, particularly in predicting excellence in jobs of all kinds, from sales to leadership. All these EI models, however, share a common core of basic concepts. Emotional intelligence, at the most general level, refers to the 'abilities to recognize and regulate emotions in ourselves and in others'. This most parsimonious definition suggests four major EI domains: *Self-awareness, Self-management, Social-awareness,* and *Relationship management* (Cherniss and Goleman, 2001). These four domains are shared by all the main variations of EI theory, though the terms used to refer to them differ. The domains of Self-awareness and Self-management, for example, fall within what Gardner (1983) calls *Intrapersonal Intelligence,* and Social-awareness and Relationship management fit within his definition of *Interpersonal Intelligence.* Some make a distinction between emotional intelligence and social intelligence, seeing EI as personal self-management capabilities like impulse control and social intelligence as relationship skills (Bar-On, 2000). The movements in education that seeks to implement curricula that teach EI skills use the general term S*ocial and Emotional Learning* or SEL (Salovey and Sluyter, 1997). The EI model seems to be emerging as an influential framework in psychology, education and organizational management fields.

Importance of Emotional Intelligence

The span of psychological fields that are now informed by the EI model ranges from neuroscience to health psychology. Among the areas with the strongest connections to EI is developmental, educational, clinical and counseling, social, and industrial and organizational psychology. Indeed, instructional segments on EI are now routinely included in many college-level and graduate courses in these subjects. One main reason for this penetration seems to be that the concept of emotional intelligence offers a language and framework capable of integrating a wide range of research findings in psychology. Beyond that, EI offers a positive model for psychology. Like other positive models, it has implications for the ways we might tackle many problems of our day — for prevention activities in physical and mental health care and for effective interventions in schools and communities, businesses, and organizations (Seligman and Csikszentmihalyi, 2000). Our increasing understanding of EI also suggests a promising scientific agenda, one that goes beyond the borders of personality, IQ, and academic achievement to study a broader spectrum of the psychological mechanisms that allow individuals to flourish in their lives, their jobs, and their families and as citizens in their communities.

Emotional Intelligence - EI - is a relatively recent behavioural model, rising to prominence with Daniel Goleman's (1995) book called 'Emotional Intelligence'. Emotional intelligence is increasingly relevant in every field because, the EQ principles provide a new way to understand and assess people's behaviours, attitudes, interpersonal skills, and potential. Emotional intelligence is an important consideration in teaching profession, human resources planning, job profiling, recruitment, interviewing and selection, management development, customer relations and customer service, and more.

Emotional intelligence can be instrumental in achieving success in many areas of professional life and also helps to achieve organizational development. Emotional intelligence can help in increasing productivity, speeding up adaptation to change, developing leadership skills, stimulating creativity and cooperation, responding effectively to competition, encouraging innovative thinking and improving retention of key employees. It can also help create an enthusiastic work environment, improve the way employees feel about them-selves and how they relate to others, reduce stress level and resolve emotional issues, improve health and well-being, improve relationships, heighten success, and enable employees to experience greater fulfillment. In work situations, EI can facilitate in resolving past issues, help employees attain emotional power, enable them to resolve external and internal conflicts, enable them to accomplish their goals at all levels- physical, mental, emotional and spiritual and improve their mental abilities such as memory, clarity of thinking and decision-making or coordinating the work of their subordinates.

Need for Emotional Intelligence for Higher Secondary Teachers

The level of Emotional Intelligence (EI) is neither genetically fixed, nor does it develop only in early childhood. Unlike Intelligence Quotient (IQ), which does not increase after adolescence, EI is largely learned and continues to develop throughout life and is conditioned by life's experience. Unlike IQ, EI can be improved throughout life. As a person becomes more mature, he/she can acquire certain emotional competencies that lead to outstanding performance at work. The people with high EI are happier, healthier and more successful in their relationships. These people strike a balance between emotion and reason, are aware of their own feelings, show empathy and compassion for others, and have high self-esteem. Emotional intelligence can be instrumental in many situations in the work place and can help achieve organizational effectiveness. High EI is also needed for making the right decisions and solving problems. Some of the immediate benefits of high EI are that it can lead to increased productivity, enhanced leadership skills, improved responsiveness and greater creativity. It can also create an enthusiastic work environment, reduce stress levels and resolve emotional issues, improve the well-being of employers and improve relationships all around. EI can enable employees to resolve past issues and both external as well as internal conflicts, help them attain emotional power and accomplish their goals at all levels *i.e.,* physical, mental, emotional and spiritual and improve psychological abilities such as memory, clarity of thinking and decision-making.

The difference between those at the high and low ends of EI is very large indeed. Being at the top therefore confers a major competitive advantage. Hence, 'soft' skills matter even more for success in 'hard' fields. It has been argued that traditional academic aptitude, school grades and advanced credentials simply did not predict how well people would perform on the job or whether they would succeed in life. Instead, there is a set of specified competencies like empathy and initiative which distinguished the most successful from those who were merely good enough to retain their jobs. All these data indicate a common core of personal and social abilities as the key ingredient of emotional intelligence.

The teachers' of today are undergoing tremendous pressure in their professional life. If they are to face the problems of their profession with confidence and courage, a basic knowledge and discipline in service are essential. A positive attitude towards life, high level of emotional intelligence to provide a new way to understand and assess people's behaviours, management styles, attitudes, interpersonal skills and potential and optimum level of stress will help the person to cope with his personal and professional life, which results in good performance in his/her job. A teacher should have high level of emotional intelligence because it links strongly with concepts of love and spirituality bringing compassion and humanity to work. To become a successful teacher requires the effective awareness, control and management of one's own emotions, and those of the pupils. It embraces two aspects of intelligence: understanding one-self, one's own goals, intentions, responses, behaviour and understanding pupils and their feelings.

The qualities which are considered crucial for teachers these days are many like; listening and verbal communication, adaptability and creative responses to setbacks and obstacles, personal management, confidence, motivation to work towards goals, a sense of wanting to develop one's career and taking pride in accomplishment, group and inter-personal effectiveness, co-operation and team work, skills in solving disagreements, willingness to make a contribution, leadership potential, along with competencies in reading, writing and mathematics. Of these desirable traits, only reading, writing and mathematics are academic skills. All the others are related to the non-academic arena to emotional intelligence.

CONCEPT, MEANING AND DEFINITIONS OF OCCUPATIONAL STRESS

Stress and strain have become pervading features of peoples' life in modern world. Despite tremendous advancements in science and technology, and remarkable growth of economy and sources of luxury, majority of people all over the world seem to be experiencing moderate to high degree of psychological stress in various spheres of their lives. In the present day world, majority of people may be seen talking about the term, yet, significantly few people use the term in the same way or even attempt for a clear-cut definition of the term stress.

The word stress is derived from the Latin word *Stringere* which means 'to be drawn tight'. The term was used to refer to hardship, strain, adversity or affliction. The physiologist, Walter Cannon (1914), in his work on homeostasis had used the term stress to describe emotional states that had possible detrimental physical impact on the focal organism. Dunbar (1947) had described the term stress as quality of stimulus while some others defined it as the quality of both stimulus and the response. Wolff (1950) described it as a state of human organism. Basowitz *et. al.* (1958) also described stress as that class of stimuli which produce anxiety and reportable experience of tension. The term stress as is currently used was coined by Hans Seyle (1956) and is defined as 'non-specific response of the body to any demand for change'. It is the body's reaction to a change that requires a physical, mental or emotional adjustment or response. Stress is a subjective feeling or tension experienced in the physical, mental and/or emotional realms as a response to environmental events that are perceived as threatening. According to Lazarus (1966), stress is a condition or feeling experienced when a person perceives that demands exceed the personal and social resources the individual is able to mobilize. In fact, stress has been widely described as a person-environment relationship (Folkman, 1984; Quick *et.al.* 1986; Baron and Byrne, 1997). Stress, in general, can be defined as the reaction of individuals to demands (stressors) imposed upon them (Erkutlu and Chafra, 2006). It refers to situations where the well-being of individuals is detrimentally affected by their failure to cope with the demands of their environment (Erkutlu and Chafra, 2006).

Stress involves a stressor and a stress response. A stressor may be a physical insult, such as trauma or physical exertion, particularly when the body is being forced to operate beyond its capacity. Other physical stressors include noise, overcrowding, and excessive heat or cold. Stressors also include primarily psychological experiences such as time-pressured tasks, interpersonal conflict, unexpected events, frustration, isolation, and traumatic life events and all of these types of stressors may produce behavioural responses and evoke physiological consequences such as increased blood pressure, elevated heart rate, increased cortisol levels, impaired cognitive function, and altered metabolism.

OCCUPATIONAL STRESS

Stress at work resulting from increasing complexities of work and its divergent demand, has become a prominent and pervading feature of the modern organizations. The researchers in the area of organizational psychology and management have used the term job stress to denote employees' mental state aroused by a job situation or a combination of job situations perceived as presenting excessive and divergent demands. Caplan *et. al.* (1975) have accordingly defined occupational stress as 'any characteristics of job environment which poses a threat to the individual'. Some other researchers tried to define stress in terms of interaction between worker and work environment. The stressfulness of a job situation or a factor is determined not only by the divergent or threatening demands of the situation but by how the individual perceives and evaluates it with reference to his own capabilities and characteristics. In this regard, Margolis *et. al.* (1974) defined stress as 'a condition at work interacting with worker's characteristics to disrupt his psychological or physiological homeostasis'. Similarly, Beehr and Newman (1978) described job stress as a 'condition wherein job related factors interact with the worker to change his psychological conditions such that the person is forced to deviate from normal functioning'.

Occupational stress, in particular, is the inability to cope with the pressures in a job and a poor fit between someone's abilities and his/her work requirements and conditions (Rees, 1997). It is a mental and physical condition which affects an individual's productivity, effectiveness, personal health and quality of work (Comish and Swindle, 1994). Main components of the work-stress process are potential sources of stress (stressors), factors of individual differences (moderators/mediators), and consequences of stress. Stressors (job-related and extra-organizational) are objective events, stress is the subjective experience of the event, and strain is the poor response to stress. Accordingly, the nature and effects of stress might be best understood by saying that some environmental variables (stressors), when interpreted by the individual (cognitive interpretation), may lead to stress (Dua, 1994).

In a very general sense, work stress describes 'a field of study', 'area of practice or research focusing on social psychological characteristics of work that are detrimental to employee's health'. A generic definition of 'job stress' given by *National Institute of Occupational Safety and Health (1999)* is 'harmful physical and emotional responses that occur when the requirements of the job do not match the capabilities, resources or needs of the worker'. Job stress can lead to poor health and even injury. Teacher stress is a specific type of occupational stress. It is the experience by a teacher of unpleasant emotions such as tension, frustration, anger and depression resulting from aspects of his/her work as a teacher (Kyriacou, 1987). Work stress, job stress and occupational stress are often used interchangeably.

Symptoms of Stress

Stresses causing factors or environmental events that result in feelings of stress are known as stressors. In general stress is related to both external and internal factors. External factors involve the physical environment including one's job, relationships with others, home and all the situations, challenges, difficulties and expectations one is confronted with on a daily basis. It is the internal factors which determine one's ability to respond to and deal with the external stress inducing factors. Nutritional status, overall health and fitness level, emotional well-being and amount of sleep and rest one gets are some of the internal factors which influence one's stress coping ability. While internal symptoms may involve feeling sick, moody or having a headache, external symptoms may include throwing things, screaming, shaking with rage, weeping etc. Stress signals could also be behavioural and physiological. Behavioural signals include bouts of weakness, fainting, losing personal possessions, doing things in a hurried manner etc. Physiological signs of stress include hypertension, jagged nerves, anxiety backache, intolerance to heat, ulcers etc. These common symptoms of stress affect work output and disrupt the smooth functioning in the workplace (Okorie, 1997).

Work stressors or hazards or risks are defined as environmental situations or events potentially capable of producing the state of stress. Stressors may be physical or psychological in origin and both can affect physical and psychological health, and may interact with each other. Physical stressors may include biological, biomechanical, chemical and radiological, or psychosocial hazards. Psychosocial hazards are 'those aspects of work design and the organization and management of work, and their social and environmental contexts, which have the potential for causing psychological, social or physical harm'. Chronic stressor, stress or strain refers to an ongoing exposure, condition or reaction respectively. An example of a chronic stressor is workload, and presumably this would be linked with a chronic or long lasting reaction, as the exposure is ongoing. Acute stressor, stress, and strain, refers to a short lived exposure, condition or reaction respectively. An example of an acute stressor would be a violent incident that could lead to an acute response or a chronic response such as Post Traumatic Stress Disorder, depending on its nature.

The Nature and Sources of Stress

Among life situations, the workplace stands out as a potentially important source of stress purely because of the amount of time that is spent in this setting (Erkutlu and Chafra, 2006). Over the years, a large number of workplace stressors of varying degrees of gravity have been identified. The common organizational and individual stressors could be classified into five groups:

1. Organizational practices (performance reward systems, supervisory practices, promotion opportunities),
2. Job/task features (workload, workpace, autonomy),
3. Organizational culture/climate (employee value, personal growth, integrity),
4. Interpersonal relationships (supervisors, coworkers, customers), and
5. Employee personal characteristics (personality traits, family relationships, coping skills) - Hurrel *et. al.* (1993), as cited by Murphy (1995).

Burke (1988) grouped job stressors into the following six categories: *(i)* physical environment, *(ii)* role stressors, *(iii)* organizational structure and job characteristics, *(iv)* relationships with others, *(v)* career development, and *(vi)* work-family conflict, while Cooper *et. al.* (1988) identified six sources of stress at work: factors intrinsic to the job, management role, relationship with others, career and achievement, organizational structure and climate, and home/work interface. More simply, Antoniou *et. al.* (2006) point that specific conditions that make jobs stressful can be categorized either as exogenous (*i.e.,* unfavorable occupational conditions, excessive workload, lack of collaboration, etc.) or endogenous pressures (*i.e.,* individual personality characteristics, etc.).

When we add the complexity and turbulence of contemporary working environment and organizational life, altogether, causes of occupational stress can be grouped into two main groups:

1. *Job related stressors*, with three major subgroups – job specific, organization specific, and environment specific stressors and
2. *Individual-related stressors,* which can be either a consequence of individual characteristics or a consequence of individual life circumstances.

1. Job Related Stressors

(a) *Job-Specific Stressors:* It must not be seen as a sum of many individual problems, but rather it is an issue to be approached from the perspective of the organization - how jobs and workplaces are designed and the way in which work is organized and managed. It is these organizational obstacles that hinder the teacher in serving their profession with a quality that lives up to the standards set by society, the school and the teacher. Yet defining the problem as 'organizational' clearly makes stress an issue of occupational health and safety, and hence it merits to be treated as such. One can defer from a number of studies that it is neither the personal

characteristics of the teacher nor the type of school, but rather the amount of stress present in the job that distinguishes different stress levels. Some of the most influential factors mentioned as causes of job stress are: lack of professional skills; new teaching methods; changes in curriculum and courses; adaptation to changes in information and communication technology; inadequate training and continuing education etc. Although there are variances in impact and job satisfaction, the presence of stress with common causes across countries and school systems, is undeniable.

The job specific stressors are also associated with the performance of specific tasks that make up an individual's job, sometimes referred to as task content factors as well as work environment and work scheduling factors (Kahn and Byosiere, 1990). They include variables such as the level of job complexities, the variety of tasks performed, the amount of discretion and control that individuals have over the pace and timing of their work, and the physical environment in which the work is performed. Early investigations aimed to identify the links between physical conditions and productivity (Roethlisberger and Dickson, 1939), and the importance of relationships between environmental factors and health was soon realized. Kornhauser (1965) observed that factors related to poor mental health include unpleasant working conditions and the requirements to operate at a fast pace, expend considerable physical effort for long periods, and work excessive and inconvenient hours. The amount of work that has to be performed is another significant stressor for many individuals. Both overload and under load can generate physical and psychological stress. Having to work under time pressure to meet deadlines is a major source of quantitative overload (Narayanan, Menon, and Spector, 1999) and has been related to high levels of strain, anxiety and depression, as well as low levels of job performance (Cooper and Roden, 1985; Kushmir and Melamed, 1991; Westman and Eden, 1992). Qualitative overload occurs when individuals believe they do not have the skills or capacities to satisfactorily perform job tasks, and it has been linked to low levels of self-esteem - as cited in International Labour Office (1981).

Teachers are perennially exposed to high level of stress cutting across all cultures (Copper and Kelly, 1993; Reglin and Reitzammer, 1997; Chan 1998; Mokdad, 2005). The combination of long working hours, insufficient pay, role ambiguity, poor teaching facilities, lack of social recognition, poor organizational climate, strained relationship with colleagues makeup a stressful recipe. As Kyriacou (1987) points out, it is the insidious day to day sources of stress with their cumulative effect, and not the less frequent but occasionally intent sources of stress, which teachers are concerned with.

Although the students were not noted as the main source of stress, it is rather that the organizational structure has not determined how to empower teachers to best deal with specific student issues. They are not always equipped with proper means to handle the increase in violence and aggression; the lack of attention, interest and motivation; disciplinary problems; drugs and; an expanding class size per teacher. These challenges are only worsened by increasing poor parent - teacher relations and decreased parent participation. The teacher experiences greater pressure from parents and society as a whole to play a larger role in the upbringing of a child - not only concerning ethical issues but also providing assistance and counseling for issues such as poor academic performance, increasing indiscipline, suicide, etc. The responsibility for students' overall welfare and well-being is a strain resulting in stress for teachers. It was also noted that women are often more susceptible to work-related stress due to a number of other outside pressures, such as having the same type of emotional and psychological responsibilities at home and at work, for her family and her students.

(b) *Organization Specific Stressors:* According to Cooper and Marshall (1976), stress could be due to factors intrinsic to the job, such as poor physical working conditions, work overload or time pressures. Often, one's role in the organization and the ambiguity associated with the job resulting from inadequate information concerning expectations, authority and responsibilities to perform one's role as well as the conflict that arises from the demands placed on the individual by superiors, peers and subordinates could also result in stress. A third factor is the impact of status incongruence, lack of job security and thwarted ambition on one's career progression. It is theorized that relationships at work with bosses and colleagues, including bullying in the workplace could result in a lot of stress. At an organizational level, the structure and climate, including the degree of involvement in decision-making and participation in office politics could result in a stressful climate. Organizational roles encompass the behaviours and demands that are associated with the job an individual performs. The importance of role related stress was first identified by kahn *et. al.* (1964). According to Beehr (1995) and; Robertson, Cooper, and Wiliams (1990), *role ambiguity, role conflict, role-overload and role under-load* are the most widely studied occupational stressors.

(i) *Role ambiguity* – as defined by kahn *et. al.* (1964), refers to unpredictability of the consequences of one's role performance. Later conceptualizations have extended the definition to include a lack of information needed to perform the role, and the typical measure of this construct assesses both unpredictability of consequences and information deficiency regarding expected role behaviour (Pearce, 1981). The role characteristic has been defined as a job situation in which there are inadequate or misleading pieces of information about how an individual is supposed to do the job (Beehr, 1985a). Additionally, role ambiguity is said to result when an individual's role is not clear, including lack of clarity about the objective of a job or the scope of an individual's responsibilities (Ivancevich and Matteson, 1980). The real stress of role ambiguity is experienced when individuals are prevented from being productive and achieving. In addition, stress resulting from role ambiguity is experienced when an individual loses a sense of certainty and predictability in the work role (Schuler, 1984). Beehr (1976) and Schuler (1980) conceptualize role ambiguity as the lack of specificity and predictability concerning an employee's job or role functions and responsibilities. Others (Beehr, 1985; Cooper, 1981; and Terborg, 1985) subsequently added that role ambiguity is an objective situation at work in which there is, insufficient, misleading, or restricted flow of information pertaining

to one's work role (Pearce, 1981). Role ambiguity is a situation in which there is lack of clearly defined role expectations (Kemery, 1991). Role ambiguity is often perceived when there are changes in technology, social structures, new personnel entering the organization (McGrath, 1976) and changes in jobs or new work place (Cooper *et. al.* 1988; Ivancevich and Matteson, 1980). Therefore, role ambiguity is the lack of clarity about duties, objectives and responsibilities needed to fulfill ones' role-often due to an inadequate understanding of colleagues' work expectations of job behaviours (Cooper, Cooper, and Eaker, 1988a; Peterson *et. al.* 1993).

(ii) *Role conflict* – reflects incompatible demands on the person, can reduce negative emotional reactions due to perceived inability to be effective on the job (Schaubroek *et. al.* 1989). Several studies have confirmed this detrimental effect of role conflict on both self reported strain (O'Driscol and Beehr, 1994) and physiological indicators of strain (Kahn and Byosiere, 1990). Quick and Quick (1984) differentiated four kinds of role conflict:

1. *Intra-sender role conflict*: when a supervisor or manager communicates expectations that are mutually incompatible.
2. *Inter-sender role conflict*: when two or more people communicate expectations that are incompatible.
3. *Person-role conflict*: when an individual perceives a conflict between his or her expectations and values and those of the organization or key people in the work environment, and
4. *Inter-role conflict*: when a person occupies two or more roles may have conflicting expectations or requirements.

Role conflict has been defined as two or more sets of incompatible demands concerning work issues (Bacharach, Bamberger, and Conley, 1990; Beehr, 1995; Kahn *et. al.* 1964; Katz and Kahn, 1978; Kemery, 1991). Specifically, incompatible demands may be between the expectations placed on an individual by concerned parties or by the interface between two or more roles of the same person (Cooper *et. al.* 1988; Peterson *et. al.* 1995). Rizzo *et. al.* (1970) maintain that role conflict also exists when organizational requirements clash with personal values and obligations to others. They express role conflict as feelings torn by pressures; *i.e.,* differing expectations placed on the individual cause the individual to feel divided in having to choose between, or to deal with, the varying demands or expectations. A commonly studied type of inter-role conflict deals with work and family roles. Gupta and Jenkins (1985) wrote that people in such relationships can experience many types of conflicts, depending on whether the conflicts are with one's spouse, one's work role, or between the two. When family problems spillover to one's work domain, there are work role related problems, including withdrawal behaviours and poor performance (Frone, 2003).

(iii) *Role overload* refers to the number of different roles a person has to fulfill and that occurs when an individual is not able to complete the work that is part of a particular job (Ross and Altmaier, 1994). Not only can role overload lead to excessive demands on an individual's time, but it also may create uncertainty about his or her ability to perform these roles adequately. An individual in a group

might malfunction where there is too much work to be done. Along with role ambiguity and role conflict, role overload has been found to be a major correlate of job related stress (Cooper, 1981). In fact, Narayanan *et. al.* (1999) found that work overload was mentioned more frequently by respondents as a source of stress than either role ambiguity or role conflict. Role overload is considered to be caused by too much work, time pressures and deadlines (Sofer, 1970), and lack of personal resources needed to fulfill duties, commitments, and responsibilities (Peterson *et. al.* 1995). In other words, it is an incompatibility between work demands and time available to satisfy the demands (Bacharach *et. al.* 1990; French and Caplan, 1973). Role overload is usually defined as the inability to fulfill organizational expectations in the time available (Kahn, 1980).

(iv) *Role under-load* is the other role characteristic related to being stressed in a particular job occurs when a person's skills are underutilised. The resulting stress is called role under-load. While role overload represents a demand, role under-load is characterized by constraint. Role under load is said to be present when employees have too much ability for the job they hold. As early as 1911, in his discussion of scientific management, Taylor (1911) noted that the negative effects that can arise when an individual is over skilled for a job.

Teachers are expected not only to work as pedagogues but also juggle multiple roles of an administrator, resource person, innovator, counsellor, and role model for society which subsequently leads to high levels of stress. In the prevailing educational setup, teachers continue to reel under the pressure of working under too many constraints imposed by too many bodies, meeting the norms and standards, rules and regulations of concerned state government, the ever changing eligibility criteria for becoming teachers and its implications and their professional lives also acts as a stressor. A vast majority of teachers employed in self-finance institutions work under autocratic organizational conditions where they are grappled with work overload, role ambiguity and job insecurity. Poor infrastructure facilities, outmoded curricula with little scope for innovation prove detrimental to the stress levels of teachers. Paucity of career advancement opportunities also contribute to stress among teachers (Basu, 2009).

The school is also viewed as a stressful working environment both physically and psychologically. Lack of financial resources for sufficient materials, class rooms and equipment, environmental noise, poor ventilation, and problems with hygiene and safety are just some of the bad working conditions. These are coupled with a lack of time and unrealistic workload, excessive paperwork and administrative duties, lack of personnel and allocation, and a strong administrative hierarchy with a lack of support. A combination of these factors places the environment in a position of low morale and lack of solidarity, and often the teacher experiences enormous isolation, being alone against their class. This causes a great deal of stress because these feelings clash with the teacher's personal ambitions and goals for fulfilling their job and providing a quality education, and the educator is left at a loss. The role of administration is crucial in handling these risks, and it must aim to balance the organization of work, human resources management, employee supervision and job performance evaluation.

(c) *Environment Specific Stressors*: Additional sources of stress include the impact a person's working life has on their life outside of work (work-life balance), the amount of satisfaction people derive from their work, the degree of control and autonomy people have in the work place, and the levels of commitment in the work place both from the employee to the organization and from the organization to the employee (Sheena *et. al.* 2005).

Managing the interface between one's job and various roles and responsibilities off the job is another potential source of strain (O'Driscol, 1996). Sometimes referred to as work/non-work conflict, this issue received considerable attention from researchers in recent years (Cooper and Lewis, 1998). Changes in family structures, increased participation by women in the workforce, and technological changes that enable job tasks to be performed in a variety of locations have blurred the boundaries between the job and life off the job for many workers and have created the potential for conflict to occur between job and off-job roles (Hill, Miller, and Colihan, 1998). The rise of families in which both partners are earning and increasing female participation in the sphere of employment has transformed the ways in which couples manage work and family responsibilities. Work and family integration can result in both negative (*i.e.,* work-family conflict) and positive interactions (*i.e.,* work-family enrichment). Work-family conflict and work-family enrichment can occur in either direction – 'work-to-family or family-to-work'. This inter-role conflict has consistently been linked with psychological strain (Frone, Russel, and Cooper, 1992; O'Driscol, Ilgen, and Hildreth, 1992) and is especially prevalent among women, employed parents, and dual-career couples (Aryee and Luk, 1996; Brayfield, 1995; Greenhaus and Parasuraman, 1994; Williams and Alliger, 1994). Work demands, family demands and work flexibility are recognized to be important determinants of the work-family interaction.

The quality of relationships that individuals have at work has consistently been linked to job stress (Payne, 1980). Poor co-worker relationships are associated with low trust, low supportiveness and low interest/willingness to listen and be emphatic (French and Caplan, 1973). Conversely, those individuals who report the greatest amount of group cohesion are best able to cope with stress on job (Ketz de Vries, 1984). It is apparent that the majority of causes are related to how work is organized, and following that are societal and personal pressures related to the teaching profession. With regard to professional development, there is a lack of training and continuing education available to keep up with the changes in teaching methods, curriculum, and aid materials. Furthermore, education policy reform and political restructuring tend to bring a heavy burden upon teachers, not only relating to the implementation of changes but also in terms of job security. Teachers are not remunerated according to the same salary scale as a majority of other professions, and this weighs heavily upon them financially and sends a message that their work is not highly valued.

2. *Individual Related Stressors*

Individual differences affect our perceptions and interpretations of events around us. They contribute to our experience of stress (primary appraisal), and our decisions what to do to deal with the stressor – our choice of coping process (secondary appraisal). Vast individual differences in vulnerability to stress alter an individual's perception of a potential source of stress (direct effect), impact on the transformation of perceived stress into various consequences of stress (indirect effect), and ameliorate these stress consequences (direct effect).

The personality variables that have been linked to stress include locus of control, self-esteem, Type- A behaviour pattern, hardiness and negative affectivity (Ganster and Schaubroeck, 1991b; Murphy, 1995). Demographic variables that are proven to relate to someone's job stressor/health relationships include gender, age, marital status, job tenure, job title and hierarchical level (Dua, 1994; Murphy, 1995), among which gender, age and hierarchical level were found to be the most significant, as further explanations reveal.

A general tendency exists in the literature according to which females experience higher levels of occupational stress regarding gender-specific stressors and have different ways of interpreting and dealing with problems related to their work environment (Antoniou *et. al.* 2006). For example, Sharpley *et. al.* (1996) found that males have statistically significant lower job stress scores. Fotinatos-Ventouratos and Cooper (2005) found that female managers are under much more pressure than their male counterparts; and Antoniou *et. al.* (2006) found that female teachers experienced significantly higher levels of occupational stress compared to their male counterparts. Ganster and Schaubroeck (1991a) point that women experience the greater level of stress as they are more vulnerable to the demands of work to the extent that they often have more non-work demands than men. Gregory (1990) notifies that, for the female professional, gender stereotyping in the workplace adds to the role conflict stress experiences, while Comish and Swindle (1994) explain that role demands such as that of being wife, mother and professional provoke role conflict. Finally, the results of the bivariate analysis conducted by Fotinatos-Ventouratos and Cooper (2005) revealed significant differences in terms of physical and psychological well-being amongst the male and female sample.

Concerning the relationship between age and occupational stress, the ability to handle stress associated with job and organization was found to increase with age (experience). For example, researches revealed that younger staff members reported more job stress than older staff (Dua, 1994), that employees who are less than 30 years old experience the highest levels of stress (Ben-Bakr *et. al.* 1995), that staff between the ages 31 and 40 suffered the most from job stress (Sharpley *et. al.* 1996), and that younger teachers experienced higher levels of burnout, specifically in terms of emotional exhaustion and disengagement from the profession (Antoniou *et. al.* 2006). The major explanation for such a finding is that older employees have often reached a stage where career development is not their major concern, and hence a number of job characteristics which may cause stress to younger staff, who have their career ahead of them, do not cause stress to older staff (Dua, 1994).

Lastly, staff employed at the higher job levels were found to be less stressed than those employed at the lower job levels (Dua, 1994). As well, different levels of management influence preference for stress coping styles, specifically, as it is progressed towards the more senior levels of management, delegation and maintaining style relationships are considered the most useful forms (Kirkcaldy and Martin, T., 2000).

Work Stress Theories/Models

Work stress theories are important as they attempt to describe, explain and predict stress/strain according to a coherent set of hypotheses. Many theories differ in emphasis, but their content is often overlapping and complementary. The work stress taxonomies include the following dimensions: stimulus/response combinations, sociological *vs.* psychological paradigms, and environmental *vs.* individual emphasis.

Cox *et.al.* (2000) assert that most current stress theorizing is psychological and conceptualizes work stress in terms of a negative psychological state, and the dynamic interaction between the person and the work environment. This includes: *Interactional Theories*, focusing on the structural features of a person's interaction with their work environment; and *Transactional Theories*, focusing on the cognitive processes and emotional reactions associated with the person's interaction with their environment.

Interactional Theories

Interactional models explain work stress in terms of the individual's interaction with the work environment. These are:

(a) Demand-Control/Support Model, and

(b) Burnout Theory.

(a) Demand-Control/Support Model

The Job Demand-Control (JDC, or DCS) Model put forward by Karasek (1979), argues that work stress primarily arises from the structural or organizational aspects of the work environment rather than from personal attributes or demographics of the situation. According to Karasek *et. al.* (1981) 'strain results from the joint effects of the demands of the work situation and environmental moderators of stress, particularly the range of decision-making freedom available to the worker facing those demands'. Strain is understood to result for people with objective high job demand and objective low control over their work, irrespective of individual differences in appraisal or coping. This conceptualization of stress views environmental causes as the starting point, although it does not strictly preclude the importance of personal factors.

Karasek argues that high demand jobs produce a state of normal arousal (*i.e.*, increased heart rate, increased adrenalin, increased breathing rate). This enables the body to respond to the demand. However, if there is an environmental constraint, such as low control, the arousal cannot be channeled into an effective coping response. Unresolved strain may in turn accumulate and as it builds up can result in anxiety, depression, psychosomatic complaints and cardiovascular disease.

According to the model, workers in high strain jobs (*e.g.*, machine paced assemblers, and service- based cooks and waiters) experience the highest levels of stress. High status workers, such as executives and professionals, have frequent opportunities to control or regulate high levels of demands. Further, potential personal health related behaviours did not appear to be responsible for the associations. Jobs with high demands, low control, and low support from supervisors to co- workers carry the highest risk for psychological or physical disorders. The model helps to develop links between productivity and healthy work. It takes account of the work environment imperative of productivity and postulates that increased productivity will occur when workers have jobs that combine high demands and high control.

(b) Burnout Theory

An interactional psychological model that is particularly relevant for people-oriented professions is the Theory of Burnout. Burnout is thought to result from prolonged exposure to chronic interpersonal stressors on the job from working with troubled people. Burnout has been described as a three-dimensional syndrome characterized by emotional exhaustion, depersonalization, and reduced personal accomplishment (Maslach and Jackson, 1981). Burnout is conceptualized as 'an individual stress experience embedded in a context of complex social relationships, and it involves the person's conception of both self and others' (Maslach, 1982).

Although human service work is argued to impose special stressors on workers because of the client's emotional demands, it is found that some stressors such as client's emotional demands, or problems associated with the professional helping role, such as failure to live up to one's own ideals, are less potent in predicting stress than those more common with other non-helping professionals. The job factors are more strongly related to burnout that is biographical or personal factors. Burnout process begins inevitably with some frustration or loss of autonomy with which the individual failed to cope in an adequate way. Burnout is largely a result of the organizational context. Further, the job is viewed more broadly to encompass the organizational context.

Maslach and Jackson (1981) note that although personality variables are certainly important in burnout, the problem is best understood in terms of job related stress. The prevalence of the phenomenon and the range of seemingly desperate professionals who are affected by it suggest that the search for causes is best directed towards uncovering the operational and structural characteristics of stressful situations. One concept of interest to researchers is the job- person fit model, not in the narrow sense of how an individual personality fits with the job, but rather how their motivations, emotions, values and job expectations fit with the job, or the organizational context.

Job-Person mismatch is hypothesized to lead to burnout, the greater the mismatch the greater the burnout. The burnout is an important mediator in the earlier job-person fit models that predict that better fit produces certain outcomes such as commitment, satisfaction, performance and job tenure (Maslach 1982). Maslach outlined six areas where mismatch can occur and the result is increased exhaustion, cynicism, and efficiency of burnout. The six mismatches are briefly described as follows.

- *Work overload* occurs when the job demands exceed limits;
- *Lack of control* occurs when people have little control over the work they do, either because of rigid policies and tight monitoring, or because of chaotic job conditions;
- *Insufficient reward* involves a lack of appropriate rewards for the work;

- *Breakdown of community* occurs when people lose a sense of positive connection with others in the work place, often due to conflict;
- *Absence of fairness* occurs with the perceived lack of a just system and fair procedures which maintain mutual respect in the work place; and
- *Value conflict* occurs when there is a mismatch between the requirements of the job and people's principles.

Transactional Theories

Transactional models explain the work stress in terms of cognitive processes and emotional reactions associated with person's interactions with his environment. These are:

(a) Effort-Reward Imbalance Model, and

(b) Cognitive Phenomenological Theory,

(a) Effort-Reward Imbalance Model

The Effort-Reward Imbalance (ERI) Model (Siegrist, 1996, 1998) is a more recently evolved model. This model is a transactional theory of stress in the sense that it focuses more on the interaction between environmental constraints or threats and individual coping resources. It also relates to the social framework of the job.

According to this model, workers expend effort at work and they expect rewards as part of a socially organized exchange process of work. It assumes that the 'work role in adult life provides a critical link between self-regulatory functions such as self-esteem and self-efficacy and the social opportunity structure'. ERI theory emphasizes rewards rather than job control. When an imbalance occurs, measured empirically as the ratio of efforts/reward, between the efforts a worker puts in and the rewards that are received, strain results. For ex, workers who have high job demands and low pay are likely to experience strain as a result of this imbalance. Similarly strain is expected when workers experience a threat to their job security.

ERI further identifies extrinsic effort and intrinsic efforts. Extrinsic effort is conceptually similar to the job demands concept in the DCS model. On the other hand, intrinsic effort refers to a personal characteristic of coping, a pattern of excessive striving in combination with a strong desire of being approved and esteemed. This pattern is referred to as over-commitment. A worker may have a high need for control which results in over-commitment and immersion in the job and likely, a personal perception of rewards. In empirical tests of the model, the idea is that over-commitment could moderate or mediate the demand between demands and rewards. This is a major departure from the DCS model which specifies no such individual variable.

(b) Cognitive Phenomenological Theory

A transactional theory that has sometimes been used in work stress research is the widely discussed Cognitive-Phenomenological Theory of Stress. Stress is defined in this approach as a relationship between the person and the environment that is appraised as taxing or exceeding resources, and endangers well-being (Lazarus and Folkman, 1984). In this cognitive model, appraisal of stress is necessary: 'for threat to occur, an evaluation must be made of situation to the effect that harm is signified' (Lazarus, 1966). Stress in these stimulus- response based models is not just the property of the body. It is the result of transactional psychobiological processes. The theory emphasizes how individuals perceive or primarily appraise a stimulus 'is this a problem?' and then secondarily appraises their coping resources 'what am I able to do about it?' Both appraisal processes, primary and secondary, are key mediators in the relation between stressor and strain. If a situation is perceived as stressful and important then coping is activated. It may involve attempts to modify person-environment relationship or attempt to regulate resulting emotional distress. The situation is then re-appraised and the process repeated. If the situation is resolved, coping ceases. If it is unresolved, then psychological physiological strain persists resulting in longer term negative effects on health and well-being.

The essence of the cognitive model is the meaning given by individuals to events. The usefulness of this is that when workers are in employment contexts that are taxing, recommended coping approaches may help alleviate strain. The theory has limitations in the work stress context, as it can not specify which aspects of the work environment would be stressful, because, according to the theory each individual might see the environment in a different way.

Consequences of Occupational Stress

At a general level, there has been a great deal of investigation of the association between the various sources of occupational stress and the resulting manifestations of stress. Stress produces a range of undesirable, expensive, and debilitating consequences, which affect both individuals and organizations. In organizational setting, stress is now-a-days becoming a major contributor to health and performance problems of individuals, and unwanted occurrences and costs for organizations. Consequences of occupational stress can be grouped into those on individual and those on organizational level. On the individual level, there are three main subgroups of stress (Cooper and Payne, 1990);

1. *Unwanted Feelings and Behaviours:* such as job dissatisfaction, lower motivation, low employee morale, less organizational commitment, lowered overall quality of work life, absenteeism, turnover to other jobs, intention to leave the job, lower productivity, decreased quantity and quality of work, inability to make sound decisions, sabotage and work stoppage, occupational burnout, alienation, and increased smoking and alcohol intake.
2. *Physiological Diseases (poor physical health):* such as increased blood pressure and pulse rate, cardiovascular diseases, high cholesterol, high blood sugar, insomnia, headaches, infections, skin problems, suppressed immune system, injuries, and fatigue. It also leads to psychosomatic illness and depleted energy reserves (Milstein and Golaszewski, 1985).
3. *Psychological Diseases (poor emotional/mental health):* psychological distress includes depression, anxiousness, passiveness/aggressiveness, boredom, loss of self-confidence and self-esteem, loss of concentration, feelings of futility, impulsiveness and disregarding of social norms and values, dissatisfaction with

job and life, losing of contact with reality, and emotional fatigue. Fimian and Santoro (1981), claim that, emotional manifestations are often precursors for behavioural and physiological manifestations of stress in teachers, and so these should never be seen as discrete in nature.

On the organizational level, consequences of occupational stress can be grouped as - discontent and poor morale among the workforce, poor performance, poor relationships with students and co-workers, loss of valuable staff, increased sick-leave, permanent vacancies, premature retirement, diminished cooperation, poor internal communications, more internal conflicts, and dysfunctional workplace climate. As it is evident, consequences of occupational stress, both on individual and organizational level can be associated with both pleasant and unpleasant events, and only becomes problematic when it remains unresolved (Erkutlu and Chafra, 2006). In other words, one could argue that not all stress is dysfunctional and that, in fact, stress is not inherently bad, while a limited amount of stress combined with appropriate responses actually can benefit both the individual and the organization. Namely, as low and high stress predict poor performance, and moderate stress predicts maximum performance (Yerkes and Dodson, 1908 in Sharpley *et. al.* 1996), the total elimination of stress should not be aimed at.

The ways in which stress manifests itself are generally referred to in terms of *behavioural, physical or psychological* outcomes. Overall, teachers manifesting high levels of stress also show signs of high levels of psychological distress, usually demonstrated by high anxiety and low psychological well-being, as well as decreased job satisfaction *i.e., mental ill-health, burnout and job dissatisfaction* among the teachers (Traverse and Cooper, 1996).

Mental ill-health: Poor mental well-being can be directly related to unpleasant working conditions, the necessity to work fast, expenditure of physical effort and inconvenient hours (Argyris, 1964; Kornhauser, 1965). A review by Miner and Brewer (1976) suggests that, certain stresses in the occupational sphere can be a source of emotional disorder. A number of studies have highlighted a positive relationship between self-reported teacher stress and overall measures of mental ill-health (Pratt, 1978; Galloway *et. al.* 1982b; Tellenbeck *et. al.* 1983). Emotional reaction may take the form of depression, anxiety, helplessness, insecurity, vulnerability and inadequacy, general uneasiness, irritability, emotional fatigue, resentment towards administration, negative self-concept and self-esteem. Dunham (1976a) has identified the two most common types of mental ill-health *i.e.,* frustration and anxiety. Frustration can be associated with the physiological symptoms of headaches, sleep disturbances, stomach upsets, hyper tension and body rashes and, in severe cases, depressive illness, where as anxiety can be linked to loss of confidence, feelings of inadequacy, confusion in thinking and sometimes panic. In severe cases, anxiety can lead to the physiological psychosomatic symptoms of a nervous rash, twitchy eye, loss of voice and weight loss. In prolonged cases, a nervous breakdown may result.

Burnout: A more extreme result of long term effects of teacher stress is total emotional exhaustion (Hargreaves, 1978). This state of burnout may lead to out-of school apathy, alienation from work and withdrawal into a number of defensive strategies. Burnout may be identified as a type of chronic response to the cumulative long term negative impact of work stress (Blasé, 1982). This is different to the short term acute stress, which is far more intense and refers to the negative working conditions, when job stress seems unavoidable to an individual, and sources of satisfaction or relief appear unavailable (Moss, 1981). Burnout may be defined as a reaction to job related stress that varies in nature with the intensity and duration of the stress itself, resulting in individuals becoming emotionally detached from their jobs altogether (Daley, 1979). The major symptoms of burnout as defined by Pines (1982a) are; high *emotional exhaustion, high depersonalization, and low personal accomplishment.* It would appear that it is experienced mainly by those professionals who deal with other people *i.e.,* lawyers, accountants, managers, nurses, police officers, social workers and, in particular, teachers (Blasé, 1982). Another view expressed by Harvey and Brown (1984) is that those who experience job burnout as a result of job related stress are those who are professionals and/or self-motivating achievers seeking unrealistic or unattainable goals. As a consequence of this, they cannot cope with the demands of their job and their willingness to try drops dramatically. Studies into burnout in teachers have shown that it is largely a result of excessive work stress over extended periods of time and relentless work demands (Begley, 1982).

A relationship between a teacher's personality and burnout has also been identified by researchers. Teachers with a negative attitude towards students, external locus of control and intolerance of ambiguity were reported to have higher levels of burnout than other teachers in Fielding's study (1982). Pines and Aronson (1981) found that different organizational environment can significantly affect burnout rates within an organization. Studies of Westerhouse (1979) and Schwab (1981) have shown that role conflict and role ambiguity were significantly related to teacher burnout. A study of 40 American teachers by Cooley and laviki concluded that individual, social-psychological and organizational factors were all strongly associated with burnout. Lowenstein's (1991) study revealed that teacher stress and burnout was caused by a lack of social recognition of teachers, large class size, lack of resources, isolation, fear of violence, lack of classroom control, role ambiguity, limited professional opportunities, and a lack of support. Of major concern to the teaching profession is that burnout can detract from the quality of teaching. Mancini *et. al.,* (1982-84) have shown that burned-out teachers give significantly less information and less praise, show less acceptance of their pupils' ideas and interact less frequently with them.

Job Dissatisfaction: One of the major significant behavioural manifestations of the experience of stress at work is low job satisfaction. A study of UK teachers by Fletcher and Payne (1982) of 148 teachers found that the majority of this sample liked their job, but at the same time felt a considerable amount of pressure. A study of Moracco *et. al.* (1983) discovered a high level of dissatisfaction with teaching as a career, with stress being seen as a major contributory factor. More detailed analysis of the issues relating to this job dissatisfaction reveals that factors such as salary, career structure, promotion opportunities, and occupational status are involved (Tellenbeck *et. al.* 1983). Needle *et. al.* (1980) also found that teachers reporting higher level of job stress reported job dissatisfaction. Kyriacou and Sutcliffe (1979a) found that self-reported teacher stress was negatively correlated with job satisfaction and also to some of the stressors such as poor career structure, individual misbehaving pupils, inadequate salary, inadequate disciplinary policy of school, noisy pupils, difficult classes, trying to uphold/maintain standards, and too much work to do. However, they found that there was no significant difference in terms of age, length of experience and position held in school.

Stress is a major risk factor in the physical and mental health of a teacher, and the effects may be both short and long term. Many surveys have concluded that work-related pressure has dramatically increased for teachers in the 1990s. Teachers experiencing high levels of work-related stress can develop a sort of 'stress syndrome' that combines their stress with negative emotions like anger, fear and helplessness. This syndrome can make it difficult for them to relax in their spare time, have a negative impact on their health and well-being, greatly interrupt their interpersonal transactions, and negatively interfere with their non-professional and family life. It is important that teachers understand that, in education, there is a profound need for restoration, relaxation and rejuvenation, and they should be allowed these things without feeling guilty. Prevalence of stress or a stress-related illness is often associated with shame, guilt and a loss of pride and dignity. Besides from feeling a lack of support for their job, most teachers feel that their employers also fail to look after their health and safety. Some of the more commonly reported stress-related illnesses are high blood pressure, migraine headaches, recurrent virus infections, irritable bowel syndrome, stomach ulcers, asthma, and depression.

However, one of the greatest risks of stress is the decrease in the quality of education and the reduction in teacher effectiveness. The combination of all of these elements means that the overall quality of education provided by the institutions also suffers. The ramifications of stress for the entire organization can be widespread. An organization affected by stress may display some of the symptoms such as: high levels of sickness and absenteeism, frequent and severe accidents, dysfunctional personal relationships, apathy among the workforce, poor quality and low levels of performance.

CONCEPT, MEANING AND DEFINITIONS OF JOB PERFORMANCE

Job performance is a commonly used, yet poorly defined concept in industrial and organizational psychology, the branch of psychology that deals with the workplace. Despite the confusion over how it should be exactly defined, performance is an extremely important criterion that relates to organizational outcomes and success. Among the most commonly accepted theories of job performance comes from the work of John Campbell and colleagues. Coming from a psychological perspective, Campbell (1990) describes job performance as an individual level variable. That is, performance is something a single person does. This differentiates it from more encompassing constructs such as organizational performance or national performance which are higher level variables. First, Campbell defines performance as behaviour. It is something done by the employee. This concept differentiates performance from outcomes. Outcomes are the result of an individual's performance, but they are also the result of other influences. In other words, there are more factors that determine outcomes than just an employee's behaviours and actions. On the other hand, it is less restrictive than defining job performance solely in terms of task performance. This is important because many behaviours that are not strictly considered part of task performance often contribute to organizational goals (Organ, 1994; Organ and Ryan, 1995).

Campbell (1990) allows for exceptions when defining performance as behaviour. For instance, he clarifies that performance does not have to be directly observable actions of an individual. It can consist of mental productions such as answers or decisions. However, performance needs to be under the individual's control, regardless of whether the performance of interest is mental or behavioural. Campbell distinguishes job performance from *effectiveness, productivity and utility*. The first is performance and the second is the effectiveness of that performance. These two can be decoupled because performance is not the same as effectiveness. *Effectiveness* is defined as the evaluation of the results of an employee's job performance. This is an important distinction to make because effectiveness is determined by more than just employee job performance. For example, it is possible for an employee to perform very well but receive a poor performance rating because he or she does not get along well with the person providing the rating. Another closely related construct is *productivity*. This can be thought of as a comparison of the amount of effectiveness that results from a certain level of cost associated with that effectiveness. In other words, effectiveness is the ratio of outputs to inputs — those inputs being effort, monetary costs, resources, etc. *Utility* is another related construct which is defined as the value of a particular level of performance, effectiveness, or productivity. Utilities of performance, effectiveness and productivity are value judgements. Another key feature of job performance is that it has to be *goal relevant*. Performance must be directed toward organizational goals that are relevant to the job or role. Therefore, performance does not include activities where effort is expended toward achieving peripheral goals. For example, the effort put toward the goal of getting to work in the shortest amount of time is not performance (except where it is concerned with avoiding lateness).

In general, instructor performance is defined as the capacity of an instructor to accomplish the work assigned. It is his or her competence to get things done. In university, teaching performance is considered as bottom line of instructors. It refers to the quality and quantity of task accomplishments by an instructor or group of instructors at work. It is a cornerstone of productivity and has great contribution to achievements of university. Viswesvaran and One's (2000) generated a relatively general view of profession performance as 'scalable actions, behaviour and outcomes that employees engage in or bring about that are linked with and contribute to organization goals'. Job performance is typically conceptualized as 'actions and behaviours that are under the control of the individual that contribute to the goals of the organization' (Rotundo and Sackett, 2002).

Viswesvaran (1993) provides an excellent comprehensive review of historical developments in the conceptualization of job performance. As he notes, the literature examining the structure of job performance is fragmented and incomplete. Early conceptualizations (*e.g.,* Brogden and Taylor, 1950) focused largely on the economic value of individual behaviours to the organization. With the emergence of the literature on expectancy theory, many researchers began to focus on measures that reflected the effort expenditure and productivity of workers (Viswesvaran, 1993). In the 1970s and 1980s, research on pro-social and organizational citizenship behaviours proliferated (*e.g.,* Bateman and Organ, 1983; Smith, Organ, and Near, 1983). This resulted in the introduction of a variety of criterion measures such as teamwork and altruism. Finally, in recent years, the impact of counterproductive behaviour in the workplace has been studied extensively (*e.g.,* Collins, 1996; Ones, Viswesvaran, and Schmidt, 1993). This literature has yielded a number of criterion measures related to honesty and integrity in the workplace.

According to Motowidlo *et. al.* (1997) job performance is *behavioural, episodic, evaluative,* and *multidimensional* and it is the aggregated value to the organization of the discrete behavioural episodes that an individual performs over a standard interval of time. It is predicted that individual differences in personality and cognitive ability variables, in combination with learning experiences, lead to variability in knowledge, skills and work habits that mediate the effects of personality and cognitive ability on job performance. An important aspect is that it predicts the kinds of knowledge, skills, work habits and traits that are associated with task performance that are different from the kinds that are associated with contextual performance.

Determinants of Performance

Campbell *et. al.* (1993) and Campbell *et. al.* (1996) presented a theory of performance formalizing relations that Hunter (1983) showed between ability, job edge and skill, and job performance. They argued that there are three direct determinants of job performance: *declarative knowledge, procedural knowledge and skill,* and *motivation. Declarative knowledge* is knowledge of facts, principles, goals and procedures, knowledge that might be measured, for example, by the kind of paper-and-pencil tests included in Hunter's meta-analysis. It is assumed to be a function of a person's abilities, personality, interests, education, training, experience, and aptitude-treatment interactions. *Procedural knowledge and skill* is actually doing what should be done. It is the combination of knowing what to do and actually being able to do it. It includes skills such as cognitive skill, psychomotor skill, physical skill, self-management skill, and inter-personal skill. Predictors of procedural knowledge and skills are again abilities, personality, interests, education, training, experience, and aptitude-treatment interactions — and additionally practice. *Motivation* is the combination of choice to exert effort, choice of how much effort to exert, and choice of how long to continue to exert effort. Campbell does not make specific assumption about the predictors of motivation. Individual differences in personality, ability, and interests are presumed to combine and interact with education, training, and experience to shape declarative knowledge and procedural knowledge and skill.

Campbell (1990) also mentioned several performance parameters that may have important implications for the job performance setting and should be investigated by industrial and organizational psychologists. The first one is the distinction between *speed and accuracy*. This distinction is similar to the one between quantity and quality. Important questions that should be considered include: which is most valued by the organization, maximized speed, maximized accuracy, or some balance between the two? What kind of trade-offs should an employee make? The latter question is important because speed and accuracy for the same task may be independent of one another. The second distinction is between *typical and maximum performance.* Sackett, Zedeck, and Fogli (1988) did a study on supermarket cashiers and found that there was a substantial difference between scores reflecting their typical performance and scores reflecting their maximum performance. This study suggested the distinction between typical and maximum performance. Regular work situations reflect varying levels of motivation which result in typical performance. Special circumstances generate maximum employee motivation which results in maximum performance.

McCrae and Costa (1996) presented a meta-theoretical framework that started from a very different intellectual tradition from that represented in work by Hunter (1983) and Campbell *et. al.* (1993), but ended with remarkably similar implications for the pattern of relations between traits such as ability and personality, job knowledge and skill, and job performance. Their framework was designed to summarize the kind of variables that all theories of personality, including the five-factor model, must be concerned with. It describes relations between five broad categories of variables-basic tendencies, characteristic adaptations, objective biography, self-concept, and external influences.

These empirical and theoretical contributions by Hunter (1983), Campbell *et. al.* (1993), and McCrae and Costa (1996) have in common the idea that effects of basic individual difference variables, such as ability and personality, on job performance are mediated by other variables. In Hunter's model, the mediating variables are knowledge and skill (work sample performance), in Campbell's *et. al.,* model, they are declarative knowledge, procedural knowledge, skill, and motivation and in McCrae and Costa's model, they are characteristic adaptations that include variables such as knowledge and skill.

Perspectives on Performance

Researchers have adopted various perspectives for studying performance. On the most general level Viswesvaran and One's (2000) differentiated between three different perspectives:

1. An individual differences perspective which searches for individual characteristics (*e.g.,* general mental ability, personality) as sources for variation in performance,
2. A situational perspective which focuses on situational aspects as facilitators and impediments for performance, and
3. A performance regulation perspective which describes the performance process.

These perspectives are not mutually exclusive but approach the performance phenomenon from different angles which complement one another. Motivational constructs related to performance can be partly subsumed under the individual differences perspectives (*e.g.*, need for achievement), partly under the situational perspectives (*e.g.*, extrinsic rewards), and partly under the performance regulation perspective (*e.g.*, goal setting).

Individual Differences Perspective

The individual differences perspective focuses on performance differences between individuals and seeks to identify the underlying factors. The core question to be answered by this perspective is: Which individuals perform best? The basic idea is that differences in performance between individuals can be explained by individual differences in abilities, personality and/or motivation. Campbell (1990) proposed a general model of individual differences in performance which became very influential (Campbell *et. al.*, 1993). In his model, Campbell differentiates performance components (*e.g.*, job specific task proficiency), determinants of job performance components and predictors of these determinants. Campbell describes the performance components as a function of three determinants:

1. Declarative knowledge,
2. Procedural knowledge and skills, and
3. Motivation.

He assumes that there are interactions between the three types of performance determinants, but does not specify them in detail (Campbell *et. al.* 1996). In his model, Campbell (1990) largely neglects situational variables as predictors of performance (Hesketh and Neal, 1999). Campbell *et. al.* (1996) summarized studies that identified job knowledge and job skills as measured by work sample tests as predictors of individual performance. Moreover, ability and experience were predictors of job knowledge and job skills, but had no direct effect on job performance. Campbell *et. al.*, interpret these findings as support for their model with declarative knowledge, procedural knowledge, and motivation acting as the only direct determinants of performance.

Empirical studies in this area are not always explicitly linked to the models proposed by Campbell (1990) or Motowidlo *et. al.* (1997). Nevertheless, virtually all studies on individual predictors of job performance can be subsumed under the individual differences perspective. More specifically, cognitive ability, personality, motivational factors and experience are the predictors of job performance. Meta-analytic evidence speaks for a strong relationship between cognitive ability and job performance. Individuals with high cognitive abilities perform better than individuals with low cognitive abilities across a broad range of different jobs (Bobko, Roth, and Potosky, 1999; Hunter and Hunter, 1984; Schmidt and Hunter, 1998). Most authors assume an underlying mechanism of cognitive ability helping to acquire job knowledge and job skills which in turn have a positive impact on job performance (Schmidt, Hunter, Outerbride, and Goff, 1988; Schmidt, Hunter, and Outerbridge, 1986).

Researchers also addressed the question whether personality accounts for performance differences across individuals. Meta-analyses showed that the general relationships between personality factors and job performance are relatively insignificant, but a strong relationship emerged for neuroticism/emotional stability and conscientiousness (Barrick and Mount, 1991; Tett, Jackson, and Rothstein, 1991). However, the relevance of specific personality factors for performance varies between different jobs (Vinchur, Schippmann, Switzer, and Roth, 1998). Individual differences in motivation may be caused by differences in motivational traits and differences in motivational skills (Kanfer and Heggestad, 1997). Motivational traits are closely related to personality constructs, but they are narrower and more relevant for motivational processes, *i.e.*, the intensity and persistence of an action. Kanfer and Heggestad (1997) described achievement and anxiety as two basic work-relevant motivational traits. Vinchur *et. al.*'s (1998) meta-analysis provides evidence for the need for achievement to be related to job performance. Motivational skills refer to self-regulatory strategies pursued during goal striving. In contrast to motivational traits, motivational skills are assumed to be more domain-specific and influenced by situational factors as well as learning and training experiences. Motivational skills comprise emotional control and motivation control (Kanfer and Heggestad, 1997; Kuhl, 1985). Self-efficacy — the belief that one can execute an action well is another construct in the motivational domain which is highly relevant for performance (Bandura, 1997; Stajkovic and Luthans, 1998). More specifically, self-efficacy has been shown to be related both to task performance, such as business success in small business owners, as well as to contextual performance, such as personal initiative (Speier and Frese, 1997) and developing ideas and suggestions within an organizational suggestion system (Frese, Teng, and Wijnen, 1999). Additionally, self-efficacy has been of particular importance in the learning process. For example, in a careful process analysis, Mitchell, Hopper, Daniels, and George-Falvy (1994) have looked at the effects of self-efficacy on learning. In the beginning of the learning process, self-efficacy is a better predictor of performance than goals, while this relationship is reversed at a later stage. Moreover, professional experience shows a positive, although small relationship with job performance (Quinones *et. al.* 1995). Additionally, there are interactions between predictors from several areas. For example, high achievement motivation was found to enhance the effects of high cognitive ability (O'Reilly and Chatman, 1994). Some practical implications follow from this individual differences perspective. Above all, the individual differences perspective suggests a focus on personnel selection. The individual differences perspective also suggests that training programmes should be implemented which aim at improving individual prerequisites for high performance. More specifically, training should address knowledge and skills relevant for task accomplishment. Furthermore, exposing individuals to specific experiences such as traineeships and mentoring programmes are assumed to have a beneficial effect on individuals' job performance.

Situational Perspective

The situational perspective refers to factors in the individuals' environment which stimulate and support or hinder performance. The core question to be answered is: In which situations do individuals perform best? The situational perspective encompasses approaches which focus on workplace factors but also specific motivational approaches which follow for example from expectancy theory (Vroom, 1964) or approaches which aim at improving performance by reward systems or by establishing perceptions of equity and fairness (Adams, 1963; Greenberg, 1990). Most of the existing leadership research can be subsumed under this perspective.

With respect to workplace factors and their relationship to individual performance two major approaches can be differentiated:

1. Those that focus on situational factors enhance and facilitate performance, and
2. Those that attend to situational factors which impede performance.

A prominent approach within the first category is the job characteristics model (Hackman and Oldham, 1976). In this model, Hackman and Oldham assumed that job characteristics (*i.e.,* skill variety, task identity, task significance, autonomy, feedback) have an effect on critical psychological states (*i.e.,* experienced meaningfulness, experienced responsibility for work outcomes, knowledge of the results of the work activities) which in turn have an effect on personal and work outcomes, including job performance. Additionally, they expected an interaction effect with employee growth need strength. In essence, the job characteristics model is a motivational model on job performance (Wall and Jackson, 1995). Meta-analytic findings suggest that there is a small, but positive relationship between job characteristics and job performance (Fried, 1991; Fried and Ferris, 1987). Guzzo, Jette and Katzell (1985) also reported positive effects of work redesign interventions on performance. The cross-sectional nature of many studies does not allow for a causal interpretation. For example, it might be that individuals who show high performance get the better jobs. However, intervention studies showed that job design suggested by a job characteristics model has a positive effect on performance (Griffin, 1991; Wall and Clegg, 1981). Socio-technical systems theory (Trist and Bamforth, 1951) also falls in this first category of job design approaches which specify workplace factors that enhance performance. Basically, socio-technical systems theory describes work systems as composed of social and technical subsystems and suggests that performance improvement can only follow from the joint optimization of both subsystems. In more detail, socio-technical systems theory suggests a number of job design principles such as the compatibility between the design process and its objectives, a minimal specification of tasks, methods, and task allocations, and the control of problems and unforeseen events as near as to their origins as possible (Cherns, 1976; Clegg, 2000). As Parker and Turner pointed out, socio-technical systems theory is more concerned with group performance than with individual performance. However, one can assume that work situations designed on the basis of this approach have also positive effects on individual performance.

Performance Regulation Perspective

The performance regulation perspective takes a different look at individual performance and is less interested in person or situational predictors of performance. Rather, this perspective focuses on the performance process itself and conceptualizes it as an action process. It addresses as its core questions: 'How does the performance process look like?' and "What is happening when someone is 'performing'?" Typical examples for the performance regulation perspective include the expert research approach within cognitive psychology (Ericsson and Lehmann, 1996) and the action theory approach of performance (Frese and Sonnentag, 2000; Frese and Zapf, 1994; Hacker, 1973; Hacker, 1998). It is one of the main goals of expertise research to identify what distinguishes individuals at different performance levels (Ericsson and Smith, 1991). More specifically, expertise research focuses on process characteristics of the task accomplishment process. It aims at a description of the differences between high and moderate performers while working on a task. Crucial findings within this field are that high performers differ from moderate performers in the way they approach their tasks and how they arrive at solutions (Sonnentag, 2000). For example, during problem comprehension, high performers focus on abstract and general information, they proceed from general to specific information, and apply a 'relational strategy' in which they combine and integrate various aspects of the task and the solution process (Isenberg, 1986; Koubek and Salvendy, 1991; Shaft and Vessey, 1998). Moreover, high performers focus more on long-range goals and show more planning in complex and ill-structured tasks, but not in well-structured tasks. The action theory approach (Frese and Zapf, 1994) describes the performance process as any other action from both a process and a structural point of view. The process point of view focuses on the sequential aspects of an action, while the structural point of view refers to its hierarchical organization.

From the process point of view, goal development, information search, planning, execution of the action and its monitoring, and feedback processing can be distinguished (Frese and Zapf, 1994; Hacker, 1998). Performance depends on high goals, a good mental model, detailed planning, and good feedback processes. Frese and Sonnentag (2000) derived propositions about the relationship between these various action process phases and performance. For example, with respect to information search they hypothesized that processing of action-relevant, important but parsimonious and realistic information is crucial for high performance. Roe (1999) suggested a very broad approach to performance regulation, in which he incorporated the action theory approach as one of five perspectives. The other four components of performance regulation are: energetic regulation, emotional regulation, vitality regulation, and self-image regulation. Roe assumes that all these five types of regulation are involved in performance regulation.

The process regulation perspective is closely linked to specific performance improvement interventions. The most prominent interventions are goal setting (Locke and Latham, 1990) and feedback interventions (Ilgen, Fisher, and Taylor, 1979). The basic idea of goal setting as a performance improvement intervention is that setting specific and difficult goals results in better performance than no or 'do-your-best' goals (Locke and Latham, 1990). Goal-setting theory assumes that goals affect performance via four mediating mechanisms: effort, persistence, direction, and task strategies. The benefits of goal setting on performance have been shown in virtually hundreds of empirical studies (Locke and Latham, 1990). Meta-analyses showed that goal setting belongs to one of the most powerful work-related intervention programmes (*e.g.*, Guzzo *et. al.* 1985). The performance regulation perspective suggests that an improvement of the action process itself improves performance. For example, individual should be encouraged to set long-range goals and to engage in appropriate planning, feedback seeking, and feedback processing. This perspective assumes that training interventions can be useful in achieving such changes. Additionally, job design interventions can help to improve the action process (Wall and Jackson, 1995).

There is a long tradition within psychology which assumes that feedback has a positive effect on performance (Kluger and DeNisi, 1996). Indeed, there is broad evidence that feedback enhances performance if the feedback is task related. Feedback which refers primarily to self-related processes however, has no effect or at least a detrimental effect on performance, even if it is 'positive' feedback (Kluger and DeNisi, 1996). Moreover, a combination of a goal-setting intervention with a feedback intervention results in better performance than a goal-setting intervention alone (Neubert, 1998). A rather different approach to performance regulation is the behaviour modification perspective. Based on reinforcement theory (Luthans and Kreitner, 1975) this approach is not primarily interested in the processes within the individual which regulate performance but in regulative interventions from outside the individual, particularly positive reinforcement. Such reinforcements can comprise financial interventions, non-financial interventions such as performance feedback, social rewards such as attention and recognition, or a combination of all these types of reinforcements. Meta-analytic findings suggest that such behaviour modification interventions have a positive effect on task performance, both in the manufacturing and in the service sector (Stajkovic and Luthans, 1997).

Relationships among the Various Perspectives

The three perspectives represent different approaches to the performance phenomenon and our description stresses the differences between these perspectives. However, researchers often combine two or more approaches when explaining performance. For example, there are combinations between the individual differences and the situational perspective (*e.g.*, Barrick and Mount, 1993; Colarelli, Dean, and Konstans, 1987). In essence, the job characteristic model assumes that a combination of situational factors (*i.e.*, job characteristics) and individual differences factors is crucial for individual performance (Hackman and Oldham, 1976). Similarly, Waldman (1994) suggested a model of performance in which he integrated the individual differences perspective with the situational perspective. He assumes that both person factors (*i.e.*, individual difference variables) and system factors (*i.e.*, situational variables) have an effect on job performance. In addition, he assumes that system factors moderate the effects of the person factors. Mitchell (1997) proposed a model on job performance in which he explicitly combined the individual differences and situational perspective. He postulated that both 'individual inputs' (*i.e.*, individual difference variables) and 'job context' (*i.e.*, situational variables) have a direct effect on motivated behaviour by providing necessary skills in the case of individual inputs, and by enabling *vs*. limiting behaviour in the case of the job context. Motivated behaviour in turn affects performance. Mitchell assumes that individual differences and job context additionally affect motivated behaviour via motivational processes such as arousal, attention, direction, intensity, and persistence. Despite these efforts, a comprehensive model which integrates all the various performance perspectives is still missing. Particularly, it is largely unclear how individual and situational variables come into play within the performance process. It would be particularly helpful to develop a model which combines the individual differences and situational perspective with the performance regulation perspective. Such a model should specify how cognitive ability and motivational factors probably in interaction with situational variables translate into the performance process, *i.e.*, how they affect the setting of goals, problem comprehension, planning and feedback processing, as well as the 'choice' of the appropriate hierarchical level of action regulation.

Different Types of Performance

Performance is a multi-dimensional concept. On the most basic level, Borman and Motowidlo (1993) divided performance in terms of *task* and *contextual* (citizenship and counterproductive) behaviours. *Task performance* describes obligatory behaviours. It can be defined as the effectiveness with which job incumbents perform activities that contribute to the organization's technical core either directly by implementing a part of its technological process, or indirectly by providing it with needed services (Borman and Motowidlo, 1993). Examples of task performance dimensions for a teachers' profession includes proficiency in content, reading and writing skills, efficiency in handling teaching aids, knowledge enrichment and attitude and aptitude towards teaching. *Contextual behaviours* are behaviours that do not fulfill specific aspects of the job's required role. Contextual activities are important because they contribute to organizational effectiveness in ways that shape the organizational, social, and psychological context that serves as the catalyst for task activities and processes. Contextual activities include volunteering to carry out task activities that are not formally part of the job and helping and cooperating with others in the organization to get tasks accomplished.

Task Performance

Task performance refers to an individual's proficiency with which he or she performs activities which contribute to the organization's 'technical core'. This contribution can be both direct and indirect. Task performance in itself is multi-dimensional. For example, among the 8 performance components proposed by Campbell (1990), there are 5 factors which refer to task performance (Campbell, Gasser, and Oswald, 1996; Motowidlo and Schmit, 1999):

1. Job-specific task proficiency,
2. Non-job-specific task proficiency,
3. Written and oral communication proficiency,
4. Supervision — in the case of a supervisory or leadership position — and partly
5. Management/administration.

Each of these factors comprises a number of sub-factors which may vary between different jobs. For example, the management/administration factor comprises sub-dimensions such as:

(i) Planning and organizing,

(ii) Guiding, directing, and motivating subordinates and providing feedback,

(iii) Training, coaching, and developing subordinates,

(iv) Communication effectively and keeping others informed (Borman and Brush, 1993).

Contextual Performance

Researchers have developed a number of contextual performance concepts. On a very general level, one can differentiate between two types of contextual performance: behaviours which aim primarily at the smooth functioning of the organization as it is at the present moment, and proactive behaviours which aim at changing and improving work procedures and organizational processes. Contextual performance refers to activities which do not contribute to the technical core but which support the organizational, social, and psychological environment in which organizational goals are pursued. Contextual performance includes not only behaviours such as helping co-workers or being a reliable member of the organization, but also making suggestions about how to improve work procedures. The 'stabilizing' contextual performance behaviours include organizational citizenship behaviour with its five components altruism, conscientiousness, civic virtue, courtesy, and sportsmanship (Organ, 1988), some aspects of organizational spontaneity (*e.g.,* helping co-workers, protecting the organization; George and Brief, 1992) and of pro-social organizational behaviour (Brief and Motowidlo, 1986). The more pro-active behaviours include personal initiative (Frese, Fay, Hilburger, Leng, and Tag, 1997; Frese, Kring, Soose, and Zempel, 1996), voice (Van Dyne and LePine, 1998), and taking charge (Morrison and Phelps, 1999). Thus, contexual performance is not a single set of uniform behaviours, but is in itself a multidimensional concept (Van Dyne and LePine, 1998).

Relationship between Task and Contextual Performance

Task and contextual performance can be easily distinguished at the conceptual level. There is also increasing evidence that these two concepts can also be separated empirically (*e.g.,* Morrison and Phelps, 1999; Motowidlo and Van Scotter, 1994; Van Scotter and Motowidlo, 1996; Williams and Anderson, 1991). Additionally, task performance and contextual performance factors such as job dedication and interpersonal facilitation contributed uniquely to overall performance in managerial jobs (Conway, 1999). Moreover, contextual performance is predicted by other individual variables, not only by task performance. Abilities and skills tend to predict task performance while personality and related factors tend to predict contextual performance (Borman and Motowidlo, 1997; Hattrup, O'Connell, and Wingate, 1998; Motowidlo and Van Scotter, 1994). However, specific aspects of contextual performance such as personal initiative have been shown to be predicted both by ability and motivational factors (Fay and Frese, in press).

Motowidlo *et. al.* (1997) agree that cognitive ability variables have an effect on task knowledge, task skills, and task habits. However, personality variables are assumed to have an effect on contextual knowledge, contextual skill, contextual habits and, additionally, task habits. Task knowledge, task skills, and task habits in turn are seen as predictors of task performance; contextual knowledge, contextual skill, and contextual habits are regarded as predictors of contextual performance. This implies that task performance is predominantly a function of cognitive ability and contextual performance is predominantly a function of personality. However, cognitive ability has a minor effect on contextual performance mediated by contextual knowledge and personality has a minor effect on task performance, mediated by task habits (Motowidlo and Van Scotter, 1994).

Three basic assumptions are associated with the differentiation between task and contextual performance (Borman and Motowidlo, 1997; Motowidlo and Schmit, 1999):

1. activities relevant for task performance vary between jobs whereas contextual performance activities are relatively similar across jobs;
2. task performance is related to ability, whereas contextual performance is related to personality and motivation;
3. task performance is more prescribed and constitutes in-role behaviour, whereas contextual performance is more discretionary and extra-role.

Citizenship behaviours are defined as behaviours which contribute to the goals of the organization through their effect on the social and psychological conditions. Smith, Organ, and Near (1983) and Bateman and Organ (1983) introduced the notion of organizational citizenship behaviour (OCB). These authors also pointed out that OCB itself draws significantly from earlier writings by Barnard (1938), Katz (1964), and Katz and Kahn (1978). OCB is defined as extra-role discretionary behaviour intended to help others in the organization or to demonstrate conscientiousness in support of the organization. Generally, two factors emerge as constructs of OCB, *i.e.,* altruism, or helping others, and generalized compliance, following the rules and procedures of the organization (Organ, 1988). *Counterproductive behaviours,* on the other hand, are intentional actions by employees which circumvent the aims of the organization. The performance constructs relevant to this are important for unit effectiveness but that fall outside technical proficiency kinds of performance requirements (Borman, Motowidlo, Rose, and Hanser, 1985). The concepts of organizational socialization, organizational commitment, and morale essentially combine to define three major performance dimensions. Commitment and socialization merge to define allegiance; socialization and morale come together to define teamwork; and morale and commitment combine to yield determination.

Theories of Job Performance

Job performance is, perhaps, the most important construct in Industrial and Organizational (I/O) psychology and Human Resource Management (HRM). However, despite its importance, relatively little is known about the latent structure of performance. Indeed, many authors (*e.g.,* Campbell, 1990; 1990c) have noted that of the parameters in the classic prediction model, performance has been the most ignored. As noted by Viswesvaran (1993), very few efforts have been directed toward developing generalizable models of performance. It has typically been assumed that what constitutes performance differs from job to job. As a result, researchers have used countless numbers of measures as indicators of performance.

More recently, however, researchers (*e.g.,* Borman and Motowidlo, 1993; Campbell, 1990; Campbell, McCloy, Oppler, and Sager, 1993; Viswesvaran, 1993; and Murphy, 1995) have developed theories of job performance which posit that some latent performance dimensions generalize across a broad range of jobs. For instance, Campbell (1990) asserts that core task proficiency, demonstrating effort, and the maintenance of personal discipline are components of every job. Models that posit the existence of core sets of performance dimensions which exist across a broad range of jobs are appealing for a number of reasons. First, as noted by Campbell (1990c), theory building is becoming an increasingly important component of research in I/O psychology. Since job performance is arguably the most important construct in our domain, a more complete understanding of its structure is a necessity (Viswesvaran, 1993). Second, if substantiated, such models could provide the basis for developing approaches to measuring and predicting performance which are useful in the field of education. The latter proposition is a primary focus of the present study.

Campbell's (1990) Taxonomy of Job Performance

Despite the emphasis on defining and predicting job performance, it is not a single unified construct. There are vastly many jobs each with different performance standards. Therefore, job performance is conceptualized as a multidimensional construct consisting of more than one kind of behaviour. Campbell (1990) proposed an eight factor model of performance based on factor analytic research that attempts to capture dimensions of job performance existent (to a greater or lesser extent) across all jobs. Campbell (1990; Campbell *et. al.* 1993) provided one of the first large scale attempts to integrate the numerous dimensions of performance into a comprehensive model. According to Campbell, the latent structure of job performance can be modeled using the following eight general factors:

1. Job-specific task proficiency,
2. non-job-specific task proficiency,
3. written and oral communication,
4. demonstrating effort,
5. maintaining personal discipline,
6. facilitating peer and team performance,
7. supervision/leadership, and
8. management/administration.

- *Task Specific* — The first factor is task specific behaviours which include those behaviours that an individual undertakes as part of a job. They are the core substantive tasks that delineate one job from another.
- *Non-task Specific* — On the other hand, non-task specific behaviours, the second factor, are those behaviours which an individual is required to undertake which do not pertain only to a particular job. A non-task specific behaviour of a person might be training new staff members.

- *Written and Oral Communication Tasks* — Written and oral communication tasks refer to activities where the incumbent is evaluated, not on the content of a message necessarily, but on the adeptness with which they deliver the communication. Employees need to make formal and informal oral and written presentations to various audiences in many different jobs in the work force.
- *Effort* — An individual's performance can also be assessed in terms of effort, either day to day, or when there are extraordinary circumstances. This factor reflects the degree to which people commit themselves to job tasks.
- *Personal Discipline* — The performance domain might also include an aspect of personal discipline. Individuals would be expected to be in good standing with the rules and regulations of the organization.
- *Role Model* — In jobs where people work closely or are highly interdependent, performance may include the degree to which a person helps out the groups and his or her colleagues. This might include acting as a good role model, coaching, giving advice or helping maintain group goals.
- *Leadership Qualities* — Many jobs also have a supervisory or leadership component. The individual will be relied upon to undertake many of the things delineated under the previous factor and in addition will be responsible for meting out rewards and punishments. These aspects of performance happen in a face to face manner.
- *Managerial Performance* — Managerial and administrative performance entails those aspects of a job which serve the group or organization but do not involve direct supervision. A managerial task would be setting an organizational goal or responding to external stimuli to assist a group in achieving its goals. In addition a manager might be responsible for monitoring group and individual progress towards goals and monitoring organizational resources.

According to Campbell (1990; Campbell *et. al.* 1993), these eight factors represent the highest-order factors that can be useful for describing performance in every job in the occupational domain, although some factors may not be relevant for all jobs. As mentioned previously, he contends that core task proficiency, demonstrating effort, and maintaining personal discipline are important components of performance in every job. While this model represents one of the most comprehensive treatments of the latent structure of job performance currently available, it has rarely been empirically tested. In fact, Campbell *et. al.* (1993) admit that direct evidence in support of the model is sparse. In response, they call for future construct validation efforts to test the adequacy of the eight factor model.

Borman and Motowidlo's (1993) Theory of Conceptual Performance

The term contextual performance was coined by Borman and Motowidlo (1993) who argued that performance measures used in selection research and practice ignored activities such as persisting, helping and endorsing organizational objectives. Borman and Motowidlo (1993) outlined the conceptual basis for expanding the criterion domain beyond task performance to include elements of contextual performance. Drawing from the literature on organizational citizenship behaviour (Barnard, 1938; Smith *et. al.* 1983), pro-social organizational behaviour (Brief and Motowidlo, 1986; Organ, 1988), and findings from Project-A (Campbell, 1990b), Borman and Motowidlo (1993) described the structure of contextual performance. Within this framework, contextual performance is defined as behaviours that support the broad organizational, social, and psychological environment of the organization in contrast to behaviours that support the organization's technical core (Borman and Motowidlo, 1993). Contextual performance is further distinguished from task performance in that it is typically more discretionary as opposed to role prescribed. The authors describe five categories of contextual performance as follows:

- Volunteering to carry out task activities that are not formally part of the job,
- Persisting with extra enthusiasm when necessary,
- Helping and cooperating with others,
- Following organizational rules and procedures, and
- Endorsing, supporting, and defending organizational objectives.

Borman and Motowidlo (1993) postulated that ability will predict task performance more strongly than individual differences in personality. On the other hand, individual differences in personality were hypothesized to predict contextual performance better than ability. Motowidlo *et. al.* (1997) developed a more nuanced model where contextual performance was modeled as dependent on contextual habits, contextual skills and contextual knowledge. Although habits and skills were predicted on personality, contextual knowledge was influenced both by personality and cognitive ability. Similarly, task performance is influenced by task habits, task skill and task knowledge. Whereas task skill and task knowledge are influenced solely by cognitive ability, task habits are affected by both cognitive ability and personality variables. Thus, this more nuanced model implies that both ability and personality have a role in explaining task and contextual performance. The bottom line appears to be that each performance dimension is complexly determined so that it is impossible to specify different individual differences variables as sole cause or antecedent of a particular dimension of job performance. This is also to be expected given the positive correlations across the various dimensions.

Viswesvaran's (1993) Theory of Job Performance

Using meta-analytic techniques, Viswesvaran (1993) cumulated studies reporting correlations between various measures of job performance. Further, he grouped the large number of measures into 25 conceptually distinct categories (*e.g.*, quality of performance, communication skills, compliance and acceptance of authority). Based on an extensive literature review, he identified five themes which captured the vast number of performance measures utilised in the literature and sorted the 25 measures into these groups. The groups he utilised are as follows:

- Productivity,
- Conscientiousness,
- Interpersonal Skills,
- Withdrawal (*e.g.*, absenteeism, turnover), and
- Measures of overall Job Performance.

Finally, he tested the adequacy of a three-level hierarchical model of job performance with a general performance factor at the highest level, the five-group factors at the second level, and the 25 categories of performance measurements at the lowest level. His results indicated a positive manifold of true score correlations among the 25 performance dimensions.

Viswesvaran (1993) listed job performance measures (486 of them) used in published articles over the years. Two raters working independently then derived 10 dimensions by grouping conceptually similar measures. The 10 dimensions were: overall job performance, job performance or productivity, effort, job knowledge, interpersonal competence, administrative competence, quality, communication competence, leadership, and compliance with rules. Overall job performance captured overall effectiveness, overall work reputation, or was the sum of all individual dimensions rated. Job performance or productivity included ratings of quantity or ratings of volume of work produced. Ratings of effort were statements about the amount of work an individual expends in striving to do a good job. Interpersonal competence was assessments of how well an individual gets along with others whereas administrative competence was a ratings measure of the proficiency exhibited by the individual in handling the coordination of the different roles in an organization. Quality was an assessment of how well the job was done and job knowledge was a measure of the expertise demonstrated by the individual. Communication competence reflected how well an individual communicated regardless of the content. Leadership was a measure of the ability to successfully bring out extra performance from others, and compliance with or acceptance of authority assessed the perspective the individual has about rules and regulations.

Murphy's (1994) Theory of Job Performance

The U.S. military has invested considerable resources in developing approaches to measuring job performance. Considerable information about specific job content is often required to develop performance measures using these approaches. The military has developed a general measure of performance based on recent conceptualizations of the structure of performance which assert that aspects of performance generalize across different jobs. One appealing aspect of such models rests in the ability to develop approaches to measuring and predicting performance which are useful across a broad range of jobs. Another Taxonomy of Job Performance was proposed and developed for the US Navy by Murphy (1994). This model is significantly broader and breaks performance into only four dimensions.

1. Task-oriented behaviours are similar to task-specific behaviours in Campbell's model. This dimension includes any major tasks relevant to someone's job.
2. Interpersonally oriented behaviours are represented by any interaction the focal employee has with other employees. These can be task related or non-task related. This dimension diverges from Campbell's taxonomy because it included behaviours (small talk, socializing, etc.) that are not targeting an organization's goal.
3. Down-time behaviours are behaviours that employees engage in during their free time either at work or off-site. Down-time behaviours that occur off-site are

only considered job performance when they subsequently affect job performance (for example, outside behaviours that cause absenteeism).

4. Destructive/hazardous behaviours correspond to compliance with or without rules.

Murphy (1994) describes the construct of job performance as comprising of four dimensions: downtime behaviours, task performance, interpersonal, and destructive behaviours. Task performance focuses on performing role-prescribed activities whereas downtime behaviours refer to lateness, tardiness, absences or, broadly, to the negative pole of time on task (*i.e.,* effort exerted by an individual on the job). Interpersonal behaviours refer to helping others, teamwork ratings, and pro-social behaviours. Finally, destructive behaviours correspond to compliance with rules (or lack of it), violence on the job, theft, and other behaviours counterproductive to the goals of the organization.

The review of the literature on the factor structure of performance provided indicates that no clear consensus exist concerning the structure of the criterion domain. However, models such as those provided by Campbell (1990), Borman and Motowidlo (1993), and Viswesvaran (1993) represent a much needed foundation in the development of comprehensive theories of work performance. As with Campbell's (1990) model of performance, much remains to be accomplished with regard to providing empirical evidence for the adequacy of the task versus contextual performance distinctions. However, the model proposed by Borman and Motowidlo (1993) has recently received empirical support. Motowidlo and Van Scotter (1994) demonstrated that task and contextual performance contributed independently to overall performance in a sample of 421 U.S. Air Force mechanics. Further, their findings suggested that job experience was more highly correlated with task performance than with contextual performance, and personality variables (*e.g.,* dependability) were more predictive of contextual performance than of task performance. These findings are logically consistent with Borman and Motowidlo's (1993) description of task and contextual performance dimensions. That is, within their framework, variation in task performance is posited to reflect individual differences in the proficiency with which task activities are carried out. Thus, individual differences in the knowledge, skills, and abilities associated with a given task should be more predictive of task performance than personality characteristics. Additionally, experience and training performance should be more highly correlated with task performance (Motowidlo and Van Scotter, 1994). Conversely, behaviours such as cooperation, persistence, and compliance would likely be more strongly related to personality variables than to experience, training performance, or ability.

While somewhat similar in the treatment of criterion domain, neither the model proposed by Campbell (1990a), nor that proposed by Borman and Motowidlo (1993) fully examines the possibility of a general performance factor at the highest level of a hierarchical structure. In fact, as noted previously, Campbell (1990) explicitly argues that his eight factors describe the highest order latent variables that can usefully describe performance. In contrast, a model proposed by Viswesvaran (1993) posits the existence of a strong general performance factor which explains substantial variation in virtually all measures of job performance that have appeared in the literature.

RELATIONSHIP BETWEEN EMOTIONAL INTELLIGENCE, OCCUPATIONAL STRESS AND JOB PERFORMANCE

Emotional Intelligence and Occupational Stress

The process and outcomes of emotional intelligence development also contain many elements known to reduce stress for individuals and organizations, by decreasing conflict, improving relationships and understanding, and increasing stability, continuity and harmony. By developing their emotional intelligence individuals can become more productive and successful at what they do, and help others become more productive and successful too.

Emotional intelligence may be considered as the only differentiator when it comes to managing stress at workplace. Emotionally intelligent work-forces have got tendencies to perceive and interpret a threatening environment differently and also to find effective solutions to it. Researchers observed that there is an inverse relationship between perceived role stress and emotional intelligence of undergraduate students of the UK Dental School and were found that people with low emotional intelligence report more of perceived stress at workplace. Similarly, Nikolaou and Tsaousis (2002) found emotional intelligence to predict 12 per cent of the variance in perceived role stress of paraprofessionals. These research findings speak volumes of the role of emotional intelligence in mitigating the negative impact of perceived stress on personal as well as organizational health. In other words, modern day organizations where stress is inevitable, emotionally intelligent employees are needed in plenty to provide competitive edge to the organizations.

Researches revealed that the female nurses who were relatively high on emotional intelligence developed fewer symptoms of burnouts. Ogniska Bulik (2005) reports that the ability to effectively deal with emotions and emotional information in the workplace assists employees in coping with occupational stress; therefore, it should be developed in stress managing trainings. Thus, the implications of these findings are to help employees develop their level of emotional intelligence for them to be effective in their professional lives. Furthermore, in a study where the UK managers attended a developmental EI training programme once a week for four weeks and pre and post measures were taken relating to EI, stress, and health and management performance, it was found that the training resulted in increased EI and improved health and well-being (Slaski and Cartwright 2003). It indicates that the EI training may be useful in reducing stress and improving health, well-being, and performance. Petrides and Furnham (2006) found that trait emotional intelligence had a positive effect on perceived job control among both employed male and female adults and also noted that emotionally intelligent men felt lesser job stress. It may be because; the emotionally intelligent individuals are able to maintain positive mental status due to their ability to effectively and productively manage their felt emotions.

The stress at workplace is in plenty and needs adequate attention of the management thinkers and practitioners. If it is not addressed to the satisfaction of the organizations, it is sure that majority of the humanity in the organizations may develop psychosomatic diseases which will affect personal as well as organizational productivity.

Occupational Stress and Job Performance

Various studies have been conducted to examine the relationship between job stress and job performance. Job performance can be viewed as an activity in which an individual is able to accomplish the task assigned to him/her successfully, subject to the normal constraints of reasonable utilisation of the available resources. At a conceptual level, four types of relationships were proposed to exist between the measures of job stress and job performance. One is a negative linear relationship, when productivity decreases with stress (distress). Productivity can also increase as a consequence of stress, thereby implying a positive linear relationship between the two. Thirdly, there could be a U-shaped or a curvilinear relationship wherein, mild stress could increase the productivity initially up to a peak and then it declines as the person descends into a state of distress. Alternately, there need not be any quantifiable relationship between the two (Guptha and Chandwani, 2011).

Approaches in the individual performance category focus on factors that have a detrimental effect on performance. Within role theory (Kahn, Wolfe, Quinn, Snoek, and Rosenthal, 1964), role ambiguity and role conflict are conceptualized as stressors that impede performance. However, empirical support for the assumed negative effects of role ambiguity and role conflict is weak (Jackson and Schuler, 1985). In a recent meta-analysis Tubbs and Collins (2000) found a negative relationship between role ambiguity and performance in professional, technical, and managerial jobs. Additionally, they found a negative relationship between role ambiguity and self-ratings of performance. However, the 90 per cent credibility interval of all other effect sizes included zero. Similarly, neither Jackson and Schuler (1985) nor Tubbs and Collins (2000) found a significant relationship between role conflict and job performance. Situational constraints include stressors such as lack of necessary information, problems with machines and supplies as well as stressors within the work environment. Situational constraints are assumed to impair job performance directly. For example, when a machine breaks down one cannot continue to accomplish the task and therefore performance will suffer immediately. Moreover, situational constraints, as other stressors, can have an indirect effect on performance by requiring additional regulation capacity (Greiner and Leitner, 1989). Additional regulation capacity over and above the one needed for accomplishing the task is required for dealing with the constraints. Because human regulatory capacity is limited, less capacity is available for accomplishing the task and, as a consequence, performance decreases. However, empirical support for the assumed detrimental effect of situational constraints and other stressors on performance is mixed (Jex, 1998). Recently, Fay and Sonnentag (2000) have shown that stressors can even have a positive effect on personal initiative, *i.e.*, one aspect of contextual performance. These findings suggest that within a situational perspective, the performance enhancing factors (*e.g.*, control at work, meaningful tasks) play a more important role than stressors. Framed differently, the lack of positive features in the work situation such as control at work threatens performance more than the presence of some stressors (Karasek and Theorell, 1990).

In terms of practical implications, the task and situational perspective suggests that individual performance can be improved by job design interventions. For example, empirical job design studies have shown that performance increases when employees are given more control over the work process (Wall; Corbett, Martin, Clegg and Jackson, 1990; Wall, Jackson, and Davids, 1992).

Emotional Intelligence and Job Performance

Wider areas of intelligence enable or dictate how successful we are. Toughness, determination, and vision help. But emotional intelligence, often measured as an emotional intelligence quotient, is more and more relevant to important work-related outcomes such as individual performance, organizational productivity, and developing people because its principles provide a new way to understand and assess the behaviours, management styles, attitudes, interpersonal skills, and potential of people. It is an increasingly important consideration in human resource planning, job profiling, recruitment, interviewing and selection, learning and development, and client relations and customer service, among others. The work conducted in most organizations has changed dramatically in the last 20 years. Since modern organizations always look to improve performance, they recognize that objective, measurable benefits can be derived from higher emotional intelligence. Naturally, the criteria for success at work are changing too. Staff is now judged by new yardsticks: not just by how smart they are, or by their training and expertise, but also by how well they handle themselves and one another. And that is strongly influenced by personal qualities such as perseverance, self-control, and skill in getting along with others. Increasingly, these new yardsticks are being applied to choose who will be hired and who will not, who will be let to go and who will be retained, and who will be passed over or promoted. Emotional intelligence may be the (long-sought) missing link that unites conventional 'can do' ability determinants of job performance with 'will do' dispositional determinants. Modern organizations now offer learning and development that is explicitly labeled as 'emotional intelligence' or 'emotional competence' training. In support, their leaders create and manage a working environment of flexibility, responsibility, standards, rewards, clarity, and commitment.

Expressing organizationally desired emotions during interpersonal interactions at work can be tiresome and counter-productive for employees. The true challenge arises when employees have to project one emotion while simultaneously feeling another (Robbins, Judge, 2009). This disparity is called *emotional dissonance*. Accumulated feelings of frustration, anger, and resentment lead to exhaustion and burnout (Murray, 2009). Felt emotions are an individual's actual emotions. In contrast, displayed emotions are those that the organization requires workers to show and considers appropriate in a given job. Several studies suggest that EI plays an important role in job performance. One study looked at the successes and failures of eleven American presidents – from Franklin Roosevelt to Bill Clinton. They were evaluated on six qualities:

(i) Communication,

(ii) Organization,

(iii) Political skill,

(iv) Vision,

(v) Cognitive style, and

(vi) emotional intelligence.

It was found that the key quality that differentiated the successful from the unsuccessful was emotional intelligence (Robbins, Judge, 2009).

Low emotional intelligence brings a plethora of negative emotions, like fear, anxiety, anger and hostility which results in using up a lot of energy, lower morale, absenteeism, apathy, and are an effective block to collaborative effort at the workplace. Negative emotions create negative energy – anger, resentment, revenge or at least discomfort to the one we perceive as opposing us. On the contrary, positive emotions create positive energy as can be seen in the excitement of conceiving a vision, designing an ambitious new product, or winning a football match. When we open the doors to emotional reactions, the emergence of hunches, guesses, and intuition enhances the expansion of existing knowledge. One costly consequence of the relentless demands on leaders' time is their propensity to turn away from emotional issues and to stick as closely as possible to the realm of facts and intellect - to value only things that can be ordered, analyzed, defined, dealt with, rationalized, controlled, and contained. However, research shows that emotions, if properly managed, can instill trust, loyalty and commitment - and drive many of the greatest productivity gains, innovations, and accomplishments of individuals, teams and organizations. Emotion can be harnessed to increase work motivation, enhance customer service and work performance.

Goleman (2001), attempts to theoretically clarify the relationship between IQ and EQ, and their respective applicability to job performance. He theorizes that IQ is a strong predictor of what jobs individuals can enter as well as a strong predictor of success among the general population as a whole. Emotional intelligence, on the other hand, is described by Goleman as a stronger predictor of who will excel in a particular job when levels of IQ are relatively equal. When the individuals are being compared to a narrow pool of people in a particular job in a certain organization, specifically in the higher levels, the predictive power of IQ for outstanding performance among them weakens greatly. In this circumstance, EQ would be the stronger predictor of individuals who outperform others.

The literature presented in above clearly indicates that there is a relationship between emotional intelligence, occupational stress and job performance. The emotional intelligence is the strong predictor of occupational stress and work performance. Specific studies focusing on the emotional intelligence, occupational intelligence and job performance of teachers will go a long way to understand the teachers' stress in relation to their emotional intelligence and job performance. Such studies are immense use for selection and training of personnel, both pre-service and in-service, in teaching profession. The present study is an attempt to identify the emotional intelligence, occupational stress and job performance of higher secondary teachers and the influence of certain personal and demographical variables on teachers' emotional intelligence, occupational stress and job performance.

The review of literature specifically related to the present problem under investigation is given in Chapter 2.

REVIEW OF RELATED LITERATURE

INTRODUCTION

THE REVIEW forms an important chapter in a thesis where its purpose is to provide the background to and justification for the research undertaken (Bruce 1994). Bruce, who has published widely on the topic of the literature review, has identified six elements of a literature review. These elements comprise:

1. A list,
2. A search,
3. A survey,
4. A vehicle for learning,
5. A research facilitator, and
6. A report (Bruce 1994).

According to Cooper *et. al.* (1988) '... a literature review uses as its database reports of primary or original scholarship, and does not report new primary scholarship itself. The primary reports used in the literature may be verbal, but in the vast majority of cases reports are written documents. The types of scholarship may be empirical, theoretical, critical/analytic, or methodological in nature. Second, a literature review seeks to describe, summarize, evaluate, clarify and/or integrate the content of primary reports'.

Sufficient, if not extensive, literature search and review throughout a research project is a must in order to gather data and discover the previous works of other researchers on related topics. The type of literatures can range from journals, theses, websites, scientific magazines and textbooks. However, one has to appraise the information collected especially from non-established websites because, not all information is valid as it claims.

At this stage, the objective of current literature search and review is to understand the relationship between emotional intelligence, occupational stress and job performance of primary teachers, secondary teachers, special education teachers and teachers working at higher secondary level in particular. It helps to gain in-depth knowledge of the topic and logical sequence intended for the thesis write up. It serves as a guideline from the previous results and reviews to get a clear picture of the present study. The studies reviewed and collected are presented in an alphabetical order under the headings; Studies Conducted in India and Studies Conducted Abroad.

The Studies Conducted in India is further grouped into the following sub-headings;

- Studies on Emotional Intelligence of Teachers.
- Studies on Emotional Intelligence of Students and Student Teachers.
- Studies on Emotional Intelligence of other Professionals.
- Studies on Occupational Stress of Teachers.
- Studies on Stress of Students and Student Teachers.
- Studies on Occupational Stress of other Professionals.
- Studies on Job Performance of Teachers and other Professionals.
- Relationship Studies on Emotional Intelligence, Occupational Stress and Job Performance.

Similarly, the Studies Conducted Abroad is placed under the following sub-headings;

- Studies on Emotional Intelligence of Teachers.
- Studies on Emotional Intelligence of Students.
- Studies on Emotional Intelligence of other Professionals.
- Studies on Occupational Stress of School Teachers.
- Studies on Occupational Stress of Higher Education Teachers.
- Studies on Occupational Stress of other Professionals.
- Studies on Job Performance of Teachers.
- Relationship Studies on Emotional Intelligence, Occupational Stress and Job Performance.

Finally, an overview of the studies conducted in India and abroad is presented at the end of this chapter.

STUDIES CONDUCTED IN INDIA

In India, many studies are being conducted in the field of emotional intelligence and occupational studies of teachers and other professionals. But, the studies related to the job performance of teachers as well as the relationship studies on emotional intelligence, occupational stress and job performance of teachers are limited and handy. Some of the studies related to these aspects are presented hereunder.

Studies on Emotional Intelligence of Teachers

Emotional intelligence pertains to an individual's capacity to reason about emotions and to process emotional information to enhance cognitive processes and regulate behaviour. The ability to recognize one's own emotions and identify how others are feeling requires attention to multiple internal and external cues and the analysis of both verbal and non-verbal communication in oneself and others. Devoting adequate time and attention to fostering such emotional awareness is extremely important in optimizing teacher effectiveness in multiple domains and also essential to identify the emotional intelligence of teachers to enhance the quality of education. In this regard, some of the studies related to the emotional intelligence and teachers' competencies; emotional intelligence of teachers with respect to their gender, age, experience and some other demographic variables; emotional intelligence and teacher effectiveness; emotional intelligence and personality characteristics of teachers; and also some other studies related to the emotional intelligence of teachers are presented hereunder.

Amirtha and Kadhiravan (2006) examined the *influence of personality on the emotional intelligence of teachers.* The sample consisted of 207 school teachers working in different schools of Chennai city. The results revealed that gender, age and qualification influence the emotional intelligence of teachers. Teachers also differ in their personality dimensions with respect to different descriptive variables. It was also found that extraversion, introversion and feeling dimensions of personality have a negative impact on emotional intelligence of teachers where as thinking and judging dimensions have a positive impact on their emotional intelligence.

Bansibihari and Pathan (2004) studied the *level of emotional intelligence of secondary school teachers in relation to their gender and age.* Emotional Intelligence Test was administered to the sample of 500 secondary school teachers of Dhule district in Maharastra. The results indicate that nearly all (98.4%) of the teachers fall under low category of emotional intelligence. There is no difference between emotional intelligence of male and female teachers and age is independent of emotional intelligence.

David and Roy (2010) explored the *relationship between emotional intelligence and teacher competencies.* Eighty secondary school teachers working at Secunderabad city were the sample of the study. The results of the study revealed that there was a moderate relationship between emotional intelligence and teacher competencies of secondary teachers. The differential study of teacher competencies among high and low emotional intelligence teachers was also found to be positive.

Edannur (2010) studied the *emotional intelligence of teacher educators.* Twenty-one teacher educators of five teacher education institutions in Barak Valley of Assam state form the sample of the study. The investigator used Emotional Competence Inventory of Goleman and Boyatzis to assess the different skills of emotional intelligence. The results show that the group under study possessed average emotional intelligence. The gender and locality of the teacher educators did not make any differential influence on their emotional intelligence.

Jayanthi and Agarwal (2006) examined the *socio-emotional climate of the classroom with respect to teaching experience, total income, age, subject teaching and gender of secondary school teachers.* Hundred secondary school teachers were chosen as a sample for the study. The findings revealed that the teachers creating different socio-emotional classroom climates do not differ significantly with respect to their teaching experience; teachers teaching science subjects are positively and significantly correlated with socio-emotional classroom climate and teachers creating positive classroom climate differ significantly from the teachers creating negative classroom climate with respect to the teaching subject.

Khan and Kumar (2008) explored the *relationship between emotional intelligence and achievement motivation among women teachers of secondary schools of Delhi.* Forty secondary school teachers were chosen for the study. The findings revealed that 33 per cent of teachers demonstrated high levels of emotional intelligence and 70 per cent of teachers had high levels of achievement motivation. Also, there was a positive moderate correlation between emotional intelligence and achievement motivation.

Latha *et. al.* (2005) carried out a *study of emotional intelligence and its effects on teacher effectiveness among school teachers.* The results of the study revealed that emotional intelligence does not influence teacher effectiveness in general. But, emotional intelligence affects the aspects of teaching process *i.e.,* teachers sense of humor and mastery in the subject.

Lenka and Kant (2012) studied the *emotional intelligence of secondary school teachers in relation to their professional development.* All the teachers (secondary) of Rampur District, U.P. constituted the population for the purpose of this study. The study was confined to both government and private school teachers. The study was conducted on a sample of 120 senior secondary/higher secondary teachers drawn from 12 schools of Rampur District (UP). A stratified random sampling technique was employed for collecting the data. The tools used in the study include Emotional Intelligence Scale (EIS) of Hyde, Pethe, and Dhar, and Scale on Professional Development. The statistical techniques employed were t-test and Correlations. The findings of the study revealed that there was a significant relationship between emotional intelligence along with its dimensions and professional development of secondary school teachers. Also, there was a significant difference between emotional intelligent of male and female secondary school teachers.

Manoharan (2007) carried out a correlation analysis on *emotional intelligence and personality characteristics among high school teachers.* The main objective of the study was to find out whether emotional intelligence is related to any particular type of personality *i.e.,* extrovert, introvert and neurotic. Stratified random sampling technique was employed to choose a sample of 195 high school teachers from Pondicherry. To assess the personality, Eyesenck Personality Inventory and to find the emotional intelligence of high school teachers, standardized tool developed by Reuven Bar-On was used. The statistical techniques used were mean, SD and t-test. The findings of the study revealed that:

- Post graduate teachers have better emotional intelligence than the graduate teachers.
- Arts teachers have a significantly higher emotional intelligence than science teachers.
- Experienced teachers have better emotional intelligence.
- Urban school teachers have better emotional intelligence and
- Neurotic teachers have lower emotional intelligence than extrovert teachers.

Neelakandan (2007) carried out a study on *emotional competence of primary school teachers.* Emotional Competence Scale was administered to 300 primary school teachers of Cuddalore district of Tamil Nadu. The results revealed that the primary school teachers have average level of emotional competence and teachers having higher qualifications are found to have better emotional competence than teachers with essential qualifications. It was also found that there was no significant difference between any two categories of sub-samples of teachers belonging to different groups in relation to their experience, with respect to their emotional competence. Similarly, there was no significant difference between the teachers of government schools and private schools in respect to their emotional competence.

Padhi and Verma (2011) examined the *effectiveness of secondary school teachers in relation to emotional intelligence and life satisfaction:* Teacher Effectiveness Scale, Emotional Intelligence Scale and Life Satisfaction Scale were used on a sample of 120 secondary school teachers to collect the data. The data was analyzed using t-test, co-efficient of correlation, chi-square test and two-way ANOVA. The study revealed that:

- The teachers working in secondary schools do not differ significantly in their variables like teacher effectiveness, emotional intelligence and life satisfaction with respect to type of school management and place of habitation,
- There is a significant correlation found between teacher effectiveness and emotional intelligence,
- Only levels of life satisfaction are dependent on types of school management, and
- The interaction effect of emotional intelligence and life satisfaction on the teacher effectiveness of secondary school teachers is insignificant.

Poornima (2010) explored the *emotional intelligence of special education teachers with respect to certain demographic variables* such as age, community, educational qualification, nature of special schools the teachers working in, training received in special education, level of classes handled, nature of job, years of experience and the salary they received. The Emotional Intelligence Rating Scale developed by the investigator was administered to the sample of 202 special teachers working in the schools for VI, HI, and MR children in Chennai city. The data was analyzed using the statistical techniques mean, SD, t-test, F-test, correlations and stepwise multiple regression analysis. The results of the study revealed that more than 85 per cent of the teachers working in special schools possess moderate and low level of intelligence. The age and community has not significantly influenced the emotional intelligence of special teachers as a whole. Lower the age lower was the emotional intelligence of teachers working in MR schools. Teachers belonging to BC community had high level of emotional intelligence than OC and MBC / SC and ST communities in MR schools. Further, educational qualification, years of experience and the salary the teacher receive slightly influenced the emotional intelligence of special teachers working in MR schools *i.e.,* higher the educational qualification higher was the emotional intelligence; the teachers receiving higher salary possess high level of emotional intelligence and the teachers with more years of experience had high level of emotional intelligence than their counterparts with less years of experience.

Subrmaniam and Cheong (2008) explored the emotional *intelligence of mathematics and science teachers.* The findings revealed that there was no significant difference in the emotional intelligence between mathematics and science teachers, even though, a higher mean value of emotional intelligence was noted for mathematics teachers as compared to the science teachers.

Tyagi (2004) examined the *emotional intelligence of secondary teachers in relation to gender and age.* Emotional Intelligence Test of Chadha and Singh was administered to 500 secondary teachers consisting of 350 male teachers and 150 female teachers of Dhule District in Maharshtra. The results of the t-test revealed that the level of emotional intelligence is low with respect to gender and age.

Usha Rao (2008) studied the *emotional maturity and role of the teachers*. Emotional maturity was exemplified in various response patterns like attention getting: clowning, affected speech, bizarre appearance; rationalization: giving foolish reasons or undesirable behaviours; projection: placing blame on another for one's own short comings; day dreaming: refusing the reality; others ego: satisfying reactions include undue criticism of others, display of jealous and generally inconsistent behaviour. Those teachers who do not show such response patterns definitely are emotionally matured and will run after their own professional development.

Williams (2008) did a research on *characteristics that distinguish outstanding urban principals' emotional intelligence, social intelligence and environmental adaptation.* The focus of this study was to identify emotional and social competencies and related contextual characteristics that distinguish outstanding urban principals based on data from behavioural event interviews using a double coding method. The design utilised a criterion group of 20 principals from a population size of 120 urban school principals. Results revealed that outstanding principals demonstrate a broader repertoire of competencies related to emotional and social intelligence.

Studies on Emotional Intelligence of Students and Student Teachers

It is clear that emotions and emotional intelligence of a person starts from home and continues to develop through school, peers and with the interaction of the society. A child's emotional life does not exist in a vacuum but is determined by the relationships and environment in which he/she interacts with others. In education, this means, considering the context of the organization, *i.e.,* the school as a whole. The values of respect, co-operation and consideration for others need to exist within the structure of the school. In this connection, some of the studies related to the emotional intelligence of students and student teachers with respect to their academic achievement, motivation, type of family and parental involvement, self-concept and personality traits and some other related studies are presented here under.

Bai (2009) carried out a *study of anxiety proneness and emotional intelligence in relation to academic achievement of pre-university students.* The sample included 500 pre-university students selected from Bangalore urban and rural areas who were studying in Science, Arts and Commerce streams by using stratified random sampling procedure. The study was conducted on 269 male and 231 female students of government, private colleges. Data was collected by using Sinha's Comprehensive

Anxiety Test (SCAT) and Emotional Intelligence Scale for Adolescents (EISA) developed by the investigator. The results of the study revealed that; Arts, Science and Commerce students of PUC have significant difference in academic achievement, anxiety proneness and emotional intelligence and its dimensions. Arts and Science students of PUC have significant difference in anxiety proneness and emotional intelligence.

Indu (2009) carried out a study on *emotional intelligence of secondary teacher trainees.* The main objective of the study was to study the influence of type of family and type of institutions on emotional intelligence of teacher trainees. Descriptive survey method was employed for data collection. The sample consisted of 502 teacher trainees studying in five different Colleges of Education in Coimbatore district. Emotional Intelligence Scale (EIS) developed by the researcher based on Bar-On's conceptualization of the dimensions of emotional intelligence was used in the study. The statistical techniques employed were mean, standard deviation, t-test and analysis of variance. The findings revealed that the sample possessed average emotional intelligence and there was no significant difference in the emotional intelligence of teacher trainees based on the type of family or type of institution.

Koneri (2010) carried out *a study of emotional intelligence in relation to parental involvement and self concept of adolescents.* Sample of 800 students studying in 10th standard of Bangalore rural and urban schools were chosen for the study. The tools used for the study were Bar-On Emotional Quotient Inventory Youth Version by Bar-On and Parker, Parental Involvement Rating Scale (PIRS), Self-concept Inventory and Socio-economic Status Scale. Mean, t-test, ANOVA and correlation co-efficient were used to analyze the data. The findings revealed that; the adolescents with high parental involvement have higher levels of emotional intelligence as compared to the adolescents with low parental involvement, girls have higher level of emotional intelligence as compared to the boys and rural students were higher in emotional intelligence when compared to their urban counterparts.

Mahajan (2011) studied the *academic achievement in relation to emotional intelligence and spiritual intelligence* of 140 students studying in class XI from four schools of Hoshiarpur district. Co-efficients of correlation and t-test were used to analyze the data. The findings revealed that there exists no significant difference between emotional intelligence and spiritual intelligence of boys and girls; there exists a positive and significant relationship between academic achievement and emotional intelligence of boys and girls.

Nagpal (2009) studied the *emotional intelligence and self-concept among prospective teachers.* The main objective of the study was to see the relation between emotional intelligence and self-concept of would be teachers. A random sample of 120 prospective teachers from Education Colleges of Rohtak city was taken. The statistical techniques include central tendency, t-test and Pearson product moment correlation. The results of the study show that there is a significant relationship between emotional intelligence and self-concept of prospective teachers. It was also found that there is a significant difference between self-concept of male and female prospective teacher.

Panda (2009) carried out a study on *emotional intelligence and personality traits of pupil-teachers.* Sample of 130 pupil-teachers were selected from Kurukshetra University College of Education in Ambala. The tools used in the study were, Emotional Intelligence Test by Anokool and Kundu's Neurotic Personality Inventory. The results of mean, SD and t-test revealed that there was a significant positive correlation between emotional intelligence and normal behaviour of pupil-teachers and there was no significant difference between male and female pupils in their emotional intelligence.

Panday (2006) examined the *deprivation among emotionally intelligent girls, studying in 9th standard* of four Hindi medium secondary schools in Varanasi. The findings revealed that girls with low emotional intelligence perceive various insufficiency, meager educational opportunities, unavailability of reasonable share of pleasant emotional experiences, lack of warmth and parental care as compared to girls with high and moderate level of emotional intelligence.

Punia and Sangwan (2011) had studied the *emotional intelligence and social adaptation of school children.* The study was carried out in Hisar district of Haryana with an objective to find out the emotional intelligence level of school children and its relation with their adjustment. A total of 120 children falling in the age group of 16 to 18 years, 60 each from randomly selected schools of urban and rural areas were selected for the study. Further, thirty children, equally representing both the sexes, were considered on random basis. Majority of the respondents had normal to high emotional intelligence and average to excellent adjustment. Urban children comparatively had slightly better emotional intelligence and adjustment than the rural children. The emotional intelligence had significant positive relationship with adjustment of children. Caste, income and father's occupation were the main contributing factors in deciding the emotional intelligence and adjustment of respondents.

Saranya and Velayudhan (2008) conducted a study on *analyzing pro-social behaviour and emotional intelligence among university students.* The objective of the study was to find out the difference among hostel students and day scholars in pro-social behaviour and emotional intelligence. Emotional intelligence and pro-social behaviour questionnaires were administered to 60 hostellers and 60 day scholars in the university departments of Bharathiar University, Coimbatore. The statistical techniques employed were mean, standard deviation and ANOVA. The findings of the study suggested that hostellers seem to be higher in pro-social behaviour and have better emotional intelligence than the day scholars.

Shah and Thingujam (2008) carried out a *study on perceived emotional intelligence and ways of coping among students.* The sample comprised of 197 students, between the age group of 18 and 25 years. Participants completed self-reported measures of emotional intelligence and ways of coping. It was found that appraisal of emotions in the self was positively correlated with problem solving and positive reappraisal coping styles. Emotional regulation was positively correlated with problem solving, confronting coping, self-controlling, positive reappraisal and with distancing, but negatively correlated with escape avoidance. No gender differences were found in perceived emotional intelligence and ways of coping except for self-control, where males reported higher than females.

Shanwal (2003) carried out *a study of correlates and nurturance of emotional intelligence in primary school children.* The main objective of the study was to examine the differences in emotional intelligence in different eco-cultural groups, to study the relationship between emotional intelligence and academic achievement, social performance and attentive abilities. The sample consisted of 200 children studying in the IV standard of the municipal corporation of Delhi. The original tool of Mayer and Salovey (1997) was adapted into a paper pencil Hindi version. The results revealed that, among the different eco-cultural groups, rural children have higher emotional intelligence and rural boys have higher emotional intelligence than urban boys while urban girls are best at identification of emotions. Emotional intelligence did not show any relationship with social performance or deftness and attentive skills.

Shrivastava and Mukhopadhyay (2009) had investigated the a*lienation and emotional intelligence of adolescents with internalizing symptoms.* Multi-dimensional assessment of personality test was used as screening tool in the first phase of the study. Total 510 adolescents in the age group of 14-18 years studying in various schools of Varanasi were screened for internalizing symptoms. Those who scored above the cut-off point were identified as the 'affected group' having internalizing symptoms showing more than 6 symptoms, the sample showing 4-5 symptoms as 'moderate group', sample showing 1-2 symptoms as 'mild group' and adolescents without internalizing symptoms were identified as 'normal group'. Student Alienation Scale and Mangal Emotional Intelligence Inventory were then administered on all the four groups each having 15 subjects for the final study. The result obtained from ANOVA revealed that the affected group is significantly alienated and emotionally immature in awareness and management compared to their comparative normal group.

Sobha (2006) did a study on *emotional intelligence and frustration tolerance of adolescents.* The main objective of the study was to find out the relation between emotional intelligence and frustration tolerance of adolescents with respect to few variables. The study was carried out on a sample of 400 students in various higher secondary schools located in Thiruvananthapuram district of Kerala. An Emotional Quotient Inventory and a Frustration Tolerance Scale developed by the investigator were used in the study. The analysis of data was done by t-test. The study revealed that emotional intelligence of adolescents was positively and significantly related to frustration tolerance. The positive correlation reveals that adolescents with a high emotional intelligence can tolerate setbacks to a great extent.

Tiwary and Srivastava (2004) studied the *schooling and development of emotional intelligence.* Emotional Intelligence Scale of Schuttle was administered to the sample of 270 primary school children of Gorakhpur. The results of ANOVA revealed that the perceived environmental quality of home as well as school was positively related to emotional intelligence scores.

Umadevi (2009) examined the *relationship between emotional intelligence, achievement motivation and academic achievement* of primary school student teachers of Davanagere in Karnataka. Emotional Intelligence Scale and Achievement Motivation Test were administered on 200 D.Ed. students and the data obtained was subjected to descriptive, correlation and differential analysis. The results revealed that there was a positive relationship between emotional intelligence and academic achievement and, achievement motivation and academic achievement. Male and female student teachers and arts and science student teachers do not differ in emotional intelligence and achievement motivation.

Upadhyaya (2006) analyzed the *emotional intelligence of student teachers.* The sample consisted of 78 student teachers from Allahabad. The findings of the study indicated that student teachers with low emotional intelligence are more uneasy and worried about future and failures. They are less cautious, irregular and like to take more rest, restrain others, feel tired, uninterested and confirmed to the opinion or accepted path taken by most people. Whereas, student teachers with high emotional intelligence are more competent, have more self-confidence, hard working, help others in a constructive way, motivated, energetic and full of enthusiasm.

Vijayalakshmi *et. al.* (2008) examined the *emotional intelligence and social reticence of post-graduate female students.* The present study is exploratory in nature and makes an attempt to explore the relationship between emotional intelligence and social reticence among women day scholars (N=26) and women hostel boarders (N=21), pursuing their post graduate courses. The influence of birth order on their emotional intelligence and social reticence has also been studied. Product moment correlation was used to study their relationship and significance of difference between the means of the two groups was computed with the aid of t-test. Results revealed that emotional intelligence and social reticence are negatively correlated and there was no significant difference in the emotional intelligence of women day scholars and women hostel boarders.

Studies on Emotional Intelligence of other Professionals

It is now recognized that emotional intelligence plays an important role in many areas of life, including work. Researchers have examined the skills and aptitudes required to succeed in certain kinds of jobs, the role of emotional intelligence and the actual level of it required for various jobs. If the requisite level of emotional intelligence is lacking, it is difficult to cope with the jobs and also it will be less satisfying. In this regard, some of the studies on emotional intelligence of individuals working in the field of software sector, corporate sector, police and some other professionals are presented hereunder.

Faye *et. al.* (2011) carried out the *study of emotional intelligence and empathy in medical postgraduates.* This study aims to: *(i)* assess emotional intelligence focusing specifically on empathy; *(ii)* to study the level of anger; and *(iii)* correlating level of anger with *(a)* EI and *(b)* empathy in medical postgraduates. Subjects were assessed randomly after obtaining informed consent, through semi-structured pro-forma and various scales, including Emotional Quotient Self-Assessment Checklist, Multi-Dimensional Emotional Empathy Scale, and Clinical Anger Scale. Data was analyzed using multivariate analysis with analysis of covariance test. Results of the study revealed that, on Emotional Quotient Self-Assessment checklist, more than 70 per cent had poor emotional intelligence. Married males in the study were more confident and empathizing. Those with some major problem at home were more aware of their own emotions and other's feelings. Residents who had voluntarily chosen their specialty post-graduation training course (*i.e.,* medicine, surgery, and others), those who had less work load, those who had time for recreational activities, and exercise had scored high on EI. Good control of emotions in self was associated with good relationship with superiors and colleagues. Score on Clinical anger was moderate to severe in 10.6 per cent of the subjects. EI and clinical anger correlated negatively.

Jadhav and Havalappanavar (2009) examined the *emotional intelligence and self-efficacy of police constable trainees.* The sample consisted of 200 police constable trainees from two different police training schools of Dharwad. Emotional Intelligence Scale developed by Hyde, Pethe and Dhar, Self-efficacy Scale developed by Schwartzer and Jerusalem was administered to all the trainees. The t-test and Pearson Product Moment Correlation were applied for analyzing the data. Results revealed that women police constable trainees have scored significantly high on emotional intelligence than their counterparts. Whereas men police constable trainees score was significantly higher on self-efficacy than the women police constable trainees. There was a positive correlation between emotional intelligence and self-efficacy.

Krishnaveni and Deepa (2009) carried out a study on *diagnosing employees' emotional intelligence in the IT/ITES sector of South India.* The study involved 533 respondents of the software sector in South India. It was found that the IT/ITES work force has high emotional intelligence and that gender and age have an impact on emotional intelligence.

Prashanthi and Devi (2009) examined the *relationship between emotional competence and family variables.* Sharma and Bhardwaj's (1995) Emotional Competence Scale was administered to a sample of 240 couple of Chittor District in Andhra Pradesh. The results revealed that family income and family type were positively correlated with emotional competence, whereas, family size was negatively correlated with the emotional competence level of the respondents.

Punia (2005) explored the *impact of demographic variables (gender, age and marital status) on emotional intelligence and leadership behaviour of corporate executives.* Data was collected from 250 executives working in different organizations in Delhi by applying convenience-cum-purposive sampling. Data was collected using three scales such as Leadership Orientation Scale, Leadership Development Scale and Emotional Intelligence Test. The results of the study revealed that the respondents above 25 years but less than 45 years of age have witnessed comparatively more emotional stability, whereas the gender level of emotional intelligence shows that women are more emotionally stable due to their high level of emotional intelligence than their counterparts. The level of emotional intelligence in both married and unmarried executives has been found to be average or high, however unmarried executives have registered higher amount of emotional stability.

Puri, Anju. (2011) studied the *emotional intelligence of business executives in the Indian corporate sector.* The purpose of the study was to identify the weak components of emotional intelligence of business executives for the purpose of identifying their training needs, to ascertain the relationship between emotional intelligence and job stress, to relate the emotional intelligence of business executives with their respective newline overall performance and to broadly assess whether the existing training and newline development programmes aim at strengthening emotional intelligence components of business executives. The sample consisted of 400 managers working at the middle level managerial positions with a minimum of three years of experience and post graduation as their minimum level of education spread over 2 major sectors, namely, Service and Manufacturing from the area covering Delhi and National Capital Region, Haryana and Punjab. The tools used in the study were Emotional Intelligence Scale developed by Hyde, Pethe and Dhar (2002), Occupational Stress Index developed by Srivastava and Singh (1981) and Self Performance Assessment (SPA) scale developed by the investigators. T-test, F-test and Correlations were used to analyze the data. Business executives were found to have high emotional intelligence and they also achieved high score on the individual dimensions of emotional intelligence. Role overload and responsibility of persons have been found to be a major source of job stress. Emotional intelligence has a significant impact in reducing overall and specific occupational stress among the business executives. No gender differences were found in the total emotional intelligence scores of male and female executives. However, differences in emotional intelligence scores across different emotional intelligence competencies for male and female were found. Overall emotional intelligence was found to be more in females than males. Higher emotionally intelligent behaviour was witnessed in the age group 40-45 years. Business executives falling in the age group 35-40 years are more prone to occupational stress. High emotional intelligence was witnessed in business executives who have a work experience between 15-20 years. Maximum occupational stress has been observed in business executives having less than 5 years of work experience. High emotional intelligence was demonstrated by the executives working in the manufacturing units and their stress levels were also found to be low. The group which perceived emotional intelligence to be important scored higher on emotional intelligence scales. Business executives high on emotional intelligence were found to be low on total occupational stress score. High emotional intelligence group exhibited higher performance assessment score. The study's results further show that the mostly business organizations offer training programmes which are aimed more towards developing the business acumen skills of their employees. The results of the study also show that emotional intelligence can be used as a potential moderating variable in the stress process and improving the performance of the business executives.

Rajkhowa (2002) studied the *emotional intelligence of IAS officers*. Incidental sampling technique was employed to select a sample of 60 IAS officers belonging to Assam cadre. The sample was further divided into two groups on the basis of the age. Group I consisted of officers in the age group of 30 to 45 years and group II consisted of officers in the age group of 46 to 60 years. Emotional Intelligence Test of Chadha was administered to the sample. The analyses of the results revealed that the sample falls under average to high level of emotional intelligence and it was also found that, even though there was no significant difference in the emotional intelligence of IAS officers across their ages, group II was slightly higher on emotional intelligence scores than the group I officers.

Ramachandran *et. al.* (2011) examined the *emotional intelligence, emotional labour and organizational citizenship behaviour in service environments.* In this study, the impact of Emotional Intelligence (EI) on Emotional Labour (EL) and Organizational Citizenship Behaviour (OCB) in the Malaysian service industry was erxamined. Data was collected from 131 front desk employees across four resorts within a Malaysian hotel chain. In line with expectations, analyses revealed that EL partially mediated the relationship between EI and OCB.

Singh (2005) carried out an international study on *EQ and managerial effectiveness.* A sample of 204 managers, comprising of 83 middle-level managers and 121 senior-level managers consisting of 149 males and 55 females were selected from four organizations, with Indian, American, Japanese and European management operating in India. Emotional Intelligence Test and Managerial Effectiveness Test were administered to the sample and the correlation analyses revealed that there was a positive relationship between emotional intelligence and managerial effectiveness of managers. It was also found that emotional intelligence and experience are positively and significantly related to each other and females were higher on their emotional scores than their male counterparts.

Sinha and Jain (2004) analyzed the *emotional intelligence, imperative for the organizationally relevant outcomes.* The study explored the relationship between emotional intelligence and job satisfaction, personal effectiveness, organizational commitment, reputational effectiveness, general health, trust, turnover intention, organizational effectiveness and organizational productivity. The data was obtained from 250 middle-level executives of two wheeler automobile manufacturing organizations. The results revealed that personal effectiveness and reputational effectiveness were predicted by assertiveness and positive self-concept; organizational productivity was positively predicted by controlled problem solving dimension of emotional intelligence; positive attitude about life predicted sense of accomplishment and contribution and botheration free existence positively; reality awareness dimension of emotional intelligence predicted sense of attachment and normative commitment dimensions of organizational commitment are conceptualized as true kinds of commitment; job satisfaction and turnover intention was found to be negative predictor of conditional continuance commitment and resource acquisition related organizational effectiveness. Also, vertical trust was positively predicted by controlled problem solving, reality awareness and impulse control.

Studies on Occupational Stress of Teachers

Looking at the wider question of stress, it is important to consider the point that stress is probably present and indeed inherent in all school organizations. We must, therefore, in the stress equation, consider both the individual and the school or other educational organization in which he/she works and hence, some of the studies on teachers' job related stress with respect to certain demographic variables, sources of stress, coping strategies, correlates of stress, teacher effectiveness, personality characteristics and also some other factors concerned with teaching profession are presented hereunder.

Aftab and Khatoon (2012) studied the *demographic differences and occupational stress of secondary school teachers.* The present study examined the relationships of a set of independent variables (gender, qualification, teaching experience, salary, subjects taught and marital status) with occupational stress among secondary school teachers. The population in this study consists of 608 teachers from 42 schools of Uttar Pradesh (India). The Teachers Occupational Stress Scale was used for data collection, while t-test and F-test are used for statistical analysis. According to the results of the analysis, nearly half of the secondary school teachers experience less stress in their job and male teachers displays more occupational stress towards job than the female teachers. Moreover, the trained graduate teachers are found to have higher occupational stress than post-graduate and untrained teachers. Teachers with an experience of 6-10 years had higher occupational stress and teachers with 0-5 years experience had the least stress; while those falling in the remaining two groups slide in between these two. Findings also reveal no significant differences between monthly salary, subjects taught, marital status and occupational stress of secondary school teachers.

Anbuchelvan (2010) carried out a study on *occupational stress of high school teachers.* The purpose of the study was to find out the level of occupational stress of high school teachers in terms of gender, educational qualifications, marital status, teachers experience of teaching and locality of school. Occupational Stress Inventory was administered to the selected sample of 60 teachers from Salem, T.N. The results of the t-test revealed that there was a significant difference between male and female high school teachers in their occupational stress and there was no significant difference between male and female high school teachers in their occupational stress on the basis of educational qualifications, marital status, locality and teaching experience.

Balaswamy (2011) carried out a study on *occupational stress of primary school teachers in Kuppam Mandal.* Sample of 100 primary teachers (60 teachers from government schools and 40 from private schools) were administered with Occupational Stress Rating Scale developed by Reddy (2006). The statistical techniques employed were mean, mean ± 1, SD, t-test and F-test. The results of the study revealed that primary teachers defer in their occupational stress with 15 per cent of the teachers having low level of stress, 74 per cent of teachers having moderate level of stress and 11 per cent of teachers were having high level of occupational stress. The variables gender, age and educational qualification has not significantly influenced the occupational stress of primary teachers while, the variables community, type of school, years of experience and monthly salary has significantly influenced the occupational stress of primary teachers. Teachers belonging to BC community had higher occupational stress; government teachers had less occupational stress than the private stress; teachers with 11-20 years of experience had more stress than other age group teachers; and teachers receiving more than Rs. 10,000/- salary per month had more stress than teachers receiving less than Rs. 10,000/- salary per month.

Chand and Monga (2007) examined the *correlates of job stress and burnout.* The objective of the study was to find out the correlates of job stress and burnout among university faculty. One hundred faculty members were included from two universities of Himachal Pradesh. Pearson's Product Moment Co-efficient of Correlation and t-test were used to determine the significant relationships with different variables used for this study. The overall findings of the study suggested that respondents with internal locus of control, high social support and high job involvement experience less stress and burnout. Results also reveal that maximum job stress was reported by professors and minimum by the assistant professors.

Chaturvedi and Purushothaman (2009) investigated the *coping behaviour of female teachers with respect to demographic determinants.* The sample consisted of 150 female teachers selected by stratified sampling method from various schools of Bhopal. The Occupational Stress Indicator was used for measuring the stress-coping behaviour of the teachers. The results of t-test and F-test revealed that marital status, age and experience were found to be the significant determinants of stress coping, whereas the scores did not differ significantly on the basis of level of teaching. Further, the married teachers in the age range of 40-60 years, with higher experience had coped better with the job stress than their counterparts.

Chopra and Gartia (2009) explored the *accountability of secondary school teachers in relation to their occupational stress.* A sample of 120 teachers from private and government secondary schools of Kurukshetra were chosen for the study. The results revealed that occupational stress had a negative impact on accountability of secondary school teachers. Teachers who had high occupational stress are less accountable towards their job and teachers with low occupational stress are more accountable towards their job. It was also found that female teachers were more accountable towards their job than their male counterparts.

John (2007) carried out a study on *occupational stress of teachers working in the schools for visually impaired children in the Malabar region of Kerala.* The purpose of this study was to find the occupational stress of teachers working in the school for visually impaired children due to variations in their gender, age, community, educational qualifications and training in special education, salary/month, years of experience, locale and type of school, and visual impairment of the teacher. The study had covered 14 schools for visually impaired with 150 teachers from six districts of Malabar region of Kerala state. Rating scale was used to measure the extent of occupational stress experienced by the teachers. The results of multiple regression analysis revealed that nearly 70 per cent of teachers are experiencing high and moderate levels of occupational stress. Gender, age and years of experience do not influence the occupational stress of teachers, whereas, community, educational qualifications, monthly salary, locale and type of school have significant influence on the occupational stress of teachers working in the schools for visually impaired children.

Kaur (2008) studied the *occupational stress in relation to teacher effectiveness among secondary school teachers in Punjab.* The tools used for the study were The Teacher Effectiveness Scale and Occupational Stress Scale. The results revealed that less effective teachers are under a higher level of occupational stress than the highly effective teachers, while the female secondary school teachers were significantly under more occupational stress than their male counterparts. The correlation analysis revealed that occupational stress was negatively correlated with the teacher effectiveness.

Kumar (2007) studied the *influence of certain psycho-social factors on the occupational stress among the public and private school teachers of Orissa.* It was found that men and women teachers differed in their level of occupational stress, while male teachers expressed high level of occupational stress than the female teachers. Job satisfaction, job involvement, achievement motivation and personality characteristics were significantly related with the stress factors and private school teachers expressed significant stress in all the factors compared to the public school teachers.

Manoj Kumar (2006) studied the *occupational stress and coping styles of high school teachers in Nellore District.* It was found that nine out of twelve job stressed factors, *i.e.,* role overload, role ambiguity, role conflict, unreasonable group and political pressure, responsibility to parents, powerlessness, intrinsic impoverishment, low status and strenuous working conditions were the significant factors causing stress among teachers. It was also found that men and women teachers differed significantly in their level of occupational stress; teachers working in rural schools had more occupational stress than the teachers in the urban schools; age, experience, educational qualifications of the teachers were found to be the significant predictors of the occupational stress among teachers.

Mathew (2005) conducted an experimental study to examine the *sources, effects and the coping strategies of occupational stress among special educators in India.* The sample of the study consisted of randomly selected 35 special educators who had more than two years of experience. Occupational Stress Indicator developed by Cooper *et. al.* (1988) was used to evaluate different factors of occupational stress. Results revealed that sources of stress included school structure and climate, home work interface, relationship with other people and intrinsic job factors. The common effect of stress on special educators was found to be health related problems and job satisfaction. Job security, over workload and high student teacher ratio were also the sources of job stress.

Mathews (2005) carried out a research on *occupational stress of teachers.* The objective of the study was to find out the occupational stress among higher secondary school teachers of Idukki and Kotayam districts of Kerala. A sample of 30 higher secondary school teachers, each from the districts of Idukki and Kotayam were chosen for the study. The occupational stress index by Srivasthava and Singh was used in the study. The statistical technique employed to assess the occurrence and the magnitude of stress was t-test. The results revealed that there was no significant relationship between the occupational stress among higher secondary school teachers of Idukki and Kotayam districts of Kerala.

Naik (2011) studied the *occupational stress of Anganawadi teachers working in Kuppam Mandal.* Occupational Stress Rating Scale developed by Reddy (2006) was administered to the sample of 60 Anganawadi teachers. The statistical techniques employed were mean, mean ± 1 SD, t-test and F-test. The results of the study revealed that age, community, educational qualification, years of experience and monthly salary do not significantly influence the occupational stress of Anganawadi teachers, whereas, locality alone has a significant influence on the occupational stress of Anganawadi teachers.

Padmaja and Prabhakar (2011) examined the *Stress of assistant professors in ANGRAU,* Rajendranagar, Hyderabad. A study was conducted to compare the level of stress among assistant professors of the College of Agriculture, Acharya NG Ranga Agricultural University, Rajendranagar, Hyderabad, Andhra Pradesh. 22 assistant professors completed a questionnaire and the collected information was processed and tabulated. Majority of the assistant professors (86.3%) belonged to the middle-age group (35-55 years). The annual income of 45.4 per cent assistant professors was Rs. 4.01/ - to Rs. 6.00/- lakhs and 18.11 per cent assistant professors had an annual income above Rs. 6.01/- lakhs. Teaching experience of 72.7 per cent assistant professors was medium, 63.6 per cent had low training exposure, and 68.19 per cent had medium achievement motivation. Regarding merits and awards, 27.2 per cent assistant professors had ICAR level awards, followed by national level (18.1%), university level (4.5%) and state level (4.5%). Personal stress was negatively and significantly correlated with training received (r=-0.4370). Family stress was positively correlated with teaching experience (r=0.4980). Teaching experience (r=-0.4176) and training received (r=-0.5141) were negatively and significantly correlated with job stress. Overall stress was negatively correlated with training received. Majority of the assistant professors (59.9%) were categorized as moderately stressed with reference to overall stress.

Padmaja and Prabhakar (2011) examined the *Stress of professors in ANGRAU,* Rajendranagar, Hyderabad. A study was conducted to compare the level of stress among professors of the College of Agriculture, Acharya NG Ranga Agricultural University, Rajendranagar, Hyderabad, Andhra Pradesh. Thirty professors completed a questionnaire and the collected information was processed and tabulated. Appropriate statistical tools were used for data interpretation. Seventy percentage of the professors belonged to the old age group (≥56 years), 90 per cent belonged to a nuclear family, and 73.3 per cent had an annual income ranging from Rs 4.01/- to Rs. 6.00/- lakhs. Majority of the professors (46.67%) had a medium teaching experience, whereas 26.67 per cent received less training and 23.38 per cent received more training. Majority (60.0%) of them had a medium achievement motivation. In case of merits and awards, 26.67 per cent had awards at international level, followed by national level (13.33%), university level (6.67%), state level (6.67%) and other awards (6.67%). Family income was significantly and negatively correlated with personal stress (r=-0.3694) and family stress (r=-0.3787). Job stress was negatively and strongly correlated with experience and training received. Overall stress was strongly and negatively related with experience. Majority of the professors (73.3%) were categorized as moderately stressed with reference to overall stress.

Poornima (2010) examined the *occupational stress of special education teachers with respect to certain demographic variables* such as age, community, educational qualification, nature of special schools the teachers working in, training received in special education, level of classes handled, nature of job, years of experience and the salary they received. The modified version of Occupational Stress Rating Scale of Reddy (2006) was administered to the sample of 202 special teachers working in the schools for VI, HI, and MR children in Chennai city. The data was analyzed using the statistical techniques mean, SD, t-test, F-test, correlations and stepwise multiple regression analysis. The results of the study revealed that 86 per cent of special teachers experience moderate and high level of occupational stress. The variable age has significantly influenced the occupation of teachers working in MR schools with teachers of 30 years and below age group experiencing higher level of occupational stress followed by teachers belonging to 46 years and above and 31 to 45 years age group. The variables community, educational qualification and years of experience have not influenced the occupational stress of special teachers. With respect to salary, the teachers receiving Rs. 10,000/- to Rs. 20,000/- per month as salary have low occupational stress than the teachers receiving salary of Rs. 20,001/- and above and Rs. 10,000/- and below.

Ramkumar (2007) explored the *occupational stress of special education teachers working in schools for mentally retarded children in Malabar region of Kerala*. The Occupational Stress Rating Scale of special education teachers developed by the investigators was administered to the sample of 200 teachers chosen from 28 special schools covering the 6 districts of Malabar region of Kerala. Mean, SD, t-test, F-test and step wise regression analysis was used to analyze the data. The findings of the study revealed that more than 73 per cent of teachers are experiencing high and moderate level of occupational stress and the sources of stress were development of materials to meet the individual needs of each child, inadequate salary, too much demand and over expectation of the job and lack of opportunities for promotion. The variables gender, educational qualification, nature of special educational training received, monthly salary, years of experience have not significantly influenced the occupational stress of special education teachers. On the other hand, age, community, and location of the school influenced the stress of special teachers. Teachers under the age group of 21-30 years, teachers belonging to OC community and teachers in the rural schools experience more stress than their counterparts.

Rao (2010) examined the *occupational stress of teachers* working in Dravidian University, Andhra Pradesh. The Occupational Stress Rating Scale developed by Reddy (2006) was administered to 50 teachers working in the university. The results revealed that the inadequate supportive staff and poor equipments for teaching and learning process have evoked high level of stress among the teachers. It was also found that 84 per cent of teachers experience moderate and high levels of stress. The personal variables of the teachers have not significantly influenced their stress levels.

Ravichandran and Rajenderan (2007) carried out a study on *Perceived sources of stress among the teachers*. The main objective of the study was to investigate the various sources of stress experienced by higher secondary teachers. A sample of 200 higher secondary teachers were randomly selected and administered Teacher's Stress Inventory developed by Rajenderan, which measures eight independent factors of sources of stress. The result of one way ANOVA indicated that sex, age, educational levels, years of teaching experience and type of school, play a significant role in the perception of various sources of stress related to the teaching profession.

Reddy (2006) in his research project on *occupational stress, professional burnout and job satisfaction among special education teachers in south India,* had selected 480 teachers working in 54 special schools of two districts each in the southern states of Tamil Nadu and Andhra Pradesh. The main objective of the study was to find out the relationship between occupational stress, professional burnout and job satisfaction of teachers due to the variations in the nature of special schools for VI, HI, MR, OH, MD and Special School as a whole and also to find out the infrastructure facilities that are available in the special schools. Rating scales developed by the investigator were used to assess the occupational stress, professional burnout and job satisfaction of special education teachers where as checklist was used to identify the infrastructure facilities. The statistical techniques employed were t-test, F-test, correlations and stepwise multiple regression analysis. The results of the study indicate that 70 per cent of the teachers in special schools are experiencing high and moderate level of occupational stress, 60 per cent are experiencing high and moderate professional burnout and 70 per cent are working with low and moderate levels of job satisfaction, Out of 22 infrastructure facilities needed for children with disabilities, only 6 facilities are available in more than 70 per cent of the special schools.

Reddy (2011) carried out a major project work on *occupational stress, professional burnout and job satisfaction of teachers working at university level in south India.* Rating scales were administered to the sample of 995 university teachers working in the states of Andra Pradesh and Tamil Nadu under the faculties of Humanities, Social Science and Science. The statistical techniques employed in the study includes mean, SD, t-test, F-test, correlations and stepwise regression analysis. The findings of the study revealed that 73.93 per cent of the university teachers were experiencing moderate and high levels of stress, and organizational structure and climate was the contributing factor for this. On the other hand, the university teachers had moderate level of burnout and low level of job satisfaction. The variables 'gender' and 'age' has significant bearing on the occupational stress owing to environmental factors. Male teachers were experiencing more stress than their counterparts, whereas teachers belonging to higher age group had higher level of occupational stress due to intra and inter personal interactions followed by lower and middle aged teachers. 'Community' and 'years of experience' has significantly influenced the occupational stress of university teachers *i.e.,* teachers belonging to MBC category were experiencing higher level stress and teachers with 11-20 years experience were exhibiting low level stress. 'Educational qualification' has not influenced the occupational stress of university teachers.

Reddy and Poornima (2007) carried out *a study on occupational stress of teachers working in the special schools for visually impaired children.* The study was conducted in the two districts each in the two states of Andra Pradesh and Tamil Nadu. The sample consisted of 87 teachers working in the schools for visually impaired children in the area. A five point rating scale to assess the occupational stress of teachers and a checklist to identify the infrastructure facilities in the schools for visually impaired children were used. The results revealed that 70 per cent of the teachers were experiencing high and moderate levels of occupational stress. Further lack of opportunities for promotion, lack of materials to meet the individual needs of each child, insufficient time for planning instructional activities, inadequate salary, long school hours, students indiscipline, inadequate professional training, feeling of physical and mental discomfort, inadequate funding for school programmes and lack of time for individual attention are the potential sources of stress for the teachers working in the schools for visually impaired children. The study also revealed that the teachers working in the schools with good and moderate infrastructure facilities were experiencing low levels of stress compared to the teachers working in the schools with poor infrastructure facilities.

Sabu and Jangaiah (2005) examined the correlation between *stress and teaching competence.* The main objective of the study was to find out any relation between stress and teaching competence of secondary school teachers with respect to few variables. Using random sampling method, 60 secondary school teachers of Kollam district in Kerala were selected for the study. The Teachers Stress Scale and Teaching Competency Scale were used in the study. The data was analyzed using mean, SD, t-test, correlation and ANOVA. The findings of the study revealed that there is a negative correlation between stress and teaching competence of secondary school teachers. Teachers with high stress have low teaching competence, and teachers with high teaching competence have low stress. Female teachers have high stress than male teachers and stress experienced by teachers who are above 45 years was greater than that of others. It was found that stress experienced by teachers with pre degree and language teachers training is higher than that of teachers with post graduation and B.Ed. training.

Jayamma *et. al.* (2007) examined the prevalence of *occupational stress of primary school teachers in relation to their personality factors.* The main objective of the study was to find out whether differences in personality factors of primary school teachers would account for significant differences in their occupational stress. By stratified random sampling technique, 150 teachers were chosen for the study. Teachers Occupational Stress Scale developed by Clark and R.B. Cattle's modified 16 personality factors questionnaire were used for data collection. The data collected was analyzed by t-test. It was found that teachers with low personality factor H, low personality factor M and high personality factor Q found to have low occupational stress.

Ushasri (2007) carried out *an analysis of occupational stress of special education teachers of Salem district.* The objective of the study was to find the occupational stress of special education teachers working in special schools for VI, HI, MR and children with MD. Sample of 52 teachers from 8 special schools in and around Salem were chosen for the study and the occupational stress rating scale developed by Reddy (2006) was employed to assess the data. The results showed that the overall occupational stress was moderate. Teachers with high level of occupational stress were: men, young teachers, teachers of HI and MR schools, temporarily employed teachers and teachers from rural location.

Ushasree and Jamuna (1990) conducted a study to examine the *role conflict and job stress among special and general school teachers.* The sample comprised of 40 special school teachers (20 men and 20 women) of Tirumala Tirupati Devasthanam's (TTD) school for the deaf and dumb, and a random sample of 60 teachers (30 men and 30 women) from TTD's high school. All the subjects were in the 35-40 years age group. Bhushan's Teacher's Role Conflict Inventory and an adapted version of Seidman and Zager's Teacher's Burnout Scale were used to assess role conflict and job stress. The analysis of data did not reveal any gender differences among the teachers from special schools on role conflict and job stress. However, women teachers in general schools were found to experience greater role conflict and had poor attitudes towards their students and were less satisfied with their careers as compared to their male counterparts in general schools. Teachers from special schools, both men and women, were found to experience significantly greater role conflict and job stress compared to their counterparts in general schools.

Vijayalakshmi (2004) studied the *stress among women lecturers working in colleges in relation to some variables.* The randomly selected sample of 220 women lecturers included 15 professors, 20 readers, 77 lecturers and 88 junior lecturers. The questionnaire consisting of 50 items was administered to the sample. The results of the study revealed that teachers working in junior colleges had more stress than degree college lecturers. Lecturers working in women's colleges had more stress than their counterparts working in co-educational institutions. The results also revealed that the teachers working in private institutions had more stress than the teachers working in government institutions. It could be concluded that the variables among subject of teaching, cadre of teachers, level of college, type of college and management where the teachers were working had significant impact on their stress.

Studies on Stress of Students and Student Teachers

Stress is inevitable in any educational institution. In optimal limits, it mobilizes the potentialities of the students to perform more effectively. However, increasing amount of academic stress for prolonged periods may create stress in the students which may affect their mental health, study habits and academic achievement. Failure in examination, underachievement and the resulting stress are becoming prominent features of educational life at school as well as the higher educational levels, leading to a wide range of health problems having far-reaching consequences for individual as well as societal well being. In this connection, research conducted on stress of students and student teachers in relation to their academic achievement, motivation, study habits, mental health, stress coping strategies and also some other variables are presented hereunder.

Adsul and Kamble (2009) had done a study on *academic stress, achievement motivation and academic achievement as predictors of adjustment among high school students.* A total of 160 students studying in the 9th and 10th standard of Sangli and Kolhapur districts were selected by random sampling method. The tools used for the study were Bisht Battery of Stress Scale to measure the four components of stresses *i.e.,* frustration, conflict, pressure and anxiety; Achievement Motive Test developed by Bhargav; Bells' Adjustment Inventory and academic achievement of the students. Multiple regression analysis was used to analyze the collected data. The findings of the study revealed that academic stress and adjustment is negatively related to each other, while achievement motivation and academic achievement are positively related to adjustment. Academic achievement and stress was found to be the most successful predictors of adjustment among high school students.

Behere *et. al.* (2011) carried out *a comparative study of stress among students of medicine, engineering, and nursing.* A cross-sectional questionnaire-based survey of 100 randomly selected students each from Medical College and Engineering College and 50 Nursing College was done. Stress was measured by using stress measurement scale having 24 Yes/No questions. Stress as an entity is universally present among students of all three streams, irrespective of age, sex, and other variables. Students in all three streams have shown denial to existence of problems, with maximum among nursing students. Medical and Engineering students had stress level of such a degree that requires clinical attention, while none of the nursing students belonged to this category.

Bramaiah and Rao (2009) studied the *stress of student teachers*. Three Hundred and Ten student teachers studying in the Colleges of Education in Andhra Pradesh were formed the sample of the study. The analysis of data revealed that the student teachers are having an average level of stress irrespective of their gender, locality, teaching methodology and educational qualification. However, the student teachers belonging to female category, graduate qualification with science methodology are having more stress than male students, post graduates and in arts methodology respectively.

Kashyap and Sidhu (2005) examined the *difference in stress and coping mechanism used by adolescents of science and commerce streams.* This study aims to assess the level of different stresses with regard to their frequency and amount among the adolescents studying in science and commerce. The Bisht Battery of Stress Scale developed by Bisht Abha Rani was used to assess the level of frequency and amount of stress. It further examined the correlation between various defense mechanisms adopted by these adolescents to cope with stress. The Defense Mechanism Inventory developed by Mrinal and Singhal was used to assess the defense mechanism adopted to cope with stress by adolescents under study. The sample size was 100. The results of the t-test revealed different levels of frequency and amount of stress among adolescents of both the streams.

Rao (2008) carried out a study on *academic stress of college students in relation to their study habits and mental health.* It was conducted on a sample of 240 college students of both boys and girls from government and private junior colleges. The tools used for the study were:

- Students Academic Stress Scale by Kim which was adapted to Indian condition by Rajenderan and Kaliappan,
- Study Habits Inventory adapted to Indian conditions by Bengalles and
- Mental Health Inventory by Jagadesh and Srivastava.

The collected data was analyzed by t-test and ANOVA. The results revealed that boys had more academic stress when compared to girls. The study habits of college students had a significant influence on the stress factor-personal inadequacy. The type of management of the institution and the mental health of the college students had not bearing any significant effect on their academic stress.

Reddy and Reddy (2004) analyzed *the stress and coping strategies in children.* Stress and coping inventories developed by the researchers were used to measure stress and coping strategies of children studying in 8th, 9th, and 10th classes in and around Tirupati in Andhra Pradesh. Two hundred and five students of primary school level and 195 students of high school level were selected through stratified random sampling. Stress Inventory was given to the children to measure the areas in which they were experiencing stress and was measured on a three point scale. Coping Behaviour Inventory was given to assess the adjusting methods used in their day today problem solving. The results revealed that children at primary level face more stress in psychological and physical areas. Appraisal focused coping and problem focused coping are used more by high school children than children at primary level.

Reddy, Koteswari, and Rao (2005) carried out a study on *sources of stress among adolescents.* The objective of the study was to identify the various potential sources of stress in adolescents with respect to their gender. A sample of 50 boys and 50 girls were selected from various schools and junior colleges of Tirupati. Mooney's Problems Checklist was administered to identify the problems faced by the adolescents. The analysis of data was done by the t-test. The findings revealed that the adolescent girls have experienced less stress in all areas when compared to adolescent boys. Social and psychological relations, financial conditions, health and physical development are the chief sources of stress in adolescent boys. Social recreational activities, adjustment to college/school, personal and psychological factors, financial conditions, home and family, health and physical development are the sources of stress in adolescent girls.

Satapathy (2003) had investigated *stress and behavioural problems among visually impaired adolescents with respect to their grade and gender differences*. The objective of the study was to examine the grade and gender differences on stress perception and behavioural problems of visually impaired adolescents, relationship between these two variables and also to find out the familial correlates of stress and behavioural problems. Hopkins's Symptom Checklist was used to measure the stress of 79 visually impaired adolescents and teachers were asked to rate the students frequently occurring behavioural problems. The analysis of data was done by using mean, SD, t-test and correlation analysis. The results revealed that the students in grade 8th and the visually impaired females were significantly more stressed than their counterparts. Stress had significant negative association with many of the family's socio-economic status variables.

Vaijayanthi and Sunny (2010) conducted a study on *stress among student teachers in Coimbatore city.* A sample of 650 student teachers of B.Ed. course were administered the standardized multi-dimensional stress inventory. The statistical techniques employed in the study were mean, SD, t-test and F-test. The results of the study revealed that 86 per cent of the sample was found to have moderate level of stress. The results of F-test revealed that there was no significant difference among the respondents' different colleges of education and different optional subjects in the average stress scores.

Studies on Occupational Stress of other Professionals

Work is experienced as stressful when the individuals realize that they are having difficulty in coping with the demands of work and when coping is important to them. There has been a considerable amount of research about those features of the work place that pose a threat to health through stress. Some of the research literature concerning the workplace stress *i.e.,* stress of managers, police personnel, working women, its sources, consequences, prevention or management is given hereunder.

Bakshi *et. al.* (2008) carried out an analytical study to investigate the *impact of occupational stress on home environment of working women of Ludhiana city.* The objectives of the study were:

- To know socio personal characteristics of selected categories of working women and their families,
- To examine working conditions of selected categories of working women, and
- To analyze the impact of occupational stress on home environment.

Total sample of 150 respondents were selected from three categories of working women namely; doctors, university teachers and bank employees with 50 respondents in each category. The interview schedule was used to collect the data and was analyzed using statistical techniques such as, percentages, SD, chi square, F-ratio and critical differences. The results showed an impact of stress on house care and up keep as 'pay full attention towards orderliness in home' had scored maximum and 'my dependency on servants has not changed' scored minimum. Impact of stress on social and leisure life revealed that 'going out on holidays' scored maximum and 'enjoy meeting social obligation' was least preferred. Impact of stress on miscellaneous work showed that maximum scoring statement was 'pay attention towards bill payments, cheques, deposits etc. and least scoring statement was 'keeping an eye over kitchen needs is easy for me'.

Basu *et. al.* (2004) carried out a study on *qualitative explanation of the stress and strengths of mothering the mentally challenged child.* The purpose of the study was to understand the maternal cognition about mental retardation and their reaction to their mentally challenged children. Sample of 80 middle class Bengali mothers of 25 to 50 years of age were chosen for the study. All the children belonged to mild retardation category (IQ 50 to 69) and were between 5 and 20 years of age. Among these children, 23 were between 5 and 10 years, 35 were between 10 and 15 years, and 22 were between 15 and 20 years. Detailed demographical information sheet was prepared to collect relevant information from the participant about their family. A detailed open-ended interview schedule had been prepared for the collection of data from mothers. The results revealed that there were some intrinsic conditions within the mothers. Thus the study as a whole reveals that mothering of a mentally challenged child is a complex experience with various shades of emotions and various levels of stress.

Chandraiah *et. al.* (2003) studied the *occupational stress and job satisfaction among managers.* The objective of the study was to investigate the effect of age on occupational stress and job satisfaction among managers of different age groups.

Sample of 105 industrial managers working in different large scale organizations were selected randomly for the study. The Organizational Stress Index developed by Srivastava and Singh and Job Descriptive Index developed by Smith Kendal were used to assess the level of job stress and job satisfaction of the sample. The findings of the study revealed higher levels of job stress and less job satisfaction among managers of 25-35 years age than their counterparts in the middle age (36-45 years) and the old age groups (46-55 years). The study also found that age found to be negatively correlated with organizational stress and positively correlated with job satisfaction.

John (2012) examined the *role of gender and maternal coping of Stress among mothers of children with intellectual disabilities in urban India.* The study assessed stress among mothers of young children with intellectual disabilities in urban India and examined the extent to which child functioning and maternal coping predict maternal stress. Through qualitative analyses, the study identified negative and positive dimensions of Indian mothers' care giving experiences. Mothers completed Parenting Stress Index-Short Form, and children's teachers completed Vineland-II teacher rating form. Maternal responses to a semi-structured interview were rated to assess maternal coping and content analysed to derive qualitative themes. Three-fourths of the sample obtained a clinically significant stress score, and maternal coping emerged as a robust predictor of stress for mothers of boys with intellectual disabilities. Qualitative analyses indicated positive and negative maternal experiences related to self, child, family and community.

Katyal *et. al.* (2011) carried out a *comparative study of job stress and type of personality of employees working in nationalized and non-nationalized banks.* Hundred employees from Nationalized and Non-Nationalized Banks having minimum one year of job experience in the same bank in Chandigarh were selected randomly for the study. The data was collected through standardized Occupational Stress Index and Eysenk's Maudsley Personality Inventory. The findings revealed highly significant difference in job stress of employees working in nationalized and non-nationalized banks, with employees of non-nationalized banks having higher job stress as compared to their counterparts working in nationalized banks. Highly significant difference also existed between the mean scores of nationalized and non-nationalized bank employees with regard to neuroticism. The employees working in non-nationalized banks were found to be more neurotic than those working in nationalized banks.

Kaur and Kaur (2007) conducted a study on *occupational stress and burnout among women police.* In this study, an attempt was made to study occupational stress and burnout among women police. The sample comprised of 80 women police, selected randomly from various police stations, women's cell from Jalandhar and Phillaur, whose age range was between 25 and 45 years. Occupational Stress Index developed by Srivastava and Singh was administered to the sample. The data thus collected was subjected to correlation co-efficient. The results indicated positive correlation between occupational stress and burnout. As the level of occupational stress increases, the level of burnout also increases among women police.

Latha and Panchanatham (2010) examined *the work life stress of call centre employees*. This study aims to identify the problems in the sector and the nature of the stress created by such problems. First hand information regarding the problems, the sources of stress and the experience on stress situations is collected from a project leader who has five years of experience. A questionnaire is circulated to measure the stress level of employees. It also identifies the various stressors prevailing among the employees. The impact of job satisfaction, feedback, working conditions, work family balance and workload in creating stress among the employees are analyzed.

Mishra *et. al.* (2011) evaluated the *work place stress in health university workers from rural India.* A cross-sectional study was designed and carried out at a Rural Health University. Both the General Health Questionnaire (GHQ)-12 and Holmes – Rahe Scale were used to evaluate 406 participants. The statistical techniques include multivariate analysis, correlation, and ANOVA. The minimum age of the participants was 19 years and the maximum age was 64 years, with an average age at 35.09 years. On the GHQ scale 239 (58.9%) recorded psychiatric morbidity out of which 201(49.5%) had moderate and 38 (9.3%) severe morbidity. Doctors were the highest stressed group ($P \leq 0.04$). Prominent work environmental stressors were poor departmental reorganization, lack of cohesiveness in department, difficult superiors and juniors ($P \leq 0.001$, Pearson correlation). Stressors associated with work organization and work nature were: non-involvement in departmental decision-making and lack of proper feedback, work load, lack of clarity in job, and an erratic work schedule ($P \leq 0.001$ on Pearson correlation). Harassment, favoritism, discrimination, and lack of self-expression ($P \leq 0.003$) were other factors responsible for work dissatisfaction. A high stress level was detected in the study population.

Mukhopadhyay (1999) carried out a study on *stress in the lives of working women and coping mechanism.* In this study, a mixed group of 45 middle and junior level women administrators, managers and professionals from government organizations and public sector organizations were interviewed on job related variables like work culture, peer-subordinate relations support mechanism and facilitating behaviour of their bosses. The respondents reported that 'boss is always right' approach makes them get going in the workplace. Respondents who were under pressure reported that their bosses did not give them criticism in a helpful way, played favourites and pulled ranks and took advantage of them whenever they got a chance.

Ojha and Rani (2004) carried out *a comparative study of the level of life stress and various dimensions of mental health among working and non-working Indian women.* The main purpose of the study was to examine and compare the level of life stress and various dimensions of mental health, the nature of relationships between life stress and mental health among the working and non-working women's respectively. The sample consisted of 60 Indian women belonging to two categories, working (30) and non-working (30). The working women comprised of official and teaching staff working in different institutions of Varanasi with at least 5 years of job experience and the nonworking women comprised of house wives. Presumptive Stressful Life Events Scale had been used for the assessment of life stress in modified form by the researchers.

To assess the positive aspects of mental health, Mental Health Inventory developed by Jagadish and Srivastava had been used. The results indicated that working women significantly scored higher on life stress compared to non-working women. The results of co-relational analysis revealed that, in case of both working and non-working women significant negative correlations were found between life stress and integration of personality. The results of stepwise regression analysis indicated that three dimensions of mental health namely autonomy, positive self-evaluation and integration of personality were important predictors of amount of life stress among working and non-working women.

Sinha *et. al.* (2011) carried out *an empirical study on measuring stress among hospital nurses*. The nursing profession is increasingly characterised by occupational stress leading to psychological and physical problems. Studies using fuzzy evaluation with special reference to government hospital nurses particularly in Indian context are very rare. Consequently, the investigators tried to minimize the uncertainty in human judgement using triangular fuzzy numbers. Findings show that among the major factors, dealing with the patients suffering from critical illnesses, lack of reward/recognition/ apprehension and fatigue induces maximum stress among nurses.

Vashishtha and Mishra (2005) carried out a study on *occupational stress and social support as predictors of affective commitment.* This study explored the relative contribution of organizational stress and social support to affective commitment of supervisors. The study was done on 200 supervisors employed in Scooters India Limited at Lucknow. The following psychometric devices such as:

(i) The general population form of Interpersonal Support Evaluation list (ISEL) developed by Cohen Mermelestein, Kamarck and Hoberman,

(ii) Occupational Stress Index (OSI) developed and standardized by Srivastava and Singh, and

(iii) Organizational Commitment Scale (OCS) developed by Meyer and Allen were used in the study.

The stepwise multiple regression analysis revealed that social support and occupational stress significantly predict the degree of affective commitment of supervisors.

Verma and Choudhary (2009) explored the *stress in farmers*. This study attempted to study the nature of stressors in farmers and also their attitude towards these stressors. A sample of 43 farmers of Mainuddinpur village in Ambedkar Nagar district in Uttar Pradesh were interviewed with semi structured interview schedule. The major stressors reported by them were repeated financial loss, fatal disease to any member in the family, constant fear of natural disaster, health problems, insecurity and domestic violence in joint families. Greater number of small and marginal families reported higher stress as compared to farmers having large land holdings.

Vijalakshmi *et. al.* (2004) carried out *a study of work motivation and stress coping behaviour of technical personal working at a railway workshop.* The sample comprising of 30 technical personnel working in the railway repair workshop at Hubli in Karnataka were administered the Work Motivation Questionnaire developed by Agarwal and another tool to measure the peoples' stress coping behaviour developed by cooper *et. al.* (1998). The results of product moment correlation co-efficient revealed that overall work motivation scores of railway technical personnel significantly correlated with their overall stress coping behaviour.

Viswesvaran *et. al.* (1999) carried out a Meta analysis on the *role of social support in the process of work stress.* After summarizing the literature on the various models for the role of social support in the process of work stress, two studies are reported. The first study was related to correlations between *(i)* social support and workplace stressors; and *(ii)* between social support and strains. Potential moderators of these relationships were weak, suggesting the presence of three general constructs of stressors, strains, and social support. In the second study, the various models for the role of social support in the process of workplace stress were tested for the general constructs identified in the first study. Results indicated that social support had a threefold effect on work stressor–strain relations. Social support reduced the strains experienced, social support mitigated perceived stressors, and social support moderated the stressor–strain relationship. Evidence for mediational and suppressor effects of social support on the process of work stress was weak. In addition, the argument that social support is mobilized when stressors are encountered was not consistent with the available empirical evidence. A similar lack of support was found for the arguments that support is mobilized when strains are encountered and that support is provided when individuals are afflicted with strains.

Studies on Job Performance of Teachers and Other Professionals

Generally speaking, differences in performance are caused by the interaction between ability, motivation, and situational factors that may facilitate or inhibit performance (Muchinsky, 1993). Thus, for an employee to perform well, it is certainly important for that person to possess job-relevant abilities. Ability alone will not lead to high levels of performance, though, unless the employee is motivated to perform and does not experience severe situational constraints. In relation with this, studies on job competence and job performance; emotional maturity and job performance; organizational culture and job performance; and some other related studies are presented hereunder.

Anuradha and Sreedevi (2007) studied the *job competence and job performance of ICDS supervisors*. Using purposive sampling technique, 220 supervisors were selected from 45 ICDS projects in Andhra Pradesh. The results of t-test, F-test and multiple regression analysis revealed that majority of the supervisors possessed high job competence and high job performance.

Bansibihari and Surwade (2006) examined the *emotional maturity of secondary teachers and its effect on teacher effectiveness and performance*. The results indicate that female teachers working in secondary schools are emotionally more matured and stable than their male counterparts. It was also found that emotionally matured and stable teachers are more effective in their teaching and performance.

Biswas *et. al.* (2007) examined the *organizational culture and communication process and their influence on individual and organizational performance.* Data was collected from 357 managers/executives and analyzed using structured equation modeling technique. The results revealed that organizational culture and communication had a significant influence on the individual's performance and the organizational effectiveness. Also, the results indicate the need to consider cultural factors and communication procedures to shape human resource development practices in Indian organization.

Garg and Rastogi (2006) had examined the *climate profile and OCBs of teachers in public and private schools of India.* This research aims to assess the significant differences in the climate profile and organizational citizenship behaviours (OCBs) of teachers working in public and private schools of India. The sample comprised of 100 teachers, out of which 50 teachers were from public school and 50 teachers were from private schools. Following data collection, significant differences regarding climate profile and OCBs were examined by using t-test. The findings indicated significant differences in the climate profile of public and private schools. Also, there was significant difference in the exhibition of citizenship behaviours of teachers working in public and private schools.

Giri and Kumar (2007) explored the *impact of organizational climate on job satisfaction and job performance.* The sample consisted of 380 managers of three levels from different Indian organizations. The results revealed that the organizational climate had a significant effect on job satisfaction and job performance. Also, it was observed that both organizational climate and job satisfaction differed significantly across the three levels of hierarchy, namely; top, middle and junior level managers. However, job performance of the employees did not differ significantly across the hierarchy.

Kumaran (2003) had studied the *organizational health and academic performance.* The organizational health of the school was studied by adopting the Ispative method, where the measures of organizational health of the schools were studied through the responses given by the teachers of the concerned schools. Eight hundred and fifty two higher secondary school teachers from Kanchipuram, Chennai and Thiruvallur were studied. The study shows that the variables academic emphasis and principal's influence had direct impact on academic performance of the schools.

Kumaraswamy and Sivanandam (2004) had done a research on the *performance of primary school teachers.* The main objectives of the study were:

(i) To find out the influence of personal and demographic variables on the performance of primary school teachers,

(ii) To assess the impact of attitude, school facilities and teacher characteristics on the performance of the primary school teachers, and

(iii) To know the amount of contribution of each of the independent variables *viz.*, gender, age, locality, caste, education, experience, attitude, income, school facilities and teacher's characteristics.

For the purpose of the research, the investigators developed tools related to attitude, school facilities, teacher's characteristics and measure of performance and were administered to the sample of 180 primary school teachers working in Nellore district, Andrapradesh. Percentages, t-test, F-test and multiple regression analysis were utilised for analysis of the data. The findings revealed that gender, age, caste, education, income and experience have significantly influenced the performance of teachers, whereas, locality did not exert significant influence on the performance of teachers. Teachers possessing better educational qualifications, experience and income (post graduates with B.Ed/M.Ed, 6 years and above experience, and Rs. 80,000 and above income) have obtained better performance scores when compared with their counterparts. Further, teachers who had obtained higher scores on attitude have obtained higher performance scores. The school facilities do not have any influence on the performance of teachers. Teacher's characteristics have significantly influenced the performance of teachers.

Muralidharan and Sundararaman (2011) examined the *teacher opinions on performance pay*. The practical viability of performance-based pay programmes for teachers depends critically on the extent of support the idea will receive from teachers. This study presents evidence on teacher opinions with regard to performance-based pay from teacher interviews conducted in the context of an experimental evaluation of a programme that provided performance-based bonuses to teachers in the Indian state of Andhra Pradesh. Four main findings in this study are: over 80 per cent of teachers had a favorable opinion about the idea of linking a component of pay to measures of performance; exposure to an actual incentive programme increased teacher support for the idea; teacher support declines with age, experience, training, and base pay; and the extent of teachers' stated ex ante support for performance-linked pay (over a series of mean-preserving spreads of pay) is positively correlated with their *ex post*-performance as measured by estimates of teacher value addition. This suggests that teachers are aware of their own effectiveness and that implementing a performance-linked pay programme could not only have broad-based support among teachers but also attract more effective teachers into the teaching profession.

Raju and Srivastava (1994) presented a study on *factors contributing to commitment to the teaching profession.* The study presents a need to look at commitment of teachers to their profession in terms of effective performance, goals and values of the profession. Measuring commitment on this basis, explores the contributing factors and variables to commitment. Empirical evidence on 454 senior secondary school teachers of Delhi, with the help of discriminant analysis, revealed that perceived characteristics of profession, work related personality and desire to improve one's own skills were contributing in that order. The constituent variables that discriminated more and less committed teachers were perceived status, expectations of significant persons, interest in the profession, intrinsic motivation, social support, positive group attitudes, perceived advancement and desire to improve skills for professional purpose.

Reddy (1992) had conducted a study on *discrepancy between ideology and practice of instructor-role performance as perceived by the national adult education programme instructors*. The objectives of the study were (1.) to estimate the amount of discrepancy that exists between idealized performance of the instructor and that discharged in actual practice and (2.) to know the causes and amount of discrepancy existing between the ideal and the actual role performance of the instructors in relation to their sex, caste and education. Role performance questionnaire developed by the investigator was given to the randomly selected sample of 240 instructors working in Srikalahasti and Naidupet projects of Chittoor district, Andrapradesh. Here the statistical techniques employed were mean, SD, and analysis of variance. The results of the study indicated that; *(i)* the instructors with better educational qualifications appear to be more successful in discharging their roles, *(ii)* instructors belonging to other castes appear to be comparatively more active than instructors belonging to the scheduled castes in discharging their roles successfully and *(iii)* women instructors appear to be more successful in discharging their roles than men instructors.

Reddy (2007) had investigated the *classroom performance of teacher trainees in colleges of education.* The main purpose of this study was to identify the general level of classroom performance prevailing among the trainees of colleges of education. The multistage stratified random sampling was employed in selecting the sample of 420 B. Ed. trainees from the state of Andhra Pradesh. Rating scale was used to measure the class room performance of the B. Ed trainees. Statistical techniques such as t-test, F-test and chi square test were employed to analyze the data. The findings of the study revealed that the level of class room performance of B. Ed trainees was more than average and the female trainees show significantly better performance than male trainees in teaching.

Relationship Studies on Emotional Intelligence, Occupational Stress and Job Performance

Emotional intelligence is the ability of a person to control impulses and persist in the face of frustration and obstacles, prevent negative emotions from swamping the ability to think, feel motivated and confident. By developing emotional intelligence, one can build a bridge between stress and better performance. Every individual has a rational-self, but when exposed to stressors, it is often pushed aside by stress-building thoughts and disrupts performance. One can learn to avoid stress-building thoughts and replace them with stress-busting thoughts for better performance. In this connection, some of the relationship studies on emotional intelligence, occupational stress and job performance are given hereunder.

Bajwa (2007) explored the *effect of yoga exercises on emotional stability and academic stress of high school students.* Sample of sixty students were taken for the study. Pre-test post-test control group design was used. The sample was randomly divided into two groups. One of the two groups was randomly assigned as the experimental (yoga) group and the other as the control group. The experimental group has given training in yoga exercises for two months and the control group was not exposed to any training in yoga exercises. The data was analyzed by using t-test. Compared to the control group the yoga group showed significant improvement in emotional stability and significant reduction in stress.

Bhagat and Allie (1989) examined the *organizational stress, personal life stress, and symptoms of life strains.* Self-competence is often regarded as an important determinant of how an individual copes with various stressful experiences. It was hypothesized that the relationships between both personal life stress and organizational stress and symptoms of various life strains would be stronger for individuals with low levels of perceived sense of competence and weaker for those with higher levels of such sense of competence. In this study of 276 teachers, it was found subjective feelings of competence concerning their ability to interact effectively with one's work environment, moderate satisfaction with work, satisfaction with co-workers, satisfaction with supervision, emotional exhaustion, and feelings of depersonalization. No significant moderating effects were found for absenteeism and job performance.

Darolia and Darolia (2005) had examined the *role of emotional intelligence in coping with stress and emotional control behaviour.* A sample of 400 adults (218 male and 182 female) in the age range of 25 to 40 years was drawn randomly from Kurukshetra, India, which covered people from all walks of life. The subjects were categorized into low and high emotional intelligence groups on the basis of lower and upper quartile of scores on Multidimensional Measure of Emotional Intelligence. The findings reveal that emotionally intelligent people cope with stressful situation by realistically accepting it or sometimes successfully detaching themselves from stress generating events. High EI subjects scored low on avoidance coping as compared to low EI subjects. It indicates that low EI subjects involve in maladaptive coping style by engaging in denial of stressful event or just giving up on account of stress.

Garg and Rastogi (2009) carried out the relationship study on *the emotional intelligence and stress resiliency.* Sample of 140 students pursuing post-graduate and research programmes from Indian Institute of Technology, Roorkee, were selected for the study. Emotional Intelligence Scale developed by Hyde, Pethe and Dhar (2002) and Stress Resiliency Profile developed by Thomas and Tymon were used to collect the data. The analysis was done by Pearson product moment method and stepwise regression analysis. The results of the study revealed that the students had high level of emotional intelligence and had significantly low relationship with deficiency focusing. It was also revealed that higher the self-motivation, emotional stability, managing relations, self-development, value orientation, commitment and altruistic behaviour, the lower is the perception of deficiency focusing.

Kauts and Saroj (2010) studied the *teacher effectiveness and occupational stress in relation to emotional intelligence among teachers at secondary stage.* Six hundred secondary school teachers were selected as a sample for the study. Emotional Intelligence Scale (EIS) by Anukool Hyde, Sanjyot Pethe, and Upinder Dhar, Teacher Effectiveness Scale by Pramod Kumar and Mutha and Occupational Stress Index by Srivastava and Singh were used to measure the emotional intelligence, teacher effectiveness and occupational stress among teachers respectively. After analysis it was found that teachers with high emotional intelligence were having less occupational stress and more teacher effectiveness, whereas, teachers with low emotional intelligence were having more occupational stress and less teacher effectiveness.

Latha and Panchanatham (2007) carried out a study on *job stress related problems and the coping strategies.* The main objective of the study was to find out the job stressors and their implications on the job performance and significance, job clarity, job feedback, job security, work load, working conditions and interpersonal relations at work in creating stress among software professionals. A job stressors questionnaire was administered on 40 software professionals. Participants answered the questionnaire on a three point scale. Low score on each item indicated low stress and high score indicated high stress. The average score was calculated for each subject, which indicates the job stress. Results of the study indicate that 73.5 per cent of the software professional had medium level of stress. Job insecurity, job dissatisfaction and work load are found to impart stress on software professionals.

Mishra and Mohapatra (2010) carried out an empirical study on *relevance of emotional intelligence for effective job performance.* The aim of the current study was to explore the relationship between emotional intelligence and workplace performance among corporate executives. The research was carried out in various organizations in Delhi. A questionnaire design was used to explore whether there was a relationship between emotional intelligence scores and scores from performance assessment checklist for a sample of 90 males and females from different streams of population were taken. The relationship was explored using an analysis of correlation. The effect of demographic variables, such as, gender, academic qualification, and work experience on EI score was also explored. The analysis found statistically significant positive correlations between scores on the emotional intelligence scale and scores on the performance scales. This means that increased emotional intelligence scores were associated with increased performance among executives working in various sectors. These results provide evidence of the concurrent validity of the emotional intelligence scale and also support the notion that emotional intelligence is associated with more or less workplace performances. Out of the different demographic variables, only work experience was found to correlate positively with EI score. Experienced executives scored significantly higher on EI scale compared to less experienced executives.

Poornima and Reddy (2011) conducted a study on *emotional intelligence and occupational stress of special education teachers working in the schools for hearing-impaired children.* A five-point rating scale was used to assess the emotional intelligence and occupational stress of 72 special education teachers working in the schools for hearing-impaired children. The results revealed that around 90 per cent of the teachers encompass only low and moderate levels of emotional intelligence and more than 80 per cent of the special education teachers experience moderate and high level of occupational stress due to various stressors. The variable 'nature of job and salary' had significantly influenced emotional intelligence and the variable 'level of classes handled' had significant bearing on the occupational stress of special education teachers. Significant negative relationship between emotional intelligence and occupational stress was observed through correlation studies. The variable 'salary' is the major predictor of both the emotional intelligence and occupational stress of the special education teachers; the nature of the job has predicted emotional intelligence to certain extent.

Apart from salary, the other variables 'training in special education' and 'level of classes handled' have also contributed to the special education teachers' occupational stress. Emotional intelligence had emerged as a significant predictor of occupational stress of the special education teachers working in the schools for hearing impaired.

Rathi and Rastogi (2009) carried out a study on *assessing the relationship between emotional intelligence, occupational self-efficacy and organizational commitment.* Data was collected from 120 employees working in various organizations in India. The tools used for the study were Emotional Intelligence Scale (EIS) by Hyde, Pethe and Dhar, Organizational commitment Questionnaire developed by Mowday, Steers and Porter and Occupational Self-efficacy Scale by Pethe, Chaudhari and Dhar. The collected data was analyzed by factor analysis, bivariate analysis and regression analysis. The results of the study indicate that employees with a high level of emotional intelligence exhibit a high level of occupational self-efficacy. Employees with higher emotional intelligence are more aware of themselves in terms of their abilities and limitations. It is also observed that there is a positive relationship between emotional intelligence and organizational commitment and performance.

Singh and Koteswari (2006) explored the *emotional intelligence and coping resources of stress among project managers.* The sample consisted of 50 project managers belonging to different information technology companies in Hyderabad. Effect of emotional intelligence and coping resources of stress across their ages was also explored. The findings of the study revealed that highly emotional intelligent people use more of coping resources of stress and emotional intelligence increases with increase in age.

Singh and Singh (2008) carried out a study of *Indian medical professionals* on *managing role stress through emotional intelligence.* The study was designed to investigate the relationship as well as the impact of emotional intelligence on to the perception of role stress of medical professionals in their organizational lives. It was conducted on a sample size of 312 medical professionals consisting of 174 male and 138 female doctors working for privately managed professional hospital organizations. The findings of the study indicate no significant difference in the level of emotional intelligence and perceived role stress between genders, but significantly negative relationships of emotional intelligence with organizational role stress for both the gender and the medical professionals as a whole. The study also found emotional intelligence of both the gender and the medical professionals as a whole to predict significant amount of variance in the total variance in their perceived role stress.

STUDIES CONDUCTED ABROAD

Many research studies have been conducted on emotional intelligence, occupational stress and job performance in western world. Enormous amount of work has been carried out in each of these fields. Similarly, studies related to the relationship between emotional intelligence, occupational stress and job performance are also done in good number with special reference to teachers, and such studies are reviewed hereunder.

Studies on Emotional Intelligence of Teachers

Alfredo (2012) carried out *a case study of urban high school mathematics teachers' perceptions of how their emotional intelligence facilitates instruction and learning in the classroom in closing the mathematical achievement gap through the heart to the brain.* The study focused on the voices of sixteen urban mathematics teachers and was undertaken in reaction to the significant mathematics achievement gap between urban students and their suburban counterparts. Data gathered during individual teacher interviews was transcribed and sorted into emergent categories using open coding. Urban math teachers reported passion for their students, their feelings affect teaching and learning, and that humor is an important tool in mediating emotions.

Beach (2010) examined the *emotional intelligence among elementary learners, parents, and teachers in Korean English Language Institutes.* In this exploratory mixed methods study, the role of EI in English language education in Korea was investigated. The study combined descriptive quantitative and qualitative approaches. Sixty-four Korean students, 21 teachers of English as a second language, and 25 Korean parents completed surveys designed for this study to measure elements of EI in second language acquisition. Interviews and observations were also conducted with a subset of the participants. Translation was provided from English to Korean as needed in interviews and surveys. Survey scores were above the scale midpoint for all participants, indicating that participants believed that they were able to recognize, identify, and forecast emotions accurately. Qualitative results differed in some areas from survey results, suggesting that social desirability may have influenced survey responses. The students interviewed demonstrated anxiety when speaking English, even though on the survey most denied being anxious. Parents who reported being sure of their emotions on the survey lacked empathic behaviours and appeared not to understand the learning processes of their children. However, results from teacher interviews and observations were similar to those found in the survey as they supported the students in learning English. In conclusion, data suggest that the concept of EI has been introduced in Korean education, but its application is evolving.

Brackett *et. al.* (2010) examined the *Emotion-Regulation* Ability, *burnout, and job satisfaction among British secondary-school teachers,* as assessed by the Mayer-Salovey-Caruso Emotional Intelligence Test (MSCEIT), with a sample of 123 secondary-school teachers. It also examined the mediating effects of affect and principal support on these outcomes. ERA was associated positively with positive effect, principal support, job satisfaction, and one component of burnout *i.e.,* personal accomplishment. Two path models demonstrated that both positive affect and principal support mediated independently the associations between ERA and both personal accomplishment and job satisfaction.

Broli *et. al.* (2011) carried out *an investigation on Italian high-school teachers in terms of emotional intelligence as a protective factor in times of educational reforms.* Three hundred and fifty teachers from 15 high schools located in two regions of northern Italy (Lombardy and Piedmont) were recruited to participate in the study. The tools used in the study were Teachers' Self-efficacy Scale, the Italian version of the Bar-on Emotional Quotient Inventory and the Organizational Satisfaction Questionnaire. The results of the study revealed that EI could be considered both a protective factor against teachers' vulnerability in times of change implying an increased performance demand, and a plausible predictor of well-being.

Chan (2008) examined the *emotional intelligence, self efficacy, and coping among Chinese prospective and in-service teachers in Hong Kong.* The study assessed the emotional intelligence (intrapersonal and interpersonal) and general teacher self-efficacy to represent resources facilitating active and passive coping in a sample of 273 Chinese prospective and in-service teachers in Hong Kong. Intrapersonal and interpersonal emotional intelligence were found to predict significantly the active coping strategy, but teacher self-efficacy has not contributed independently to the prediction of active coping, even though, there was some evidence that teacher self-efficacy might interact with intrapersonal emotional intelligence in the prediction of active coping, especially for male teachers.

Dominguez-Cruz (2003) explored the *relationship of leadership orientations to emotional intelligence of public elementary, intermediate and high school principals in Puerto Rica.* The results indicated motivation as one of the dimensions of emotional intelligence that had no relationship with leadership orientation. The study also indicated that principals viewed themselves in different ways when leading and there was absence of social skills and self-awareness among them.

Fernandez (2011) examined *the relationship between teachers' emotional intelligence and sense of humor, and student achievement.* This study examined the role of teachers' emotional intelligence (EI) and sense of humor and its impact on students' academic achievement. Utilising the Bar-On Emotional Intelligence Inventory (EQ-i) to measure teachers' emotional intelligence and Thorson and Powell's Multidimensional Sense of Humor Scale to measure teachers' sense of humor, 40 reading teachers in grades 2–8 of a K-8 public school in South Florida completed the self-reporting survey instruments. Students of the teachers participated in baseline (pre) and interim (post) benchmarked reading assessments to determine changes in academic achievement. A correlational research design was implemented. Descriptive statistics were used to examine the variables of the study and Pearson product-moment correlation procedures were used to determine the strength and nature of the relationships. The findings of this research demonstrated that there are significant and positive relationships between all variables of the study. Through regression analysis and partial correlation, emotional intelligence, in comparison to sense of humor, was found to have a stronger relationship to students' positive score changes.

Hasket (2003) studied the *emotional intelligence and teaching success in higher education.* This study compared the emotional intelligence of 286 faculty members with their teaching effectiveness. Based on the findings of the study, a significant link was found between specific emotional intelligence competencies and behaviours of effective teaching. Based on the findings, it was concluded that, not only the actions/behaviours taken by faculty that are important, but the underlying attitude behind the actions that had the greatest influence on effective teaching.

Hosotani and Imai-Matsumura (2011) studied the *emotional experience, expression, and regulation of high-quality Japanese elementary school teachers.* The present study investigates the emotional experience, expression, and regulation processes of high-quality Japanese elementary school teachers while they interact with children, in terms of teachers' emotional competence. Qualitative analysis of interview data demonstrated that teachers had various emotional experiences including self-elicited negative emotions. The major expression patterns were identified as direct staging and the suppression of emotions. Teachers considered emotion expression in front of children as a skill, and their emotion regulation processes involved considering various purposes, appropriately using emotion expression, and ideal teacher images. The findings suggest that high-quality teachers effectively use emotional competence in teaching.

Jose Maria Augustolanda *et. al.* (2006) had carried out a study on *perceived emotional intelligence and life satisfaction among university teachers.* Sample of 52 university teachers completed the Spanish version of the Trait Meta Mood Scale for emotional intelligence, TAS-20 for Alexithymia and SWLS for life satisfaction. By using stepwise regression analysis, the results yield a strong correlation between life satisfaction and work satisfaction. Further analysis show that the life satisfaction's most significant predictors were positive and negative affect and emotional clarity.

Kafetsios and Zampetakis (2008) *tested the mediatory role of positive and negative affect at work* on *emotional intelligence and job satisfaction.* The study tested the extent to which positive and negative affect at work mediate personality effects (Emotional Intelligence) on job satisfaction. Participants were 523 educators who completed the Wong Law Emotional Intelligence Scale, a version of the Job Affect Scale and the General Index of Job Satisfaction. Results using structural equation modeling indicated that positive and negative affect at work substantially mediate the relationship between EI and job satisfaction with positive affect exerting a stronger influence. In males, affect at work fully mediated the EI effect on job satisfaction. Among the four EI dimensions, use of emotion and emotion regulation were significant independent predictors of affect at work. The results confirm expectations deriving from Affective Events Theory regarding the role of work affectivity as an interface between personality and work attitudes and extend the literature on EI effects in organizational settings.

Kaplan (2003) conducted a *study on emotional intelligence training for early childhood teachers and caregivers.* The intervention programme was designed for the teachers and caregivers to develop their ability to perceive, understand and manage emotions and to successfully implement a social-emotional learning programme with children. Findings suggested that, the emotional intelligence appeared to be weak in pre-programme and it improved significantly after post-training.

Karakus (2012) presented the *emotional intelligence and negative feelings in a gender specific moderated mediation model.* This study aims to clarify the effect of emotional intelligence (EI) on negative feelings (stress, anxiety, burnout and depression) in a gender specific model. Four hundred and twenty-five primary school teachers (326 males, 99 females) completed the measures of EI, stress, anxiety, burnout and depression. The multi-group analysis was performed using a structural equation approach. The moderated mediation results show that there are gender related differences in the relationships of age, emotional intelligence, stress, anxiety, burnout and depression.

The results imply that school managers should take into consideration the teachers' personal variables such as gender and age in order to assess the use of emotional intelligence in coping with negative feelings at the place of work effectively.

Karim and Weiz (2007) examined the *emotional intelligence as a moderator of affectivity/emotional labour and emotional labour/psychological distress relationships.* The moderating role of emotional intelligence dimensions (self-emotional appraisal; others' emotional appraisal, use of emotion, and regulation of emotion) in the affectivity (a general positive or negative tendency to experience a particular mood) / emotional labour and emotional labour/psychological distress relationships were examined among 210 university teachers. Specifically, it was found that:

(a) regulation of emotion was a particularly important emotional intelligence dimension in influencing the use of deep acting, both directly and indirectly through the interaction with negative affectivity;

(b) positive affectivity emerged as an important affectivity dimension in influencing the use of deep acting both directly and indirectly through the interaction with self-emotional appraisal;

(c) negative affectivity was a particularly important affectivity dimension in influencing the use of surface acting, both directly and indirectly through its interaction with emotional intelligence dimensions of self-emotional appraisal and use of emotion; and finally

(d) regulation of emotion interacted with deep acting to influence the psychological distress arising from EL requirements.

Kinman *et. al.* (2011) examined *the role of workplace social support on emotional labour, burnout (emotional exhaustion, depersonalization and personal accomplishment) and job satisfaction in UK teachers.* The relationship between job experience and emotional labour was also investigated. Six hundred and twenty-eight teachers working in secondary schools in the UK completed questionnaires. Significant associations were observed between emotional labour and all outcomes, with a positive relationship found between emotional labour and personal accomplishment. Some evidence was found that social support mitigates the negative impact of emotional demands on emotional exhaustion, feelings of personal accomplishment and job satisfaction. More experienced teachers reported higher levels of emotional labour. Findings highlight the need for teacher-training programmes to raise awareness of the emotional demands of teaching and consider ways to enhance emotion regulation skills in experienced as well as recently qualified staff.

Lee (2003) studied the *conflict management styles and emotional intelligence of faculty and staff of selected colleges in Southern Taiwan.* Two Hundred and Ninety faculty and staff were selected for the study. Analyses of the data indicated that the majority of faculty and staff members used the integrating style most often and the obliging style least often. With regard to the five dimensions of emotional intelligence *i.e.,* self-awareness, managing emotions, self-motivation, empathy and handling relationships, the faculty and staff members' scores were highest in self-motivation and lowest in managing emotions. The results of ANOVA showed that EI level, gender and position affected faculty and staff members' conflict-management styles. In addition, gender, academic rank and position influenced emotional intelligence. Significant interaction effects were found between emotional intelligence level and academic rank as well as between emotional intelligence and age in faculty/staff members' conflict-management styles. The results of Pearson Product Moment correlations revealed that both integrating and compromising styles have significant and positive relationships with emotional intelligence. The findings also showed that self-motivation, managing emotions and self-awareness of emotional intelligence were significant predictors in predicting both the integrating and compromising conflict-management styles.

Lordanoglou (2007) carried out a study on *the relationship between emotional intelligence and leadership effectiveness, commitment and satisfaction.* Sample of 332 primary school teachers were participated in the study conducted in Greece. Results, using structural equation modeling showed that emotional intelligence, especially interpersonal and intrapersonal dimensions has a positive effect on leadership roles. A strong positive correlation was also apparent on teacher's commitment and effectiveness, and as measured by teacher's perception. Leadership role such as performance evaluation, motivation support and development had a strong influence on effectiveness.

Malik *et. al.* (2011) examined the *perceived learning environment and emotional intelligence among prospective teachers*. The purpose of this study was to explore relationship of perceived classroom learning environment on emotional intelligence of prospective teachers. Data was collected from 100 male and female prospective teachers of public and private sector universities and degree awarding institutions in Islamabad, Pakistan. Respondent's age range was 20 years to 30 years and their family income level ranged from Pak. Rs. 25, 000/- to Rs. 50, 000/-. Two questionnaires were used for data collection from sample for measuring perceived Classroom Learning Environment (CLE) and other for measuring Emotional Intelligence (EI) of prospective teachers. The major findings of the present study were that classroom learning environment was highly correlated with emotional intelligence; married prospective teachers had higher level of emotional intelligence than unmarried ones. Results revealed gender differences in prospective teacher's perceptions where female teachers perceived CLE positively when compared to men. Gender differences were found in emotional intelligence where female were found more emotionally intelligent than their male counterparts. Respondents from higher income showed higher emotional intelligence as well as they perceived CLE as favorable. Older respondents possessed high emotional intelligence and they considered CLE as positive as compared to young ones. Respondents having first birth order showed higher emotional intelligence and positive response on CLE.

Nahid (2012) examined the *teachers' emotional intelligence, job satisfaction, and organizational commitment.* The purpose of this study was to investigate the relationship between emotional intelligence and job satisfaction, between emotional intelligence and organizational commitment as well as the relationship between job satisfaction and organizational commitment among high school English teachers. Furthermore, the study examined the role of gender and age in emotional intelligence, job satisfaction and organizational commitment. The participants were selected by proportional stratified sampling and simple random selection. This study adopted a survey research design that utilised an ex post facto research type in which the researcher used questionnaires to collect data from the respondents. The results of the study indicate that there was a positive significant relationship between emotional intelligence and job satisfaction, between emotional intelligence and organizational commitment and also between job satisfaction and organizational commitment. It was also found there is no significant difference among high school English teachers with different genders and age concerning their job satisfaction and organizational commitment. But concerning emotional intelligence, findings in this study provide support for gender differences, with females reporting higher emotional intelligence, but the results show no age differences among the participants.

Platsidou (2011) investigated the *trait emotional intelligence of Greek special education teachers in relation to burnout and job satisfaction*. EI was measured by the Emotional Intelligence Scale (EIS) developed by Schutte *et. al.* (1998). Factor analysis revealed that four factors can be identified in the EIS. Results showed that Greek teachers reported fairly high scores in the specific factors and the overall EI. Perceived EI was significantly related to burnout syndrome and job satisfaction, indicating that teachers of high-perceived EI are likely to experience less burnout and greater job satisfaction. Regression analysis revealed that emotional exhaustion can be predicted by satisfaction with the job itself and with the principal sub scales; depersonalization is predicted by satisfaction with the job and with prospective promotions; personal accomplishment is predicted by satisfaction with the job itself as well as by an EI factor, optimism/mood regulation and a demographic variable, age.

Rastegar and Memarpour (2009) examined *the relationship between emotional intelligence and self-efficacy among Iranian EFL teachers.* Sample of the study were the Iranian EFL teachers. The tools used to collect the data were Emotional Intelligence Scale (Schutte *et. al.* 1998) and Teacher Sense of Efficacy Scale. The statistical techniques employed were Pearson product moment correlation, t-test and ANOVA. The results of the analysis revealed that there was a positive significant correlation between perceived emotional intelligence and self-efficacy and there was no significant difference among EFL teachers with different gender, age and teaching experience concerning their emotional intelligence and self-efficacy.

Salami (2007) explored the research on *relationship of emotional intelligence and self-efficacy to work attitude among secondary school teachers in south western Nigeria.* The purpose of this study was to investigate the relationship of emotional intelligence and self-efficacy to work attitude of secondary school teachers in Southwestern Nigeria. Measures of demographic data from career commitment, organizational commitment, emotional intelligence, self efficacy and work-family conflict were administered to the randomly selected 475 secondary school teachers. The statistical technique employed was hierarchical multiple regression analysis. Results of the study indicate that emotional intelligence and self-efficacy had significant relationship with work attitude. However, age, gender and work experience had no significant relationship with work attitude.

Syed *et. al.* (2012) examined the *role of emotional intelligence on job satisfaction among school teachers.* A total of 1200 primary and secondary school teachers from 60 schools in Malaysia participated in this research. The objective of this research was to ascertain the role of Emotional Intelligence (EI) on job satisfaction and the effect of gender on the relationship between EI and job satisfaction. A set of questionnaires containing Emotional Competence Inventory for measuring EI and Job Diagnostic Survey for measuring job satisfaction was used. Results of this study showed a significant positive relationship between EI and job satisfaction and no effect of gender on the relationship between the two variables.

Trapp (2010) explored the *association among emotional intelligence, resilience, and academic performance of pre-service teachers*. This quantitative study examined the association among emotional intelligence, as measured by the Emotional Skills Assessment Process, resilience, as measured by the Resilience Scale, grade point average, and Praxis I scores of three different groups of teacher candidates at a state university in western Pennsylvania. A total of 118 teacher candidate participated in the study. The results revealed significant differences in emotional intelligence scores of participants across the three groups. The difference was attributed to leadership, change orientation, and self-esteem scores. Furthermore, the correlation between emotional intelligence scores and resilience was significant.

Tseng (2011) studied the *influence of emotional intelligence and burnout on public elementary school teachers' quality of life.* The sample of study included teachers from Taipei, Taiwan. The research method used was the questionnaire survey method. The data was statistically analyzed with t-test, ANOVA, Pearsons' Product-Moment Correlation, and hierarchical regression analysis. The findings of the study revealed that the emotional intelligence of elementary school teachers was high-to-medium. Emotional intelligence is negatively correlated with emotional exhaustion and depersonalization, and it is positively correlated with personal accomplishment perspective in burnout.

Tsouloupas *et. al.* (2010) analyzed *the importance of teacher efficacy beliefs and emotion regulation* in *exploring the association between teachers' perceived student misbehaviour and emotional exhaustion.* Data was collected from 610 elementary, middle and high school teachers using an online survey. Results indicate that despite the significant direct effect between the two emotion regulation strategies (cognitive reappraisal, expressive suppression) on emotional exhaustion, both strategies failed to show a mediating effect between perceived student misbehaviour and emotional exhaustion. However, teacher efficacy in handling student misbehaviour was found to mediate the relationship between perceived student misbehaviour and emotional exhaustion. In turn, a significant relationship was found between emotional exhaustion and turnover intentions. Furthermore, teacher perception of student misbehaviour was found to have a considerable indirect effect on teacher turnover intentions.

Wong *et. al.* (2010) investigated the *effect of middle-level leader and teacher emotional intelligence on school teachers' job satisfaction.* The main purpose of this study was to empirically investigate the potential effect of school leaders' (*i.e.,* senior teachers) EI, as measured by the 16-item scale developed by Wong and Law (2002), on teachers' job satisfaction in Hong Kong. In Study 1, 107 teachers were asked to list the attributes of successful senior teachers/mentors in their schools. In Study 2, 3866 school teachers and middle-level leaders were surveyed on their EI and job satisfaction level. For the 3866 teachers, the correlation between their EI and job satisfaction scores was 0.30. Middle-level leaders' average EI was significantly related to the average of ordinary frontline teachers' job satisfaction. Results showed that school teachers believe that middle-level leaders' EI is important for their success, and a large sample of teachers surveyed also indicated that EI is positively related to job satisfaction.

Studies on Emotional Intelligence of Students

Bradshaw and Bell (2008) explored *the relationship between emotional intelligence and academic achievement in African American female college students.* A purposive sample of 60 successful undergraduate female African American college students at local colleges and universities in a Mid-Atlantic area were asked to voluntarily participate in this research study. Participants were asked to complete quantitative testing instruments which included; The Subject Demographic Survey, The Mayer-Salovey-Caruso Emotional Intelligence Test, The Bar-On Emotional Quotient Test and The Kaufman Brief Intelligence Test. Next, in-depth qualitative interviews were conducted with twenty academically successful college-aged African American females to clarify understanding and supplement findings presented in the quantitative portion of the study. The methodology chosen solicited the students' perceptions about emotional intelligence as they relate to academic achievement. Quantitative findings from the current study revealed that, there was no statistically significant correlation between African American female college students' emotional intelligence level and their academic performance, a weak correlation between stress management and the academic performance of African American female college students and no statistically significant difference between African American female college students' emotional intelligence level and their academic level.

Frederickson *et. al.* (2012) examined the *trait emotional intelligence as a predictor of socio-emotional outcomes in early adolescence.* Trait emotional intelligence (EI) refers to a constellation of emotional self-perceptions located at the lower levels of personality hierarchies. This study investigated the predictive and incremental validity of this construct in a sample of 1140 pupils aged 11–13 years. Trait EI showed strong concurrent and predictive validity in relation to three measures of socio-emotional competence: self-reported psychopathology as assessed by the Strengths and Difficulties Questionnaire, a socio-metric measure of peer relations, and a peer-assessed measure of social behaviour. Socio-emotional measures were taken twice over a period of seven months. Structural equation modeling revealed trait EI and IQ effects on socio-emotional competence (SEC), the former being stronger than the latter. Hierarchical regression analyses suggested an association also of trait with level of change in SEC (controlling for both IQ and SEC at time 1). The findings corroborate an important role for trait emotional-intelligence in peer relations and socio-emotional competence.

Han and Johnson (2012) explored the *relationship between students' emotional intelligence, social bond, and interactions in online learning.* The purpose of the study was to investigate the relationship between students' emotional intelligence, social bond, and their interactions in an online learning environment. The research setting in this study was a 100 per cent online master's degree programme within a university located in the Midwest of the United States. Eighty-four students participated in the study. Using canonical correlation analysis, statistically significant relationships were found between students' emotional intelligence, social bond, and the interactions that occurred naturally in the educational setting. The results showed that students' ability to perceive emotion by facial expression was negatively related to the number of text and audio messages sent during synchronous interaction. Additionally, the ability of students to perceive emotion was positively related to peer bonding. Lastly, students' bond to their online programme was associated with management type interaction during synchronous discussion sessions.

Lomas *et. al.* (2011) presented a *brief report on emotional intelligence, victimization and bullying in adolescents.* In order to better understand bullying behaviours, the relationship between emotional intelligence (EI) of adolescents, bullying behaviours and peer victimization was studied. The sample consisted of 68 adolescents from a secondary college. Participants completed a self-report questionnaire which assessed their EI, how frequently they engaged in bullying behaviours and how often they were the target of peer victimisation. Results of the study indicated that the EI dimensions of Emotions Direct Cognition and Emotional Management and Control, significantly predicted the propensity of adolescents to be subjected to peer victimisation. The EI dimension of Understanding the Emotions of Others was found to be negatively related with bullying behaviours.

Rahim *et. al.* (2002) carried out a study on *model of emotional intelligence and conflict management strategies in seven countries.* The study investigated the relationships of the five dimensions of emotional intelligence: *(i)* self-awareness, *(ii)* self-regulation, *(iii)* motivation, *(iv)* empathy, and *(v)* social skills of supervisors to subordinates' strategies of handling conflict: problem solving and bargaining. Data from 1,395 MBA students in seven countries (U.S., Greece, China, Bangladesh, Hong Kong, South Africa, and Portugal) were collected using questionnaires. Psychometric properties of the measures were tested and improved with exploratory and confirmatory factor analysis and analysis of indicator and internal consistency reliabilities, and the hypotheses were tested with a structural equations model for each country. Results in the U.S. and in the combined sample provided support for the model which suggests that self-awareness is positively associated with self-regulation, empathy, and social skills; self regulation is positively associated with empathy and social skills; empathy and social skills are positively associated with motivation; which in turn, is positively associated with problem solving strategy and negatively associated with bargaining strategy.

Ruiz-Aranda *et. al.* (2012) examined the *Short and midterm effects of emotional intelligence training on adolescent mental health.* The purpose of the study is to analyze the effects that an emotional intelligence (EI) educational programme based on the EI ability model had on adolescent mental health immediately and 6 months after completion of the training. A pretest–post test quasi-experimental design with a treatment and a control group was used; 479 Spanish adolescents (47.4% male, mean age of 13 years) were involved in the study. Adolescents were recruited through several schools in three Spanish cities. The two year training programme involved 24 sessions lasting one hour each, conducted weekly during six months of 2009 and 2010. Data on psychological adjustment, mental health, and negative affect were collected at baseline, at the end of the training programme, and six months later. Data were analyzed by multivariate analysis of covariance. Students who participated in the EI educational programme reported fewer clinical symptoms compared with students in the control group, and these differences persisted six months after the conclusion of the programme. These results suggest that EI programmes created to develop skills in perceiving, facilitating, understanding, and managing emotions can be effective at promoting mental health in adolescents.

Studies on Emotional Intelligence of other Professionals

Goleman's (1998) research indicated that emotional intelligence is a significant predictor of the success of leaders in a variety of organizations. In a study of over 2,000 supervisors, middle managers, and executives, all but two of the sixteen abilities that distinguished star performers from average performers were emotional competencies.

Goleman, Boyatzis, and McKee (2002) analyzed data from close to 500 competency models (including the likes of IBM, Lucent, PepsiCo, British Airways, and Credit Suisse First Boston), as well as a wide range of global companies, healthcare organizations, academic institutions, and government agencies. They found that when star performers were matched against average performers in senior leadership positions, emotional intelligence competencies accounted for 85 per cent of the differences in their profiles. For successful executives emotional intelligence was the most frequent relevant characteristic, with relevant experience a close second and IQ coming in a significantly distant third. For the executives who were classified as failures, the most frequent relevant characteristic was previous relevant experience, followed closely by IQ. The failures almost inevitably had a weakness in overall emotional intelligence. The biggest difference between the successful executives and the executives that failed was emotional intelligence.

Jung-Hoon and Chihyung (2012) analyzed the *critical role of hotel employees' emotional intelligence and emotional labour in reducing burnout and enhancing job satisfaction.* This study investigated direct and indirect effects of employees' EI on two different forms of emotional labour (*i.e.,* emotional effort: EE; emotional dissonance: ED): burnout and job satisfaction. Data was collected from 309 customer-contact hotel employees and managers in the United States. Results of structural equation modeling showed that EI had a direct, positive effect on EE and personal accomplishment and a direct, negative effect on ED and depersonalization. EI was also found to indirectly affect job satisfaction and emotional exhaustion through the mediating roles of personal accomplishment and ED, respectively. Additionally, ED was found to directly affect depersonalization and indirectly affect job satisfaction through emotional exhaustion while EE directly affects personal accomplishment and indirectly affects job satisfaction through personal accomplishment. Finally, personal accomplishment was found to mediate the depersonalization–job satisfaction relationship.

Nelis *et. al.* (2009) carried out an explorative study to find out *whether it is possible to increase emotional intelligence.* The construct of emotional intelligence (EI) refers to the individual differences in the perception, processing, regulation, and utilisation of emotional information. As these differences have been shown to have a significant impact on important life outcomes (*e.g.,* mental and physical health, work performance and social relationships), this study investigated, using a controlled experimental design, whether it is possible to increase EI. Participants of the experimental group received a brief empirically-derived EI training (four group training sessions of two hours and a half) while control participants continued to live normally. Results showed a significant increase in emotion identification and emotion management abilities in the training group. Follow-up measures after 6 months revealed that these changes were persistent. No significant change was observed in the control group. These findings suggest that EI can be improved and open new treatment avenues.

Qin-Hu (2011) studied the *relationship between emotional labour, emotional intelligence and job burnout.* With 203 employees as the subjects, the relationship of emotional labour and emotional intelligence with job burnout was studied. The results showed that perceived emotional display rule had significant positive impact on emotional regulation strategies; received demands to suppress negative emotions may positively forecast job burnout. Deep action fully mediated the relation of perceived demands to suppress negative emotions and job burnout. Emotional intelligence acts as the moderator between emotional labour and job burnout.

Woitaszewski and Aalsma (2004) portrayed emotional intelligence as critical to human success, sometimes even more important than IQ. The results of hierarchical multiple regression analysis revealed that emotional intelligence did not contribute to the social and academic success of gifted children.

Zeidner (2004) carried out a critical review of *emotional intelligence in the workplace*. Conceptualizations and empirical evidence in support of emotional intelligence (EI) and its claimed role in the occupational environment were critically reviewed. Consideration is given to the purported status of EI in occupational and career assessment (with particular emphasis on personnel selection and placement), job performance, and satisfaction. Overall, this review demonstrates that recent research has made important strides towards understanding the usefulness of EI in the workplace. However, the ratio of hyperbole to hard evidence is high, with over-reliance in the literature on expert opinion, anecdote, case studies, and unpublished proprietary surveys.

Studies on Occupational Stress of School Teachers

Al-Amri (2004) had conducted a study on *job stress among teachers.* The objective of this study was to determine the relationship between demographic and work variables and job stress. The target population for this study was all 472 male teachers in government schools in Riyadh city. The sample was selected by simple random means. The questionnaire consisted of three parts: job stress measurement, work variables, and demographic variables. The use of multiple regressions revealed the following significant relationships:

(i) There were negative relationships between demographic variables and job stress.

(ii) There were positive relationships between work variables and job stress.

(iii) The work variables affect job stress more than demographic variables.

Antoniou *et. al.* (2000) had investigated the *sources of stress and professional burnout of teachers of special education needs (SEN) in Greece.* The aim of this study was to investigate the specific sources of stress which make the work of Greek SEN teachers especially demanding and the specific mechanism that they use to cope with the stress. Questionnaires were administered to a representative sample of 110 SEN teachers of special classes and special schools across Greece. The results of multiple regression analysis revealed that the SEN teachers possess high levels of stress.

Borg and Riding (1991) had analyzed the *occupational stress and satisfaction in teaching.* Teacher stress, job satisfaction, absenteeism, career intention, career commitment and self image of teachers were investigated in a context which allowed many of the characteristics of an educational system to be incorporated in the design. A questionnaire survey of 545 teachers in Maltese secondary schools revealed that some of the demographic characteristics of the sample were related to self reported teacher stress, job satisfaction and career commitment. Results also showed that teachers who reported greater stress were less satisfied with teaching, reported greater frequency of absence and a greater number of total days absent, were more likely to leave teaching (career intention), and less likely to take up a teaching career again (career commitment).

Burke *et. al.* (2007) examined the *effects of work stress, social support, and self-doubts on burnout and its consequences in predicting teacher burnout over time.* This longitudinal study examined antecedents and consequences of psychological burnout among 362 teachers and school administrators. Antecedents included red tape, disruptive students and lack of supervisor support. Consequences of burnout included heart symptoms and depressive mood. Respondents completed questionnaires sent to them at their schools at two points in time, one year apart. LISREL analyses indicated that the predictors had significant relationships with burnout levels one year later, and that burnout served as a mediator between the predictors and emotional and physical health outcomes.

Chan *et. al.* (2010) examined the *work stress of teachers from primary and secondary schools in Hong Kong.* This study was done to comprehensively investigate the occupational health problems among teachers of primary and secondary schools in Hong Kong. A self-reporting questionnaire was administered to the randomly selected sample of 1,710 teachers. The results of t-test and ANOVA indicated that comparing with one year and five years ago, 91.6 per cent and 97.3 per cent of the responding teachers reported an increase of perceived stress level, respectively. Heavy work load, time pressure, education reforms, external school review, pursuing further education and managing student's behaviour and learning were the most frequently reported sources of work stress. The four most frequently reported stress management activities were sleeping, talking to neighbors and friends, self-relaxing and watching television, where as the least frequently reported activity was doing more exercises or sports.

Chaplain (1995) examined the *stress and job satisfaction of English primary school teachers.* Using a self report questionnaire, a picture of the sources of stress and job satisfaction amongst a sample of 267 teachers, drawn from primary schools in the North and Eastern regions of England, was established. Teachers scored the frequency and intensity of 18 items on a stress scale. A principal components analysis was carried out and three factors were identified: professional concerns, pupil behaviour and attitude, and professional tasks. The strongest correlations were found between professional concerns and occupational stress. Biographical factors were examined and significant differences were found between men and women, and teachers of different ages and length of teaching experience. Men reported more stress than women on professional tasks, and pupil behaviour and attitude. Women scored higher than men on professional concerns. Just over one third of teachers were satisfied with their job. When specific facets of job satisfaction were examined, teachers were most satisfied with their professional performance and least satisfied with teaching resources. Stress and job satisfaction were found to be negatively correlated. High reports of occupational stress were related to low levels of job satisfaction.

Chona and Roxas (2009) examined the *stress among public elementary school teachers.* Using descriptive survey method, this study dealt on stress among the public elementary school teachers in Baguin city, Phillipines with a sample size of 320 teachers. The researcher found that the stress felt by the teacher is at normal level. Moreover, it was revealed that gender, age and civil status do not have significant influence on the level of stress experienced by the teachers.

Cooper and Kelly (1993) investigated the *occupational stress in head teachers in UK.* This study assessed occupational stress amongst 2,638 head teachers of primary and secondary schools, together with principals/directors of further and higher education establishments, throughout the United Kingdom. Data was collected on personal/job demographics, sources of job stress, mental health, job satisfaction and coping strategies. This data was analyzed by SPSS-X, producing univariate, bivariate and multivariate techniques. It was found that, from the further/higher education level to secondary to primary sectors, the levels of job dissatisfaction and mental ill health rose. In addition, it was found that, with the exception of primary schools, female head teachers in secondary and further/higher secondary seem to be suffering significantly greater job dissatisfaction than their male counterparts, although this does not translate itself into mental ill health. Male head teachers, on the other hand, seem to suffer more mental ill health than their female counterparts. And finally, the two main sources of occupational stress that appear in many of the multivariate analyses as predictors of job dissatisfaction and mental ill health are 'work overload' and 'handling relationships with staff'.

Crothers *et. al.* (2011) carried out a *comparison study between samples from the United States and Zimbabwe* on the *job stress and locus of control in teachers*. Multiple regression analyses are used to identify significant relationships in the US sample between teachers' external locus of control and the severity of the job stress that they experience, coupled with the perceived degree of organizational support received. However, this relationship between the locus of control and stress indices could not be identified for the Zimbabwean sample. Significant differences between the two samples were noted in terms of educators' perceptions of the frequency of poor organizational support, with the Zimbabwean teachers reporting greater dissatisfaction. To explain these differences, a qualitative approach was utilised to illuminate the contextual stressors that educators face in Zimbabwe.

Darmody and Smyth (2011) had analyzed the *job satisfaction and occupational stress among primary school teachers and school principals in Ireland.* The findings of this study indicate that an overall majority of Irish primary school teachers (98%) and principals (93%) were happy in their job, though some experienced occupational stress (45% of teachers and 70% of principals). Job satisfaction and occupational stress were associated with a number of background and school-level factors.

De Nobile and McCormick (2007) studied the *occupational stress of catholic primary school staff by investigating biographical differences.* This study aimed at investigating the relationship between biographical variables and occupational stress of staff members of catholic primary schools in New South Wales, Australia. Data was collected using teacher's attribution of responsibility for stress questionnaire. Multivariate analysis and comparison of means were employed to test research hypotheses. The results revealed that biographical differences, particularly age, gender and position were related to several aspects of occupational stress. It was also revealed that as from student domain appear to decrease with age overall, with the exception of the 41-50 year age group. There was no relationship exists between stress arising from a lack of administrative support and unpleasant school climate and biographical characters. In general, males reported greater stress than their female colleagues.

Fimian *et. al.* (1983) studied the *sources and manifestations of occupational stress as reported by full-time special education teachers.* Three hundred and sixty five full-time special education teachers with low, moderate, and high stress were administered a Teacher Stress Inventory. Results indicate that many special education teachers exhibited frequent and strong manifestations of job-related stress. Becoming frustrated, mentally exhausted, excessively worried, and feeling pressured, depressed, and anxious were the 6 strongest emotional manifestations reported. Having a near-total separation of job from personal life, acting defensively with others, allowing social and professional performance to deteriorate, sleeping for more than usual time, and dealing with students only on an intellectual and impersonal basis were the 6 strongest behavioural manifestations of teacher stress. Teachers' ratings of stress manifestation variables across low, moderate, and high stress levels were quantitatively different. In the case of almost every aforementioned variable, high-stress teachers exhibited significantly more frequent and stronger emotional, behavioural, and physiological manifestations than did all other teachers including those in the moderate-stress group.

Hsiu-Ju Lin (2011) carried out *a study to know the relationships among job stress, emotional management and job satisfaction of elementary school teachers in Kaohsiung city*. This study aimed to explore the relationship among job stress, emotional management and job satisfaction of elementary school teachers. The tools used were the questionnaire of Job Stress, Emotional Management and Job Satisfaction of elementary school teachers. The sample of this investigation was 657 public elementary school teachers in Kaohsiung City. The collected data were analyzed with t-test, one-way ANOVA, Pearson product-moment correlation and stepwise multiple regression analysis. The major results of the study were as follows; generally, elementary school teachers felt their jobs stressful but satisfactory, and had good skills in emotional management. The elementary school teachers who were younger, junior or in the smaller-scale school, or those who were language-teachers felt their jobs more stressful. The language-teachers of elementary schools had better performance and emotional management. As to the elementary school teachers' jobs, it was more stressful and less satisfactory.

Kokkinos (2007) had conducted a cross-sectional study on the *job stressors, personality and burnout in primary school teachers* from Cyprus. The study also investigated the relative contribution of these variables on the three facets of burnout – emotional exhaustion, depersonalization and reduced personal accomplishment. A representative sample of 447 primary school teachers participated in the study. Teachers completed measures of burnout, personality and job stressors along with demographic and professional data. Results showed that both personality and work-related stressors were associated with burnout dimensions. Neuroticism was a common predictor of all dimensions of burnout although in personal accomplishment had a different direction. Managing student misbehaviour and time constraints were found to systematically predict dimensions of burnout.

Kyriacou and Chien (2004) studied the *teacher stress in Taiwanese primary schools.* A questionnaire was used to explore the teacher stress among 203 teachers in primary schools. Results of the study revealed that 26 per cent of the teachers reported being a teacher was either very or extremely stressful. The main source of stress identified was the changing education policies of the government. The most effective coping action reported by teachers was having a healthy home life and the most effective action that schools or the government could take to reduce teacher stress was to decrease teachers workload.

Lanre Olaitan *et. al.* (2010) studied the *prevalence of job stress among primary school teachers in south-west Nigeria.* The study aimed at determining the job stress among primary school teachers in south-west Nigeria. A total of 624 teachers were chosen as subjects using a multistage sampling technique and questionnaire was used to collect the data. ANOVA was employed to analyze the data. There was a significant difference for age and gender. Majority of the teachers had headache as symptom of poor health and majority of them engaged in watching television as a strategy for coping with stress. The major source of stress for the subjects was the society.

Leung *et. al.* (2009) investigated the *occupational stress, mental health status and stress management behaviours among secondary school teachers in Hong Kong.* This study aimed to examine occupational stress and mental health among secondary school teachers in Hong Kong, and to identify the differences between those actively engaged in stress management behaviours and those who were not. The sample consisted of 89 secondary school teachers who attended a professional development course offered by the University of Hong Kong, Hong Kong. Survey design was adopted using validated instruments including Occupational Stress Inventory (OSI-R), Depression Anxiety Stress Scale (DASS-21), and Health Promoting Lifestyle Profile (HPLP). The results of the study revealed that majority of participants (75.3%) reported fair to very low satisfaction with the teaching career, and 82 per cent of them felt unaccountably tired or exhausted. Results of OSI-R showed that 38.6 per cent had experienced strong maladaptive stress due to vocational strain but coping resource was limited with most deficits on rational and cognitive coping. Analysis of DASS-21 indicated that 30.3 per cent had severe to extremely severe anxiety and 12.3 per cent had severe to extremely severe depression. HPLP revealed that participants paid little attention to their health and the management of stress.

Leung *et. al.* (2011) studied the *feasibility and potentials of online support for stress management among secondary school teachers* in Hong Kong. Following 7 days of forum use, content analysis and post-intervention evaluations were carried out to examine the anonymous communications of 75 secondary school teachers who participated in one of five online discussion forums. Consensus on the coding and categorization of the data was reached among three experienced researchers in qualitative analyses. The online forums were well received by the participants. Most participants reported that they received support from the forum and considered it useful for stress management. These results suggest that online support can be used for stress management among secondary school teachers.

Ling-Feng (2005) explored the *relationship between mental health status and stress of kindergarten teaches* and provided basis for improving mental health. Self administered questionnaires were adapted to test the kindergarten teachers' status of mental health and stress at Huzhou. Results of the study revealed that 39.2 per cent and 4.7 per cent of the teachers felt that they were under medium and heavy stress and the higher stress was caused by the infants and their parents. The prevalence of mental problems was 10.38 per cent. Mental health of kindergarten teachers under 39 years of age was poorer than that of 40 to 49 years of age and the teachers with first grade title of the technical post had the poorest mental health. Some of the kindergarten teachers had mental disorders.

Litt and Turk (1985) analyzed the *sources of stress and dissatisfaction in experienced high school teachers.* High school teachers (N = 291) were surveyed to identify sources of stress and dissatisfaction that may induce teachers to leave teaching. Data on four sets of independent variables (perceived role, school climate, coping resources, and specific work problems) were entered into a canonical correlational analysis to predict a multidimensional cossnstruct of teacher stress encompassing job satisfaction, negative well-being, absence, and intention to leave teaching. Three significant canonical variates were extracted in the canonical correlation procedure, with the independent variables accounting for a total of 86 per cent of the variance in the dependent sets. Certain commonly cited work problems, such as inadequate salary and low status, were found to be important in predicting job stress, but another often-cited problem, pupil misbehaviour was not found to be a factor. The results further suggested that the role teachers perceived for themselves and the school climate, particularly the relationship with administrators, may be extremely important in predicting job stress. Unexpectedly, teachers' coping resources were found to be unrelated to job satisfaction or physical stress but were related to intention to leave teaching.

Majid (1998) conducted a study on *occupational stress and teacher's job satisfaction to find out the implications to the human relations management approach.* The aim of this study was to investigate the prevalence of teacher stress with special emphasis on the human relations management approach; to identify the stress factors and to examine the relationship between teacher stress and job satisfaction. Questionnaires were used on a sample of 204 teachers in seven secondary schools in Jasin district in Malacca. The results of the t-test revealed that there was a significant negative relationship between overall stress and job satisfaction. For both overall stress and human relations stress, female teachers indicated higher level of stress as compared to the male teachers. It also revealed that less experienced teachers had significantly high level of stress as compared to the teachers with more experience.

McCormick (2007) analyzed *an attribution model of teachers' occupational stress and job satisfaction in a large educational system.* A cognitive model based on the attribution of responsibility for stress was used as a framework for a study of the occupational stress and job satisfaction of teachers in New South Wales, Australia. One thousand questionnaires were distributed among 109 New South Wales Department of School Education schools of various types: single teacher, infants/primary, central and high school, throughout the state. There was a total response rate of approximately 49 per cent ($n = 487$). The proposition that externalization of responsibility for stress may be explained in terms of self-defense styles was also investigated. Stress attributable to student misbehaviour was found to be associated with immature defense styles. Occupational stress and job satisfaction were treated as multidimensional phenomena and associations between the dimensions were explored. Teachers satisfied with their occupation attributed greater responsibility for stress to self than did dissatisfied teachers.

McCormick and Barnett (2011) investigated the *teachers' attributions for stress and their relationships with burnout.* The participants were 416 classroom teachers in 38 randomly selected high schools in New South Wales, Australia. Two established instruments, the Maslach Burnout Inventory, and the Teachers' Attribution of Responsibility for Stress Scale were employed in a postal survey. Data were analysed using confirmatory factor analysis and multilevel modelling. Findings suggest the centrality of stress attributed to student misbehaviour in predicting each of the three dimensions of burnout: depersonalisation, emotional exhaustion, and personal accomplishment. Occupational stress attributed to personal feelings and also negatively predicted personal accomplishment.

Mearns and Cain (2003) examined the *relationships between teachers' occupational stress and their burnout and distress: roles of coping and negative mood regulation expectancies.* The current study has a cross-sectional self-report design, focusing on teachers' negative mood regulation (NMR) expectancies as predictors of their coping, burnout and distress, in response to occupational stress. NMR expectancies are people's beliefs that they can control the negative moods they experience. Participants were 86 primary and secondary school teachers, who filled out questionnaire measures of teacher stress, NMR expectancies, coping, burnout, and distress. Simultaneous regression analyses showed that higher stress on the job did indeed predict greater burnout and distress. Additionally, stronger NMR expectancies predicted more active coping. NMR expectancies also predicted less burnout and distress, independent of stress level and coping. Believing one could control one's negative moods was associated with more adaptive outcomes for teachers. Results argue for the value of examining individual difference variables in research on occupational stress, in particular negative mood regulation expectancies.

Mogojo and Williams (2010) examined the *occupational stress and work engagement among special needs educators in the Umlazi District of KwaZulu-Natal, Durban.* A quantitative, non-experimental, cross-sectional, ex post facto research design was employed for the collection and analysis of data. Data was gathered from seven special schools in the Umlazi District of KwaZulu-Natal. These special schools provide high levels of support to learners with severe intellectual (learning) disabilities. A sample of 86 voluntaries comprising 12 men and 74 women participated in the study. Data was generated via self-report survey-type questionnaires. The results revealed that inadequate pay and benefits was a major source of perceived occupational stress. Support for the hypothesis of an inverse relationship between work engagement and perceived occupational stress was attained. In addition, analyses of biographical variables in relation to perceived occupational stress provided support for the Transaction Model of Stress.

Mokdad (2005) conducted a study on *occupational stress among Algerian teachers.* The main objective of the study was to find the sources of occupational stress among the Algerian primary school teachers. Questionnaire was used on a sample of 126 teachers working in the Biskara government primary schools. The results of the study indicated that the major sources of stress among the teachers were society, parents, teaching, the teaching-environment, pupils, supervisors, the curriculum, colleagues and administration.

Muto *et. al.* (2007) analyzed the *job stressors and stress among teachers engaged in nursing activity.* This study evaluated job stressors and job stress among such teachers using a cross-sectional study design. The subjects were all 1,461 teachers from all 19 prefectural schools for handicapped children in Shizuoka Prefecture, Japan. Job stress questionnaire was administered to the sample and 831 teachers completed the questionnaire. Job stressors among teachers engaged in nursing activity were compared with those among teachers not engaged in nursing activity. Job stress among such teachers was estimated by the score for total health risk, and was compared with the score in the Japanese general population. Male and female teachers engaged in nursing activity had a significantly higher level of job stressors for physical work load and job control compared with those not engaged in nursing activity.

Prakke *et. al.* (2007) conducted a study related to *challenging parents, teacher occupational stress and health in Dutch primary schools.* The aim of this study was to examine teacher's perception of their own ability to handle challenging parent behaviour and to establish positive relationship as a possible influence on the quality of teacher-parent relationships. Sample of 212 elementary school teachers in the middle and middle-east region of Western-Holland, the Netherlands were chosen for the study. Questionnaire was used to collect the data. Using multivariate analysis and canonical correlations, it was found that unsatisfied parents, over protective parents, neglectful parents and excessively worried parents have the largest impact on teacher stress. Teacher's who experience stress from challenging parent behaviour, suffer mostly from negative feelings toward parents, frustration on working with parents, loss of satisfaction with teaching and to a lesser extent, health problems.

Russel *et. al.* (1987) examined the *job-related stress, social support, and burnout among classroom teachers.* A mail survey of a random sample of public school teachers in Iowa was conducted. Consistent with findings in previous research, teacher characteristics such as age, gender, and grade level taught were predictive of burnout. It was also found that the number of stressful events experienced and social support were predictive of teacher burnout. Some evidence of the stress-moderating role of social support was also found. Teachers who reported that they had supportive supervisors and indicated that they received positive feedback concerning their skills and abilities from others were less vulnerable to job related stress.

Soyibo (1994) investigated the *occupational stress factors and coping strategies among Jamaican high school science teachers.* This study reports on data from 230 high school science teachers in Jamaica using a 40 item self-report questionnaire. 'Difficulty in obtaining science teaching equipments' was perceived as the most stressful factor by the teachers. There were no significant differences in the degree of stress experienced by the teachers based on their gender, school location, teaching experience and subjects taught.

Sprenger (2011) examined *the stress and coping behaviours among primary school teachers.* One hundred per cent of teachers interviewed for this study reported that the teaching profession is stressful, with 72 per cent describing the profession as extremely or very stressful. This study recognizes and investigates the stressors that affect primary school teachers, and identifies the coping behaviours that are used in response to these stressors. A mixed method design was used to assess stress and coping behaviours among current primary school teachers. Two quantitative focus groups provided insight into stress and coping behaviours through the perspectives of current primary school teachers at a specific school in rural North Carolina. The results indicate that unrealistic expectations set forth by school officials and parents are the most frequent source of stress followed by excessive paperwork, and school administration. The results also indicate that primary school teachers will most often employ neutral coping behaviours, followed by positive coping behaviours and negative coping behaviours.

Torres *et. al.* (2009) carried out *a comparison study to examine the job-related stress among secondary agricultural education teachers.* The study sought to explore and compare the current level of job stress among secondary agriculture teachers in Missouri and North Carolina. The accessible populations consisted of secondary agriculture teachers in Missouri (n = 252) and in North Carolina (n = 118). Data was collected using the Job Stress Survey (Spielberger and Vagg, 1999). From the findings, it was concluded that agriculture teachers in Missouri and North Carolina are not in an overall state of stress compared with norm data. However, time-related job tasks were found to be a source of stress among both teacher samples, and 'excessive paperwork' was identified as the highest stressor. The number of hours per week at work was the largest predictor on each index scale used to measure job stress. The second predictor was gender, with women showing higher stress levels than men in this study. Low stress items among teachers fell into three broad job-related categories best described as supervision, advancement, and inactivity.

Traverse and Cooper (1993) studied the *mental health, job satisfaction and occupational stress among UK teachers.* Data was collected through questionnaire, from a random sample of 1790 teachers drawn from a cross-section of school types, sectors and teaching grades. Univariate analysis of the results revealed that teachers, as compared with other highly stressed occupational groups, experienced lower job satisfaction and poor mental health. With regard to various subgroups in the sample, bivariate analysis revealed that it is necessary to consider the relationship between the level and nature of stress experienced and membership of a particular subgroup within the teaching profession (*e.g.,* being a head teacher). Further examination of the data via use of multivariate analysis revealed that ten reliable factors regarding 'sources of job pressure' could be obtained for this sample of teachers. Teachers were found to be reporting stress-related manifestations that were far higher than the population norms and of other comparable occupational groups. Multiple regression analysis was performed on the total sample and various subgroups, and it was discovered that the 'job pressure factors' of 'management/structure of the school' and 'lack of status and promotion' were the major predictors of job dissatisfaction. Mental ill-health was predicted by a variety of job pressure and personal factors, but predominantly linked to job pressure from 'ambiguity of the teacher's role'. Intention to leave was found to be most highly related to mental ill-health in teachers.

Tsai *et. al.* (2006) explored the *sources and manifestations of stress in female kindergarten teachers.* Sample of 113 female kindergarten teachers working in Hong-Kong city were given the Teacher Stress Inventory by Fimian and Fastenu measure the sources and manifestations of stress. The statistical approach employed was Structural Equation Modeling (SEM) and LISREL 8.5 was used for assessing the fit of the data to the model. Results suggested that time management and work related stressors are more common sources of stress whereas feelings of fatigue and emotional related symptoms are more common manifestations of stress.

Vance *et. al.* (1989) carried out a study on *sources and manifestation of occupational stress as reported by fulltime teachers working in a Bureau of Indian*

Affairs (BIA) school. This study was an investigation of occupational stress as measured by the Teacher Stress Inventory of 30 teachers working in a BIA school. The sample consisted of 22 women, six men (two respondents did not indicate their gender); nineteen were white, 10 were Native Americans and one Hispanic. New and completely one-way analysis of variance was used to analyze the data. The Scheffe procedure was used for post-hoc analysis. The level of significance was set at $p < .05$ to overcome the alpha effect because of the small sample size. The findings indicated that the major source of stress for these teachers was in managing his/her job. There were no significant differences found between the men and women with respect to the stressors. There was no significant difference even between the Native American and White samples.

Wang *et. al.* (2001) conducted *a study on the resources coping with occupational stress in teachers.* Occupational Stress Inventory Revised edition (OSI-R) was used to measure the occupational stress, strain and psychological coping resources of 1,460 teachers in primary and secondary schools and 319 non-teacher intellectuals. Analyses were focused on coping resources of teachers. The results of the study revealed that the higher the level of coping resource of teachers, the lower the personal strain in them. Coping resource in the teacher group was significantly higher than that in the non-teacher group. Coping resource in teachers decreased with the increase of age. Coping resource in the female teachers was significantly higher than that in the male teachers. Coping resource in the primary school teachers was significantly higher than that in the secondary school teachers.

Wu *et. al.* (2006) carried out a research on *intervention on occupational stress among teachers in the middle schools in China.* The purpose of this study was to evaluate the effectiveness of the interventions on occupational stress among teachers in the middle schools. The study group consisted of 459 teachers from four middle schools. The control group consisted of 502 teachers. The three dimensions of occupational adjustment such as occupational stress, psychological strain and coping resources were measured with the occupational stress-revised edition and the work ability was assessed with the Work Ability Index (WAI) among the teachers. The integrated interventions were taken to the teachers in the study group. The results revealed that the scores of some scales of occupational role questionnaire and personal strain questionnaire decreased significantly and the scores of some scales of personal resources questionnaire and WAI increased significantly after intervening.

Yagil (1998) examined the *occupational stress among inexperience teachers.* The purpose of the study was to examine the sources of stress encountered by inexperienced teachers when compared to experienced teachers. Sixty nine female teachers in elementary schools and kindergartens in Israel participated in the study. A questionnaire measuring job related stress factors, emotional involvement in the job and active coping with stress factors was administered to the sample. The results revealed that inexperienced teachers experienced high level of stress when compared to experienced teachers and their sources of stress were interaction with pupil's parents and workload and were emotionally less involved in their work.

Yang *et. al.* (2009) carried out a study to find out the *Relationship between quality of life and occupational stress among teachers.* The aim of this study was to explore the relationship between quality of life and occupational stress in primary and middle school teachers. A cross-sectional study was conducted using cluster sampling. The study population was composed of 3570 school teachers working in 64 primary and middle schools in Heping District in Shenyang, China. A demographic questionnaire, the 36-item Short-Form Health Survey (SF-36) and the Occupational Stress Inventory Revised Edition were employed to collect demographic variables and assess quality of life and occupational stress. Multivariate stepwise linear regression analyses were performed to study the relationship between quality of life and occupational stress. Male teachers scored significantly higher than female teachers for physical functioning, body pain, vitality and physical health. Age, role overload, role insufficiency, vocational strain, psychological strain, physical strain, recreation and rational coping were significantly associated with both the physical and mental component summaries of the SF-36. Gender, physical environment and self-care appeared to be robust indicators of physical health, while role insufficiency, interpersonal strain and social support were strong indicators of mental health.

Studies on Occupational Stress of Higher Education Teachers

Ahsan *et. al.* (2009) carried out *an empirical study of job stress and job satisfaction among university staff in Malaysia.* Sample of 203 university academicians from Klang valley area in Malaysia were chosen for the study. Job Stress Questionnaire with dimensions; workload, role conflict, role ambiguity and performance pressure, and Job Descriptive Index were the tools used in the study. The statistical techniques employed were cross sectional analysis, descriptive analysis and regression analysis. The results showed that there was a significant relationship between the four dimensions of occupational stress and also there was a significant negative relationship between job stress and job satisfaction.

Blix *et. al.* (1994) analyzed the *occupational stress among university teachers.* In this study Person-Environment Fit model was used to analyze the lack of fit between motivational style and job rewards as a contributing factor in developing occupational stress symptoms in university teachers. Three motivational styles and corresponding job rewards were measured using instruments derived from Porter's motivational theory in a questionnaire mailed to 400 randomly selected tenure-track university teachers. Occupational stress symptoms were measured by items reflecting burnout, stress-related health problems, perceived work stress, productivity, job satisfaction and consideration for job change. The majority of teachers indicated a good fit between motivational style and job rewards. Female teachers were a noted exception with higher misfit scores than their male counterparts. Despite the 'good' fit, two-thirds of the teachers indicated they perceived stress at work at least 50 per cent of the time. Teachers also reported burnout, stress-related health problems, lowered work productivity, inability to cope with work stress and job change consideration. Heavy workload was the most frequently cited reason for considering job change. Female teachers were more likely to consider job change as a result of job stress. Research-related activities were considered to be more stressful than either teaching or service. A positive perception of ability to manage work stress was negatively correlated with stress symptoms.

Bradley and Eachus (1995) investigated the *occupational stress in a U.K. higher education institution. All* employees, including academic, support and manual staff, were invited to participate anonymously in the survey. The results, based on the Occupational Stress Indicator, showed that employees reported significantly poorer mental and physical well-being, and greater job dissatisfaction, than a normative group. The findings suggested that female employees were at greater risk from adverse effects of occupational stress. Predictors of distress and job dissatisfaction were identified.

Doyle and Hind (1998) examined the *occupational stress, burnout and job status of female academics.* The study investigated perceived occupational stress in a sample of 582 academic staff members working in institutions of higher education in the UK. Data was collected using the Maslach Burnout Inventory, The Job Diagnostic Survey) and the Faculty Stress Index. The results indicate that women academics perceive the structure and content of their jobs similarly to men. However, women generally experience higher overall levels of stress in their jobs and results indicate that they may cope better with the demands placed upon them than their male counterparts. There is some evidence of the presence of a 'glass ceiling' in the institutions studied, with women holding more junior positions, and remaining in them longer, than men. A difference in effect size was found between those women who do achieve senior positions and men in similar posts. Higher grades predict greater job strain for women but not for men.

Gillespie *et. al.* (2001) investigated the *occupational stress in universities and the staff perceptions of the causes, consequences and moderators of stress.* A total of 22 focus groups were conducted with a representative sample of 178 academic and general staff from 15 Australian Universities. The groups focused on understanding staffs' experience of occupational stress, and perceptions of the sources, consequences and moderators of stress. Both general and academic staff reported a dramatic increase in stress during the previous 5 years. As a group, academic staff reported higher levels of stress than general staff. Five major sources of stress were identified including: insufficient funding and resources; work overload; poor management practice; job insecurity and; insufficient recognition and reward. The majority of groups reported that job-related stress was having a deleterious impact on their professional work and personal welfare. Aspects of the work environment (support from co-workers and management, recognition and achievement, high morale, flexible working conditions), and personal coping strategies (stress management techniques, work non-work balance, tight role boundaries and lowering standards), were reported to help staff cope with stress.

Jackson and Rothmann (2006) conducted a study on o*ccupational stress, organizational commitment and ill-health of educators in the North-west Province of Nigeria.* A cross sectional survey design was used and a stratified random sample of about 1170 educators in the north-west province was taken for the study. The results of Organizational Stress Screening Tool (ASSET) and a biographical questionnaire confirmed the internal consistency of the ASSET. Difference between the organizational stress, organizational commitment and ill-health of educators in different types of schools, age and qualification were found. Occupational stress and low organizational commitment explained 15 per cent of the variance in physical ill-health and 30 per cent of the variance in psychological ill-health. Although, organizational commitment had major effects on occupational stressor, namely job insecurity, on the physical and psychological health of educators.

Liu and Zhu (2009) carried out a *numerical analysis and comparison on stress between male and female academic faculty in Chinese universities.* The primary objective of the study was to verify the sex gap between male and female faculty's stress by numerical analysis. Self-made questionnaire on source of stress was used to collect the data. By descriptive statistics, chi-square test and numerical analysis, the results indicate that both male and female faculty are experiencing stress slightly strong and female faculty experience less stress than their male counterparts, but male faculty report shares strong and slightly strong ability to cope with the stress than female faculty.

Moreno *et. al.* (2010) conducted a *descriptive study of stress and satisfaction at work in the Saragossa University services and administration staff.* This research is an exploratory research to improve the stress management programme. Twenty four people from the services and administration staff in the University of Saragossa participated in the study. A personal interview was carried out and additionally, participants were given the Maslach Burnout Inventory and the Scale of Satisfaction at Work of Warr, Cook and Wall. The correlation of data was tested by using Spearman Correlation Analysis. The results of the study revealed that most of the participants were in low burnout level. The results also revealed that not only the personality or temperament has an influence on stress, but the job conditions are also related with it.

Pithers and Fogarty (1995) studied the *occupational stress among vocational teachers.* Data was obtained, using the OSI, from a group of vocational teachers and compared to a group of professional non-teachers. Overall the results showed a significantly higher level of teacher stress, although only one of 10 stress and strain measures contributed to this effect.

Sun *et. al.* (2011) investigated the *Occupational stress and its related factors among university teachers in China.* University teachers in China are expected to suffer serious occupational stress due to the expanding enrollment in universities without a proportional increase in teacher resources and the fact that all promotions for university teachers are determined based on not only teaching but also the outcome of scientific research. This study was designed to assess the occupational stress among university teachers in China and clarify its risk factors. A cross-sectional study was performed in Liaoning Province, the centralized area of higher education in Northeast China. Eight universities (2 multidiscipline and 6 specialized) and 10 per cent of academic staff were randomly selected. Questionnaires pertaining to occupational stress indicated by the Chinese Version Personal Strain Questionnaire (PSQ) and demographic characteristics, health status, work situations, and personal and social resources were distributed in October 2008. A total of 827 effective respondents (response rate 76.4%) participated in the study. The average raw score of PSQ was 91.0 among the university teachers. General linear model analysis showed that the factors significantly associated with the PSQ score were, in standardized estimate (β) sequence, mental health, role overload, role insufficiency, social support, monthly income, role limitations due to physical problems, research finance and self-rated disease with adjustment for age and gender.

Yahaya *et. al.* (2010) explored the *factors that contributed stress and the level of occupational stress among the technical teachers* who are currently teaching in technical schools in Johore, Malacca, and Negeri Sembilan. The five teachers stress sources that were included in this study are pupil misbehaviour, teacher workload, time and resources difficulties, interpersonal relationships, and recognition. A total of 92 teachers from nine technical schools in three states were chosen for the study. Modified version of Teacher Stress Inventory was used to collect the data and was analyzed using both descriptive (mean, frequency, and percentage) and inferential (t-test, Pearson Correlation and One Way ANOVA) methods. The results revealed that the overall stress level of respondents was moderate. Among the five stressors, pupil misbehaviour was the strongest determinant of teacher stress with a mean of 3.67, followed by teacher workload (M=3.00), time and resources difficulties (M=2.97), recognition (M=2.90), and interpersonal relationships (M=2.85) respectively. The workload and other factors had caused a moderate stress on the respondents. The results also indicate that there was no significant difference of work stress among the respondents based on gender, marital status, and highest academic qualification. Furthermore, the results were failed to indicate a significant correlation between teacher stress and demographic factors such as age, length of teaching experience, and the respondent's monthly salary.

Yong (2011) presented a research paper on *the sources of occupational stress of college teachers* focusing on college teachers, a specific working group. The author conducted a survey and made this paper in order to search their overall feeling of stress and its source. It turns out that college teachers are vulnerable to great stress, which is mostly attributed to heavy workload, desire for self-development, income, and college management.

Studies on Occupational Stress of other Professionals

Bokthi and Talib (2009) carried out *a preliminary study on occupational stress and job satisfaction among male navy personnel at a naval base in Lumut, Malayasia.* The main objective of the study was to have a valid measure of job satisfaction and occupational stress. A total of 40 male officers and non-officers from the seaman and engineering and supply brands in the Lumut naval base were chosen for the study by using random sampling techniques. The data was collected using a questionnaire, the job satisfaction survey and job related tension index. The correlation analyses revealed that majority of the male navy personal reported moderate levels of Job Satisfaction in the favorable nature of work faculty. On the other hand, high occupational stress was related to an unknown superior's evaluation of one's workplace performance.

Landsbergis (1988) *tested the job demands-control model by studying the occupational stress among health care workers.* A survey instrument was distributed to 771 hospital and nursing home employees in New Jersey, and 289 (37.5%) were returned. The results support the hypothesis that reported job strain (job dissatisfaction, depression, psychosomatic symptoms) and burnout is significantly higher in jobs that combine high workload demands with low decision latitude. This association remained significant after controlling for age, gender, education, marital status, children, hours worked per week and shift worked. Other job characteristics (job insecurity, physical exertion, social support, hazard exposure) were also associated with strain and burnout.

Mark and Smith (2012) *investigated the effects of occupational stress, job characteristics, coping, and attributional style on the mental health and job satisfaction of university employees.* This study investigated the relationships between job demands, control, social support, efforts, rewards, coping, and attributional style in predicting anxiety, depression, and job satisfaction in a sample of 307 university employees from the UK. Results were compared to those from a sample of 120 members of the general population. Workplace demands, intrinsic and extrinsic effort, and negative coping and attributional behaviours were associated with high levels of depression and anxiety and low job satisfaction in university employees. Rewards, social support, job control, and positive coping and attributional behaviours were associated with lower levels of depression and anxiety and high job satisfaction. The study adds to the growing research on university samples by showing that a transactional approach should be adopted.

Mazzola *et. al.* (2011) carried out a *qualitative research on occupational stress.* The researchers reviewed the qualitative studies on occupational stress that met two criteria:

1. the studies employed qualitative methods;
2. the stressors, strains and/or coping strategies were grouped into identifiable, higher-order categories.

Results indicated that the nature of the stressors experienced varied by:

(a) Occupation,
(b) Country,
(c) Seniority, and
(d) Gender.

The review further revealed that organizational constraints, work overload and interpersonal conflict were relatively universal stressors. Anger and annoyance were the most frequently reported psychological strains in the United States and the United Kingdom, while Chinese workers exhibited tension and anxiety and Indian workers exhibited acceptance. Coping strategies also varied by gender, occupation and country. Research on gender differences suggested that, compared to men, women tend to report more interpersonal stressors. Differences in the ways in which the two types of methodologies are applied, as well as their relative strengths and weaknesses, underline the value of qualitative approaches to the study of occupational stress, especially when used in conjunction with quantitative methods in mixed-methods studies.

Okoza *et. al.* (2010) carried out a study on *the jailer or the jailed: stress and prison workers in Nigeria.* This study examined the sources of stress among prison workers in Nigeria. A total of 150 prison staff drawn from the Oko and Benin prisons in Edo state, Nigeria participated in the study. Questionnaire was used to collect the data. The results of the ANOVA revealed that riots in prisons were the highest sources of stress to prison staff and the least source of stress was dilapidating building. Results also revealed that gender and length of service have significant effect on stress experienced by prison workers, while age has no significant effect.

Poloskivokic and Bogdanic (2007) carried out *a survey in Croatian on individual differences and occupational stress perceived.* The research had two objectives:

1. to measure occupational stress levels among different categories of employees working in Croatian enterprises; and
2. to study and analyze stress in Croatian employees in relation to individual differences (gender, age, marital status, parenthood, number of children, hierarchical level, department and working hours).

Occupational Stress Intensity Questionnaire was administered to the sample of 147 Croatians working in different enterprises. The results of t-test and ANOVA revealed that the greatest level of stress perceived by the respondents who have three or more children; who are more than 50 years age; and those employed in marketing, at middle levels or in procurement; while the lowest level of stress perceived by employees younger than 30 years of age; those employed in HR, finances and production; and parents of one child.

Smith *et. al.* (2000) *analyzed the impact of demographic factors and type of job while developing the scale of organizational stress.* The aim of the analyses was to identify factors associated with perceptions of stress at work. This demographical survey of 17000 randomly selected people from the Bristol electoral register revealed that approximately 20 per cent of the working people regretted that they had very high or extremely high levels of stress at work. Further analysis using chi-square test, Fisher's exact test revealed that gender had little overall effect although it did interact with other factors such as full time/part time employment. The middle aged workers (30-50 years old) and those educated to degree level have showed high related stress category. Marital status *i.e.,* widowed/divorced or separated has showed high levels of stress. Reported stress was found to be highest among teachers, nurses and managers.

Vagg *et. al.* (1998) studied the *occupational stress while measuring job pressure and organizational support in the workplace.* Person environment fit and demand-control theoretical models developed to explain stress and strain, in the workplace have guided the construction of most measures of occupational stress. The strengths and limitations of 8 job stress measures are briefly reviewed, and the Job Stress Survey (JSS), designed to assess the severity and frequency of occurrence of 30 specific sources of occupational stress, is described in some detail. Factor analyses of responses to the JSS items identified Job Pressure and Lack of Organizational Support as major dimensions of occupational stress for male and female employees in a wide variety of work settings. JSS Index, scale, subscale, and item scores assess general and specific aspects of the work environment that is most distressing for individual workers and that adversely affect groups of employees.

Wu *et. al. (2011)* examined the *factors associated with occupational stress among Chinese female emergency nurses.* The study sample consisted of 655 female emergency nurses from 16 hospitals in the Liaoning province, China. Occupational stress was measured by questionnaires that included the Chinese version of the Personal Strain Questionnaire, and data were collected on respondents' demographic characteristics, work situations, occupational roles and personal resources. A total of 510 effective respondents comprised the study (response rate 77.9%). A general linear model was applied to analyse the factors associated with occupational stress. The mean Personal Strain Questionnaire score of the emergency nurses was 91.2 and this score was correlated, in descending order of standardised estimate, with role overload, role boundary, role insufficiency, social support, chronic disease and self-care. The factors role overload, role boundary and role insufficiency had the highest association with occupational stress.

Yang *et. al.* (2004) carried out a research to *compare the occupational stress and work ability among the police-officers, doctors and teachers.* The sample of the study included 288 doctors, 191 police-officers and 343 teachers. Occupational Stress Inventory (OSI-R) and Work Ability Index (WAI) were used to measure the occupational stress and work ability of the sample respectively, and then comparative and correlation analyses were made. The results of the study revealed that, the difference in occupational stress and strain between the groups was statistically significant, and the score of the police-officers was higher than that of the doctors and teachers, but the personal resources of police-officers were lower than those of the doctors and teachers Analysis of the 6 items of Occupational Role Questionnaire revealed that the scores of role ambiguity, role boundary and responsibility were obviously higher in police-officers than in doctors and teachers, while the scores of role overload and physical environment were higher in teachers. Analysis of all items of personal strain revealed that the scores of vocational strain, psychological strain, physical strain, but not of interpersonal strain, were significantly higher in police-officers than in doctors and teachers. As to the personal resource, the results indicated that recreation and self-care of doctors and teachers were superior to those of police-officers. The score of social support was highest in doctors. The score of rational conduct was highest in teachers. Occupational role and personal strain were positively correlated, and both were correlated negatively to the personal resources. The correlations of work ability, occupational stress and strain, and personal resources were significant in teachers.

Studies on Job Performance of Teachers

Akram (2010) examined the f*actors affecting the performance of teachers at higher secondary level in Punjab.* The purpose of this study was to improve the job performance of teachers by measuring the factors affecting the performance of teachers at higher secondary level. Main objectives of the study was to measure and summarize the perceptions of principals, teachers themselves and students about the factors that influence teachers' performance; to compare teachers' performance on each factor in the light of perceptions of principals, teachers themselves and students; to determine the rating of principals, teachers themselves and their students on each factor; and to discover the level of presence of each factor on teachers' job performance in the light of perceptions of principals, teachers themselves and students. The study was descriptive in nature. The principal, five teachers and ten students were included in the sample from each institution, thus the sample consisted of 1920 individuals *i.e.,* 120 principals, 600 teachers and 1200 students. Three types of closed ended questionnaires on five point rating scale were prepared separately for principals, teachers and students. The data obtained were tabulated, analyzed and interpreted by using statistical techniques such as, mean, standard deviation, average rating and analysis of variance (ANOVA). The main conclusions of the study were that the factor of subject mastery was perceived by the principals, teachers themselves and students to be at the highest level among the four factors of teachers' job performance. The factor of attitude toward students was viewed to be at the lowest level among the four factors of teachers' job performance. Teaching methodology and teachers' personal characteristics were factors considered to be present in teachers' performance at intermediary level. The average rating of teachers was the highest whereas that of students was the lowest on all the four factors, namely the attitude toward students, subject mastery, teaching methodology and personal characteristics of teachers' job performance. The rating of the principals was at intermediary level. There was no real difference among the views of principals, teachers themselves and students about teachers' performance on the factors of attitude toward students, subject mastery and teaching methodology. However, the views of principals, teachers themselves and students were found different on the factor of teachers' personal characteristics.

Akram *et. al.* (2011) investigated the *principals' perception regarding factors affecting the performance of teachers.* This study investigated the perception of principals on how the factors of subject mastery, teaching methodology, personal characteristics, and attitude toward students affect the performance of teachers at higher secondary level in the Punjab Province of Pakistan. All principals of higher secondary level in the Punjab were the population of the study. From the population, 120 principals were selected as the sample. A questionnaire was developed and validated through pilot testing. The data obtained were tabulated and analyzed by using statistical techniques of mean and standard deviation. The major conclusions of the study were that the factor of subject mastery was perceived to be influencing the performance of teachers maximally, but the factor of attitude toward students was affecting the performance of teachers minimally. The remaining two factors -teaching methodology and personal characteristics -were perceived to be at the intermediary level.

Anjum *et. al.* (2011) examined the *performance appraisal systems in public sector universities of Pakistan.* The current research investigates different aspects of performance appraisal system, and how performance appraisal system can play its role in improving the performance of teachers in higher education institutions of Pakistan. In the present study multi-methods approach was used which consist of survey questionnaire and in depth interviews. Survey questionnaire was used in order to investigate various aspects of current performance appraisal system and in depth interview to study the perception of teachers on performance appraisal approach. The focus of the study was on the employees of Bahauddin Zakariya University (BZU) Multan, Pakistan. The researchers undertook the public sector University of Pakistan, as a case study in the present study. Results show that although employees of BZU are aware of the useful outcomes of performance appraisal but there are some hindering factors *e.g.,* untrained raters, exclusion of multiple raters, absence of feedback in the way of successful implementation of performance appraisal system.

Bowling (2007) carried out *a meta-analytic examination to know whether the relationship between the job satisfaction and job performance is spurious.* Many researchers and most lay people believe that a causal relationship exists between satisfaction and performance. In the current study, however, analyses using meta-analytic data suggested that the satisfaction–performance relationship is largely spurious. More specifically, the satisfaction–performance relationship was partially eliminated after controlling for either general personality traits (*e.g.,* Five Factor Model traits and core self-evaluations) or for work locus of control and was almost completely eliminated after controlling for organization-based self-esteem.

Cohen and Liu (2011) examined the *relationships between in-role performance and individual values, commitment, and organizational citizenship behaviour among Israeli teachers.* This study examines the relationship between individual values, organizational and occupational commitment, and organizational citizenship behaviour (OCB) and in-role performance in a sample of 192 teachers employed in 10 secular Jewish schools (response rate of 64%). The results showed that individual values were related to all commitment forms examined here, but contrary to expectations, there was no clear distinction between values that represent conservation and self-transcendence and values that represent openness to change and self-enhancement in terms of their relationship either to commitment or to behavioural outcomes. Likewise, there was no clear distinction between the three dimensions of commitment (affective, continuance, and normative) or two commitment foci (organizational and occupational) in terms of their relationships to different values. The findings showed a strong effect of commitment on OCB and in-role performance. The findings show that both individual values and commitment are concepts that can increase the understanding of employees' behaviour in the workplace.

Chughtai and Zafar (2006) studied the *antecedents and consequences of organizational commitment among Pakistani university teachers.* The purpose of this study was to determine if selected personal characteristics, facets of job satisfaction, and the two dimensions of organizational justice (distributive justice and procedural justice) significantly explained variance in the organizational commitment of Pakistani university teachers. In addition, the present study examined the influence of organizational commitment on two organizational outcomes — job performance and turnover intentions. Data were gathered from 125 full-time teachers from 33 universities in the three major cities of Pakistan: Lahore, Islamabad/Rawalpindi, and Peshawar. The results of the study indicate that the personal characteristics, facets of job satisfaction and two dimensions of organizational justice as a group were significantly related to organizational commitment of teachers. Individually, distributive justice and trust in management were found to be the strongest correlates of commitment. Moreover, commitment was found to be negatively related to turnover intentions and positively related to a self-report measure of job performance.

Cooper-Hakim and Viswesvaran (2005) *tested an integrative framework on the construct of work commitment.* This study meta-analytically examined extensive literature associated with work commitment. The primary purposes were to *(a)* cumulate correlations among dimensions of work commitment to see which were inter-correlated and *(b)* determine impact of work commitment dimensions and sub-dimensions on specific outcome variables (job satisfaction, job performance, turnover intentions, and turnover). Results were cumulated across 997 articles. The positive manifold of correlations suggests the presence of a common psychological construct underlying different commitment forms, with the exception of calculative, continuance, and union commitment. Most of the 94 meta-analyzed correlations were small, suggesting that concept redundancy is not a major concern. Meta-analyses of the correlations of 24 commitment constructs with 4 outcome variables suggest that different commitment forms have similar patterns of correlations with outcome variables.

Elstad *et. al.* (2011) explored the *social exchange theory as an explanation of organizational citizenship behaviour among teachers.* Social exchange theory is a theoretical explanation for organizational citizenship behaviour. This study examines a model of clear leadership and relational building between head and teachers as antecedents, and organizational citizenship behaviour as a consequence of teacher–school exchange. One purpose of this study is to explore the nature of exchanges between parties in the organization of teachers' work and examine the relative impact of these aspects on organizational citizenship behaviour. The methodology adopted was a cross sectional survey of 234 secondary teachers. The structural equation analysis indicates a strong support for the importance of principal–teacher trust on social exchange and indirectly an impact on organizational citizenship behaviours. Some moderate support for the importance of clear leadership on organizational citizenship behaviours were also found in the study.

Enueme and Egwunyenga (2008) carried out *a case study on principal's instructional leadership roles and effect on teacher's job performance of secondary schools in Asaba Metropolis, Delta State, Nigeria.* The main objective of the study was to find out how the principals play their instructional leadership roles and to what extent these roles affect the work performance of the teachers. The questionnaire titled Questionnaire on Instructional Leadership Employed by Principal's was administered to 240 teachers selected randomly from all the government owned secondary schools in Asaba metropolis of delta state. The statistical technique employed was Pearson's product moment correlation co-efficient. The results indicate that the principal's play their instructional leadership roles to high extent and these roles affect the work performance of their teachers.

Jamal and Baba (2009) examined the relationship between *type-A behaviour, job performance and well-being in college teachers.* Well-being was related in terms of burnout, social support, work satisfaction and turnover motivation. Data were collected by means of a structured questionnaire from 420 college teachers in Canada. Pearson correlation and moderated multiple regressions were used to analyze the data. Global type-A behaviour was not related to three measures of job performance: teaching hours, number of course preparation per semester and number of students. However, type-A behaviour correlated positively with burnout and turnover motivation and negatively with perceived social support and work satisfaction.

Munaf and Seema (2009) carried out a *comparitive study of public and private sectors in Pakistan and Malaysia* on *motivation, performance and satisfaction among university teachers.* The research aims to determine the difference in performance, achievement motivation and job satisfaction of teaching faculties of selected private and public sector higher educational institutions of Pakistan and Malaysia. The sample consisted of 120 Heads of the departments and teaching faculties of Pakistan (N = 60) and Malaysia (N = 60). With the consent of the Vice Chancellors/Registrars/Deans of the faculties, the Heads of the Department (HODs) were requested to rate the performance of their teaching faculty on University Teacher's Evaluation Rating Questionnaire. Then two senior and regular teachers from each teaching faculty of the department completed Personal Information Form following Costello Achievement Motivation Scale (adapted English version by Misra and Srivastava) and Job Satisfaction Scale (Singh and Sharma). T-test was used to analyze the data. The results indicate that when comparison was made separately between private and public higher educational institutions of Pakistan and Malaysia, the achievement motivation of teaching faculties of Malaysian private and public sector is higher than that of Pakistan. Similarly, the performance of public sector Malaysian teaching faculties seems to be better than public sector Pakistani faculties, although their evaluation mean score fall in the good range. However, the performance of private sector teachers of Pakistan and Malaysia do not differ. Furthermore, Pakistani public sector faculties seems to be more satisfied with their teaching jobs than Pakistani private sector teachers, although their performance and achievement motivation are alike. Whereas Malaysian public sector faculties not only seem to perform better than private sector Malaysian teachers but they are also more satisfied with their teaching profession than the latter group, regardless of similarity in their achievement motivation.

Ng, Sorensen and Yim (2009) carried out a study to know *whether the relationship between job satisfaction and job performance vary across cultures.* The purpose of this study was to examine whether culture moderates the relationship between job satisfaction and job performance. Multiple theoretical frameworks regarding culture were used as the theoretical guide. Based on meta-analytical moderator tests, the authors found some support for their hypotheses that the effect size for the job satisfaction — job performance relationship is likely to be stronger in individualistic (*vs.* collectivistic) cultures, in low-power-distance (*vs.* high-power-distance) cultures, in low-uncertainty-avoidance (*vs.* high-uncertainty-avoidance) cultures, and in masculine (*vs.* feminine) cultures. They also observed stronger evidence of these effects for task performance than for contextual performance.

Ololube (2006) assessed the *differences and relationship between the level of teachers' job satisfaction, motivation and their teaching performance in Rivers State of Nigeria.* Data was collected by using the questionnaire. The statistical techniques employed were mean, standard deviation, t-test and ANOVA. The survey results revealed that teacher related sources of job satisfaction seem to have a greater impact on teaching performance, as teachers are also dissatisfied with the educational policies and administration, pay and fringe benefits, material rewards and advancement.

Patricia (*2011*) carried out a study on *enhancing job performance.* The impact of the Self-Determined Career Development Model on the job performance of four adults with moderate intellectual disability employed in competitive work settings was examined. Employees learned to set work-related goals, develop an action plan, implement the plan, and adjust their goals and plans as needed. A multiple baseline design across employees was implemented. All participants achieved their self-selected goal at levels that exceeded the expectations of their supervisor and job coach. Findings extend the current line of research utilising the Self-Determined Career Model and support the use of this model by personnel providing support to individuals with disabilities in work settings.

Poropat (2011) analyzed the *Eysenckian personality factors and their correlations with academic performance.* This meta-analysis assessed the validity of the Eysenckian personality measures for predicting academic performance. Statistics were obtained for correlations with Psychoticism, Extraversion, and Neuroticism (20–23 samples; *N* from 8,013 to 9,191), with smaller aggregates for the Lie scale (7 samples; *N*= 3,910). The Hunter — Schmidt random effects method was used to estimate population correlations between the Eysenckian personality measures and academic performance. Moderating effects were tested using weighted least squares regression. Significant but modest validities were reported for each scale. Neuroticism and Extraversion had relationships with academic performance that were consistent with previous findings, while psychoticism appears to be linked to academic performance because of its association with conscientiousness. Age and educational level moderated correlations with neuroticism and extraversion, and gender had no moderating effect. Correlations varied significantly based on the measurement instrument used.

Rahman (2006) studied the *attitudes of Malaysian teachers toward a performance-appraisal system.* This study investigated the attitude of teachers of different ethnic origins in Malaysia toward an outcome-oriented performance appraisal, the New Performance Appraisal System (NPAS). It also investigated the relationship between teachers' attitude towards the system and their job satisfaction and professional commitment. Teachers of the major ethnic origins in Malaysia — Malays, Chinese, and Indians — were selected randomly from 6 public high schools in the state of Kedah. The study found that teachers of all ethnic origins reported less favorable attitudes toward the NPAS, and that their cultural dimension had no bearing on attitudes toward the NPAS. Teachers, who received appropriate explanation and supervision of their performance, despite low performance-appraisal results, reported high levels of job satisfaction and professional commitment.

Rose *et. al.* (2009) studied the *effect of organizational learning on organizational commitment, job satisfaction and work performance.* From the sample of public service managers in Malaysia, it was found that organizational learning was found positively related to organizational commitment, job satisfaction, and work performance. Organizational commitment and job satisfaction are also positively related with work performance and these variables partially mediate the relationship between organizational learning and work performance.

Roth *et. al.* (2011) carried out a *meta-analysis of gender group differences for measures of job performance in field studies.* The investigators conducted a meta-analysis of job performance measures from field studies. They found that females generally scored slightly higher than males (mean d = ".11, 80 per cent credibility interval of ".33 to .12). Other analysts suggested that, although job performance ratings favored females, ratings of promotion potential were higher for males. Thus, ratings of promotability may deserve further attention as a potential source of differential promotion rates.

Sukirno (2011) presented the research paper on *Does participative decision-making affect lecturer performance in higher education?* The purpose of this paper was to empirically examine the impact of participation in decision-making on lecturer performance in higher education. Mail survey was used to collect the data. Open-ended questionnaires were distributed to the lecturers in Yogyakarta Province in Indonesia. A total of 347 usable questionnaires were obtained which is about 46.3 per cent rate of return. Factor analysis was used to identify the constructs. All Cronbach's alpha values are more than 0.7 and factor loading is more than 0.50. Regression analysis was employed to test research hypotheses. In addition, t-test and ANOVA test were also conducted to investigate the different impact of demographic data on the job performance of the lecturers. This study finds that participative decision-making and academic rank have significant effect on lecturer performance. This finding implies that involving lecturers in educational decision-making would be useful to improve not only lecturer performance but also organizational performance. In addition, among all demographic variables taken into account, only academic rank significantly affects lecturer performance.

Tett *et. al.* (2006) carried out *a meta-analytic review on personality measures as predictors of job performance.* The purpose of this study was to investigate conflicting findings in previous research on personality and job performance. Meta-analysis was used to *(a)* assess the overall validity of personality measures as predictors of job performance, *(b)* investigate the moderating effects of several study characteristics on personality scale validity, and *(c)* appraise the predictability of job performance as a function of eight distinct categories of personality content, including the 'Big Five' personality factors. Based on review of 494 studies, usable results were identified for 97 independent samples (total N= 13,521). Consistent with predictions, studies using confirmatory research strategies produced a corrected mean personality scale validity (0.29) that was more than twice as high as that based on studies adopting exploratory strategies (0.12). An even higher mean validity (0.38) was obtained based on studies using job analysis explicitly in the selection of personality measures. Validities were also found to be higher in longer tenured samples and in published articles versus dissertations. Corrected mean validities for the "Big Five" factors ranged from 0.16 for Extroversion to 0.33 for Agreeableness. Weaknesses in the reporting of validation study characteristics are noted. Contrary to conclusions of certain past reviews, the present findings provide some grounds for optimism concerning the use of personality measures in employee selection.

Relationship Studies on Emotional Intelligence, Occupational Stress and Job Performance

Adeyemo and Ogunyemi (2007) carried out a research on *emotional intelligence and self-efficacy as predictors of occupational stress among academic staff in a Nigerian University.* This study seeks to explain the interactive and relative effects of emotional intelligence and self-efficacy on occupational stress of university academic staff. A sample of 300 academic staff of Olabisis-Onabanjo University, Ago-Lwaye, Nigeria was chosen for the study. The tools used in the study were Emotional Intelligence Scale, General Perceived Self-Efficacy Scale and Organizational Stress Scale. The data collected was analyzed using Pearson correlation and multiple regression techniques. The results indicated that the two independent variables, when taken together were effective in predicting organizational stress. Each of the variables contributed significantly to the prediction of organizational stress with self-efficacy making higher contribution.

Akhlaq *et. al.* (2010) carried out an *evaluation of the effects of stress on the job performance of secondary school teachers.* The study was designed to identify the Sources and Effects of Stress on the Job Performance of Federal Government (FG) Secondary School teachers of Rawalpindi Region. The main objectives of the study were to find the sources of stress among the teachers and the effects of stress on the performance of teachers. The findings of the study revealed that:

- The teachers taught to the students as per their level,
- They were not fair in grading,
- Majority of students agreed that teachers did not let their domestic obligations interfere with professional responsibilities,
- Teachers focused on teaching in the classroom,
- They were regular to school/class, and
- Exhibited stress related symptoms.

Akintayo (2010) studied the *impact of emotional intelligence and work-family role conflict in work organizations in Nigeria.* Survey method was used for the study and the data was collected by using Emotional Intelligence Scale, Work-Family Role Conflict Scale and Managerial Effectiveness Scale. Linear regression analysis was used to test the hypotheses. The findings revealed that there was a significant combined contribution of emotional intelligence and work family role conflict to managerial effectiveness. Besides, the findings indicate that the role conflict experienced by the managers resulting from work-family role interface has deleterious effects on their performance effectiveness.

Bar-On, Handley, and Fund (2006) present the results of a study examining the *emotional intelligence and occupational performance in the US Air Force.* In this study of 1,171 Air Force recruiters, high performers had significantly higher emotional intelligence scores than the low performers. The study also determined that geographic area, gender, ethnicity, education, age, and hours worked were not related to the job success of the recruiters.

Brand (2007) explored the *relationship between burnout, emotional intelligence and occupational stress in the nursing industry.* Sample of 220 nurses working in medical field were administered with Sources of Work Stress Inventory, Maslach Burnout Inventory and Emotional Intelligence Test. The results revealed that significant positive relationship exists between occupational stress and two dimensions of burnout, *i.e.,* emotional exhaustion and depersonalization. Significant negative relationship was found between emotional exhaustion and two dimensions of emotional intelligence, *i.e.,* emotional management and emotional control and between depersonalization and emotional management and emotional control. Accomplishment showed significant positive relationship with four of the five dimensions of emotional intelligence. Further, the sources of stress found to be the strongest predictor of burnout. Understanding emotions, emotional management and emotional control were all significant contributors to variance on occupational stress.

Chang *et. al.* (2012) examined the *interactive dynamics between leaders and members in finding the team emotional intelligence and performance.* In this study, it was proposed that average member EI indirectly affects team performance by shaping emergent team dynamics. The results based on 91 teams show that both average member EI and leader EI are positively associated with intra-team trust, which in turn positively relates to team performance. Average member EI and leader EI have a compensatory relationship in predicting team performance. Either high average member EI or high leader EI (not necessarily both) is sufficient to explain a high level of team performance. This pattern is particularly strong with the emotion appraisal and social skills dimensions of EI.

Chen (2012) studied *the relationship between principal's organizational citizenship behaviour and teacher's organizational citizenship behaviour on Tainan city's public elementary school along with teacher's organizational commitment and teacher's job stress as mediators.* Using Stratified Sampling method, 571 public elementary school teachers from Tainan city were chosen for the study. To ensure validity of the questionnaire, LISREL was first used to execute the confirmatory factor analysis and Structural Equation Modeling (SEM) was used to examine the relationship between the variables. The results of the study revealed that: there was no significant influence on principal's OCB and teacher's job stress towards teacher's OCB; there was a positive influence on teacher's organizational commitment towards teacher's OCB; there was a negative influence on teacher's job stress towards teacher's organizational commitment; principal's OCB towards teacher's OCB shows a positive relationship via the mediating effect of teacher's organizational commitment; and teacher's job stress towards teacher's OCB shows a negative relationship via the mediating effect of teacher's organizational commitment.

Chen and Cheng (2012) explored the *leadership behaviour and job performance of teachers in public and private kindergartens and the perspectives of institutionalization, reason, and feeling.* This study sample included 1,058 subjects from public and private kindergartens, using structural equation modeling (SEM) and LISREL software. According to the results, public and private kindergarten teachers believed that the charismatic and persuasive behaviour of directors could best promote teachers' job performance; in other words, the use of reasons (reason giving) has great significance for job performance. Furthermore, empathy and model behaviours were shown to be conducive to the job performance of teachers in private kindergartens, while there was no significant effect on public school teachers. Clear reward and punishment behaviours were shown to have a slightly negative effect on the job performance of public school teachers.

Farouk (2011) investigated *the relationship between emotional intelligence and high managerial performance in selected corporations in Belgium and Malaysia.* A correlational study was conducted to examine the relationship between EI and high managerial performance. In addition, other known correlates of performance such as behavioural competencies, personality traits, motivation, and team culture were also examined as a comparison to EI. Results of this study indicate that EI, as measured by the Mayer-Salovey-Caruso Emotional Intelligence Test (MSCEIT V2.0) was not significantly and positively related to managerial performance in either of the two corporations despite interpersonal and teamwork behavioural competencies being distinguishing competencies between high and average performing managers. Additionally, team leadership, achievement orientation, self confidence, development of others, and cognitive abilities are key competencies that are significantly correlated to high managerial performance in both corporations. In predicting managerial performance using logistic regression, team leadership and self management competencies correctly classified 83 per cent of managers' performances. The small sample sizes may limit the generalizability of the findings, though the multi-sample approach revealed consistent findings to suggest that behavioural competencies seem to be the best predictor of managerial performance and that further conceptualization and operationalization of the EI construct across cultural contexts may still be needed before implementing the measure at large.

Gardner (2005) examined the *emotional intelligence and occupational stress* among 320 employees. The results of the study revealed that four dimensions of emotional intelligence were particularly important in the occupational stress process, *i.e.,* emotional recognition and expression, understanding emotions, emotional management and emotional control. Further, the intervention of emotional intelligence training programmes demonstrated the effectiveness in terms of improving the levels of emotional intelligence, decreasing feelings of stress and strain, and improving the outcomes of stress.

Ghanizadeh and Moafian (2009) investigated *the role of EFL teacher's emotional intelligence in their success.* This study examined the relationship between EFL teacher's emotional quotient (EQ) and their pedagogical success in language institutes. In addition, the role played by their years of teaching experience in their EQ and the relationship between their age and EQ were also studied. For this purpose, 89 EFL teachers were chosen from different language institutes in Mashhad, a city in north-eastern Iran. They were asked to complete Bar-On's 'EQ test'. Simultaneously, a questionnaire entitled 'Characteristics of successful EFL teachers' was filled in by the students taught by each teacher with the aim of evaluating the teachers' performance. Subsequent data analysis revealed that there is a significant relationship between teachers' success and EQ. Furthermore, significant correlations were found between teachers' EQ, their teaching experience, and their age.

Hanif *et. al.* (2011) examined the *personal and job related predictors of teacher stress and job performance among school teachers*. The present study was conducted to find out the role of personal and job related variables in teacher stress and job performance of school teachers. Furthermore, levels and sources of stress and their relationship with job performance among teachers were also explored. The tools used in this study were self developed Teacher Stress Inventory (TSI-Urdu), Teachers Job Performance Scale and personal and job related information sheet. Two independent samples were selected from government and private Schools of Islamabad (Pakistan). Sample I was comprised of 400 teachers (men and women) from Primary and secondary schools. For the evaluation of teachers' job performance another sample of 1200 students from the classes of teachers of sample I was selected. Three students were randomly selected from each teacher's class. The students were requested to evaluate their respective teachers' job performance. The findings revealed that negative significant relationship exists between teachers stress and job performance. The stepwise regression analysis revealed school system, gender, job experience, number of family members, and number of students as significant predictors of teacher stress and gender, school system, family members, job experience and age as significant predictors of teachers' job performance.

Hülsheger *et. al.* (2010) analyzed the *emotional labour, strain, and performance by testing reciprocal relationships in a longitudinal panel study.* Models of emotional labour suggest that emotional labour leads to strain and affects job performance. Goal of the study was to test the direction of effects in a two-wave longitudinal panel study using a sample of 151 trainee teachers. Longitudinal lagged effects were tested using structural equation modeling. Results revealed that the emotional labour strategy of surface acting led to increases in subsequent strain while deep acting led to increase in job performance. In contrast, there was no indication of reverse causation: Neither strain nor job performance had a significant lagged effect on subsequent surface or deep acting. Overall, results support models of emotional labour suggesting that surface and deep acting causally precede individual and organizational well-being.

Ismail *et. al.* (2010) carried out a study in Malaysia to find out *the relationship between occupational stress, emotional intelligence and job performance*. Sample of 104 academic employees who work in private institutions of higher learning in Kuching city, Malaysia were chosen for the study. Questionnaire was used as a research tool. The analysis of the data using stepwise regression revealed that relationship between occupational stress and emotional intelligence are significantly correlated with the job performance.

Jude (2011) investigated the *emotional intelligence, gender and occupational stress among secondary school teachers in Ondo state, Nigeria.* An ex-post factor design was used to gather 392 usable copies of the questionnaires from secondary school teachers. Stratified random sampling technique was used to choose the sample. Two tools, Emotional Intelligence Scale and Occupational Stress Scale were used to collect the data. The t-test analysis indicated that there was a significant difference between the occupational stress of secondary school teachers with low and those with high emotional intelligence. There was no significanct difference between the occupational stress experienced by male and female secondary school teachers.

Kazmi *et. al.* (2008) carried out a case study on the *organizational stress and its effect on job performance of medical house officers of district Abbottabad, Pakistan.* The purpose of the study was to investigate the effect of job stress on job performance. Complete population of 55 house officers of Ayub Medical College, Abbottabad, were chosen for the study. The data obtained through questionnaire was analyzed using descriptive statistics, Spearman's correlation and multiple regression analysis. The results revealed that there was a high job stress among the house officers, resulting in low job performance.

Khan *et. al.* (2012) investigated the *teachers' stress, performance a resources and the moderating effects of resources on stress and performance.* The present study has carried out a non-systematic narrative overview of the teachers' stress, performance and resources by conceptualizing them for understating the phenomenon of moderating effect of teachers' resources on the teachers' stress and performance. It has been found that the teachers' stress is a reaction of teachers to the unwanted environment factors furthermore the performance of teachers is both tasks and non task related. The teachers' stress negatively affects the performance of teacher by lowering the productivity of individual teacher and of educational institution. The teachers' resources act as moderator by minimizing negative effects of stress.

Manning *et. al.* (1986) carried out two studies on *occupational stress: its causes and consequences for job performance.* The first study, in which 104 nurses participated in group discussions and 96 nurses completed a questionnaire, identified 45 stressful events for nurses. In the second study, 171 nurses who completed another questionnaire were also rated by a supervisor and-or a co-worker. Ratings of interpersonal aspects of job performance (such as sensitivity, warmth, consideration, and tolerance) and cognitive-motivational aspects (such as concentration, composure, perseverance, and adaptability) correlated significantly with self-reported perceptions of stressful events, subjective stress, depression, and hostility. Models developed through path analysis suggest that the frequency and subjective intensity of the 45 events identified in Study 1 cause feelings of stress, which lead to depression, which, in turn, causes decrements in interpersonal and cognitive-motivational aspects of job performance.

Mohammadyfar *et. al.* (2009) examined the *effect of emotional intelligence and job burnout on mental and physical health.* The aim of this study was to determine the effect of emotional intelligence and occupational stress on mental and physical health of primary and high school teachers. Two Hundred and Fifty teachers were selected using stratified random sampling from schools of Tehran, Iran. Three questionnaires, *i.e.,* Emotional Intelligence Scale (EIS), Teachers' Occupational Stress Questionnaire, and Mental Health Inventory, and one checklist (Physical Health Checklist) were administered to the school teachers. The results showed that emotional intelligence and job burnout were explained 43.9 per cent of mental health and 13.5 per cent of variance in physical health.

Nguyen (2008) examined *the relationship between emotional intelligence and instructor performance in Ho Chi Minh City University of Foreign Languages and Information Technology (HUFLIT), Vietnam.* The purpose of this study was to investigate the relationship of emotional intelligence and instructor performance. The questionnaire containing demographic information, self-report emotional intelligence test and self-evaluation of job performance was administered to the sample of 201 university teachers. The statistical techniques employed were Pearson's correlation co-efficients, ANOVA and Post Hoc Multiple Comparisons. The findings revealed that HUFLIT instructors were overall proficient in emotional intelligence. For each emotional intelligence dimension, they were vulnerable in emotional literacy and proficient in EQ competency, EQ values and beliefs. Regarding each emotional intelligence facet; HUFLIT instructors were optimal in intentionality, resilience and compassion and trust radius; proficient in emotional awareness of others, interpersonal connections and personal power.

Oginska-bulik (2005) investigated the *emotional intelligence in the workplace by exploring its effects on occupational stress and health outcomes in human service workers.* The purpose of the study was to explore the relationship between emotional intelligence and perceived stress in the workplace and health-related consequences in human service workers. Sample of 330 participants representing various human service professions (physicians, nurses, teachers, probation officers and managers) were chosen for the study. The tools used in the study were the Emotional Intelligence Questionnaire with Polish modification, the Subjective Work Evaluation Questionnaire developed in Poland, and the General Health Questionnaire with Polish modification. The results confirmed an essential, but not very strong, role of emotional intelligence in perceiving occupational stress and preventing employees of human services from negative health outcome.

Ross Azura and Normah (2008) studied the *teacher stress and examined the factors influencing teaching performance in the rural elementary schools.* The sample was 102 teachers and the elements studied were the relationship between stress, self-efficacy and teaching performance, comparison of stress and self-efficacy with genders and prediction of factors influencing teaching performance. The results revealed that self-efficacy had significant positive correlations with stress, particularly time management stress and work related stress. Teachers' performance had weak negative correlations with emotional manifestations. Level of stress among male differs significantly in terms of discipline and motivation compared to female. Emotional manifestation of stress and fatigue manifestation significantly influenced teaching performance.

Siu (2003) examined the *job stress and job performance among employees in Hong Kong in relation to the role of Chinese work values and organizational commitment.* A three component (affective, continuance, and normative) conception of commitment (Meyer and Allen, 1991) is used. A self administered questionnaire was used to collect the data from two samples of Hong Kong employees. These samples included 386 (197 males, 179 females, 10 unidentified) and 145 (51 males, 94 females) respondents. The purpose of recruiting two samples was to replicate the stress–performance relationship in a Chinese setting to enhance generalization of the results. The results consistently revealed that sources of pressure and self rated job performance were negatively related. Furthermore, organizational commitment and Chinese work values were positively related to job performance. A series of hierarchical regressions, while controlling for age, tenure, and job level, revealed that Chinese work values and organizational commitment were significant stress moderators. Chinese work values were found to be significant moderators of the stress–performance relationship in both samples. However, those values only safeguarded performance when work stress was low or moderately high. When work stress was very high, employees with high levels of Chinese work values reported lower job performance. Organizational commitment, in contrast, protected employees from the negative effects of stressors and moderated the stress–performance relationship in a positive direction, but for the first sample only.

Sullivan and Bhagat (1992) studied the *organizational stress, job satisfaction and job performance.* This article reviews and summarizes two decades of empirical literature concerned with both direct and moderating variable-based analyses of the relationship of organizational stress with job satisfaction and job performance. Moderating influences of various constructs operationalized at the individual, group and organizational level of analysis are classified and then reviewed systematically. An evaluative summary of this research suggests that although there have been significant improvements in the analytical methods employed to investigate such phenomena, much of this research still does not consider the role of reciprocal relationships that evolve over time.

Vergara *et. al.* (2010) examined the *emotional intelligence, coping responses, and length of stay as correlates of acculturative stress among international university students in Thailand.* This study sought to determine the relationship of acculturative stress with emotional intelligence, coping responses, and length of stay in Thailand, and to identify the best predictors of acculturative stress. The participants were 216 foreign students with the majority attending undergraduate courses from seven universities in Thailand. The findings showed that stress due to change or culture shock, perceived discrimination, and homesickness defined participants' experience of acculturative stress. Low levels of acculturative stress were found to be significantly correlated with length of stay in Thailand, emotional intelligence, active coping responses (logical analysis and seeking guidance), and passive coping responses (cognitive avoidance, acceptance/resignation, emotional discharge). However, emotional intelligence and acceptance were significant predictors of acculturative stress.

AN OVERVIEW OF THE RESEARCH REVIEWED

The above cited reviews clearly indicate that studies are attempted on emotional intelligence and occupational stress of teachers, students, student teachers and other professionals both in India and abroad. Studies on job performance of teachers were more in western world, whereas, it is limited in Indian context. It is noted that studies related to the emotional intelligence and occupational stress of teachers were mostly limited to the teachers working in primary and secondary schools, special education schools and higher educational institutions. Studies on emotional intelligence and occupational stress of teachers working in higher secondary schools were very limited. Similarly, studies on job performance of teachers working in higher secondary schools are few in number in India compared to abroad. A good number of empirical researches on relationship studies on emotional intelligence, occupational stress, and job performance were found in western world. A close look at the review clearly indicates that the studies conducted abroad are more in-depth in nature compared to the studies conducted in India. It also indicates that the studies conducted in India on relationship between emotional intelligence and occupational stress, emotional intelligence and job performance, and occupational stress and job performance are very few and are limited to teachers in all levels other than the higher secondary teachers, which requires the researchers' attention. It was also noted that, whatever may be the limited studies available on this aspect, researchers should focus on higher secondary level, as the higher secondary education is the turning point in the students' life. Higher secondary level requires the involvement of teacher not only in the academic level but also in developing the social skills as well as emotional levels of the adolescents, where the teacher has to play a crucial role apart from performing his / her job effectively. Hence, it is necessary for the researchers to focus on this aspect, so that, the factors contributing to the development of emotional intelligence, reducing occupational stress and enhancing the job performance of the teachers can be implemented, considering the complexity of the job they are involved.

A critical analysis of the studies conducted in India and abroad revealed that, the Indian studies are very much limited to self-reporting rating scales or questionnaires and here and there interview method (Basu *et. al.* 2004; Bakshi *et. al.* 2008; Williams, 2008 and so on) is being employed. Survey method and simple random sampling technique are the most commonly used methods with average sample size ranging from 250-400. The most commonly used tools to assess the emotional intelligence are Emotional Intelligence Scale of Hyde *et. al.* (2002), Singh (2003), and Bar-On (1998), and for assessing occupational stress, the Occupational Stress Rating Scale of Reddy (2007), Occupational Stress Index of Srivastava and Singh (1984), and Occupational Stress Indicator of Cooper *et. al.* (1988) are used most frequently. The job performance is assessed mostly by the self developed tools of the researchers as there is no relevant tool found to assess the job performance of the teachers. The common statistical techniques used are t-test, F-test, correlations and regression analysis. So, it can be said that most of the Indian researchers are employing single methods and techniques to carryout their research work.

In the western context, multi methodologies and multi techniques and multiple tools are used in their studies. Combined descriptive, quantitative and qualitative approaches *i.e.,* surveys, interviews and observations are carried out in a single study (Bradshaw, 2008; Beach, 2010; Sprenger, 2011 and so on). Unlike Indian survey methods, here, other methods like experimental research (Koplan, 2003; Ruiz-Aranda *et. al.* 2012; etc.), longitudinal studies (Burke *et. al.* 2007; Hosotani, 2011; etc), meta-analysis (Cooper-Hakim and Viswesveran, 2005; Roth *et. al.* 2011; etc) are also found in common. The sample of the studies are also more than 1000 in most of the Western studies (Chan *et. al.* 2010; Frederickson *et. al.* 2012; Muto *et. al.* 2007; Rahim *et. al.* 2002; etc) and other than random sampling technique, cluster sampling and multistage random sampling techniques are also used frequently. In case of statistical techniques, along with t/F tests and stepwise multiple regression analysis, structural equation modeling, hierarchical multiple regression analysis, canonical correlation analysis, LISREL analysis, post-hoc analysis, univariate, bivariate and multivariate analysis are used in most of the studies. On the whole, it is found that in the western researches multi methodologies and multiple tools are used along with in-depth higher order statistical techniques as compared to Indian researches.

The statement of the problem of the present investigation is presented in the succeeding Chapter 3.

STATEMENT OF THE PROBLEM

INTRODUCTION

ONCE THE PROBLEM has been selected, stating it is an important task that has to be carried out. Defining the problem helps to specify the problem under study in a clear manner. A proper definition of research problem will enable the researcher to be on the track. This process helps the investigator to separate his/her study in careful distinction of other previous studies. It is only on careful detailing of research problem, the researcher can work out the research design and can smoothly carryon all the consequential steps involved while doing research. Operational definition of the term helps to view the general problem in terms of more specific, measurable and observable variable.

Hypotheses are a set of suggested tentative solutions for the problem. A hypothesis is defined as a proposition or a set of propositions set forth as an explanation for the occurrence of some specified group of phenomenon either asserted merely as a provision conjecture to guide some investigation or accepted as highly probable in the light of established facts (Kothari, 1995). Hypotheses of the study with specific objectives enable the researcher to identify the variables involved in the study and suggest methodological procedures to be employed. Similarly, its scope and need show the urgency of the study.

This chapter deals with the title of the problem, operational definition of the terms used in the study, objectives, assumptions, hypotheses, scope, need, importance and delimitations of the study.

TITLE OF THE PROBLEM

"*Emotional Intelligence, Occupational Stress and Job Performance of Teachers Working at Higher Secondary Level*".

OPERATIONAL DEFINITION OF THE TERMS USED IN THE STUDY

The meaning and definition of the key terms used in the study along with the operational definitions are presented hereunder.

Emotional Intelligence

According to *The Longman's Dictionary* (1998), emotional means 'influenced by one's feelings rather than by one's thoughts or knowledge' and intelligence means 'the ability to learn, understand, and think about things. Similarly, *The Oxford Dictionary* (2003) termed emotion as 'a strong mental or instinctive feeling'; 'emotional intensity or sensibility' and emotional means 'relating to the emotions'; 'easily affected by or readily displaying emotion'; while the term intelligence refers to 'quickness of understanding'. *The Cambridge Advanced Learner's Dictionary and Thesaurus (2011)* defines emotional intelligence as 'the ability to understand the way people feel and react to use this skill to make good judgements and to avoid or solve problems'. *The Oxford On-Line Dictionary (2012)* defines emotional as 'arousing or characterized by intense feeling, having feeling that are easily excited and openly displayed, and intelligence means 'the ability to acquire and apply knowledge and skills'.

In this study, emotional intelligence of higher secondary teachers is used in terms of the ability of higher secondary teacher to understand one's own self and others in terms of his/her self-awareness, self-management, social-awareness and social-skills. Here Emotional Intelligence is a phrase that incorporates the intricate aspects of both emotion and intelligence.

Occupational Stress

The Oxford Dictionary (2003) defines occupation as 'a person's temporary or regular employment' and occupational means 'rendered more likely by one's occupation'. Stress refers to 'the demand on physical or mental energy'. *The Longman's Dictionary (1998)* termed occupation as 'a job or profession'; occupational as 'related to or caused by one's own job' and stress as 'the continuous feeling of worry that prevents a person from relaxing'. *The Cambridge Advanced Learner's Dictionary and Thesaurus (2011)* defines occupation as 'a regular activity or hobby' and stress as 'a great worry caused by a difficult situation, or something which causes this condition'. According to *the Oxford On-Line Dictionary (2012),* occupational is 'relating to job or profession' and stress is 'a state of mental or emotional strain or tension resulting from adverse or demanding circumstances'.

Kyriacou and Sutcliffe (1978) defined teacher stress as 'a response to negative effect such as anger or depression of a teacher usually accompanied by psychological and biological changes resulting from aspects of teacher's job and medicated by the perception of the demands made upon the teacher which constitute a threat to his self-esteem'.

In this study, occupational stress of higher secondary teachers is defined in terms of ability of the teacher to face the challenges posed by the organizational structure and climate; personal and professional efficiency; intra and inter-personal interactions; home-work interface and; environmental factors.

Job Performance

According to *the Oxford Dictionary (2003)* the term job is referred as 'a piece of work'; 'a paid position of employment' and; performance means 'the execution or fulfillment of a duty'; 'the process of performing or carrying out'. Likewise, *The Longmans' Dictionary* (1998) defines job as 'the regular paid work that one does for an employer' and performance as 'the act of doing a piece of work, duty etc'. Similarly, *The Cambridge Advanced Learner's Dictionary and Thesaurus (2011)* defines job as 'the regular work which a person does to earn money' and performance as 'how well a person does a piece of work or an activity. *The Oxford On-Line Dictionary (2012)* has also defined job as 'a paid position of regular employment' and performance as 'a task or operation seen in terms of how successfully it is done'. *John P. Campbell (1990) describes* job performance as 'an individual level variable, *i.e.,* a performance is something a single person does'. He also defines 'performance as behaviour'.

In this study, job performance of higher secondary teachers is defined as a multi-dimensional construct which refers to an individual's proficiency in task-oriented behaviour, inter-personally oriented behaviour, managerial capabilities and, the personal discipline and leadership qualities with which he/she performs goal relevant activities both directly and indirectly which contribute to the organization's development as well as students overall development.

Higher Secondary Teachers

The Oxford On-Lline Dictionary (2012) defines secondary as 'relating to education for children from the age of eleven to sixteen years' and teachers as 'a person who teaches, especially in schools'.

In this study, the higher secondary teachers in the Indian context refers to 'the persons who teaches to the students in the age group of sixteen to eighteen years and are studying in 11th and 12th standard, *i.e.,* the students who are going to complete their school level education'.

OBJECTIVES OF THE STUDY

The following objectives have been framed for the present study:

1. To develop a tool to assess the level of Emotional Intelligence of teachers working at higher secondary level.
2. To develop a tool to assess the level of Occupational Stress of teachers working at higher secondary level.
3. To develop a tool to assess the level of Job Performance of teachers working at higher secondary level.
4. To develop a tool to assess the level of Job Performance of teachers working at higher secondary level as perceived by their respective Principal's / Headmaster's.
5. To find out the significant difference, if any, in the self ratings of Job Performance of teachers working at the higher secondary level and the Job Performance rating by their respective school Principal's/Headmaster's.

6. To find out the significant difference, if any, in the Emotional Intelligence, Occupational Stress and Job Performance of teachers working at higher secondary level due to variations in their Gender (men/women); Age (up to 35 yrs/ 36-45 yrs/ 46 yrs and above); Community (OC/BC/MBC, SC and ST); Marital Status (married/unmarried); Educational Qualification (PG with B.Ed. and M.Ed./PG with M.Ed. and M.Phil.); Nature of the Subject the Teachers Handling *i.e.,* Languages (English, Tamil, Hindi, French) / Science (Physics, Chemistry, Botany, Zoology) / Mathematics/Commerce; Salary they Receive (up to Rs. 10,000/-, Rs. 10,001- Rs. 15,000/-, Rs. 15,001/- Rs. 20,000/-, Rs. 20,001/- and above); Type of School they are Working-in (government/private); Location of the School (rural/urban) and; Years of Experience (up to 15 yrs/ 16 yrs and above).
7. To find out the relationship between the:
   - Emotional Intelligence and Occupational Stress.
   - Emotional Intelligence and Job Performance.
   - Occupational stress and Job Performance.
8. To study how far and to what extent the independent variables (gender, age, community, marital status, educational qualification, nature of the subjects the teachers handling, salary they receive, type of school they are working-in, location of the school, and years of experience) influence the dependent variables (emotional intelligence, occupational stress and job performance).
9. To study how far and to what extent the independent variable (emotional intelligence dimensions) contribute to the dependent variables (occupational stress and job performance); independent variable (occupational stress dimensions) to the dependent variable (job performance).

ASSUMPTIONS

1. It is possible to develop tools to assess the Emotional Intelligence, Occupational Stress and Job Performance of teachers working at higher secondary level.
2. The Emotional Intelligence, Occupational Stress and Job Performance of teachers working at higher secondary level may vary.
3. It is possible to predict the contribution of independent variables (gender, age, community, marital status, educational qualification, nature of the subjects the teachers handling, salary they receive, type of school they are working-in, location of the school, and years of experience) to the dependent variables (Emotional Intelligence, Occupational Stress and Job Performance) of teachers working at higher secondary schools.
4. It is possible to predict the contribution of Emotional Intelligence dimensions to the Occupational Stress and Job Performance of teachers working at higher secondary level.

HYPOTHESES OF THE STUDY

1. There exists a significant difference in the emotional intelligence of higher secondary teachers due to variations in their gender, age, community, marital status, educational qualification, nature of the subjects the teachers handling, salary they receive, type of school the teachers are working-in, location of the school, and years of experience.
2. There exists a significant difference in the occupational stress of teachers working at higher secondary level due to variations in their gender, age, community, marital status, educational qualification, nature of the subjects the teachers handling, salary they receive, type of school the teachers are working-in, location of the school, and years of experience.
3. There exists a significant difference in the job performance of teachers working at higher secondary level due to variations in their gender, age, community, marital status, educational qualification, nature of the subjects the teachers handling, salary they receive, type of school the teachers are working-in, location of the school, and years of experience.
4. There is no significant difference in the assessment of job performance of teachers working at higher secondary level using their self rating scale and the assessment of job performance of the same teachers by their respective Principal's / Head Master's.
5. There is a positive significant correlation between the:
    - Emotional Intelligence and Occupational Stress of teachers working at higher secondary level.
    - Emotional Intelligence and Job Performance of teachers working at higher secondary level.
    - Occupational Stress and Job Performance of teachers working at higher secondary level.

SCOPE OF THE STUDY

The present study aims to identify the emotional intelligence, occupational stress and job performance of teachers working at higher secondary level. For this purpose, the Emotional Intelligence Rating Scale developed by Poornima (2010) for special education teachers based on certain emotional competencies of Goleman (2001) was adopted and modified by the investigator in accordance with the need of the present study. Similarly, the Occupational Stress Rating Scale developed by Reddy (2007), which was adopted and modified by Poornima (2010) for special education teachers has been used for the study. This scale has been re-modified here and there keeping in mind the requirements of the study and suitable for higher secondary teachers and utilised in the current study. Further, the researcher has developed the Job Performance Rating Scale of teachers to assess the job performance at higher secondary level.

As the teachers self-rating scale alone may lead to biased results, the investigator also developed the Principal's / Head Master's Assessment of Teachers Job Performance Rating Scale to assess the job performance of higher secondary teachers. Here, the investigator has adopted the multi-methodology to assess the teachers' performance through the teachers self-rating as well as the assessment of the teachers by their respective principals to get an unbiased outcome. The study also intends to find out the significant differences, if any, in the emotional intelligence, occupational stress and job performance of higher secondary teachers due to variations in their gender, age, community, marital status, educational qualification, nature of the subjects the teachers handling, salary they receive, type of school they are working-in, nature of school the teachers are working-in, and years of experience.

Further, the study deliberated the relationship between emotional intelligence and occupational stress; emotional intelligence and job performance and; occupational stress and job performance of teachers working at the higher secondary level. The study also focused on how far and to what extent the personal variables such as, gender, age, community, marital status, educational qualification, nature of the subjects the teachers handling, salary they receive, type of school they are working-in, location of the school, and years of experience are contributing to the dependent variables, *i.e.,* emotional intelligence, occupational stress and job performance of higher secondary teachers. In addition, it also focuses its attention on the contribution of emotional intelligence dimensions to the dimensions of occupation stress and job performance and; occupational stress dimensions to the dimensions of job performance of higher secondary teachers.

The tools developed in this study will serve as reference material to the other researchers working in the area of emotional intelligence, occupational stress and job performance. A comprehensive study of emotional intelligence, occupational stress and job performance of teachers working at higher secondary level will explore the factors contributing to the emotional intelligence, sources of occupational stress and which in turn, resulting in the effective job performance of teachers and the relationship among these three. Similarly, such studies will give better insight into the influence of personal variables of teachers on their emotional intelligence, occupational stress and job performance which may lead to better policy planning, development and implementation at higher secondary level and also help to develop the intervening programmes to increase the levels of emotional intelligence, reduce the degree of stress and enhance the teachers job performance.

NEED AND IMPORTANCE OF THE STUDY

Emotional intelligence has become a very popular concept in professional settings and is even analyzed in the academic domain. There is a growing consensus among the researchers, educationists and experts that in today's context, a world characterized by globalization, rapid technological change, work place diversity, and constant environmental turbulence, emotional intelligence is essential to effective individual and organizational performance. Although technical and cognitive learning continue to be very important to strategic success in the market place, most would agree that they are not sufficient. High level of emotional intelligence leads to less stress at occupational environment and positively related to organizational commitment and better performance (Ioannis Nikolaou and Ioannis Tsaousis, 2002). Numerous studies argue that personal qualities such as self-awareness, self-motivation, flexibility and integration, as well as interpersonal skills such as negotiation, listening, empathy, conflict management, and collaboration are critical ingredients for high performance (Spencer, McClelland, and Kelner, 1997; Spencer and Spencer, 1993; Hall and Associates, 1996; Boyatzis, 1982). Individuals with greater emotional intelligence show higher levels of career, life and job satisfaction (Poornima, 2010) and become more resilient to occupational stress. Emotional intelligence and self efficacy had significant relationship with work attitudes (Penrose *et. al.* 2007; Salami, 2008).

Unlike IQ, which increases upto one's teen years, emotional intelligence seems always continue to develop. As people learn from experiences, their emotional intelligence grows. Studies that have tracked people's emotional intelligence over the years indicate that people's competencies increase as they grow older (Goleman, 1998). Bar-On (2000) found that older groups scored higher on the Emotional Quotient Inventory Scale than younger groups. Individuals in their late forties and early fifties achieved the highest mean score. The study suggests that emotional and social intelligence increases with age. Mayer, Caruso, and Salovey (1999) suggest that women might have a slight advantage over men in the area of emotional intelligence. Bar-On (2000), however, suggests that no significant differences exist between men and women regarding overall emotional and social competence; but he does indicate some gender differences for a few factorial components of the construct. Bar-On theorizes that women appear to be more aware of emotions, demonstrate more empathy, relate better interpersonally, and act more socially responsible than men. Men, on the other hand, appeared to be able to have better self-regard, cope better with stress, solve problems better, and be more independent, flexible, and optimistic than women. In general, when looking at the overall ratings of men and women, far more similarities exist than differences regarding their emotional intelligence. Thus, in terms of total emotional intelligence, no gender differences exist (Bar-On, 1998).

In so far as the management of social behaviour involves the management of emotions (Hochschild, 1983), EI has the potential to be a strong predictor of performance (Mishra and Mahapatra, 2010). Linking EI with performance can provide organizations with a valid alternative for selecting and assessing employees. Many organizational researchers have called for more focus on the role of emotions at work. For example, Ashforth and Humphrey (1993) argue that emotions are an integral and inseparable part of organizational life and that more attention should be given to the employees' emotional experience. Emotional intelligence has been cited as a crucial contributor to organizational success (Goleman, 1998; Salovey and Mayor, 1990) and many organizational behaviourists have responded to the growing significance of emotional intelligence by attempting to identify factors that influence employees' performance at work. Work on emotional labour and management of emotion has highlighted those small, relatively costless changes in organizational context or managerial behaviour that can impact employees' emotional reactions and consequently, their performance (Hochschild, 1983; Huy, 1999). EI has been found to be positively related to outcomes such as job performance (Newman *et. al.* 2010; O'Boyle *et. al.*

2010) managerial thinking styles (Groves and Vance, 2009), successful life adjustment (Sjöberg, 2008), better coping and job behaviours (Gupta and Mishra, 2011), better social relations, family relations, academic achievements and psychological well-being (Carmeli *et. al.* 2009; Mayer *et. al.* 2008). Goleman (1995) claimed EI may be as important as intelligence quotient (IQ) in determining life success. Such claims have, however, been disconfirmed by the decade of rigorous empirical research that has followed. Van Rooy and Viswesvaran (2004), in a meta-analysis, showed that after correcting for statistical artifacts, the average correlation between EI and work performance was modest (*i.e.,* around 0.24).

The positive impact of the self-confidence competence of emotional intelligence on performance has been shown in a variety of studies. A high degree of self-confidence distinguishes the best from the average performers (Boyatzi's, 1982). The level of self-confidence is in fact a stronger predictor of performance than the level of skill or previous training (Saks, 1995), as revealed by a 60 years study of more than one thousand high-IQ men and women tracked from early childhood to retirement, those who possessed self-confidence during their early years were most successful in their careers. Those with a stronger sense of control over not only themselves but the events in their lives are less likely to become angry or depressed when faced with job stress, or to quit the job (Rahim and Psenicka, 1996). Superior performers tend to respond calmly with full self-control to angry attacks (Boyatzis and Burrus, 1995; Spencer and Spencer, 1993). Top performers are able to balance their drive and ambition with emotional self-control, harnessing their personal needs in the service of the organization's goals (Boyatzis, 1982).

On the other hand, there are many reasons for stress at workplace. The major sources of occupational stress are age, sex, marital status, job status and school locations. Years of teaching experience and type of school play a significant role in the perception of various sources of stress related to the teaching profession (Nhundu, T., 1992; Ravichanran and Rajendran, 2007). The other variables associated with occupational stress are role ambiguity, loss of control, isolation, lack of administration support, emotional exhaustion, depersonalization, and lack of accomplishment in the job (Weiskopf, 1980; Maslach and Jackson, 1981; Fimian, 1986). Researchers have shown that role stressors are related to burnout (Anderson, 1991; Peiro, Ganzalez-Roma, Tordera, and Manes, 2001; Shirom, 2003). Other psychological strains resulting from role stressors include lower job satisfaction (Fisher and Gitelson, 1983; Jackson and Schuler, 1985) and higher anxiety (Srivastava, Hagtvet, and Sen, 1994). Occupational stress leads to the low occupational commitment and major effects on physical and psychological ill health (Leon Jackson and Sebastiaan Rothmann 2006; Wang Pei and Zhang Guoli 2007). Occupational stress also leads to absenteeism, turnover to other jobs and job dissatisfaction and low performance (Kobasaa 1982; Fimian and Santoro 1983; Siuoi-ling 2009; Mokadad, 2005). Stress is often accepted as inescapable aspect of teaching. Teachers' lives are adversely affected by stress leading to physical ill health (Otto, 1986; Mokdad, 2005) and mental ill health (Fletcher and Payne, 1982; Finlay-Jones, 1986; Beer and Beer, 1992). Teacher stress often affects the teacher's ability to function effectively (Blasé, 1986), sometimes to the extent of causing burnout (Seldman and Zager, 1998). Other common responses listed by Brown and Ralph (1992) includes reduction in work performance and output; inability to manage time or delegate; feelings of alienation and inadequacy; loss of confidence and motivation; increasing introversion; irritability with colleagues; unwillingness to cooperate; frequent irrational conflict at work; withdrawal from supportive relationships; inappropriate cynical humor; persistent negative thoughts; increased substance abuse; loss of appetite; frequent infections; and accident proneness.

Change in organizations suggests that change can create a number of potentially stressful conditions. Change can introduce new roles and performance expectations that conflict with other roles an individual is expected to perform (Brett, 1980; Latack, 1986; Louis, 1980). Change can also introduce new uncertainties and ambiguities about organizational goals, the roles of individual in the organization and the knowledge and skills that are required to perform new roles (McGrath, 1984). Principals play their instructional leadership roles to enhance the work performance of the teacher (Murphy, 1987; Shephard, 1999; Enuchme and Egwunyena, 2008). Conducive environment also enhances teachers work performance. Job satisfaction and role clarity leads to better job performance (Nhundu, 1992; Ololube, 2006). The feelings of a leader may be an indicator and predictor of the performance of an organization (Staw and Barsade, 1993, Staw, Sutton, and Pelled, 1994).

The voluminous literature on teacher stress has yielded a substantial amount of data on the sources of teacher stress (Borg, 1990; Dunham, 1992; Travers and Cooper, 1996; Upton and Varma, 1996). Such studies not only indicated the main source of stress facing teachers as a whole, but also how the main sources of stress vary to some extent from one subgroup to another. For example, teachers in independent schools often cite the intense pressure on them from parents to ensure their children achieve unrealistically higher levels; student teachers often cite having their teaching performance assessed by tutors and mentors. Numerous studies have demonstrated a consistent link between substantial role ambiguity in the job and the high level of psychological stress and strain (O'Driscoll and Beehr, 1994; Schaubroeck, Cotton, and Jennings, 1989). From the reviews of many researches, it is evident that optimal matching between work demands and individual capabilities is required to prevent strain from exceeding limits. This may facilitate greater flexibility in the design of the jobs to tailor them more directly to the skills and interests of the individuals. To be effective in helping organizations manage change, leaders first need to be aware of and to manage their own feelings of anxiety and uncertainty (Bunker, 1997). Then they need to be aware of the emotional reactions of other organizational members and act to help people cope with those reactions. How long an individual stays in an organization and how productive he/she is, is determined by his/her relationship with the superior and the colleagues (Zipkin, 2000). Relationships can help people become more emotionally intelligent even when they are not set up for that purpose (Kram and Cherniss, 2001).

The wealth of research published on teacher stress over the last 20 years has indicated that most teachers experience some stress from time to time, and that some teachers experience a great deal of stress fairly frequently (Boyle *et. al.* 1995; Chan and Hui, 1995; Hart, Wearing and Conn, 1995; Cockburn, 1996; Travers and Cooper, 1996). However, some of the studies of Manthei, Gilmore, Tuck and Adair, (1996); Capel, (1997); and Male and May, (1997) have not consistently shown that certain subgroups of teachers report higher levels of stress than other subgroups. Studies comparing teachers with other professional occupations using a variety of measures (attitudinal, physiological, behavioural and medical) indicate that teaching is one of the high stress professions (Health Education Authority, 1988; Traverse and Cooper, 1996). Stress resulting from work is a major problem and it takes a toll on one's physical and mental well being. Moreover, the management of stress is not easy, as can be ascertained by the documented ineffectiveness of stress management interventions. However, a few pointers could be had for managers to counter and mitigate stress effectively. First and foremost, one should be able to identify the stressors at work, assess them and manage them too. One should be careful not to remove the rewarding aspects of the job (Akrani, 2011).

Stress can be either helpful or harmful to job performance, depending upon its level. When stress is absent, it limits job challenges and performance becomes low. As stress increases gradually, job performance also tends to increase, because stress helps a person to gather and use resources, to meet job requirements. Constructive stress inculcates encouragement among employees and helps them to tackle various job challenges. Eventually, a time comes when stress reaches its maximum saturation point that corresponds approximately to the employee's day to day performance capability. Beyond this point, stress shows no signs of improvement in job performance. Finally, if stress is too high, it turns into a damaging force. Job performance begins to decline at the same point because excessive stress interferes with performance. An employee, who loses the ability to cope, fails to make a decision and displays inconsistent behaviour. If stress continues to increase even further it reaches a breaking point. At this breaking stage, an employee is very upset and mentally devastated. Soon he/she completely breaks down. Performance becomes zero, no longer feels like working for their employer, absenteeism increases, eventually resulting into quitting of a job or getting fired. Stress should neither be very high nor too low. It must be within the range and limits of employee's capacity to tolerate and his performance level. A controlled stress which is within limits is always beneficial and productive than an uncontrolled one (Akrani, 2011).

In studies of job performance, outstanding effectiveness in virtually all jobs, *i.e.,* from the bottom to the top of the corporate ladder, depends on conscientiousness component of emotional intelligence (Barrick and Mount, 1991). Superior performers exhibit the adaptability component of emotional intelligence (Spencer and Spencer, 1993), who are open to new information and can let go of old assumptions and so adapt how they operate. They also found that the need to achieve is the competence that most strongly sets apart superior and average performer. Optimism is the key ingredient of better performance because it can determine one's reaction to unfavorable events or circumstances, those with high performance, are proactive and persistent, have an optimistic attitude towards setbacks, and operate from hope of success (Schulman, 1995). Initiative is the key to outstanding performance and to the development of healthy relationships with co-workers (Crant, 1995; Rosier, 1996). Empathy requires self-awareness; our understanding of other's feelings and concerns flow from awareness of our own feelings. This sensitivity to others is critical for superior job performance whenever the focus is on interactions with people (Friedman and Dimattee, 1982). In an increasingly diverse work force, the empathy competence allows us to read people accurately and avoid resorting to the stereotyping that can lead to performance deficits by creating anxiety in the stereotyped individuals (Steele, 1997). The relationship management set of competencies includes essential social skills, developing others, influence, communication and conflict management skills (Goleman, 2000). Those adept at the visionary leadership are able to articulate and arouse enthusiasm for a shared vision and mission, to step forward as needed, to guide the performance of others while holding them accountable and to lead by example. The more positive the style of the leader, the more positive, helpful, and co-operative are those in the group (George and Bettenhausen, 1990). The emotional tone set by a leader tends to ripple outward with remarkable power (Bachman, 1998). A leader's competence at catalyzing change brings greater efforts and better performance from subordinates, making work more effective (House, 1988). The collaboration and team work competence has taken on increased importance in the performance (Sweeney, 1999). Team members tend to share moods, both good and bad with better moods improving performance (Totterdell, Kellett, Teuchmann, and Briner, 1998). The positive mood of a team leader at work promotes both worker effectiveness and retention (George and Bettenhausen, 1990). Positive emotions and harmony on a top management team predict its effectiveness (Barsade and Gibson, 1998). Emotional competencies seem to operate most powerfully in synergistic groupings, with the evidence suggesting that mastery of a 'critical mass' of competencies is necessary for superior performance (Boyatzis, Goleman, and Rhee, 2000). Other researchers have reported that competencies operate together in an integrated fashion forming a meaningful pattern of abilities that facilitates successful performance in a given role or job (Nygren and Ukeritis, 1993). Spencer and Spencer (1993) have identified distinctive groupings of competencies that tend to typify high performing individuals.

Stress is an energy sapping condition. The energy that the teachers dissipate in coping with occupational stress could be put to better use, creating quality teachers. Also stress being intrinsically associated with the profession acts as an impediment in attracting and retaining high caliber teachers. In extreme cases of accumulated stress causing teacher burnout, teachers are rendered incapable of functioning as educators. Stress is also found to precipitate physical ailments such as headaches, ulcers, diabetes, heart problems, hypertension etc., among the teachers. Stress related mental health problems range from depression, anxiety, mood swings, irritability to drug abuse, sleep disorders and suicidal tendencies (Basu, 2009). The most serious implication of stress among teachers is the impact it has on the quality of teacher performance. Such stressed teachers cannot produce balanced and holistically developed students equipped to take on the challenges of the future. Ultimately it affects the quality of education in the country. Hence stress among teachers ought to be a matter of grave concern for one and all. Considering the fallouts of stress among teachers, the need of the hour is to devise appropriate coping strategies for teachers and include stress busting methods to help the teachers to come out of their stress (Basu, 2009).

Teachers or any other employee's attitude towards their work can be best measured through their work performance, achievement, motivation and job satisfaction. In higher educational institutions, teachers play an important role in development of motivation in students to strive for higher grades. Their guidance, suggestions and involvement in administrative activities help management of educational institutions to reach their goals of accomplishment and having good national and international standing. Teachers form the crux of the education system, preparing the young people to build their nation with purpose and responsibility and confront the challenges of tomorrow. They are the social engineers and custodians of the future. The most pertinent question that arises in the present scenario is whether our teachers are indeed emotionally well equipped to handle the pressures and challenges of their venerable yet vulnerable profession. Teaching is a noble and also very exacting profession. It demands much from the self, from the resilience and integrity of the person within. It has often been attributed to be a physically wearing and psychologically stressful occupation. The stressors operating in the lives of teachers is a critical issue with far reaching implications, influencing not only the quality of teachers but also the quality of the nation at large, thereby gaining prominence in academic circles.

It is a matter of great concern to all the teachers to improve the student's interest and performance in their subjects. Why do students show poor performance in any subject? Is it because of apathy, frustration, lack of motivation or aptitude, hostility, or is it because they do not understand due to lack of insight into the subject? Obviously different factors such as physiological, psychological, social, emotional and intellectual may cause aversion towards particular subject for a particular student. It is the duty of the teacher to identify and isolate these factors, especially for the students in higher secondary classes, as it is the crucial as well as transition period and a turning point in their life. The teacher has to mould and shape their ideas, expectations and ambitions into reality. For this, the teacher should have high level of emotional intelligence to understand the level of his/her pupils and help them to cope with their subjects. The teacher should also have optimum level of stress so that he/she can show good performance in his/her job there by promoting the better results of students. Many studies have supported these assumptions (Akhlaq *et. al.* 2010; Brand, 2007; Chughtai and Zafar, 2006; Gardner, 2005; Ismail *et. al.* 2010; Kazmi *et. al.* 2008; Manning *et. al.* 1986; and Ross Azura and Normah, 2008).

Studies have consistently concluded that teaching is a stressful occupation, and that a significant number of teachers are affected by work-related stress (Dunham, 1994; Kyriacou, 1987, 1997, 2001; Guglielmi and Tatrow, 1998). It is apparent that more research is needed into the complexities of teacher stress and its relationship to job performance, which may have some features unique to the profession in Indian context. All these research studies on emotional intelligence, occupational stress and job performance have been analyzed with varied applications in the western context. However, in Indian context, it is still relatively unclear what accounts for low levels of emotional intelligence, sources of occupational stress and the factors concerned with the job performance of higher secondary teachers. Also, a critical view of the research studies reviewed in Chapter-II indicates that the research on emotional intelligence, occupational stress and job performance of teachers working at higher secondary level are limited in both Indian and Western context. Only the study by Lenka and Kant (2012) is noted on emotional intelligence of teachers involved in higher secondary level. In case of occupational stress, the studies of Mathews (2005) and Ravichandran and Rajendran (2007) are noted and the studies of Kumaran (2003) and Raju and Srivastava (1994) are identified on the job performance of teachers at higher secondary level in India. Similarly, very few studies on the job performance of higher secondary teachers (Akram, 2010 and Anjum, 2011) and the relationship studies on emotional intelligence, occupational stress and job performance (Ismail *et. al.* 2010; and Jude, 2011) have focused on the need to carryout further research in this field.

As far as higher secondary education is concerned in India, the field is wide open to the researchers to explore the levels of teachers' emotional intelligence, occupational stress and job performance. Such studies facilitate to fill the research gaps in these aspects and further helps in identifying the factors contributing to the emotional intelligence, sources of occupational stress, which, in-turn helps the teacher to give better performance in his/her job. This helps to develop congenial and better working environment for the teachers, which will have positive implications for the students and quality education can be provided to the students. In fact, research in this area provide better insights to create effective organizational environment, healthy intra-personal relations, professional interactions, strengthening of the professional training and the ways and means to equip the teachers with personal and professional competencies to meet the needs of the global society (Reddy, 2011). Such studies explore the positive and negative factors associated with the levels of emotional intelligence, sources and consequences of stress on the teachers' profession. Similarly, the studies on job performance of teachers facilitate to know what factors are contributing the effective teaching and lower levels of teaching.

The review of literature has undoubtedly revealed that the last two decades had witnessed an enormous number of research studies on emotional intelligence and occupational stress at work place and among educational personal at primary and secondary levels. Unfortunately, the researches done are countable with respect to the relationship between emotional intelligence, occupational stress and job performance among the higher secondary teachers. Hence there is a need to study the emotional intelligence, occupational stress and job performance among the higher secondary teachers and the relationship between these variables. It may throw light on the teachers' level of emotional intelligence and their stress at work place which has an inverse effect on their performance. It enables the education facilitator and administrator to find the remedies and enhance the teachers' level of emotional intelligence and decrease their occupational stress which will have a positive impact on their job performance, thereby leading to a healthy and competitive school atmosphere.

DELIMITATIONS OF THE STUDY

1. The study is confined to the Vellore District of Tamil Nadu state.
2. The study is limited only to the teachers working at the higher secondary level.
3. Rating Scale is the only tool used to assess the emotional intelligence, occupational stress and job performance of higher secondary teachers.
4. The emotional intelligence and occupational stress have been assessed only based on the self-ratings of the teachers.
5. Students' academic achievement results are not included to assess the job performance of the higher secondary teachers.
6. The effect of only a few personal variables such as gender, age, community, marital status, educational qualification, nature of the subjects the teachers handling, salary they receive, type of school they are working-in, location of the school, and years of experience on emotional intelligence, occupational stress and job performance has been studied.

The methodology used in the study is given in the Chapter 4.

METHODOLOGY

INTRODUCTION

RESEARCH METHODOLOGY is a way to systematically solve the research problem. It may be understood as a science of studying how research is done scientifically. It includes the various steps that are generally adopted by a researcher in studying the research problem along with the logic behind it. It is necessary for the researcher to know not only the research methods/techniques but also the methodology (Kothari, 1995). The accuracy and adequacy of the research findings depend upon the method adopted. The scientific method encourages the rigorous, impersonal mode of procedure dictated by the demands of logic and objective procedure. Scientific method implies an objective, logical and systematic way, *i.e.,* a method free from personal bias or prejudice, a method to ascertain demonstrative qualities of a phenomenon capable of being certified, a method wherein the investigation proceeds in an orderly manner and a method that implies internal consistency. The methodology adopted should describe the details such as selection; development and validation of tools; sources of data and procedure for the collection and; analysis of data. The quality of a study depends upon the selection of suitable methods and tools for investigation. A pre-planned and well designed methodology will provide the researcher a scientific and feasible plan for the problem under analysis. The credibility of the research depends very much upon the credibility of the method used. Thus research methodology not only implies the research methods but also consider the logic behind the methods that has been used in the context of the research study.

DESIGN OF THE STUDY

The purpose of this study is to identify the emotional intelligence, occupational stress and job performance of teachers working at higher secondary level. Considering the research approaches and methodologies adopted both in India and western context, to study the concept under investigation, the researcher rationally used the appropriate methodology for the present research work. Survey method was used in the present study. Survey research is one of the most important methods of measurement in the applied social research, which is a non-experimental, descriptive research method. Survey method is concerned with describing, recording, analyzing and interpreting conditions that either exist or existed. The researcher does not manipulate the variable or arrange the events to happen. Surveys are only concerned with conditions or relationships that exist, opinions that are held, processes that are going on, effects that are evident or trends that are developing. They are primarily concerned with the present but at times do consider past events and influences as they relate to current conditions. Surveys are concerned with hypotheses formulation and testing the analysis of the relationship between non-manipulated variables (Kothari, 1995).

Surveys are an example of field research, where it may either be census or sample survey. They may also be classified as social surveys, economic surveys or public opinion surveys. Whatever be their type, the method of data collection happens to be either, observation, or interview or questionnaire/opinionnaire/rating scale or some projective techniques. Case study method can as well be used. Possible relationships between the data and the unknowns in the universe can be studied through surveys and the researcher's interest lies in understanding and controlling relationships between variables and as such correlation analysis is relatively more important in surveys.

CONSTRUCTION OF RESEARCH TOOLS USED IN THE STUDY

The broad area of survey research encompasses any measurement procedure that involves asking questions to respondents. A survey can be anything from a short paper-pencil feedback form to an intensive one-on-one in-depth interview. Rating scale is one of the most commonly used tools in the survey research. According to Moulay (1964), the rating scale is best conceived as an instrument, which permits the quantification of numerical values of ratings, cumulated points, multiple choice methods etc. were carefully examined. Rating scale involves qualitative description of a limited number of aspects of a thing or of traits of a person. When rating scales are used, an object or trait is measured in absolute terms as against some specified criteria *i.e.,* it is measured without reference to the similar objects or traits. There is no specific rule whether to use a two points scale, three points scale, or scale with still more points. In practice, three to seven point scales are generally used for the simple reason that more points on a scale provide an opportunity for greater sensitivity of measurement (Kothari, 1995). Considering the nature and purpose of study, the investigator went through various tools and the related literature, and developed Likert type Rating Scales to assess the job performance of the higher secondary teachers (self-ratings) and also by their respective Principal's/Head Master's (H.M's); adopted and modified the emotional intelligence rating scale for special education teachers developed by Poornima (2010) and; adopted and re-modified the occupational stress rating scale for special education teachers developed by Reddy (2006) and modified by Poornima (2010).

DEVELOPMENT OF THE RESEARCH TOOLS

The objectives of the present study are to identify the emotional intelligence and occupational stress of higher secondary teachers and; the job performance of higher secondary teachers as assessed by teachers themselves and by their respective Principal's/Head Master's. To achieve the above stated objectives, the researcher developed and adopted the following rating scales.

1. Rating Scale to Assess the Emotional Intelligence of Teachers Working at Higher Secondary level (adopted and modified from Poornima, 2010).
2. Rating Scale to Assess the Occupational Stress of Teachers Working at Higher Secondary Level (developed by Reddy, 2006 and modified by Poornima, 2010 has been adopted and re-modified).
3. Rating Scale to Assess the Job Performance of Teachers Working at Higher Secondary Level - Self-ratings (developed by the investigator).
4. Rating Scale to Assess the Job Performance of Teachers Working at Higher Secondary Level - ratings by their Principal's/H.M's (developed by the investigator).

Description of Rating Scale to Assess the Emotional Intelligence of Teachers Working at Higher Secondary Level

To develop the Rating Scale to assess the Emotional Intelligence of teachers working at higher secondary level, the researcher went through various tools developed earlier, both in India and abroad to assess the emotional intelligence and reviewed the extensive literature related to the emotional intelligence.

Bar-On (1997) developed a self-report Emotional Quotient Inventory (EQ-i) with 133 items. EQ-i has fifteen scales that can be divided into five larger groupings. The areas assessed are emotional self-awareness, assertiveness, self-regard, self-actualization, independence, empathy, interpersonal relationship, social responsibility, problem solving, reality testing, flexibility, stress tolerance, impulse control, happiness, and optimism. Salovey and Mayer (1990) used the 30 item self report Trait Meta Mood Scale (TMMS) to measure the attitudes about emotions and mood regulations. The scale is divided into 3 sub-scales *viz.,* attention to feelings, clarity in discrimination of feelings and mood repair. Mayer *et. al.* (1999) used 402 items Multifactor Emotional Intelligence Scale (MEIS) to measure the performance based emotional intelligence. It is designed comprehensively to assess the four branches, *i.e.,* perceiving, using, understanding and managing emotions of the emotional intelligence model developed by Mayer and Salovey (1997). Similarly, Mayer, Salovey and Caruso Emotional Intelligence Test (MSCEIT) developed by Mayer *et. al.* (1999) is an ability-based test with 141 items to measure the four branches of emotional intelligence *i.e.,* identifying emotions, facilitating thought, understanding emotions, and managing emotions.

Boyatzis *et. al.* (2000) developed 110 items Emotional Competence Inventory (ECI) which is a 360 degree measure to assess the self-awareness, self-regulation, motivation, empathy and social skills of a person. Palmer and Stough (2001) developed a self-report inventory called Swinburne University Emotional Intelligence Test (SUEIT) with 64 items to assess the way people typically think, feel and act with emotions at work. The inventory consists of five sub-scales i.e., emotional recognition and expression; understanding emotions; emotions direct cognition; emotional management and; emotional control. Cameron (2004) used Work Profile Questionnaire-Emotional Intelligence version (WPQ-EI) to measure the personal qualities and competencies that employees need to develop to manage emotion at work which includes seven components *i.e.,* innovation, self-awareness, intuition, emotions, motivation, empathy and social skills. McCann and Roberts (2008) developed the Situational Test of Emotional Understanding (STEU). This test, consisting of 42 questions, is designed to ascertain the capacity of individuals to understand emotions, *i.e.,* to predict the likely changes in emotions they will experience in response to specific events. McCann and Roberts (2008) also developed the Situational Test of Emotion Management (STEM) with 44 items. This test is intended to assess emotion management, *i.e.,* the capacity of individuals to regulate their emotions optimally, curbing negative feelings and fostering positive feelings. Both the tests were relatively independent of personality and thus assessed a form of intelligence. Petrides (2009) developed 153 items Trait Emotional Intelligence Questionnaire (TEIQUE) with 15 sub-scales to measure the four factors of emotional intelligence *i.e.,* well being, self-control, emotionality and sociability.

Kashdan *et. al.* (2010) developed a procedure to measure Emotional Differentiation. Specifically, several times every day, over the course of three weeks, participants were prompted to evaluate the extent to which they feel six negative emotions: sadness, anxiety anger, tiredness, distraction, and fatigue. For each participant, the intra-class correlation with absolute agreement across these emotions was computed. A low correlation indicates the person discriminates across emotions, reflecting emotional differentiation. A high correlation indicates the person does not discriminate across the emotions.

In Indian context, very few measures have been developed to assess the emotional intelligence. Roger and Najarian (1989) designed Emotional Control Questionnaire (ECQ) to measure the tendency to inhibit the expression of emotional responses to stress and illness. Fifty-six items ECQ taps four dimensions of emotional control, *i.e.,* rehearsal, emotional inhibition, aggression control and benign control. Sharma and Bharadwaj (1995) developed the Emotional Competencies Scale with 30 items to measure five competencies *i.e.,* adequate depth of feeling; adequate expression and control of emotions; ability to function with emotions; ability to cope with problem emotions and; encouragement of positive emotions to assess the students' emotional competencies. Emotional Quotient Test (EQT) developed by Chadha and Singh (2001) is widely accepted for the Indian population. This test has been standardized for Indian managers, businessmen, bureaucrats, and industrial workers. Hyde *et. al.* (2002) developed Emotional Intelligence Scale with 34 items that measure 10 factors of emotional intelligence, *viz.,* self-awareness, empathy, self-motivation, emotional stability, managing relations integrity, self-development, value orientation, commitment and altruistic behaviour. Multidimensional Measure of Emotional Intelligence (MMEI) developed by Darolia (2005) is comprised of 80 multiple-choice items distributed in five dimensions, each consisting of 16 items. The five measures covered by MMEI are self-awareness, empathy, managing emotions, motivating one-self and handling relationships.

Similarly, Gupta and Singh (2011) constructed an ability-based scale for emotional intelligence in the Indian context. The items were constructed in such a way that, that they tap onto the four branches as measured by the MSCEIT (perceiving emotions, facilitating thought, understanding emotions and managing emotions). The questionnaire consisted of 38 items, of which, thirty-two were situation based and six were picture based. Poornima (2010) developed an Emotional Intelligence Rating Scale (EIRS) to assess the emotional intelligence of special education teachers. This scale, based on certain emotional competencies from the Goleman's (2001) model of emotional intelligence, has 58 items and was constructed using the four dimensions of emotional intelligence, *i.e.,* self-awareness, self-management, social awareness, and social skills.

As the research on EI has been conducted mostly in western countries, the generality of existing findings remains unclear. A display of emotion that is acceptable in one culture may be deeply offensive in another. Research on EI has tended to shy away from cross-cultural analyses, but it is likely that emotionally intelligent behaviour is culturally dependent (Zeidner *et. al.* 2009). Accordingly, it is important to adopt a cross-cultural perspective in EI research. Considering the uniqueness of Indian context, uncritical adaptation of scales evolved in the context of Western cultural values may not be effective in measuring EI of Indian employees. There exists no EI measure created and tested specifically for the teachers working at higher secondary level in Indian context. While there have been efforts to develop ability-based measure of EI suitable for other countries like China (*e.g.,* Wong and Law, 2002; Wong *et. al.* 2004, 2007), there have been no such effort in the Indian context.

After going through the tools that are previously developed by the researchers, it was found that the available tools and the literature on emotional intelligence have not specifically focused on the emotional intelligence of teachers working at higher secondary school. Considering the available tools and literature, the investigator felt that the rating scale developed by Poornima (2010) to assess the emotional intelligence of special education teachers is more appropriate, as the researcher has covered many aspects of emotional intelligence of teachers. Also, this tool possesses the content, face and intrinsic validity and the calculated reliability value of the tool was found to be 0.88. However, the investigator felt the need to change some of the items, keeping in mind the requirements of the present study. Accordingly, the investigator adopted the tool, and modified certain statements. The prepared rating scale was given to the education experts and head masters of some higher secondary schools. Based on their suggestions, two statements were deleted and four statements were re-modified again. Thus a final form of 56 statements with both positive and negative items was framed and arranged under the four dimensions of emotional intelligence.

(i) *Self-awareness*: self-awareness refers to the ability to understand one's own emotions as well as understanding the impact of one's emotions on specific situations and people and recognizing the impact of particular emotions. This dimension assesses the emotional competencies like emotional awareness, accurate self-assessment and self-confidence of higher secondary teachers.

(ii) Self-management: self-management refers to the ability to use awareness of one's emotions to stay flexible to positively direct behaviour and managing emotional reactions to specific situations and people. The items in this dimension measure self-control, trustworthiness, conscientiousness, adaptability, achievement drive and initiative.

(iii) Social awareness: social awareness refers to the ability to pick up accurately on emotions in other people and react to their emotions and understanding their needs. The emotional competencies like empathy, service orientation, and the institutional awareness are included in this dimension.

(iv) Social skills: social skill is the ability to use awareness of one's own emotions and the emotions of others to manage interactions successfully. This includes clear communication and effectiveness in handling conflicts. Developing others, conflict management, leadership, change catalyst, building bonds, team work and collaboration are the emotional competencies included in this dimension.

Thus the final form of the Emotional Intelligence Rating Scale includes part-I and part-II. The demographical/personal characteristics of the higher secondary teachers like gender, age, marital status, community, educational qualification, nature of subjects the teachers handling, salary per month, type of school they are working-in, location of the school, and years of experience have been included in part-I of the rating scale. Where-in, specific directions for the respondents to fill the rating scale followed by the 56 statements are given in part-II. To avoid the tendency of giving stereotyped responses, both positive and negative items are included in the rating scale. The distribution of statements in the final form of the rating scale is given hereunder.

Distribution of Statements in the Emotional Intelligence Rating Scale

Emotional Intelligence Dimensions	Serial Number of the Statements	Total Number of Statements
Self-awareness	1,2,3*4,5,6,7,8,9*10,11,12	12
Self-management	13*,14*,15,16,17,18*,19,20*,21,22,23,24*, 25,26*27,28	16
Social awareness	29,30,31,32,33,34,35,36,37,38*	10
Social skills	39,40*41,42,43,44*45,46,47,48,49,50,51, 52*53,54*55,56*	18
	Total =	56

*represents negative statements

To measure the emotional competencies of the teachers working at higher secondary schools, five gradations against each statement are given namely, Strongly Disagree (SD), Disagree (D), Undecided (UD), Agree (A) and Strongly Agree (SA) having the scores 1, 2, 3, 4 and 5 respectively for positive items and reverse scoring for negative items.

Description of Rating Scale to Assess the Occupational Stress of Teachers Working at Higher Secondary Level

The occupational stress, being a global aspect is affected by a large array of variables such as salary, promotion, experience, primary and secondary needs, opportunities for advancement, congenial working conditions, rewards, job security, competent and fair supervision, degree of participation in goal setting and perception of the employees. Occupational stress does not always lead to distress and if challenges are dealt with effectively, then growth and positive changes can result in an individual. The challenge lies in providing the tools required to handle the effective management of workplace demands. A close look at the literature reveals that there are various tools available to measure the occupational stress both in western and Indian context.

The Occupational Stress Inventory-Revised (OSI-R) by Osipow (1981, 1998) is a concise measure of three domains of occupational adjustment: occupational stress, psychological strain, and coping resources. The instrument yields scores on 14 different scales ranging from 'role overload' and 'interpersonal strain' to 'self-care'. The OSI-R is comprised of 140 items in total, written at a seventh grade reading level. Respondents indicate on a 5-point rating scale, the frequency of a stress-related event.

Cooper, Sloan and Williams (1988) developed the Occupational Stress Indicator (OSI) to assess the causes and effects of stress and what coping strategies are currently being used in both groups and individuals. This includes six questionnaires each measuring different dimensions of stress. The OSI consists of 25 subscales with a total of 167 items. The scales look at sources of pressure (61 items, six subscales; intrinsic to the job, organizational role, relationships with others, career and achievement, organizational structure and climate, and home-work interface); type A behaviour (14 items, three sub scales; attitude to living, style of behaviour, and ambition); locus of control (12 items, three sub scales; organizational forces, management process, and individual influence); coping styles (28 items, six sub scales; social support, task strategies, logic, home-work relations, time management, and involvement); job satisfaction (22 items, five sub scales; achievement, value and growth, job itself, organizational design and structure, organizational processes, and personal relationships); and health (30 items, two sub scales; mental ill-health and physical ill-health). These six questionnaires focus on four closely defined areas like sources of stress, individual characteristics, coping strategies, and the effects on the individual and the organization. The Pressure Management Indicator (PMI) developed by Williams and Cooper (1998) is a 120-item self-report questionnaire developed from the Occupational Stress Indicator (OSI). The PMI is more reliable, more comprehensive, and shorter than the OSI. It provides an integrated measure of the major dimensions of occupational stress. The outcome scales measure job satisfaction, organizational satisfaction, organizational security, organizational commitment, anxiety-depression, resilience, worry, physical symptoms, and exhaustion. The stressor scales cover pressure from workload, relationships, career development, managerial responsibility, personal responsibility, home demands, and daily hassles. The moderator variables measure drive, impatience, control, decision latitude, and the coping strategies of problem focus, life work balance, and social support.

Job Stress Survey (JSS) developed by Spielberger and Vagg (1999) is a standardized, commercially available instrument designed to measure job stress as a function of job related items that are perceived to be a source of severe and frequent stress among teachers. The JSS contained two sections. Section one sought to determine teachers' perceived level of severity of 30 common job-related stressors using a scale from 1 to 9; 9 being the most stressful measure. The second section sought to determine the frequency at which teachers encountered the job-related stressor at work during the previous 6 months using a scale that ranged from zero days experienced to more than nine occurrences in the last six months (0–9+). The two responses (severity and frequency) were used to produce three stress index scores: Job Stress Index, Lack of Support Index, and Job Pressure Index. Index scores were calculated by multiplying severity scores by frequency scores. A third section was added to the questionnaire that sought teachers' personal, home, and work related information. The JSS was prepared for a paper-pencil and electronic format.

In Indian context, some of the measures were developed to measure the occupational stress among various professionals. Srivastava and Krishna (1991) developed a 13 item Functional Job Stress Scale to assess the extent of job stress which is caused from demanding but desirable job situation. Pareek (1983a and 1983c) developed and standardized the 5-point Organizational Role Stress (ORS) Scale to measure the role stresses. Fifty items ORS scale measures ten types of role stresses such as inter-role distance, role stagnation, self-role distance, role ambiguity, role expectation conflict, role overload, role erosion, resource inadequacy, personal inadequacy and role isolation. Similarly, Occupational Stress Index (OSI) developed by Srivastava and Singh (1984) purports to measure the extent of stress which employees perceive from various constituents and conditions of their job. The scale may be administered to the employees of every level operating in context of industries or other non-production organizations. The scale consists of 46 items, comprising 28 'true-keyed′ and 18 'false-keyed′ and each of which is rated on a five-point scale. The items are related to almost all relevant components of job life which cause stress in some way or other. The Occupational Stress Scale (OSS) developed by Hassan and Hassan (1998) measures a variety of stressful job situations. Participants respond by indicating their level of agreeableness to each of the 60-item statements using a five-point scale ranging from 1to 5 (*i.e.,* Never like me to Always like me). The OSS has also demonstrated a high internal consistency (Cronbach á ranged from 0.79 t 0.87). The scale also has a test-retest reliability coefficient of 0.76. Pethe *et. al.* (2001) developed Organizational Climate Scale (OCS) with 24 items assessing the employees' results, clarity of roles and sharing of information, and altruistic behaviour. Mathew (2005) used Stress Indicator to identify the sources, effects and the coping strategies of occupational stress among special education teachers in India.

Reddy (2006) developed Occupational Stress Scale to assess the extent of occupational stress among special education teachers with 46 items measuring four factors of occupational stress *viz.,* organizational structure; professional training; interpersonal and professional interactions and; instructional assignments and arrangements. Poornima (2010) adopted the Occupational Stress Rating Scale of Reddy (2006) to measure the occupational stress among special education teachers and modified it with 52 items under four dimensions *viz.,* organizational structure and climate; personal and professional efficiency; intra and interpersonal interactions and; environmental factors.

From the review of the research tools, it is understood that in western context, a good number of tools are available to assess the occupational stress among teachers in particular and other employees in general. In India too, some tools were designed to measure the occupational stress of special education teachers such as Mathew (2005), Reddy (2006) and Poornima (2010). But there were no tools to assess the stress of teachers working at higher secondary schools. The investigator felt that the tool developed by Reddy (2006) and modified by Poornima (2010) can be re-modified to assess the occupational stress of higher secondary teachers as this tool also possesses the content, face and intrinsic validity and the calculated reliability value of the tool was found to be 0.97. However, the investigator felt that home-work interface which has been left out in the tool, has to be included to know the role and impact of family as well as work environment on the stress of higher secondary teachers. Likewise, the investigator adopted the tool, modified some of the items and included certain statements under new dimension *i.e.,* home-work interface. Thus the prepared rating scale with 63 items was then given to the education experts and head masters of some higher secondary schools. Based on their suggestions, seven statements were deleted and few statements were re-modified again. Thus a final form of 56 statements was framed and arranged under the five dimensions of occupational stress.

(i) *Organizational Structure and Climate:* organizational structure and climate is one of the major potential sources of stress factors. This dimension includes items which identify the sources of stress experienced by the higher secondary teachers arising out of the organizational factors like role overload, role ambiguity, role conflict, little or no participation in decision making, stringent rules and regulations, resource constraints, and problematic instructional assignments and arrangements.

(ii) *Personal and Professional Efficiency:* The second major source of stress among teachers is the personal and professional efficiency. The statements in this dimension spots the causes of stress in teachers due to inadequate personal and professional training, poor self-efficacy and management, and technological advancement in higher secondary education.

(iii) *Intra and Interpersonal Interactions:* The quality of intra and interpersonal relationship at work plays a dominant role in determining the job behaviour and stress among teachers. The factors such as negative feelings in teachers; strained relationship with colleagues, students, parents, administration and paraprofessionals are included as stressors in this dimension.

(iv) *Home-Work Interface:* Potential stressors that exist in the life of the teacher, outside the work arena and affecting behaviour at work, which require consideration when assessing the sources and impact of teacher stress. Potential

stressors include stressful life events, pressure resulting from conflict between organizational and family demands, financial difficulties, and conflicts between organizational and personal beliefs. In the case of teachers, the main sources of stress from home-work interface are those resulting from dual-career couples and relationships between work and family.

(v) *Environmental Factors:* This dimension includes a set of factors in work setting causing stress among teachers that are related to the violence and danger caused by the pupils and co-workers, reward structure and recognition, negative publicity, and physical working conditions.

Thus in the final form of the occupational stress rating scale, 56 statements assessing the sources of stress along with the specific directions for the respondents to fill the rating scale was given. All the statements are framed in negative format. The distribution of statements under each dimension is given hereunder.

Distribution of Statements in the Occupational Stress Rating Scale

Occupational Stress Dimensions	Serial Number of the Statements	Total number of Statements
Organizational Structure and Climate	1,2,3,4,5,6,7,8,9,10,11,12,13,14	14
Personal and Professional Efficiency	15,16,17,18,19,20,21,22,23,24,25,26	12
Inter and Intrapersonal Relations	27,28,29,30,31,32,33,34,35,36,37,38	12
Home-work Interface	39,40,41,42,43,44	06
Environmental Factors	45,46,47,48,49,50,51,52,53,54,55,56	12
	Total	**= 56**

To measure the occupational stress of higher secondary teachers, against each statement five gradations are given namely, Strongly Disagree (SD), Disagreree (D), Undecided (UD), Agree (A), and Strongly Agree (SA) having the scores 1, 2, 3, 4 and 5 respectively.

Description of Rating Scale to Assess the Job Performance of Teachers Working at Higher Secondary Level

To develop a rating scale to assess the job performance of teachers working at higher secondary level, the investigator has prepared the statements to measure the job performance of higher secondary teachers. The investigator went through some of the tools developed to assess the job performance and reviewed the literature to frame the statements.

Kulsum Teacher Effectiveness Scale developed by Kulsum (2000) has 60 items. The items were constructed based on five areas related to teaching *i.e.,* preparation and planning for teaching; classroom management; knowledge of subject matter, its delivery and presentation including black board summary; teacher characteristics and;

interpersonal relations. This scale was developed both for the teachers self-rating as well as for the assessment of teachers by their respective head teachers. Haseen Taj (2004) developed the Teacher's Participation in School Administration Scale with 27 items. The dimensions covered in this scale are planning, organizing, communications, controlling and evaluation. This scale was also aimed at assessing the teachers' job performance by their own self-ratings and also by their respective head teachers.

Campbell (1990; Campbell *et. al.* 1993) provided one of the first large scale attempts to integrate the numerous dimensions of performance into a comprehensive model. According to Campbell, the latent structure of job performance can be modeled using the following eight general factors:

1. job-specific task proficiency;
2. non-job-specific task proficiency;
3. written and oral communication;
4. demonstrating effort;
5. maintaining personal discipline;
6. facilitating peer and team performance;
7. supervision/leadership; and
8. management/administration.

According to Campbell, these eight factors represent the highest-order factors that can be useful for describing performance in every job in the occupational domain, although some factors may not be relevant for all jobs. Similarly, Borman and Motowidlo (1993) outlined the conceptual basis for expanding the criterion domain beyond task performance to include elements of contextual performance. The authors describe five categories of contextual performance as follows:

1. volunteering to carryout task activities that are not formally part of the job;
2. persisting with extra enthusiasm when necessary;
3. helping and cooperating with others;
4. following organizational rules and procedures; and
5. endorsing, supporting, and defending organizational objectives.

Using meta-analytic techniques, Viswesvaran (1993) cumulated studies reporting correlations between various measures of job performance. Next, he grouped the large number of measures into 25 conceptually distinct categories (*e.g.,* quality of performance, communication skills, compliance and acceptance of authority). Based on an extensive literature review, he identified five themes which captured the vast number of performance measures utilised in the literature and sorted the 25 measures into these groups. The groups he utilised are as follows:

- Productivity,
- Conscientiousness,
- Interpersonal skills,
- Withdrawal (*e.g.,* absenteeism, turnover), and
- Measures of overall job performance.

For the present study, the investigator was in need of an appropriate tool to measure the job performance of higher secondary teachers. The investigator could not able to identify the suitable scale to measure the job performance of higher secondary teachers and hence decided to construct the required tool based on the literature reviewed. The theories presented by Campbell (1990), Borman and Motowidlo (1993), and Viswesvaran (1993) are the groundwork upon which the present rating scale to assess the job performance of teachers has been constructed. Understanding of the structure and composition of job performance lags behind the understanding of predictors and outcomes of successful job performance. For this reason, efforts directed at identifying generalizable dimensions are particularly valuable. As noted by Viswesvaran (1993): developing theories of job performance for each task (or even job) will hinder the development of a general theoretical understanding of the construct of job performance. Further, empirically identifying dimensions of performance with generalizable content represents the first step in the development of instruments that could be used to obtain general criterion data across a broad range of jobs.

At the initial stage, the draft pool of 106 statements were prepared and arranged under the four dimensions *viz.*, task oriented behaviour; interpersonally oriented behaviour; managerial capabilities and personal discipline and leadership qualities. Care was taken to present the statements in a clear and concise form for better understanding. This draft pool of items was given to the experts and was discussed critically about the performance of teachers at higher secondary level. Based on the discussion, the statements were further refined to avoid ambiguity and repetition. At the final stage, the rating scale with 52 statements is arranged under the following four dimensions of job performance of higher secondary teachers.

(i) *Task Oriented Behaviour:* Task oriented behaviours are the part of an individual's job. They are the core substantive tasks that delineate one job from another. An individual's or a teacher's performance can be assessed in terms of effort, either day to day, or when there are extraordinary circumstances. This factor reflects the degree to which people commit themselves to job tasks. Written and oral communication tasks refer to activities where the teacher is evaluated, not on the content of a message necessarily, but on the adeptness with which he/she deliver the communication. Besides this, a teacher is also assessed on the basis of his/her content knowledge, efficiency in handling the teaching aids, methodology adopted for teaching, evaluation process, knowledge enrichment, and attitude and aptitude towards teaching.

(ii) *Interpersonally Oriented Behaviour:* Interpersonally oriented behaviours are represented by any interaction the teacher has with others. These can be task related or non-task related. It includes behaviours that are not targeting an institution's goal. Both the quality of interpersonal relationships and lack of social support have an impact on the effective performance of teachers. Nevertheless, it is clear that negative interpersonal relations and the absence of support from colleagues, superiors, and parents will lead to unhealthy atmosphere in the work environment. Here, the interpersonal relation refers to the teachers' healthy

relationship with the students, parents, colleagues and superiors, and other staff in the institution.

(iii) *Managerial Capabilities:* Managerial and administrative performance entails those aspects of a job which serve the group or institution but do not involve direct supervision. A managerial task would be setting an institutional goal or responding to external stimuli to assist the students in achieving its goals. In addition, a teacher might be responsible for monitoring group and individual students' progress towards goals and monitoring institutional resources. Examples include planning and organizing, guiding and motivating, developing others, communicating, maintaining good working relationships, voluntarily involves in school activities, significantly contributes to the school's progress, problem solving, and monitoring and controlling.

(iv) *Personal Discipline and Leadership Qualities:* The performance domain might also include an aspect of personal discipline. Leadership effectiveness refers to the ability to influence others and achieve collective goals. In teaching profession where teachers work closely or are highly interdependent, performance may include the degree to which a teacher helps out the students and his or her colleagues. This might include acting as a good role model, coaching, giving advice, tolerance and patience, accommodativeness in work environment, or helping maintain institutional goals. The teacher will be relied upon to undertake many of the things delineated under the leadership factor and in addition will be responsible for meting out rewards and punishments.

Thus in the final form of the job performance rating scale, 52 statements under the four dimensions *i.e.,* Task Oriented Behaviour, Interpersonally Oriented Behaviour, Managerial Capabilities, and Personal Discipline and Leadership Qualities for assessing the job performance of higher secondary teachers along with specific directions for the respondents to fill the rating scale was given. To avoid the tendency of giving stereotyped responses, both positive and negative items are included in the rating scale. The distribution of statements under each dimension is given hereunder.

Distribution of Statements in the Job Performance Rating Scale

Job Performance Dimensions	Serial Number of the Statements	Total Number of Statements
Task Oriented Behaviour	1,2,3,4*5,6,7,8,9*10,11,12,13, 14*15,16,17,18*19,20,21,22,23,24	24
Interpersonally Oriented Behaviour	25,26,27,28,29*30,31,32,33,34,35,36	12
Managerial Capabilities	37*,38,39,40*41,42,43*,44*	08
Personal Discipline/ Leadership Qualities	45,46,47,48,49*50,51,52*	08
	Total =	52

* represents negative statements

To measure the job performance of higher secondary teachers, against each statement five gradations are given namely, Always (A), Often (O), Sometimes (S), Rarely (R), and Never (N) having the scores 5, 4, 3, 2 and 1 respectively for positive items and reverse scoring for negative items.

Description of Rating Scale to Assess the Job Performance of Teachers Working at Higher Secondary Level by their Principal's/H.M's

To develop the rating scale to assess the job performance of teachers working at higher secondary level by their Principal's/H.M's, the investigator has constructed the statements to measure the job performance of higher secondary teachers. The investigator went through some of the tools developed to assess the job performance and reviewed the literature to construct the statements.

The principal's/H.M's rating scale is developed based on the rating scale developed by the investigator to assess the job performance of higher secondary teachers. Twenty five statements related to the proficiency of teachers were developed considering the four main dimensions of the teachers' job performance rating scale *i.e.,* task oriented behaviour; interpersonally oriented behaviour; managerial capabilities and personal discipline and; leadership qualities. The prepared rating scale was given to the education experts for their opinion. Based on their suggestions, few statements were deleted and few statements were modified. Thus the final form of 20 statements was framed and arranged under the following four dimensions.

(i) *Task Oriented Behaviour:* In this aspect, the Principal/H.M has to assess the teacher based on the teacher's content knowledge, written and oral skills, efficiency in handling the teaching-learning materials, adaptation of proper teaching methodology, evaluation techniques, knowledge enrichment programmes, attitude and aptitude towards the teaching profession.

(ii) *Interpersonally Oriented Behaviour:* Here teachers were assessed by their relationship with others. The teachers were expected to maintain healthy relationships with the students, parents, their colleagues and their superiors for the congenial working atmosphere to coexist.

(iii) *Managerial Capabilities:* Managerial abilities of the teachers were assessed based on how well the teacher voluntarily involves in school activities, follows rules and regulations of the school and significantly contributes to the school's progress.

(iv) *Personal Discipline and Leadership Qualities:* Teachers are the role models to their students. Teachers are assessed for their discipline by observing their clean habits, punctuality, tolerance and patience in handling the students, fluency in their language while dealing with the subject, accommodativeness in their work environment and the circumstantial ability to face the situation.

Thus, in the final form of the principal's/H.M's assessment of teachers job performance rating scale, 20 statements assessing the job performance of higher secondary teachers along with the specific directions for the respondents to fill the rating scale was given. The distribution of statements under each dimension is given hereunder.

Distribution of Statements in Job Performance Rating Scale Assessed by the Principal's/H.M's

Job Performance Dimensions	Serial Number of the Statements	Total Number of Statements
Task Oriented Behaviour	1,2,3,4,5,6,7	07
Interpersonally Oriented Behaviour	8,9,10,11	04
Managerial Capabilities	12,13,14	03
Personal Discipline/ Leadership Qualities	15,16,17,18,19,20	06
	Total =	**20**

To measure the job performance of higher secondary teachers by their Principal's/ H.M's, five gradations against each statement are given namely, Always (A), Often (O), Sometimes (S), Rarely (R), and Never (N) having the scores 5, 4, 3, 2 and 1 respectively.

PILOT STUDY

A pilot study has been carried out by the investigator to find out the suitability of the test items for the investigation. The pilot study aimed to find out the reliability and validity of the rating scales developed and used in the study. The Emotional Intelligence Scale, Occupational Stress Scale, and Job Performance Scale were administrated to 30 teachers (9% of the total sample) working at higher secondary schools, randomly selected from two schools from each district and principal's assessment of teachers scale was administered to 4 principals (9% of the total sample) of the same schools where the teachers were assessed. The teachers and principals were oriented to rate the statements of the rating scales to indicate their responses using the gradations. The completed rating scales were collected and statistically analyzed to establish the reliability and validity of the tools.

RELIABILITY OF THE RESEARCH TOOLS

The test reliability means the consistency with which a set of test scores measures what they do measure. It relates the accuracy with which skills and knowledge are measured (Slavin, 1987). If a tool is reliable, it reveals similar results in various situations. Reliability is a necessary condition for validity. Reliability co-efficient provides the most revealing statistical index of validity that is ordinarily available. Garrett (1966) describes four methods of establishing the reliability of a test. They are:

(i) Test-retest method,

(ii) Alternate or parallel forms,

(iii) Split-half method, and

(iv) Rational equivalence method or Kuder-Richardson method.

Of these four procedures, the split-half method is regarded by many as the best of the methods for measuring test reliability (Garrett and Wordsworth, 1981). This method is used by many investigators because the data for calculating reliability are obtained from one occasion so that variations brought about by differences between the two testing situations are eliminated. In split-half method, the tool is divided into two equivalent halves and the correlation was found for these half-tests by using the following Karl Pearson's Correlation Co-efficient formula.

$$r_{½} = \frac{N\Sigma xy - [\Sigma x][\Sigma y]}{\sqrt{[N\Sigma x^2 - (\Sigma x)^2][N\Sigma y^2 - (\Sigma y)^2]}}$$

Where,

$r_{½}$ = Correlation co-efficient

x = Score obtained for one half of the test

y = Score obtained for second half of the test

Σx = Sum of x scores

Σy = Sum of y scores

Σx^2 = Sum of squared x scores

Σy^2 = Sum of squared y scores

(Σx^2) = Squared value of the sum of x scores

(Σy^2) = Squared value of the sum of y scores

Σxy = Sum of the products of x and y scores

N = Total number of sample

From the reliability of the half-test, the self-correlation of the whole test is then estimated by using Spearman Brown's Proficiency formula.

$$r_{11} = \frac{2r_{½}}{1 + r_{½}}$$

Where,

$r_{½}$ = Reliability co-efficient of the half test

r_{11} = Reliability co-efficient of the whole test

The obtained reliability values for the tools used in the study through split-half method are presented here under.

Name of the Scale	Reliability value through Half test Reliability $r_{½}$	Split-Half Method Whole Test Reliability r_{11}
(Emotional Intelligence Rating Scale	0.72	0.83
Occupational Stress Rating Scale	0.88	0.93
Job Performance Rating Scale	0.93	0.96
Principal's/HM's Rating Scale	0.91	0.95

From the above, it is evident that the reliability values of the rating scales used in the study is high and hence, the rating scales used in this study possess high reliability indicating their suitability for the present investigation.

VALIDITY OF THE RESEARCH TOOLS

According to Best (1989), validity is the quality of a data gathering instrument or procedure that enables it to measure what it is supposed to measure. The validity of a test enables it to measure what it is supposed to measure. It refers to the degree to which extent the test scores predict some practical criterion measures. The index of reliability is sometimes taken as a measure of validity (Garrett and Wordsworth, 1981). Several kinds of validity are ascertained to the rating scales used in the study. They are:

Content Validity

The content validity shows the adequacy of the content of a test. This form of validity is estimated by evaluating the relevance of the test items individually and as a whole. The items in the rating scales are based on the review of related literature and the tools already available. Also, a logical examination of statements of the rating scales was done by the panel of experts. Their suggestions have been taken into account to enhance the contents and quality of items. In view of the changes made in the language, content, coverage and format of the items, it can be said that the rating scales used in this study possess content validity.

Face Validity

This is the term used to characterize test materials that appear to measure what the test desires to measure and appears to those it is meant, to experts, examiners, educationists and the like. That is, the test items should be related to the variable that is being measured. It is clear that all the items in the respective tools measure the specific variable under study *i.e.,* emotional intelligence, occupational stress, and job performance of teachers working at the higher secondary level.

Intrinsic Validity

Intrinsic validity shows, how well, the obtained scores measure the test's true score component. The square root of the reliability is the intrinsic validity of the tools. The obtained intrinsic validity of emotional intelligence rating scale (0.91), occupational stress rating scale (0.96), teachers' job performance rating scale (0.98), and the principal's assessment of teacher's job performance rating scale (0.97) were high and hence the tools used in the study possessed intrinsic validity.

Criterion Validity

In a situation of some observable criterion, the tool's validity can be investigated by seeing how good an indicator it is. This approach leads to two categories of validity *i.e.,* predictive and concurrent validity. Predictive validity is concerned with how the total can forecast a future criterion and concurrent validity with how well it can describe a present one. The results in the succeeding chapter show that the four rating scales have both concurrent and predictive validity.

LOCALE AND SAMPLE OF THE STUDY

The higher secondary education of Vellore district is divided into two divisions *i.e.,* Vellore Educational District and Tirupattur Educational District with 10 blocks in each division. The 10 blocks in Vellore Educational District are; Arakkonam, Anaicut, Arcot, Vellore, Sholinghur, Nemili, Kaveripakkam, Kaniyambadi, Thimiri and Walaja and the 10 blocks in Tirupattur Educational District are; Alangayam, Gudiyatham, Kandhili, K.V.Kuppam, Jolarpet, Madhanur, Katpadi, Tirupattur, Parnambut and Natrampalli. In each block, both government and private schools are functioning. For the purpose of the study, the investigator has selected 2 blocks in each division, considering the type of the school the teachers are working-in (government/private) and location of the school (rural/urban), by using simple random sampling technique. The selected blocks are Vellore and Walaja Blocks in Vellore Educational District, and Gudiatham and Katpadi Blocks in Tirupattur Educational District.

In Vellore Block, there are 16 government and 8 private schools; Walaja Block, there are 10 government and 8 private schools; Gudiatham Block, there are 11 government and 4 private schools; and in Katpadi Block, 15 government and 10 private schools covering 52 government and 30 private schools in total, are functioning in both rural and urban areas. For the purpose of the study, the investigator has randomly selected 4 government and 4 private schools in each block taking the overall total to 16 government and 16 private schools in all the four blocks of both the Vellore and Tirupattur Educational districts, considering the location of the schools by using simple random sampling technique. All the teachers working in the selected government and private schools were the sample of the study *i.e.,* 79 teachers from Vellore Block, 83 teachers from Walaja Block, 81 teachers from Gudiatham Block and 84 teachers from Katpadi Block, taking the total to 327 higher secondary teachers. The Principal's / H.M's of the respective 32 schools were also the sample of the study to assess the job performance of the teachers working under their preview. The background characteristics of the sample are given hereunder.

Background Characteristics of the Sample

Name of the Variable	Number of Teachers
Gender	
Male	139
Female	188
Age	
Up to 35 years	114
36-45 years	129
46 years and above	84
Community	
OC	44
BC	201
MBC and SC/ST	82

Contd..

Marital Status	
Married	264
Unmarried	63
Educational Qualification	
PG with B.Ed. and M.Ed.	206
PG with M.Ed. and M.Phil.	121
Subject Teaching	
Languages	84
Science	119
Mathematics and Computers	67
Commerce	57
Salary per Month	
Upto Rs.10,000/-	91
Rs. 10,001/- to 15,000/-	77
Rs. 15,001/- to 20,000/-	88
Rs. 20,001/- and above	71
Type of School the Teachers Working-in	
Government	159
Private	168
Location of the School	
Rural	166
Urban 161	
Years of Experience	
1 to 15 years	179
16 years and above	148

Out of 139 men and 188 women, who constituted the total sample of 327 teachers, 264 teachers were married and 63 teachers were unmarried. 114 teachers were coming under 35 years and below age group, 129 teachers were falling under 36-45 years and 84 teachers were belonging to 46 years and above age group. With regard to community, 44 teachers were from OC category, 201 teachers were from BC category and 82 belonging to MBC and SC/ST category. Under educational qualification, 206 teachers possessed PG with B.Ed. and M.Ed. and 121 teachers were having PG with M.Ed. and M.Phil. When subject teaching is considered, 84 teachers were handling languages, 119 teachers were teaching science, 67 teachers were taking mathematics and computer science classes, and 57 were commerce teachers. With regard to salary, 91 teachers were receiving up to Rs. 10,000/-, 77 teachers were receiving salary between Rs. 10,001/- to Rs. 15,000/-, 88 teachers were receiving salary between Rs. 15,001/- to Rs. 20,000/-, and 71 teachers were receiving salary of Rs. 20,001/- and above per month. Of the total sample, 159 teachers were working in government schools, 168 teachers were working in private schools, 166 teachers were from rural schools and 161 were from urban schools. When experience is considered, 179 teachers possess 1 to 15 years of experience and 148 teachers were with 16 years and more.

RATIONALE BEHIND THE LOCALE AND SAMPLE SELECTION

Vellore is a fast developing city in the Vellore district of Tamil Nadu state. In 2008, the 142 year old municipality was made into a City Corporation. The Vellore city corporation, at 392 square kilometers (151 sq miles), is the largest in Tamil Nadu, surpassing Chennai City Corporation, which is 182 square kilometers (70 sq miles). It is considered as one of the oldest cities in South India and lies on the banks of the river Palar, on the site of Vellore Fort. Vellore is a major transit point for travelers, a forerunner of medical facilities and is emerging as a centre for higher education. With the population of 39, 28,106 lakhs, Vellore is economically well developing district and is one of the commercial hub in the state. Even though Vellore is very famous for its higher education in terms of medical education provided by the century old Christian Medical College, technical education provided by the world famous Vellore Institute of Technology and the newly established Thiruvalluvar University for higher education; it is very backward in providing good Higher Secondary education. Eventhough the pass percentage is 80; it stands at 28th position out of 32 districts in the state's higher secondary results of 2012. It is far behind the smallest districts, Virudhunagar, which stood at first place with 94.68 per cent and Namakkal, which bagged all the top 3 ranks for the current year in. This is the main reason for choosing Vellore as the locale of the study. The rationale behind choosing higher secondary teachers as the sample is, it is the most crucial period for both the students as well as the teachers. It is the turning point in the life of every student who is moving on to the higher ladder in his/her student career, which mainly depends on the maximum effort of the teachers. Here the teachers' role is highly motivating and it is very necessary to know how well the teacher is coping, adapting and giving his/her best in teaching and also in moulding the career of these adolescents as it will be the final years of the students in their school environment and also the students will be at the fag end of their teenage. Hence an in-depth study can be done, only if the investigator concentrates on such a sample.

DATA COLLECTION

The investigator has obtained prior permission from the Chief Education Officer of Vellore district to visit the government and private higher secondary schools in both rural and urban areas of Vellore Educational District as well as Thirupattur Educational District. The investigator personally visited the higher secondary schools to collect the data from the teachers and Principals/Head Master's working in those schools. Good rapport was established with the Principal/Head Masters and teachers before administering the tools. They were explained about the purpose of the study. It was emphasized that the data will be kept confidential and were used only for research purpose, and they were instructed not to leave any items without rating. The developed rating scales were administered to the higher secondary teachers to know their emotional intelligence, occupational stress and job performance. In the beginning, the teachers were asked to provide their personal information in part-I of the emotional intelligence rating scale. Later, they were oriented as how to rate their gradations against the statements under each dimension of emotional intelligence rating scale. Similarly, the occupational stress rating scale and job performance rating scale were administered to the higher secondary teachers. Teachers were directed to go through the instructions before rating the statements in the tools. No time limit was fixed for responding to the rating scales. The rating scales were provided to the higher secondary teachers with a request to fill and return the same within a handful of days.

The Principals/Head Masters' of the schools, from where the higher secondary teachers' data was collected, were given the rating scale with a special request to assess the job performance of the same teachers working in their respective higher secondary schools. They were asked to assess the teachers objectively in their own free time. The investigator personally went to collect the filled-in rating scales from the teachers as well as the Principal/Head Masters of the respective schools.

STATISTICAL TECHNIQUES USED IN THE STUDY

The collected data was analyzed by using appropriate statistical techniques such as number and percentage, mean, SD, t-test, F-test, correlations and stepwise multiple regression analysis with the help of SPSS package. To findout the number and percentage of higher secondary teachers coming under low, moderate and high levels of emotional intelligence, mean and standard deviation of emotional intelligence scores have been computed. By using mean ± 1SD, the number and percentage of teachers coming under low, moderate and high level of emotional intelligence was calculated. The same procedure is followed for identifying the number and percentage of higher secondary teachers with low, moderate and high levels of occupational stress and job performance. In the second stage, to identify the level of emotional intelligence of higher secondary teachers, mean and SD of the emotional intelligence scores have been computed for each statement. Mean ± 1 SD is used to categorize the statements into low, moderate and high levels of emotional intelligence among higher secondary teachers. Similar procedure was used for identifying the low, moderate and high level statements leading to occupational stress and job performance among higher secondary teachers.

To find out the effect of higher secondary teachers gender, age, community, marital status, educational qualification, nature of the subjects the teachers handling, salary they receive, type of school they are working-in, location of the school and years of experience on their emotional intelligence- mean and standard deviation; t-test and F-test had been worked out. Whenever two groups are involved in a variable, t-test had been used. F-test was used when more than two groups are involved in a variable. Similar procedure was used to find out the effect of personal variables on the occupational stress and job performance of higher secondary teachers.

Correlations were computed to findout the relationship between emotional intelligence and occupational stress; emotional intelligence and job performance and; occupational stress and job performance of higher secondary teachers.

To find out the contribution of the independent variables (gender, age, community, marital status, educational qualification, nature of the subjects the teachers handling, salary they receive, type of school they are working-in, location of the school, and years of experience) on the dependent variables (emotional intelligence, occupational stress, and job performance), stepwise multiple regression analysis was carried out. This analysis aimed to predict, to what extent and to how far the independent variables contribute to the dependent variables (emotional intelligence, occupational stress, and job performance) of higher secondary teachers. Also, using stepwise multiple regression analysis, the contribution of independent variable-emotional intelligence dimensions to the dimensions of dependent variables-occupational stress and job performance; and independent variable-occupational stress dimensions to the dimensions of dependent variable-job performance has been worked out.

The obtained results are presented and discussed in detail in the Chapter 5.

5

RESULTS AND DISCUSSION

INTRODUCTION

APPLICATION OF STATISTICAL TECHNIQUES, analyzing and interpreting the collected data plays an important role in any scientific investigation. The collected data must be carefully processed, systematically classified and tabulated, scientifically analyzed and rationally concluded. This chapter deals with the analysis and interpretation of data collected for the study. The results and discussion are presented in two parts. The Part-I deals with the descriptive analysis. In this part, the description of the sample with background characteristics; number and percentage of teachers with low, moderate, and high levels of emotional intelligence, occupational stress and job performance; mean scores and level of emotional intelligence, occupational stress and job performance of higher secondary teachers were analyzed.

The Part-II deals with the differential analysis, where the effect of personal variables (gender, marital status, educational qualification, type of school the teachers are working-in, location of the school, years of experience age, community, nature of the subjects the teachers handling, and salary they receive) on the emotional intelligence, occupational stress, and job performance of higher secondary teachers was analyzed. Further, the relationship between emotional intelligence, occupational stress and job performance dimensions of higher secondary teachers were calculated. In addition, the relationship between emotional intelligence and occupational stress; emotional intelligence and job performance; and occupational stress and job performance were worked out.

Further, the contribution of the independent variables (gender, marital status, educational qualification, type of school the teachers are working-in, location of the school, years of experience age, community, nature of the subjects the teachers handling, and salary they receive) to the dependent variables (emotional intelligence, occupational stress and job performance) of higher secondary teachers have been calculated. Likewise, the contribution of the independent variable *i.e.,* dimensions of emotional intelligence to the dependent variables *i.e.,* the dimensions of occupational stress and job performance; and independent variable *i.e.,* occupational stress dimensions to the dependent variable *i.e.,* the dimensions of job performance have been calculated.

Part — I: Descriptive Analysis

DESCRIPTIVE ANALYSIS OF EMOTIONAL INTELLIGENCE (EI), OCCUPATIONAL STRESS (OS) AND JOB PERFORMANCE (JP) OF HIGHER SECONDARY TEACHERS

In this part, the description of the background sample of the study is presented in Table 5.1. The independent variables of the higher secondary teachers like gender, marital status, educational qualification, type of school the teachers are working-in, location of the school, years of experience age, community, nature of the subjects the teachers handling, and salary they receive have been discussed in detail. In addition, the number and percentage of higher secondary teachers falling under low, moderate and high emotional intelligence, occupational stress and job performance have been calculated, as it is one of the major objectives of the study. For this, mean and standard deviations of the emotional intelligence, occupational stress and job performance scores have been calculated for each teacher working in the higher secondary schools. By using mean ± 1SD, the emotional intelligence, occupational stress and job performance scores of higher secondary teachers have been divided into three levels *i.e.,* low, moderate and high. Accordingly, the teachers coming under emotional intelligence scores of 3.70 and above are categorized as high, 3.00 to 3.69 are moderate and 2.99 and below are low. Similarly, the teachers with occupational stress scores 3.00 and above are grouped as high, 2.26 to 2.99 are moderate and 2.25 and below are grouped as low. Likewise, the teachers with mean job performance scores 4.00 and above are categorized as high, 2.71 to 3.99 are moderate and teachers with scores 2.70 and below are grouped as low. The number and percentage of teachers falling under each category have been worked out and are presented in Table 5.1.

Likewise, to identify the emotional competencies possessed by the higher secondary teachers, sources of occupational stress and job performance of the teachers, mean and standard deviation for each aspect of the emotional intelligence, occupational stress and job performance have been computed for the total sample of the study. By using mean ± 1SD, the statements have been divided in each scale into three categories *i.e.,* low, moderate and high. This analysis facilitates to identify the emotional abilities, sources of occupational stress and job performance of the higher secondary teachers. The obtained results were presented in the form of tables and are discussed in Tables 5.2 to 5.4. Further, to assess the job performance of higher secondary teachers' by their self-ratings and ratings by their respective Principal's/H.M's, mean and SD for each aspect has been computed and by using mean ± 1SD, the statements have been divided into three categories *i.e.,* low, moderate and high. The obtained results are presented together in Table 5.1.

Number and Percentage of Higher Secondary Teachers with Low, Moderate and High EI, OS and JP

Table 5.1 illustrates the number and percentage of teachers falling under low, moderate and high level of Emotional Intelligence (EI), Occupational Stress (OS) and Job Performance (JP).

Table 5.1: Number and Percentage of Teachers Working in Higher Secondary Schools with Low, Moderate and High Levels of EI, OS and JP

Level	Number and Percentage of Teachers		
	EI	OS	JP
Low	62 (18.9)	36 (11.0)	74 (22.6)
Moderate	211 (64.5)	249 (76.1)	172 (52.6)
High	54 (16.5)	42 (12.8)	80 (24.5)

Note: Number in the brackets denotes percentage

From Table 5.1 it is clear that, out of 327 teachers working in higher secondary schools, 211 (64.5%) teachers possess moderate level of emotional intelligence, followed by 62 (18.9%) teachers with low level of emotional intelligence and the remaining 54 (16.5%) with high level of emotional intelligence. The present findings are in agreement with the results of David and Roy (2010), Edannur (2010), Neelakandan (2007) and Indu (2009). In case of occupational stress too, majority of the higher secondary teachers *i.e.* 249 (76.1%) teachers were experiencing moderate level of occupational stress, followed by 42 (12.8%) teachers falling under high level of occupational stress and 36 (11.0%) with low level of occupational stress. These findings go along with the findings of John (2007), Reddy (2006), Reddy and Poornima (2007), Rao (2010), and Ushasri (2007). With regard to job performance of higher secondary teachers, 172 (52.6%) teachers were coming under moderate level of performance followed by 80 (24.5%) teachers with high level of performance and 74 (22.6%) with low level of job performance.

From the above, it is inferred that, more than 83 per cent of the teachers working in higher secondary schools possess moderate and low levels of emotional intelligence; whereas, 88 per cent of higher secondary teachers were experiencing moderate and high level of occupational stress. Likewise, around 77 per cent of higher secondary teachers were showing moderate and high level of job performance. This trend indicates that there is a need to look into the emotional competencies possessed by the higher secondary teachers that help them to balance their emotions and manage their various sources of occupational stress that enables them to perform better in their roles as teachers. It is necessary to figure out the effective ingredients of emotional intelligence, various sources of stress and the factors responsible for the better performance of teachers in the higher secondary schools.

Level of Emotional Intelligence of Higher Secondary Teachers

Gold and Roth (1993) identified self-awareness as a key component for managing stress and defined it as 'a process of getting in touch with their feelings and behaviours'. Increased self-awareness involves a more accurate understanding of how students affect the teachers own emotional processes and behaviours and how teachers affect students, as well. Teacher's self-awareness of primary emotions triggers and improves their chances of making rational decisions based on conscious choice, rather than unconscious emotional conditioning. Further, they should be aware of their own abilities and skills to carryout the multiple roles and responsibilities. Self-awareness of teachers helps them to stay with confidence in establishing the objectives, plan and conduct the activities for a balanced programme of instruction. (Table 5.2)

Table 5.2: Mean Scores and Level of Emotional Intelligence of Higher Secondary Teachers

S.No.	Statements	Mean	Level
1	2	3	4
I.	**Self-awareness**		
1.	Able to identify and distinguish my own emotions.	3.89	H
2.	Defend myself when I receive negative feedback in the work environment.	3.27	M
3.	I am unaware of my own feelings.	3.60	M
4.	I know how feelings impact my own actions.	3.92	H
5.	I acknowledge my own strengths and weaknesses.	3.33	M
6.	My ability in self-evaluation has helped me to over-come many difficult situations.	3.25	M
7.	Even under severe criticism, I do what I believe in.	2.33	L
8.	I know my priorities very clearly.	3.95	H
9.	I do not feel good about myself on many situations.	3.16	M
10.	I feel good about myself when I look at both my good and bad points.	3.09	M
11.	I am happy with the way I look at the things.	3.88	H
12.	I feel confident that I can do my Job up to the expectations.	3.17	M
II.	**Self-management**		
13.	I find it difficult to control my anger.	2.43	L
14.	I maintain patience on many occasions.	2.24	L
15.	Ready to change my ideas and goals based on new information to fit into the situation.	3.36	M
16.	I have the presence of mind in any situation.	3.00	M

Contd..

1	2	3	4
17.	I can behave calmly even in stressful situations.	2.40	L
18.	I feel restless on occasions when new ideas and information are to be accepted.	3.06	M
19.	I am ready to admit my mistakes when it demands.	3.11	M
20.	It is not possible to do the duties entrusted to me with responsibility and commitment.	3.04	M
21.	I am able to maintain the standards of honesty and integrity.	3.25	M
22.	I take calculated risks to reach the goals.	3.14	M
23.	I initiate actions to create possibilities for the future.	3.14	M
24.	I hesitate to take up new assignments.	2.45	L
25.	My optimism motivates me to overcome any hurdles and go forward.	3.15	M
26.	It is difficult for me to reach even small goals.	3.19	M
27.	Always act on my own values even when there is a significant risk.	2.90	L
28.	I am well organized in my work.	2.51	L
II.	**Social Awareness**		
29.	It is very hard to see people suffer.	3.07	M
30.	I do not interfere with the feelings of others and help them to overcome.	2.36	L
31.	I am able to confront with the unethical actions of others.	2.49	L
32.	I am capable of using teaching aids to cater to the needs of the special students.	3.17	M
33.	I am available to the students even after the school hours, if they are in need.	3.88	H
34.	Sometimes, it is difficult to relate the curriculum to the diverse backgrounds of special children.	3.09	M
35.	In many situations, I understand the organizational values and unspelt out rules.	3.23	M
36.	I always work by understanding the organizational financial constraints and act accordingly.	3.17	M
37.	I always recognize the forces in the school and work to meet the requirements of the job.	3.17	M
38.	I am not fully aware of the infrastructure facilities available in the school.	3.02	M
IV.	**Social Skills**		
39.	I encourage my colleagues to work even when things are not favourable.	3.33	M

Contd..

1	2	3	4
40.	I do not insist the students to learn what they are lacking.	3.29	M
41.	I appreciate others for their success.	3.89	H
42.	I try to provide ongoing mentoring or coaching to my colleagues.	3.32	M
43.	It is easy for me to make friends.	3.37	M
44.	It is not easy to get along with others in work situations.	3.17	M
45.	I feel it difficult to seek help from others when needed.	2.51	L
46.	I interact well and provide guidance and counseling to the students and their parents.	3.55	M
47.	I maintain good relations and co-operate with the school personnel.	3.92	H
48.	I can lead others by setting an example.	3.54	M
49.	I have clear ideas to realize the vision of the school I am working.	3.90	H
50.	I try to move away from the conflict situations.	3.08	M
51.	I always like to be the active partner in solving the conflicts in my school.	3.48	M
52.	I quarrel with others when things have not favoured me.	3.88	H
53	I adopt new teaching techniques to make learning more effective.	3.91	H
54.	I believe that working with group leads to failure.	3.25	M
55.	I establish and maintain close relationship with other professionals at work.	3.89	H
56.	I will not convince by appealing to the students and parents interest.	2.34	L

Note: Levels of Emotional Intelligence - Low: 2.99 and below; Moderate: 3.00 to 3.69; High: 3.70 and above

From Table 5.2 it is clear that, under the *self-awareness* dimension, the teachers working in higher secondary schools possess moderate level of self-awareness in defending themselves while receiving negative feedback (S.No.2), knowing their own feelings (S.No.3), acknowledging their own strengths and weaknesses (S.No.5), self-evaluating themselves to overcome difficult situations (S.No.6), feeling good about themselves (S.No.9) while looking at their own positive and negative points (S.No.10) and feeling confident in delivering their duty upto the expectations of the job (S.No.12). The same teachers are showing high level of emotional intelligence in identifying and distinguishing their own emotions (S.No.1), knowing their feelings and its impact on actions (S.No.4), knowing their priorities clearly (S.No.8) and in being happy with the way of looking at the things (S.No.11). Contrary to this, the teachers possess low level of self awareness in only one aspect *i.e.,* continuing to act on their beliefs even under criticism (S.No.7).

In the dimension *self-management*, the higher secondary teachers possess moderate level of emotional intelligence on the aspects of having ability to change ideas and goals based on new information to fit into new situations (S.No.15), having presence of mind (S.No.16), feeling restless in accepting new ideas and information (S.No.18), ready to accept the mistakes when situation demands (S.No.19), impossible to do the entrusted duties with responsibility and commitment (S.No.20), ability to maintain the standards of honesty and integrity (S.No.21), ready to take calculated risks to reach the goals (S.No.22), initiating actions to create possibilities for the future (S.No.23), motivated by optimism to overcome any hurdles to go forward (S.No.25), and sometimes it is difficult to reach even the smallest goals (S.No 26). Further, the same teachers are exhibiting low levels of self management in certain aspects such as: difficulty in controlling their over anger (S.No.13), ability to maintain patience on many occasions (S.No.14), capable of behaving calmly even in stressful situations (S.No.17), hesitate to take up new assignments (S.No.24) always acts on own values even at significant risks (S.No.27), and well organized in the work (S.No.28).

With regards to dimension of *social awareness*, the higher secondary teachers are possessing high level of social awareness by making themselves available to the students even after the school hours, if the students are in need (S.No.33). Contrary to this, the teachers are showing low level of self-management with respect to the interference in the feelings of others and helping them to overcome it (S.No.30) and ability to confront with the unethical actions of others (S.No.31). Further, the teachers are demonstrating moderate levels of social awareness on certain aspects such as; unable to see the people suffering (S.No.29), capable of handling teaching aids to cater to the needs of special children (S.No.32), sometimes finds it difficult to relate the curriculum to the diverse backgrounds of special children (S.No.34), able to understand the organizational values and unspelt rules in many situations (S.No.35), always work by understanding the organizational financial constraints and act accordingly (S.No.36), always works to meet the requirements of the job (S.No.37) and not fully aware of the infrastructure available in the school (S.No.38).

Under the *social skills* dimension, the teachers exhibit low level of social skills only in two aspects such as; difficulty in seeking help from others when it is needed (S.No.45) and not convinced by appealing to the students and parents interest (S.No.56). Their social skills are at high level in six aspects such as; appreciating others for their success (S.No.41), maintaining good relations and co-operating with the school personnel (S.No.47), having clear ideas to realize the vision of the school (S.No.49), quarrel with others when things are not in favour (S.No.52), adopt new teaching techniques to make learning more effective (S.No.53) and establishing and maintaining close relationship with other professionals at work (S.No.55). Apart from this, the higher secondary teachers are demonstrating moderate level of social skills with regard to; encouraging colleagues to work even when things are not favourable (S.No.39), do not insist the students to learn what they are lacking (S.No.40), try to provide mentoring and coaching of colleagues (S.No.42), easy to make friends (S.No.43), not easy to get along with others in the work situations (S.No.44), ready to provide guidance and counseling to the students and their parents (S.No.46), can lead others by setting an example (S.No.48), trying to move away from the conflicting situations (S.No.50), like to be active partner in solving the conflicts in the school (S.No.51) and believing that working with group leads to failure (S.No.54).

From the above, it is concluded that out of 28 personal competencies listed under 'self-awareness' and 'self-management' dimensions, the teachers working in the higher secondary schools possess moderate level of emotional intelligence in 17 aspects (self-awareness – S.No. 2, 3, 5, 6, 9, 10 and 12; self-management – S.No. 15, 16, 18, 19, 20, 21, 22, 23, 25 and 26), where as they evince low level of emotional intelligence in 7 aspects (self-awareness – S.No.7; self-management – S.No. 13, 14, 17, 24, 27 and 28) and exhibit high level of emotional intelligence in the rest of the 4 aspects (self-awareness – S.No. 1, 4, 8, 11). Likewise, in 'social competencies', out of 28 aspects, they demonstrated moderate level of emotional intelligence in 17 aspects (social awareness – S.No. 29, 32, 34, 35, 36, 37 and 38; social skills – S.No. 39, 40, 42, 43, 44, 46, 48, 50, 51 and 54). In 7 aspects (social awareness – S.No. 33; social skills – S.No. 41, 47, 49, 52, 53 and 55), the higher secondary teachers are exhibiting high level of emotional intelligence. Contrary to this, they are having low level of emotional intelligence in 4 aspects (social awareness – S.No. 30 and 31; social skills – S.No. 45 and 46).

Sources and Level of Occupational Stress of Higher Secondary Teachers

One of the major objectives of the present study is to find out the level of occupational stress of teachers working at higher secondary level. Also, this study attempts to identify the potential sources of stress among the higher secondary teachers. The potential sources of stress may be due to organizational structure and climate; personal and professional efficiency; intra and interpersonal relationships; home-work interface; and environmental factors. To identify the level of occupational stress of teachers working at higher secondary schools, mean and SD for each stressor of the occupational stress dimensions have been calculated for the whole sample of teachers working at higher secondary schools. By using mean ± 1 SD, the low, moderate and high level stressors have been identified. The same is presented in Table 5.3. (*See table on next page*)

It is a known fact that the nature of organizational structure and climate plays a vital role in promoting job involvement in the employees. At the same time, structural factors such as role ambiguity, role conflict, role overload and role under load can be the potential causes of stress. Other stressors include poor communication, an inadequate feedback about performance, features concerning participation in decision-making, lack of effective consultation and restrictions on behaviour, relationships at work, career development *i.e.,* lack of job security and the most important stressor-homework interface. This refers to the stressors resulting from a mismatch between work demands and family or social demands, which may be viewed as 'overspill' of one life into another.

Table 5.3: Mean Scores and Level of Occupational Stress of Higher Secondary Teachers

S.No.	Statements	Mean	Level
1	2	3	4
I.	**Organizational Structure and Climate**		
1.	Long working hours and expectations to do more work.	3.27	H
2.	Carrying multiple responsibilities in a short span of time.	2.08	L
3.	Lack of information in carrying out the professional responsibilities.	2.09	L
4.	Working on assignments that are not necessary to the profession.	2.05	L
5.	Lack of equipments and teaching- learning materials.	2.68	M
6.	Inadequate supportive staff in the school.	2.67	M
7.	Inadequate trained human resources to carry out the work assigned.	1.98	L
8.	Large class size with students of diverse needs.	3.32	H
9.	Lack of time to pay individual attention to each special needs student.	2.04	L
10.	Lack of involvement in the decision-making process of the activities related to the profession.	2.83	M
11.	Lack of opportunities for promotion in the school.	2.91	M
12.	Inadequate salary for the work done in the school.	2.87	M
13.	Stringent rules and regulations in the school that hinders to act independently.	2.86	M
14.	Taking responsibilities for the activities of others.	3.35	H
II.	**Personal and Professional Efficiency**		
15.	Inadequate training to meet the demands of the profession.	2.17	L
16.	Lack of opportunities for professional enhancement in the form of participation in professional meetings/ seminars/conferences.	2.96	M
17.	Inadequate knowledge in using new aids and appliances.	2.52	M
18.	Thrusting on development of curricular innovations and materials.	2.72	M
19.	Over qualified to perform the job.	2.79	M
20.	Lack of commitment and interest to perform the job.	2.01	L
21.	Problem in identification and assessment procedures.	2.57	M

Contd..

1	2	3	4
22.	Difficulty in managing students in the classroom.	2.24	L
23.	Difficulty in solving the problems that arise out of work.	2.14	L
24.	Face problems in decision-making process.	2.99	M
25.	Unable to complete the task within a stipulated period of time.	2.53	M
26.	Difficult to implement new policies and procedures in place of those already in practice.	2.79	M
III.	**Intra and Interpersonal Interactions**		
27.	Difficult to adjust with the fellow teachers in the school.	2.26	M
28.	Lack of healthy interactions between/among the teachers.	2.17	L
29.	Inadequate knowledge to give guidance and counseling to students and parents.	2.15	L
30.	Stressful interactions with parents and lack of parental support.	2.79	M
31.	Lack of teamwork and professional collaboration to meet the diverse needs of children.	2.83	M
32.	Angry with the students for their continuous failure.	2.60	M
33.	Difficulty in understanding the students' behaviour.	2.44	M
34.	Difficult to satisfy the requirements of the management.	2.51	M
35.	Misunderstood the organizational values and goals.	2.35	M
36.	Lack of pro-active communication with the management.	2.52	M
37.	Poor quality of feedback and supervision that address teacher concerns.	2.55	M
38.	Difficult to discuss the failure of the students with their parents.	2.69	M
IV.	**Home-Work Interface**		
39.	Financial problems at home are hindering my work.	2.15	L
40.	Difficult to concentrate in the class due to tension with my spouse.	2.10	L
41.	Health of my children is disturbing a lot.	2.34	M
42.	Education of my children is interfering in my job.	2.30	M
43.	Insufficient salary is troubling both my family and work environment.	2.33	M
44.	Family needs are taking priority than the teaching.	2.11	L
V.	**Environmental Factors**		
45.	Bullying and frightening by the students inside and outside the school.	2.26	M
46.	Complaints by the students.	2.58	M

Contd..

1	2	3	4
47.	Complaints by other staff members.	2.48	M
48.	Problems with students' indiscipline.	2.98	M
49.	Seldom opportunity to utilise the abilities and experience independently.	3.04	H
50.	Seldom rewarded for the hard labour and efficient performance.	2.96	M
51.	Problems faced with drug abuse by the students.	2.50	M
52.	Problems arising out of fraud and financial mismanagement within the school.	2.29	M
53.	Polluted working environment.	2.59	M
54.	Difficult to solve students disputes.	2.39	M
55.	Problems with the theft and damage of the property by the students.	2.64	M
56.	Lack of respect for teachers by the pupils, parents and the society.	2.78	M

Note: Levels of Occupational Stress - Low: 2.25 and below; Moderate: 2.26 to 2.99; High: 3.00 and above

From Table 5.3, under the dimension of *organizational structure and climate*, it is clear that, the long working hours and expectations to do more work (S.No.1), large class size with students of diverse needs (S.No.8) and taking responsibilities for the activities of others (S.No.14) are the major stressors for the teachers working in higher secondary schools, as their mean occupational stress scores fall under high level category. Contrary to this, the teachers are having low level of occupational stress in certain aspects such as; carrying multiple responsibilities in a short span of time (S.No.2), lack of information in carrying out the professional responsibilities (S.No.3), working on assignments that are not necessary to the profession (S.No.4), inadequate trained human resources to carryout the work assigned (S.No.7) and lack of time to pay individual attention to each special needs student (S.No.9). Further, the same teachers are showing moderate level of occupational stress in 6 aspects such as; lack of equipments and teaching learning materials (S.No.5), inadequate supportive staff in the school (S.No.6) lack of involvement in the decision-making process of the activities related to the teaching profession (S.No.10), lack of opportunities for promotion in the school (S.No.11), inadequate salary for the work done in the school (S.No.12) and stringent rules and regulations in the school that hinders to act independently (S.No.13).

The various aspects related to the *personal and professional efficiency* are also the sources of stress among higher secondary teachers. Some of the aspects such as; inadequate training to meet the demands of the profession (S.No.15), lack of commitment and interest to perform the job (S.No.20), difficulty in managing students in the classroom (S.No.22) and difficulty in solving the problems that arise out of work (S.No.23) are evoking low level of stress among teachers, whereas, the aspects such as; lack of opportunities for professional enhancements in the form of participation in professional meetings/seminars/conferences (S.No.16), inadequate knowledge in using new aids and appliances (S.No.17), thrusting on development of curricular innovations and materials (S.No.18), over qualified to perform the job (S.No.19), problem in identification and assessment procedures (S.No.21), facing problems in decision-making process (S.No.24), unable to complete the task within a stipulated period of time (S.No.25) and difficult to implement new policies and procedures in place of those already in practice (S.No.26) are making the teachers experience moderate level of stress.

With regard to the dimension *intra and interpersonal interactions*, the higher secondary teachers exhibit moderate level of stress with regard to; difficulty in adjusting with the fellow teachers in the school (S.No.27), stressful interactions with parents and lack of parental support (S.No.30), lack of teamwork and professional collaboration to meet the diverse needs of children (S.No.31), being angry with the students for their continuous failure (S.No.32), difficulty in understanding the students behaviour (S.No.33), difficulty in satisfying the requirements of the management (S.No.34), misunderstanding the organizational values and goals (S.No.35), lack of pro-active communication with the management (S.No.36), poor quality of feedback and supervision that address the teachers' concern (S.No.37) and difficult to discuss the failure of the students with their parents (S.No.38). On the other hand, the teachers are showing low level of stress in only two aspects *i.e.,* lack of healthy interactions between/among the teachers (S.No.28), and inadequate knowledge to give guidance and counseling to students and parents (S.No.29).

Under the dimension *home-work interface*, the higher secondary teachers experience equal amount of low and moderate levels of stress with 3 aspects in each of them. The financial problems at home (S.No.39), difficulty in concentrating in the classroom due to tension with the spouse (S.No.40) and priority for family needs (S.No.44) are placing the teachers under low level stress category, whereas, health of their children (S.No.41), education of their children (S.No.42) and insufficient salary (S.No.43) are the sources of moderate level of stress.

With regard to the dimension *environmental factors*, the higher secondary teachers are showing high level of stress due to the seldom opportunities to utilise their abilities and experience independently (S.No.49). In the remaining aspects *i.e.,* bullying and frightening by the students inside and outside the school (S.No.45), complaints by the students (S.No.46), complaints by the staff members (S.No.47), problems with students indiscipline (S.No.48), lack of reward for the hard labour and efficient performance (S.No.50), problems of students with drug abuse (S.No.51), problems due to fraud and financial mismanagement within the school (S.No.52), polluted working environment (S.No.53), difficult to solve students disputes (S.No.54), problems with the theft and damage of the school property by the students (S.No.55), and lack of respect for teachers by the pupils, parents and society (S.No.56), the teachers are experiencing moderate level of stress.

After analyzing the stressors that are responsible for causing stress among higher secondary teachers under the dimensions 'organizational structure and climate' and 'personal and professional efficiency', it is found that, out of 26 aspects, 9 stressors (organizational structure and climate – S.No. 2, 3, 4, 7 and 9; personal and professional efficiency – S.No. 15, 20, 22 and 23) are causing low level of stress, 3 aspects (organizational structure and climate – S.No. 1, 8 and 14) are causing high level of stress and the rest (organizational structure and climate – S.No. 5, 6, 10, 11,12 and 13; personal and professional efficiency – S.No.16, 17, 18, 19, 21, 24, 25 and 26) are evoking moderate level of stress among the higher secondary teachers. Further, 10 aspects in inter and intrapersonal interactions (S.No. 27, 30, 31, 32, 33, 34, 35, 36, 37 and 38); 3 aspects in home-work interface (S.No. 41, 42 and 43) and 11 aspects in environmental factors (S.No. 45, 46, 47, 48, 50, 52, 53, 54, 55 and 56) are causing moderate level of stress. Contrary to this, 2 aspects in inter and intrapersonal relations (S.No. 28 and 29), 3 aspects in home-work interface (S.No. 39, 40 and 44) evoked low level of stress and only one aspect in environmental factors (S.No. 49) causing high level of stress for the higher secondary teachers.

Level of Job Performance of Higher Secondary Teachers

Job performance is deceptively simple term. It can be distinguished from effectiveness, productivity and utility. Here, effectiveness is the evaluation of the results of the teachers' job performance. Generally speaking, differences in performance are caused by the interaction between ability, motivation, and situational factors that may facilitate or inhibit the performance of higher secondary teachers. Thus, for a teacher to perform well, it is certainly important for that person to possess job relevant abilities. Ability alone will not lead to high levels of performance, though; the teacher is motivated to perform and does not experience severe situational constraints. Ofcourse, in some cases, a high level of one of these three factors will compensate for low levels of the others *i.e.,* a highly motivated person will overcome situational constraints, but usually all three conditions are necessary for performance to be at a consistently high level. To identify the level of job performance of teachers working at higher secondary schools, mean and SD for each factor of the job performance dimensions have been calculated for the whole sample of teachers working at higher secondary schools. By using mean ± 1 SD, the low, moderate and high level job performance have been identified. The same is presented in Table 5.4. (*See table on next page*)

From Table 5.4, it is clear that, under the dimension *task oriented behaviour*, the teachers working at higher secondary schools are exhibiting low level of job performance in 5 aspects *i.e.,* reviewing the prior lesson for student understanding and assess the knowledge acquired before starting the new lesson (S.No.1), using of appropriate audio-visual aids to make teaching more effective (S.No.7), do not make varying stimuli like movements, gestures, voice modulation, pausing etc., while teaching (S.No.9), do not resort to remedial teaching whenever necessary (S.No.14) and do not require any orientation class, in-service training, workshop, short-term bridge courses etc., to update the knowledge (S.No.18). The teachers' performance is

Table 5.4: Mean Scores and Level of Job Performance of Higher Secondary Teachers

S.No.	Statements	Mean	Level
1	2	3	4
I.	**Task Oriented Behaviour**		
1.	Review prior lesson for student understanding and assess the knowledge acquired, before starting the new lesson.	2.59	L
2.	I will be confident and thoroughly prepare the content before taking the class.	4.29	H
3.	My teaching is well organized according to the objectives.	4.28	H
4.	Do not plan my teaching well in advance.	3.53	M
5.	My writing is more legible and unambiguous.	3.53	M
6.	My voice is audible to the students sitting in the last bench.	4.29	H
7.	Appropriate audio-visual aids are used to make my teaching more effective.	2.60	L
8.	I have the efficiency to handle any kind of teaching technology.	3.66	M
9.	I do not make varying stimuli like movements, gestures, voice modulation, pausing etc.	2.66	L
10.	Interactive and explorative way of teaching-learning is seen in my class.	3.79	M
11.	I use verbal and non verbal reinforces to appreciate pupils' participation.	3.52	M
12.	I will assign independent and group tasks to students to encourage their individuality.	3.68	M
13.	Try to stimulate the intellectual curiosity of my students during my class.	3.96	H
14.	Do not resort to remedial teaching whenever necessary.	2.64	L
15.	I will conduct periodical tests after completing every unit.	4.32	H
16.	Feedback will be given to the students who are unable to clear the final exams.	4.28	H
17.	I refer other books relevant to the topic I teach.	4.33	H
18.	I do not require any orientation class, in service training, work-shop, short term bridge courses etc., to update my knowledge.	2.65	L
19.	I am well informed about contemporary or current events/issues.	3.62	M
20.	My memory is fairly good.	3.88	M
21.	Students can contact me even after the school hours to clear their doubts.	3.61	M
22.	If I do not have the required skills, I acquire them.	3.73	M
23.	I enjoy my teaching to the full extent.	4.28	H

Contd..

1	2	3	4
24.	I am satisfied with my teaching.	4.31	H
II.	**Interpersonally Oriented Behaviour**		
25.	I use to discuss both the strengths and weaknesses of the students with their parents.	3.61	M
26.	I wholeheartedly welcome the suggestions of parents in the students' progress.	4.30	H
27.	I try to generate awareness and understanding among the parents on different aspects of learning difficulties in children.	3.74	M
28.	Parents and students will be given information about the courses offered and different avenues that are available after completing the higher secondary courses.	3.59	M
29.	Ignore the view points of the students.	3.58	M
30.	I do highlight the importance of vocational education to the students.	3.43	M
31.	More of written work will be given to the students to improve their writing skills.	3.48	M
32.	Students are asked to give oral presentation on different topics to improve their oral communication.	3.48	M
33.	Encourage students' creativity and stimulate their curiosity to know the hidden truth behind the scientific facts.	3.69	M
34.	I use to involve other colleagues in improving the weak students in their academics.	3.49	M
35.	Group studies among the students are encouraged.	3.52	M
36.	I do encourage bright students to help their peers who are weak in their academics.	3.55	M
III.	**Managerial Capabilities**		
37.	The needs of special children need not be emphasized and brought to the notice of the administration.	2.62	L
38.	I involve myself in the functions and programmes organized by the school even though they are not related to my subject.	3.54	M
39.	I concentrate on developing my capabilities more than my position in the school.	3.59	M
40.	I do not involve myself in the school's decisions.	2.61	L
41.	I understand the values and unspoken rules of the school.	3.62	M
42.	I Strive hard myself to maintain the identity of the school.	3.63	M
43.	It is difficult to abide by the principles and priorities of the school.	2.64	L
44.	The policies of the administration affect my teaching.	3.38	M

Contd..

1	2	3	4
IV.	**Personal Discipline and Leadership Qualities**		
45.	I have a sense of duty and responsibility.	4.34	H
46.	I am very punctual and stick to the school timings.	3.70	M
47.	My habits are clean and inspiring	3.66	M
48.	There is clarity and fluency in my language.	3.64	M
49.	I feel difficult to work effectively under the pressure of deadline.	2.70	L
50.	I can put in my best even in an unsupportive environment.	3.52	M
51.	I am easily approachable.	3.68	M
52.	I am not against corporal punishment in the schools.	2.67	L

Note: Level of Job performance - Low: 2.70 and below; Moderate: 2.71 to 3.9; and High: 4.00 and above

moderately focused on the aspects such as; not planning the lesson to be taught in advance (S.No.4), writing being more legible and unambiguous (S.No.5), efficiency in handling any kind of teaching technology (S.No.8), following interactive and explorative way of teaching-learning in the class (S.No.10), pupils participation is appreciated with both verbal and non-verbal reinforces (S.No.11), assigning independent and group tasks to students to encourage their individuality (S.No.12), well informed about the contemporary or current events (S.No.19), memory is being fairly good (S.No.20), allowing the students to contact even after the class hours to clear their doubts (S.No.21) and ready to acquire the required skills which are not present (S.No.22). The same teachers are demonstrating high level of job performance with regard to; being confident and thoroughly prepare the content before taking the class (S.No.2), teaching is well organized according to the objectives (S.No.3), voice being audible to the student in the last bench (S.No.6), try to stimulate the intellectual curiosity of the students (S.No.13), conducting periodic tests after every unit (S.No.15), feedback is given to the students who fail in the final exams (S.No.16), refer other books relevant to the topic (S.No.17), enjoy the teaching to the full extent (S.No.23) and satisfied with the teaching (S.No.24).

With regard to the dimension *interpersonally oriented behaviour*, the higher secondary teachers' job performance is high in welcoming the suggestions of parents in the students' progress (S.No.26). With regard to; discussing the strengths and weaknesses of the students with their parents (S.No.25), generate awareness and understanding among the parents on different aspects of learning difficulties in children (S.N0.27), parents and students will be given information about the courses offered and different avenues available after completing the higher secondary course (S.No.28), ignoring the view points of the students (S.No.29), importance of vocational education is highlighted to the students (S.No.30), to improve the writing skills of the students, more of written work will be given (S.No.31), to improve the oral communication, students are asked to give oral presentation (S.No.32), students creativity is being encouraged and curiosity is being stimulated to know the hidden truth behind the scientific facts (S.No.33), other colleagues are being involved in improving the weak students are being involved in improving the weak students (S.No.34), group studies among students is being encouraged and bright students are encouraged to help the students who are weak in their academics (S.No.36), the teachers job performance is at moderate level.

With regard to the dimension *managerial capabilities*, the higher secondary teachers have shown least performance in 3 aspects *i.e.,* needs of special children is not being emphasized and brought to the notice of the administration (S.No.37), not involving in the schools decisions (S.No.40) and difficulty to abide by the principles and priorities of the school (S.No.43). While the teachers are showing moderate level of job performance in the remaining 5 aspects such as; involving in the functions and programmes of the school, even though they are not related to the subject (S.No.38), concentration on developing self capabilities rather than on the position in the school (S.No.39), understanding the values and unspoken rules of the school (S.No.41), striving hard to maintain the identity of the school (S.No.42) and teaching is being affected by the administrative policies of the school (S.No.44).

Under the dimension *personal discipline and leadership qualities*, the higher secondary teachers' performance is high in their sense of duty and responsibility (S.No.45). Contrary to this, their performance is low in the aspects — difficulty to work effectively under the pressure of deadline (S.No.49) and accepting the corporal punishment in the schools (S.No.52). In the remaining aspects, the teachers exhibit moderate level of performance *i.e.,* being punctual and sticking to the school timings (S.No.46), habits being clean and inspiring (S.No.47), clarity and fluency in the language (S.No.48), gives the best in an unsupportive environment (S.No.50) and being easily approachable (S.No.51).

From the above analysis, it is concluded that, out of 24 aspects under the dimension 'task oriented behaviour', the higher secondary teachers are showing moderate level of job performance in 10 aspects (S.No. 4, 5, 8, 10, 11, 12, 19, 20, 21 and 22), high level job performance in 9 aspects (S.No. 2, 3, 6, 13, 15, 16, 17, 23 and 24) and low level job performance in 5 aspects (S.No. 1, 7, 9, 14 and 18). Under the dimension 'interpersonally oriented behaviour', out of 12 aspects, the higher secondary teachers are showing high performance in one aspect (S.No.26) and moderate performance in the remaining 11 aspects (S.No. 25, 27, 28, 29, 30, 31, 32, 33, 34, 35 and 36). Out of 16 aspects under the dimensions 'managerial capabilities' and 'personal discipline and leadership qualities', the teachers demonstrating high level performance in one aspect (personal discipline and leadership qualities – S.No.45), low level performance in 5 aspects (managerial capabilities – S.No. 37, 40 and 43; personal discipline and leadership qualities – S.No. 49 and 52) and moderate level performance in 10 aspects (managerial capabilities – S.No. 38, 39, 41, 42 and 44; personal discipline and leadership qualities – S.No. 46, 47, 48, 50 and 51).

ASSESSMENT OF JP OF HIGHER SECONDARY TEACHERS BY THEIR SELF-RATINGS AND THE RATINGS OF THEIR RESPECTIVE PRINCIPAL'S /H.M'S

Teaching profession is expected to be an oasis of idealism, devotion to duty and love for humanity amidst a vast desert of materialism, competitiveness and unconcern for the good of others. In spite of the vast expansion of education and the quantum jump in the number of teachers, there is a dearth of selfless, devoted teachers, who do not always look for material gains, who have a commitment to their profession, and a strong desire to inspire the budding and blooming adolescents who are in the verge of crossing their higher secondary stage and step into the college life. This kind of teacher will keep in touch with the latest developments in the field of education, be conversant with the modern means of curriculum transaction, and experiment with new ideas and innovative methods of curriculum teaching to make his/her performance more effective. To make their performance even more effective, it is necessary to find the flaws and problems in their work, and strengthen their weaknesses to uplift the confidence of the teachers. In this study, an attempt has been made to assess the performance of the higher secondary teachers by their self-ratings and also by the ratings of their respective Principal's/Head Master's (H.M).

Level of Job Performance of Higher Secondary Teachers in Accordance with Teachers Self-Ratings and Head Master's Ratings

One of the objectives of the present study is to find out the job performance (JP) of higher secondary teachers in accordance with their own ratings using job performance rating scale (JPRS) of teachers and also assessing the same teachers' JP by their respective Principal's/H.M's using separate rating scale but consists of the same aspects as given in JPRS of higher secondary teachers. This is done to know how far the self-ratings of the teachers are correct with regard to their JP, the ratings of their Principal's/H.M's is also taken. As the JPRS of higher secondary teachers consist of 52 items under four dimensions, it is practically not possible for the Principal's/H.M's to go through each statement for all the teachers in their school to rate their performance due to time constraint and administrative responsibility. Hence, the Principal's rating scale has been minimized to 20 sub-dimensions under the same four dimensions as in JPRS of teachers *i.e.,* task oriented behaviour (TOB), interpersonally oriented behaviour (IOB), managerial capabilities (MC), and personal discipline and leadership qualities (PDLQ). The 52 statements in JPRS of teachers have been grouped together under the following sub-dimensions in the Principal's/ H.M's rating scale.

In the principal's rating scale under the dimension TOB, the sub-dimension – *content* represents four statements in the JPRS of teachers *i.e.,* review prior lesson for student understanding and assess the knowledge acquired, before starting the new lesson (S.No.1), will be confident and thoroughly prepare the content before taking the class (S.No.2), teaching is well organized according to the objectives (S.No.3), and do not plan teaching well in advance (S.No.4). The sub-dimension – *written and oral skills* covers two statements *i.e.,* writing is more legible and unambiguous (S.No.5), and voice is audible to the students sitting in the last bench (S.No.6). Appropriate audio-visual aids are used to make teaching more effective (S.No.7), and have the efficiency to handle any kind of teaching technology (S.No.8) stands for the sub-dimension – *usage of teaching aids*. *Methodology* covers 5 statements such as; do not make varying stimuli like movements, gestures, voice modulation, pausing etc (S.No.9), interactive and explorative way of teaching-learning is seen in class (S.No.10), use verbal and non verbal reinforces to appreciate pupils' participation (S.No.11), assign independent and group tasks to students to encourage their individuality (S.No.12), and try to stimulate the intellectual curiosity of the students during class (S.No.13). The sub-dimensions – *evaluation* and *knowledge enrichment* covers 3 statements each such as, do not resort to remedial teaching whenever necessary (S.No.14), conduct periodical tests after completing every unit (S.No.15), and feedback will be given to the students who are unable to clear the final exams (S.No.16); refer other books relevant to the topic to teach (S.No.17), do not require any orientation class, in service training, workshop, short term bridge courses etc., to update the knowledge (S.No.18), and well informed about contemporary or current events/issues (S.No.19) respectively. The sub-dimension – *attitude and aptitude* represents 5 statements *i.e.,* memory is fairly good (S.No.20), students can contact even after the school hours to clear their doubts (S.No.21), ready to acquire the required skills (S.No. 22), enjoy teaching to the full extent (S.No.23), and satisfied with own teaching ability (S.No. 24).

Likewise, the dimension – IOB consisted of 4 sub-dimensions – developing good relationship with parents representing 4 statements *i.e.,* use to discuss both the strengths and weaknesses of the students with their parents (S.No.25), wholeheartedly welcome the suggestions of parents in the students' progress (S.No.26), try to generate awareness and understanding among the parents on different aspects of learning difficulties in children (S.No.27), and parents and students will be given information about the courses offered and different avenues that are available after completing the higher secondary courses (S.No.28); with students representing 5 statements such as — ignore the view points of the students (S.No. 29), highlight the importance of vocational education to the students (S.No. 30), more of written work will be given to the students to improve their writing skills (S.No.31), students are asked to give oral presentation on different topics to improve their oral communication (S.No.32), and encourage students' creativity and stimulate their curiosity to know the hidden truth behind the scientific facts (S.No.33); with colleagues stands for involving other colleagues in improving the weak students in their academics (S.No.34), and the sub-dimension between students covers two statements *i.e.,* group studies among the students are encouraged (S.No.35) and encourage bright students to help their peers who are weak in their academics (S.No.36).

In case of the dimension – MC, 4 statements represents the sub-dimension – *involves in the school's activities* such as, the needs of special children need not be emphasized and brought to the notice of the administration (S.No.37), involve in the functions and programmes organized by the school even though they are not related to the subject (S.No.38), concentrate on developing own capabilities more than the position in school (S.No.39), and do not involve in the school's decisions (S.No.40); two statements covers the sub-dimension — follows rules of the school *i.e.,* understand the values and unspoken rules of the school (S.No.41), and strive hard to maintain the identity of the school (S.No.42); and two statements represents the sub-dimension – *contributes to school's progress i.e.,* it is difficult to abide by the principles and priorities of the school (S.No.43), and the policies of the administration affect the teaching (S.No.44).

The fourth dimension – PDLQ consisted of 6 sub-dimensions – with *punctuality* representing two statements *i.e.,* have a sense of duty and responsibility (S.No.45), and very punctual and stick to the school timings (S.No.46); habits are clean and inspiring (S.No.47) stands for *clean habits*; the clarity and fluency in the language (S.No.48) represents *fluency in language*; feel difficult to work effectively under the pressure of deadline (S.No.49) stands for *tolerance and patience*; can put in the best even in an unsupportive environment (S.No.50), and easily approachable (S.No.51) stands for *accommodativeness*; and *discipline* covers the statement - not against corporal punishment in the schools (S.No.52) - refer Table 5.4.

After grouping one or more statements in JPRS of teachers into 20 sub-dimensions under Principal's/H.M's rating scale, to identify the level of JP of higher secondary teachers, mean and SD for each statement in both the teachers rating scale as well as Principal's/H.M's rating scale have been calculated. By using mean ± 1 SD, the low, moderate and high level of JP have been identified in both the scales and are presented together in Table 5.5. (*See table on next page*)

Form Table 5.5, it is found that the higher secondary teachers rated their performance as high in 3 aspects *i.e.,* written and oral skills, evaluation, and attitude and aptitude and; moderate in three aspects-content, methodology and knowledge enrichment. Whereas, 'usage of teaching aids' has been rated 'low', and TOB as a whole is moderately rated by the same teachers. On the otherhand, the Principal's/ H.M's rated the teachers' performance moderately under the dimension TOB of JP.

In case of IOB, the teachers and their Principal's/H.M's have moderately rated the performance for all the sub-dimensions *i.e.,* develops good relationship with students, colleagues, between students, and IOB as a whole; but for one sub-dimension, where the teachers placed themselves in high level in their relationship with the parents.

Under the dimension – MC, the teachers feel they are 'moderate' in following the rules of the school and 'low' in involving in school activities, contributing to schools progress, and MC as a whole. The Principal's/H.M's also opinioned that the teachers contribution to schools progress is low, but they are moderate in the remaining two sub-dimensions and MC as a whole.

With respect to the dimension – PDLQ, the teachers as well as Principal's/H.M's rated high for 'punctuality', low for 'fluency in language' and 'discipline'. Both of them rated moderately for 'clean habits', tolerance and patience, accommodativeness and also PDLQ as a whole. Further, JP as a whole is moderately rated by both the teachers themselves and their respective Principal's/H.M's.

Table 5.5: Mean and Level of Teachers Self-Ratings and Principal's/H.M's Ratings on the Job Performance of Higher Secondary Teachers

Job Performance Dimensions	Teachers Self-Ratings		Head Master's Ratings	
	Mean	Level	Mean	Level
Task Oriented Behaviour				
Content	3.67	M	3.56	M
Written and Oral Skills	3.91	H	3.78	M
Usage of Teaching Aids	3.13	L	3.05	M
Methodology	3.52	M	3.46	M
Evaluation	3.75	H	3.61	M
Knowledge Enrichment	3.53	M	3.48	M
Attitude and Aptitude	3.96	H	3.88	M
TOB as a whole	3.67	M	3.54	M
Interpersonally Oriented Behaviour				
With Parents	3.81	H	3.72	M
With Students	3.53	M	3.48	M
With Colleagues	3.49	M	3.47	M
Between Students	3.53	M	3.46	M
IOB_as a whole	3.62	M	3.53	M
Managerial Capabilities				
Involves in School's Activities	3.09	L	3.01	M
Follows Rules of the School	3.63	M	3.44	M
Contributes to School's Progress	3.01	L	2.96	L
MC as a Whole	3.20	L	3.14	M
Personal Discipline and Leadership Qualities				
Punctuality	4.02	H	3.89	H
Clean Habits	3.66	M	3.53	M
Tolerance and Patience	3.64	M	3.58	M
Fluency in Language	2.70	L	2.61	L
Accommodativeness	3.60	M	3.52	M
Discipline	2.67	L	2.61	L
PDLQ as a Whole	3.38	M	3.29	M
Job Performance as a Whole	3.56	M	3.41	M

Note: Teachers self-Ratings: High-3.71 and above; Moderate-3.21 to 3.70; Low-3.20 and below
Head Masters ratings: High-3.89 and above; Moderate-2.98 to 3.88; Low-2.97 and below

From the above discussion, it is concluded that the Principal's/H.M's rated the higher secondary teachers' performance moderately in all sub-dimensions except for 'punctuality' under the dimension-PDLQ, where it is rated high. In contrary, they rated 'contribution to progress of the school' under the dimension-MC, and 'fluency in language' and 'discipline' under the dimension-PDLQ, as low. On the otherhand, the teachers are high in their opinion about their 'written and oral skills', 'evaluation', and 'attitude and aptitude', under TOB; developing good relationship 'with parents', under IOB; and 'punctuality' under PDLQ. Further, the teachers placed themselves moderately in 3 sub-dimension *i.e.,* 'content', 'methodology', 'knowledge enrichment', and TOB as a whole, under the dimension TOB; 3 sub-dimension *i.e.,* 'relationship with students', 'colleagues', 'between students', and IOB as a whole, under the dimension IOB; only in one aspect *i.e.,* 'follows rules of the school' under the dimension MC; and 3 sub-dimensions under PDLQ *i.e.,* 'clean habits', tolerance and patience', 'accommodativeness' and PDLQ as a whole. In contrary, they rated themselves low in 'usage of teaching aids' under TOB; 'involves in school's activities', 'contributes to school's progress' and MC as a whole, under MC; and 'fluency in language' and 'discipline', under PDLQ. On the whole, the Principal's/H.M's and the teachers rated moderately about the performance of higher secondary teachers and their ratings are almost all going hand in hand.

Job Performance of Higher Secondary Teachers Assessed by Teachers Self-Ratings and Principal's/H.M's Ratings

Table 5.6 represents the mean and SD of the dimensions of job performance (JP) of higher secondary teachers in accordance with the teachers self-ratings and the ratings by their respective Principal's/H.M's. (*See table on next page*)

From Table 5.6, it is clear that the t-values with respect to the different job performance aspects under the dimensions – task oriented behaviour (TOB), interpersonally oriented behaviour (IOB), managerial capabilities (MC) and personal discipline and leadership qualities (PDLQ) are not significant at 0.05 level indicating that the JP of higher secondary teachers through their self-ratings and ratings by their Principal's/H.M's are similar. It means, the higher secondary teachers JP ratings (self-ratings) and their Principal's/H.M's ratings are going hand in hand, further indicating the validity of the tool used in the study.

Table 5.6 also shows that, out of twenty job performance aspects, only in two aspects the teachers and Principal's/H.M's differ in their ratings about the job performance of higher secondary teachers. For the aspects evaluation (t-value: 2.14) and developing good relationship with parents (t-value: 2.08), the t-values are significant at 0.05 level. When job performance as a whole is taken into account, the ratings of higher secondary teachers and their Principal's/H.M's are same, as the t-value (1.17) is not significant at 0.05 level. Hence, the formulated hypothesis 'there is no significant difference in the assessment of job performance of teachers working at higher secondary level using their self-rating scale and the assessment of job performance of the same teachers by their respective Principal's/H.M's' is accepted.

Table 5.6: Job Performance of Higher Secondary Teachers with their Self-Ratings and H.M's Ratings and the Calculated t-values

JP-Dimensions	Teachers Ratings		HM's Ratings		Calculated t-values
	Mean	SD	Mean	SD	
Task Oriented Behaviour					
Content	3.67	0.72	3.56	0.88	1.74@
Written and Oral skills	3.91	0.87	3.78	0.86	1.89@
Usage of Teaching aids	3.13	0.97	3.05	0.95	1.06@
Methodology	3.52	0.92	3.46	0.93	0.82@
Evaluation	3.75	0.81	3.61	0.86	2.14*
Knowledge Enrichment	3.54	0.74	3.48	0.71	1.05@
Attitude and Aptitude	3.96	0.86	3.88	0.78	1.24@
TOB as a whole	3.67	0.84	3.54	0.88	1.93@
Interpersonally Oriented Behaviour					
with Parents	3.81	0.46	3.72	0.63	2.08*
with Students	3.53	0.58	3.48	0.56	1.12@
with Colleagues	3.49	0.62	3.47	0.54	0.43@
between Students	3.53	0.64	3.46	0.68	1.35@
IOB as a Whole	3.62	0.59	3.53	0.58	1.96@
Managerial Capabilities					
Involves in School Activities	3.09	0.47	3.01	0.59	1.91@
Follows Rules of the School	3.63	0.68	3.54	0.78	1.57@
Contributes to School's Progress	3.01	0.61	2.96	0.63	1.03@
MC as a Whole	3.20	0.53	3.14	0.57	1.29@
Personal Discipline and Leadership Qualities					
Punctuality	4.02	0.42	3.95	0.56	1.80@
Clean Habits	3.66	0.74	3.59	0.69	1.25@
Tolerance and Patience	3.64	0.71	3.58	0.73	1.06@
Fluency in Language	2.70	0.70	2.61	0.67	1.67@
Accommodativeness	3.60	0.69	3.52	0.65	1.52@
Discipline	2.67	0.78	2.61	0.79	0.97@
PDLQ as a Whole	3.38	0.63	3.29	0.58	1.90@
JP as a whole	3.56	0.83	3.41	0.48	1.17@

Note: * Significant at 0.05 level; ** Significant at 0.01 level; @ Not Significant at 0.05 level

The dimension wise job performance of higher secondary teachers and job performance as a whole also indicate that the ratings are going hand in hand, and hence, it can be said that the tool used to assess the job performance of higher secondary teachers based on their self-ratings and the ratings of their Principal's / H.M's is valid.

Part — II: Differential Analysis

EFFECT OF GENDER, MARITAL STATUS, EDUCATIONAL QUALIFICATION, TYPE OF SCHOOL THE TEACHERS ARE WORKING-IN, LOCATION OF THE SCHOOL, YEARS OF EXPERIENCE, AGE, COMMUNITY, SUBJECTS THE TEACHERS HANDLING, AND SALARY THEY RECEIVE ON THE DIMENSIONS OF EI, OS AND JP OF HIGHER SECONDARY TEACHERS

In order to study the significant difference between two and more than two groups of samples, differential studies are made. One of the major objectives of the study is to find out the significant differences, if any, in the higher secondary teachers' emotional intelligence, occupational stress and job performance dimensions due to variations in their independent variables.

To know the significant differences, if any, in the dimensions of emotional intelligence of teachers due to variations in their gender, marital status, educational qualification, type of school the teachers are working-in, location of the school, years of experience, age, community, subjects the teachers handling, and salary they receive, mean and SD have been calculated for each group in a variable. Based on the mean and SD's, t/F-values have been worked out to know the significant differences in the dimensions of emotional intelligence of higher secondary teachers. The same procedure is adopted for occupational stress, and job performance of higher secondary teachers. The obtained results are presented in Tables 5.7 to 5.16.

Effect of 'Gender' on the Emotional Intelligence, Occupational Stress and Job Performance of Higher Secondary Teachers

Table 5.7 represents the mean and SD of the dimensions of emotional intelligence, occupational stress and job performance scores of men and women teachers working in higher secondary schools and the calculated t-values. (*See table on next page*)

From Table 5.7, it is clear that the obtained t-values of emotional intelligence of higher secondary teachers with respect to the dimensions – self-awareness *i.e.* EI_1 (2.90), social skills *i.e.* EI_4 (3.01) and emotional intelligence as a whole *i.e.* EIW (2.73) are significant at 0.01 level. It indicates that men and women teachers are significantly differ in their self-awareness, social skills and emotional intelligence as a whole. Hence, the formulated hypothesis '*there exist significant difference in the emotional intelligence of higher secondary teachers due to variations in their gender*' is accepted only for the above said emotional intelligence dimensions and emotional intelligence as a whole. Further, the mean values clearly indicate that women teachers (self-awareness – 39.80; social skills – 63.60 and emotional intelligence as a whole – 183.46) are heading over men (self-awareness – 41.71; social skills – 59.18 and emotional intelligence as a whole-175.33) in self awareness, social skills and emotional intelligence as a whole.

Table 5.7: Mean and SD of the EI, OS and JP Scores of Men and Women Teachers and the Calculated t-values

Variables	Men (N=139)		Women (N=188)		Calculated t-values
	Mean	SD	Mean	SD	
Emotional Intelligence					
EI_1	39.80	6.31	41.71	5.18	2.90**
EI_2	46.37	6.67	46.92	6.34	0.74@
EI_3	29.97	6.37	31.22	6.25	1.77@
EI_4	59.18	14.13	63.60	11.51	3.01**
EIW	175.33	28.30	183.46	24.04	2.73**
Occupational Stress					
OS_1	38.45	8.48	36.04	8.10	2.58**
OS_2	32.03	8.69	29.35	6.49	3.06**
OS_3	32.96	8.15	27.65	7.66	5.97**
OS_4	15.18	5.50	12.01	4.42	5.59**
OS_5	34.92	8.44	29.03	8.71	6.14**
OSW	153.56	32.53	134.10	27.69	5.69**
Job Performance					
JP_1	87.35	17.41	88.75	15.78	0.74@
JP_2	44.75	15.78	44.00	10.72	0.71@
JP_3	25.15	7.04	26.06	6.77	1.17@
JP_4	27.89	6.98	27.99	7.71	0.12@
JPW	184.41	37.94	185.97	35.05	0.38@

Note: @Not Significant at 0.05 level; * Significant at 0.05 level; ** Significant at 0.01 level

This may be due to the fact that, men teachers generally go for multiple frame of leadership in contrast to female teachers who are more oriented towards structural and humanistic frame and also teaching is viewed as a female profession. In Indian culture it is a general saying that female is another name of tolerance, patience and humbleness and she is good in developing rapport and comfort in dealing with students. These results are supported by the findings of Bansibihari and Surwade (2006), Jadhav and Havalappanavar (2009), Karakus (2012), Koneri (2010), Lee (2003), Lenka and Kant (2012), Malik *et. al.* (2011), Mayer *et. al.* (1999), Nahid (2012), Punia (2005) and Singh (2003). On the other hand, the t-values with respect to self-management *i.e.* EI_2 (0.74) and social awareness *i.e.* EI_3 (1.77) dimensions of emotional intelligence are not significant at 0.05 level, indicating men and women teachers are similar in these two aspects of emotional intelligence.

Further, the stated hypothesis '*there exist significant difference in the occupational stress of higher secondary teachers due to variations in their gender*' with regard to the dimensions – organizational structure and climate (OS_1), personal and professional efficiency (OS_2), intra and inter personal interactions (OS_3), home-work interface (OS_4), environmental factors (OS_5) and occupational stress as a whole (OSW) is accepted, as their obtained t-values (2.58, 3.06, 5.97, 5.59, 6.14 and 5.69 respectively) are significant at 0.01 level. It means, men and women teachers are significantly differ in their occupational stress as a whole as well as its dimensions. The trend of mean occupational stress scores of men (38.45, 32.03, 32.96, 15.18, 34.92, and 153.56) and women (36.04, 29.35, 27.65, 12.01, 29.03 and 134.10) also reveal that men teachers are experiencing more stress than the women teachers. This can be attributed to the fact that men teachers are having more pressure from managerial concerns as they are related to promotional opportunities and status, in addition to higher pressure from appraisal, which may be a factor that increases the limitations and barriers to status acquisition and promotion. These results are in line with the findings of Aftab and Khatoon (2012), Anbuchelvan (2010), Chaplain (1995), Chopra and Gartia (2009), Cooper and Kelly (1993), DeNobile and McCormick (2007), Kumar (2007), Lanreolaitan *et. al.* (2010), Liu and zhu (2009), Okoza *et. al.* (2010), Reddy (2011), Ushasri (2007) and Yang *et. al.* (2009); and contradicted by the results of Doyle and Hind (1998), Kaur (2008), Majid (1998), Mazzola (2011), Sabu and Jangaiah (2005) and Ushasree and Jamuna (1990).

With respect to job performance of higher secondary teachers, the mean scores of men and women for the task oriented behaviour *i.e.* JP_1 (87.35 and 88.75), inter personally oriented behaviour *i.e.* JP_2 (44.75 and 44.00), managerial capabilities *i.e.* JP_3 (25.15 and 26.06), personal discipline and leadership qualities *i.e.* JP_4 (27.89 and 27.89) and job performance as a whole *i.e.* JPW (184.41 and 185.97) do not differ

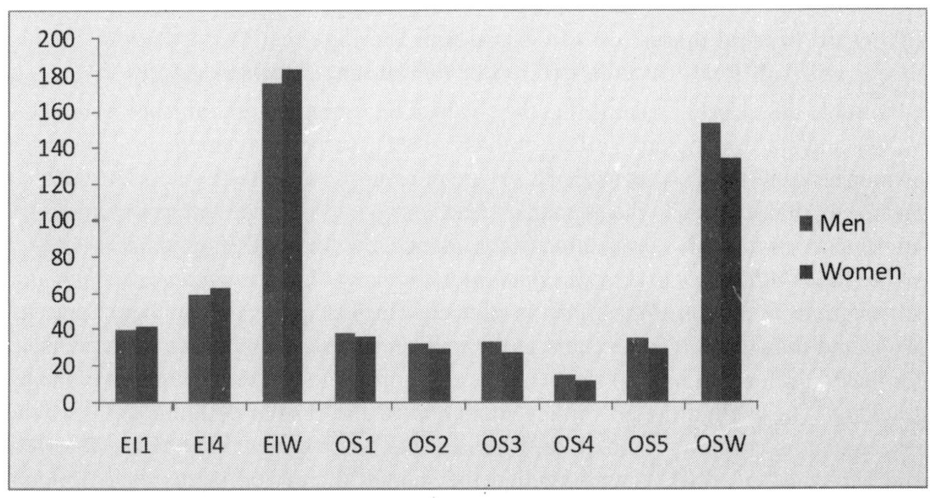

EI and OS Dimensions

Fig. 5.1: Mean Scores of the Dimensions of EI, OS and JP of Higher Secondary Teachers with Respect to their Gender

significantly as the calculated t-values are not significant at 0.05 level. Hence, the formulated hypotheses '*there exist significant difference in the job performance of higher secondary teachers due to variations in the gender*' is rejected. The present findings are supported by Giri and Kumar (2007) and contradicted by Anuradha and Sreedevi (2007), Biswas *et. al.* (2007) and Kumaraswamy and Sivanandam (2004), where the effect of gender has significant bearing on the job performance of individuals. Also, the studies by Bansibihari and Surwade (2006), Reddy (1992), Reddy (2007) and Roth *et. al.* (2011) confirmed that women are better in their performance than their counterparts. The bar diagram representing the significant mean scores of the dimensions of emotional intelligence and occupational stress are shown in Figure 5.1.

From the above discussion, it can be concluded that, the variable 'gender' has significant influence on the emotional intelligence dimensions – self-awareness, social skills and emotional intelligence as a whole; occupational stress dimensions – organization structure and climate, personal and professional efficiency, intra and interpersonal interactions, home-work interface, environmental factors and occupational stress as a whole. On the otherhand, the variable is not having significant bearing on the emotional intelligence dimensions – self-management and social awareness; and job performance dimensions – task oriented behaviour, interpersonally oriented behaviour, managerial capabilities, personal discipline and leadership qualities and job performance as a whole. Further, the mean values indicate that women teachers are better in their self-awareness skills, social skills and emotional intelligence competency as a whole compared to their counterparts; and men teachers are possessing more occupational stress compared to women teachers owing to organizational structure and climate, personal and professional efficiency, intra and interpersonal interactions, home-work interface, environmental factors and occupational stress as a whole.

Effect of 'Marital Status' on the Emotional Intelligence, Occupational Stress and Job Performance of Higher Secondary Teachers

Table 5.8 clearly explains that the t-values for emotional intelligence as a whole (0.75) and its dimensions self-awareness (1.22), self-management (1.43), social awareness (0.99) and social skills (1.20) are not significant at 0.05 level. This reflects that the marital status of higher secondary teachers do not influence neither the emotional intelligence as a whole nor its dimensions. Hence, the formulated hypothesis '*there is a significant difference in the emotional intelligence of higher secondary teachers due to variations in their marital status*' is rejected. The vast gap in the number of married (264) and unmarried (63) teachers in the present sample may be one of the reasons for the non-impact of marital status on the emotional intelligence of higher secondary teachers. These findings are in acceptance with the results of Punia (2005) who researched on corporate executives, whereas, it is contradicted by Faye *et. al.* (2011) and Malik *et. al.* (2011), who studied the impact of marital status on emotional intelligence of medical postgraduates and prospective teachers respectively.

With respect to the occupational stress of higher secondary teachers, the variable marital status has its impact only on the dimension – environmental factors, as its calculated t-value (2.57) implies its significance at 0.05 level. This is also represented in Figure 5.2.

Table 5.8: Mean and SD of the EI, OS and JP Scores of Married and Unmarried Higher Secondary Teachers and the Calculated t-values

	Married (N=264)		Unmarried (N=63)		Calculated T-values
	Mean	SD	Mean	SD	
Emotional Intelligence					
EI_1	41.10	5.62	40.04	6.27	1.22@
EI_2	46.41	6.29	47.82	7.17	1.43@
EI_3	30.87	6.14	29.92	7.03	0.99@
EI_4	62.20	12.26	59.74	15.07	1.20@
EIW	180.60	25.25	177.53	29.97	0.75@
Occupational Stress					
OS_1	37.19	8.39	36.55	8.16	0.55@
OS_2	30.58	7.84	30.09	6.61	0.51@
OS_3	29.64	8.33	31.04	8.05	1.23@
OS_4	13.09	5.12	14.47	5.15	1.91@
OS_5	30.93	9.08	34.07	8.61	2.57*
OSW	141.44	31.97	146.25	28.31	1.18@
Job Performance					
JP_1	88.65	15.73	86.09	19.30	0.97@
JP_2	43.63	10.07	43.07	11.30	0.35@
JP_3	25.53	7.06	26.25	6.12	0.80@
JP_4	27.74	7.57	28.80	6.60	1.11@
JPW	185.56	35.40	184.23	39.93	0.24@

Note: * Significant at 0.05 level; ** Significant at 0.01 level; @ Not Significant at 0.05 level

Hence, the stated hypothesis '*there exist significant difference in the occupational stress of higher secondary teachers due to variations in their marital status*' has been accepted for environmental factors only. This is because environmental factors are considered as one of the potential stressors that exist in the life of the teacher, affecting behaviour at work and outside the work arena. This requires consideration when assessing the sources and impact of teachers stress. These stressors may be life events, pressure resulting from conflict between organizational and family demands, financial difficulties and conflicts between organizational and personal beliefs. This is strongly supported by Mokdad (2005) who found that environmental factors was the main source of stress among Algerian teachers and, partially supported by Smith *et. al.* (2000) and Chaturvedi and Purushothaman (2009) who studied the coping behaviour of female teachers, confirmed that marital status is a significant determinant of stress among teachers. Further, the mean values for marital status of teachers on occupational stress as a whole (141.44) and its dimensions – organizational structure and climate

(37.19), personal and professional efficiency (30.58), intra and interpersonal interactions (29.64) and home-work interface (13.09) indicates its insignificance, as the t-values are not significant at 0.05 level. The results from the studies of Aftab and Khatoon (2012), Anbuchelvan (2010), Mathew (2005) and Yahaya *et. al.* (2010) are in tune with these findings.

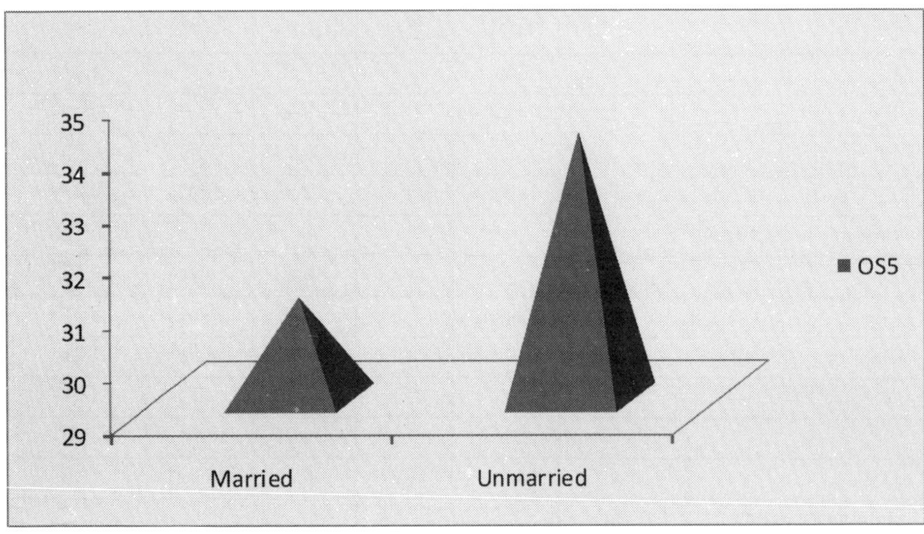

OS_5 – Environmental Factors

Fig. 5.2: Mean Scores of the OS Dimension-Environmental Factors of Higher Secondary Teachers with respect to their Marital Status

In case of job performance of higher secondary teachers, the stated hypothesis '*there exist significant difference in the job performance of higher secondary teachers due to variations in their marital status*' is rejected, as the mean scores of job performance as a whole (185.56) for married teachers along with the mean scores for its dimensions – task oriented behaviour (88.65), interpersonally oriented behaviour (43.63), managerial capabilities (25.53) and, personal discipline and leadership qualities (27.74) do not differ significantly with the mean job performance scores of unmarried teachers (184.23, 86.09, 43.07, 26.25, and 28.80 respectively) The same is statistically confirmed with t-values that are not significant at 0.05 level (0.24, 0.97, 0.35, 0.80 and 1.11 respectively). This indicates that the marital status of higher secondary teachers is not influencing their performance and this may be attributed to the basic ethics of any profession. It is the moral responsibilities of the individual to do justice to job by keeping aside ones family problems and the same is reflected in the present findings.

On the whole, it can be concluded that the variable 'marital status' has its significant influence on the occupational stress dimension – environmental factors alone and is not having any significant bearing on the emotional intelligence dimensions – self-awareness, self-management, social awareness, social skills and emotional intelligence as a whole; occupational stress dimensions – organizational structure and climate, personal and professional efficiency, intra and interpersonal interactions, home-work interface and occupational stress as a whole; and job performance dimensions – task oriented behaviour, interpersonally oriented behaviour, managerial capabilities, personal discipline and leadership qualities and, job performance as a whole of higher secondary teachers.

Effect of 'Educational Qualification' on the Emotional Intelligence, Occupational Stress and Job Performance of Higher Secondary Teachers

The results shown in Table 5.9 compel to reject the stated hypothesis '*there exist significant difference in the emotional intelligence of higher secondary teachers due to variations in their educational qualification*' as the t-values for the dimensions of emotional intelligence *i.e.,* self-awareness (1.12), self-management (0.74), social awareness (1.02), social skills (0.60) and also emotional intelligence as a whole (0.98) do not significantly differ at 0.05 level. It means, the higher secondary teachers possessing PG with B.Ed. and M.Ed. and, PG with M.Ed. and M.Phil do not differ significantly in their emotional intelligence. The reason may be that it is mandatory in Tamil Nadu to appoint teachers with PG and B.Ed. for higher secondary schools. Obtaining M.Ed. or M.phil degree is becoming very easy since, many Regular Universities and Open Universities are providing these degrees through distance mode. Here merit is not a constraint for eligibility and anybody with average grades can obtain the degrees. Hence, adding another degree to their B.Ed. or M.Ed. is not showing its effect on the emotional intelligence of higher secondary teachers. These findings are opposed by the studies of Amirtha and Kadhiravan (2006) on school teachers, Manoharan (2007) on high school teachers, Neelakandan (2007) on primary teachers and Poornima (2010) on special education teachers – claiming that higher the qualification better is the emotional intelligence among teachers.

Further, the variation in the educational qualification of higher secondary teachers is not showing any impact on their occupational stress (organizational structure and climate-0.21, personal and professional efficiency-0.05, intra and interpersonal interactions-0.89, home-work interface-0.58, environmental factors-0.58 and occupational stress as a whole-1.32) as the calculated t-values are not significant at 0.05 level. It shows that irrespective of educational qualifications, the teachers stress is same. Hence, the formulated hypothesis '*there exist significant difference in the occupational stress of higher secondary teachers due to variations in their educational qualification*' has been rejected. The trend may be due to the impact of decreasing demarcation between merit and average as there is no need to clear the entrance examination for M.Ed. and M.Phil courses in many universities, particularly in distance mode. Hence, most of the teachers are getting their additional degrees without much hard work which in turn is not causing any stress among teachers with respect to their qualification. This is supported by the studies of Balaswamy (2011) on primary school teachers, Naik (2011) on Anganwadi teachers, Poornima (2010) and Ramkumar (2007) on special education teachers, Reddy (2011) on University teachers and Yahaya *et. al.* (2010) on technical teachers; whereas, it is rejected by the studies of Aftab and Khatoon (2012), Anbuchelvan (2010), John (2007) and Manoj Kumar (2006).

Table 5.9: Mean and SD of the EI, OS and JP Scores of Higher Secondary Teachers with Respect to their Educational Qualification and the Calculated t-values

Variables	PG / B.Ed. and M.Ed (N=206)		PG / M.Ed. and M.Phil (N=121)		Calculated t-values
	Mean	SD	Mean	SD	
Emotional Intelligence					
EI_1	41.17	5.697	40.42	5.86	1.12@
EI_2	46.89	6.27	46.33	6.83	0.74@
EI_3	30.96	6.57	30.23	5.88	1.02@
EI_4	62.05	12.88	61.16	12.86	0.60@
EIW	181.09	26.52	178.16	25.66	0.98@
Organizational Stress					
OS_1	37.27	8.38	36.71	8.28	0.21@
OS_2	30.47	7.24	30.52	8.23	0.05@
OS_3	30.16	8.60	29.47	7.73	0.89@
OS_4	13.99	5.024	12.28	5.20	0.58@
OS_5	32.23	8.74	30.34	9.50	0.58@
OSW	144.14	30.87	139.35	31.96	1.32@
Job Performance					
JP_1	86.87	15.78	90.34	17.46	1.79@
JP_2	42.72	10.67	44.88	9.53	1.88@
JP_3	25.50	6.79	25.96	7.07	0.57@
JP_4	27.639	7.09	28.48	7.89	0.97@
JPW	182.74	35.87	189.68	36.64	1.66@

Note: * Significant at 0.05 level; ** Significant at 0.01 level; @ Not Significant at 0.05 level

As in the case of emotional intelligence and occupational stress, the same trend is continuing with job performance of higher secondary teachers with respect to their educational qualification. The t-values for job performance as a whole (1.66) and its dimensions task oriented behaviour (1.79), interpersonally oriented behaviour (1.88), managerial capabilities (0.57) and, personal discipline and leadership qualities (0.97) clearly demonstrates its insignificance in terms of degrees the teachers are possessing. This implies that variations in the qualification of teachers is not playing any role in differentiating their job performance and hence, the stated hypothesis '*there exist significant difference in the job performance of higher secondary teachers due to variations in their educational qualification*' is rejected. The findings of Kumaraswamy and Sivanandam (2004) on primary teachers and Reddy (1992) on role performance of adult education programme instructors are not corroborated with the present findings by claiming that higher qualification results in better performance.

Overall it can be viewed that, the variable 'educational qualification' is not significantly influencing any of the dimensions of emotional intelligence (self-awareness, self-management, social awareness, social skills and emotional intelligence as a whole), occupational stress (organizational structure and climate, personal and professional efficiency, intra and interpersonal interactions, home-work interface, environmental factors and occupational stress as a whole) and job performance (task oriented behaviour, interpersonally oriented behaviour, managerial capabilities, personal discipline and leadership qualities and job performance as a whole) of higher secondary teachers.

Effect of 'Type of School the Teachers are Working-in' on the Emotional Intelligence, Occupational Stress and Job Performance of Higher Secondary Teachers

The t-values presented in Table 5.10 clearly shows that for the dimensions – self-awareness (1.95), self-management (1.06), social awareness (0.34), social skills (1.17) and emotional intelligence as a whole (1.18) are not significant at 0.05 level. It indicates that the teachers working in government and private schools are similar in their emotional intelligence. Hence, the formulated hypothesis '*there exist significant difference in the emotional intelligence of higher secondary teachers due to variations in the type of school the teachers are working-in*' is rejected. This may be due to the fact that both the government schools as well as private schools are on par with each other in providing the qualitative facilities as well as monetary benefits. These results are in line with the findings from the studies of Indu (2009) on student teachers, Neelakandan (2007) on primary teachers and Padhi and Verma (2011) on secondary school teachers; whereas, Manoharan (2007) contradicted that, urban high school teachers are better in their emotional intelligence compared to their counterparts.

With respect to occupational stress of higher secondary teachers, the t-values for occupational stress as a whole (2.65) and the dimensions – personal and professional efficiency (3.13) and, intra and interpersonal interactions (3.10) are significant at 0.01 level and, for the dimension environmental factors (2.46) it is significant at 0.05 level. This indicates that the type of school the teachers are working-in *i.e.*, government or private schools, has its impact on occupational stress as a whole and also on its dimension – personal and professional efficiency, intra and interpersonal interactions and environmental factors. Hence the formulated hypothesis 'there exists significant difference in the occupational stress of higher secondary teachers due to variations in the type of school the teachers are working-in' is accepted only for occupational stress as a whole and it's above mentioned dimensions. John (2007) and Ravichandran and Rajendran (2007) also found the significant influence of type of school on the occupational stress of special education teachers and higher secondary teachers respectively. Further, the mean scores of teachers working in government schools for occupational stress as a whole (147.06), personal and professional efficiency (31.83), intra and interpersonal interactions (31.35) and environmental factors (32.79) are higher compared to the mean scores of their counterparts working in private schools (137.93, 29.22, 28.54 and 30.34 respectively). The mean values clearly indicate that the higher secondary teachers working in the government schools are more stressed

Table 5.10: Mean and SD of the EI, OS and JP Scores of Higher Secondary Teachers with Respect to the Type of School they are Working-in and the Calculated t-values

Variables	Government Schools (N=159)		Private Schools (N=168)		Calculated t-values
	Mean	SD	Mean	SD	
Emotional Intelligence					
EI_1	40.26	5.90	41.50	5.57	1.95@
EI_2	46.29	6.73	47.05	6.23	1.06@
EI_3	30.81	6.00	30.57	6.63	0.34@
EI_4	60.86	12.88	62.54	12.82	1.17@
EIW	178.24	26.41	181.68	25.98	1.18@
Organizational Stress					
OS_1	37.45	8.33	36.70	8.34	0.80@
OS_2	31.83	8.02	29.22	6.98	3.13**
OS_3	31.35	8.40	28.54	7.96	3.10**
OS_4	13.61	5.43	13.11	4.87	0.87@
OS_5	32.79	9.09	30.34	8.90	2.46*
OSW	147.06	32.82	137.93	29.23	2.65**
Job Performance					
JP_1	88.82	15.24	87.52	17.59	0.71@
JP_2	43.81	10.36	43.25	10.28	0.48@
JP_3	25.24	6.62	26.08	7.13	1.10@
JP_4	27.49	7.16	28.38	7.61	1.08@
JPW	185.37	35.04	185.25	37.47	0.03@

Note: * Significant at 0.05 level; ** Significant at 0.01 level; @ Not Significant at 0.05 level

due to personal and professional efficiency, intra and interpersonal interactions, environmental factors and occupational stress as a whole. This is in contradiction with the results of Balaswamy (2011) and Vijayalakshmi (2004), who found that private school and college teachers are more stressed than their counterparts respectively. On the otherhand, the t-values for organizational structure (0.80) and home-work interface (0.87) are not significant at 0.05 level, indicating the non-influence of the variable 'type of school the teachers are working-in' on their occupational stress. This was strongly opposed by Mathew (2005), who claimed that school structure and climate, and home-work interface were the main sources of stress for special education teachers. The significant mean scores of the dimensions of occupational stress for the 'type of school the teachers are working-in' are shown in Figure 5.3.

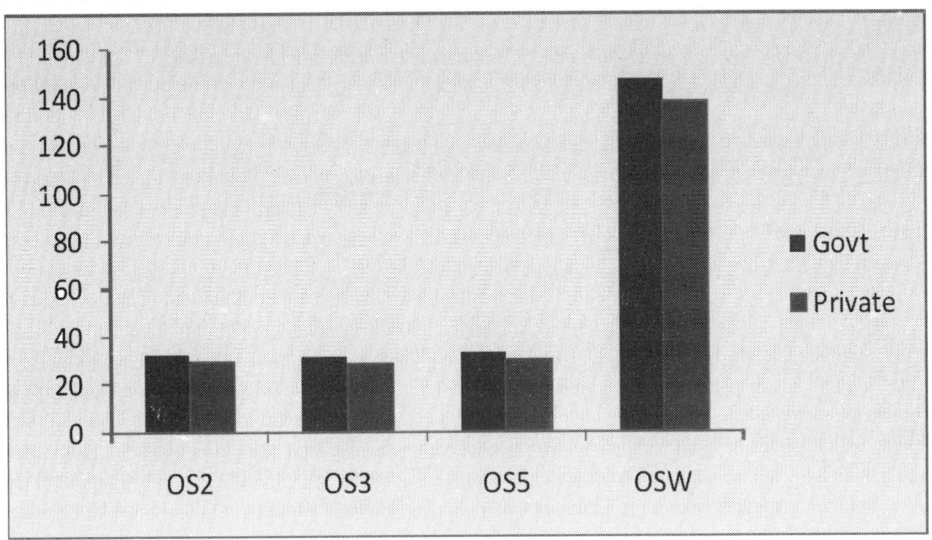

OS-Dimensions

Fig. 5.3: Mean Scores of the OS Dimensions of Higher Secondary Teachers with Respect to The Type of School they are Working-in

In case of job performance, the t-values for job performance as a whole (0.03) and its dimensions – task oriented behaviour (0.71), interpersonally oriented behaviour (0.48), managerial capabilities (1.10) and, personal discipline and leadership qualities (1.08) shows that they are not significant at 0.05 level. Hence, the stated hypothesis '*there exist significant difference in the job performance of higher secondary teachers due to variations in the type of school the teachers are working-in*' is rejected. This result is supported by Chen and Cheng (2012) who studied the public and private kindergarten teachers and contradicted by Garg and Rastogi (2006) who studied the organizational climate and behaviour of public and private schools found the significance difference in the job performance of teachers.

From the above, it can be concluded that the occupational stress dimensions – personal and professional efficiency, intra and interpersonal interactions, environmental factors and occupational stress as a whole are significantly influenced by the variable 'type of school the teachers are working-in', indicating that the teachers working in the government higher secondary schools are more stressed than their counterparts. The insignificance of the variable is found with the emotional intelligence dimensions – self-awareness, self-management, social awareness, social skills and emotional intelligence as a whole; occupational stress dimensions – organizational structure and climate and home-work interface; and job performance dimensions – task oriented behaviour, interpersonally oriented behaviour, managerial capabilities, personal discipline and leadership qualities, and job performance as a whole.

Effect of 'Location of the School' on the Emotional Intelligence, Occupational Stress and Job Performance of Higher Secondary Teachers

The stated hypothesis '*there exist significant difference in the emotional intelligence of higher secondary teachers due to variations in the location of the school* is rejected, as the t-values in Table 5.11 for self-awareness (0.54), self-management (0.08), social awareness (0.46), social skills (0.37) and emotional intelligence as a whole (0.43) are not significant at 0.05 level. It means that, the higher secondary teachers working in rural and urban schools are similar in their emotional competency. This result is supported by Edannur (2010) and Padhi and Verma (2011); and contradicted by the studies of Alfredo (2012) and Manoharan (2007) on high school teachers and, Shanwal (2003), Punia and Sangwan (2011) on primary and secondary school children respectively and Koneri (2010) found that rural adolescents are high on emotional intelligence than their counterparts.

Table 5.11: Mean and SD of the EI, OS and JP Scores of Higher Secondary Teachers with Respect to the Location of the School and the Calculated t-values

Variables	Rural Schools (N=166)		Urban Schools (N=161)		Calculated t-values
	Mean	SD	Mean	SD	
Emotional Intelligence					
EI_1	41.07	5.62	40.72	5.90	0.54@
EI_2	46.71	6.36	46.65	6.62	0.08@
EI_3	30.85	6.53	30.52	6.12	0.46@
EI_4	61.99	12.92	61.45	12.83	0.37@
EIW	180.63	26.02	179.36	26.47	0.43@
Occupational Stress					
OS_1	37.43	8.89	36.68	7.73	0.81@
OS_2	30.46	8.39	30.52	6.73	0.06@
OS_3	29.80	8.27	30.02	8.32	0.24@
OS_4	13.93	5.51	12.76	4.68	2.07*
OS_5	31.93	9.74	31.13	8.32	0.80@
OSW	143.57	33.56	141.13	28.87	0.70@
Job Performance					
JP_1	85.77	17.13	90.61	15.45	2.68**
JP_2	42.49	10.24	44.59	10.30	1.84@
JP_3	24.90	6.86	26.46	6.85	2.05*
JP_4	27.26	7.30	28.65	7.45	1.70@
JPW	180.44	36.76	190.32	35.14	2.48*

Note: * Significant at 0.05 level; ** Significant at 0.01 level; @ Not Significant at 0.05 level

With regard to occupational stress, the location of school has its significant influence on only one dimension of occupational stress *i.e.,* home-work interface, as its t-values (2.07) is significant at 0.05 level. Hence, the stated hypothesis '*there exist significant difference in the occupational stress of higher secondary teachers due to variations in the location of the school'* is accepted for home-work interface dimension and rejected for other dimensions as the t-values for organizational structure and climate (0.81), personal and professional efficiency (0.06), intra and interpersonal interactions (0.24), environmental factors (0.80) and occupational stress as a whole (0.70) are not significant at 0.05 level. From this, it is clear that the location of school plays a significant role on home-work dimension of occupational stress and do not influence the other dimensions as well as occupational stress as a whole. These findings are supported by Soyibo (1994), who found that location of school is not influencing the stress among Jamaican high school teachers and contradicted by Naik (2011) and Ramkumar (2007). Further, studies of Manoj Kumar (2006) on high school teachers and Ushasri (2007) on special education teachers also contradicted and found that rural teachers are more stressed than the urban teachers.

When job performance is taken into account, the t-values in the table shows that the managerial capabilities (2.05) and job performance as a whole (2.48) are significant at 0.05 level and another dimension – task oriented behaviour (2.68) is significant at 0.05 level. Hence, the stated hypothesis '*there exist significant differences in the job performance of higher secondary teachers due to variations in the location of the school'* is accepted for job performance as a whole and its dimensions – managerial capabilities and task oriented behaviour. Further, the mean scores of urban school teachers on the aspects of managerial capabilities (28.65), task oriented behaviour (90.61) and job performance as a whole (190.32) are higher as compared to the mean scores of rural teachers on the same aspects (27.26, 85.77 and 180.44 respectively). This implies that the job performance of teachers working in urban schools is better compared to their counterparts working in the rural schools. This better performance may be due to the availability of better facilities, better monitoring by the authorities, high level of achievement competition between the schools, bounded to respond to the parents, motivation and incentives to the teachers. All these factors which are visible and are not compulsory in the rural schools are creating the performance gap between rural and urban school teachers. On the otherhand, the t-values for the dimensions – interpersonally oriented behaviour (1.84) and personal discipline and leadership qualities (1.70) are not significant at 0.05 level, indicating that, these aspects are not affecting the job performance due to the location of the school. The study of Kumaraswamy and Sivanandam (2004) also revealed that location of the school do not influence the job performance of primary school teachers. The bar graph representing the significant mean scores of the dimensions of OS and JP are shown in Figure 4. (*See fig. on next page*)

From the above discussion, it is clear that the variable 'location of the school' has its significant bearing on the occupational stress dimension – homework interface and the mean values indicating rural teachers having more stress due to this dimension

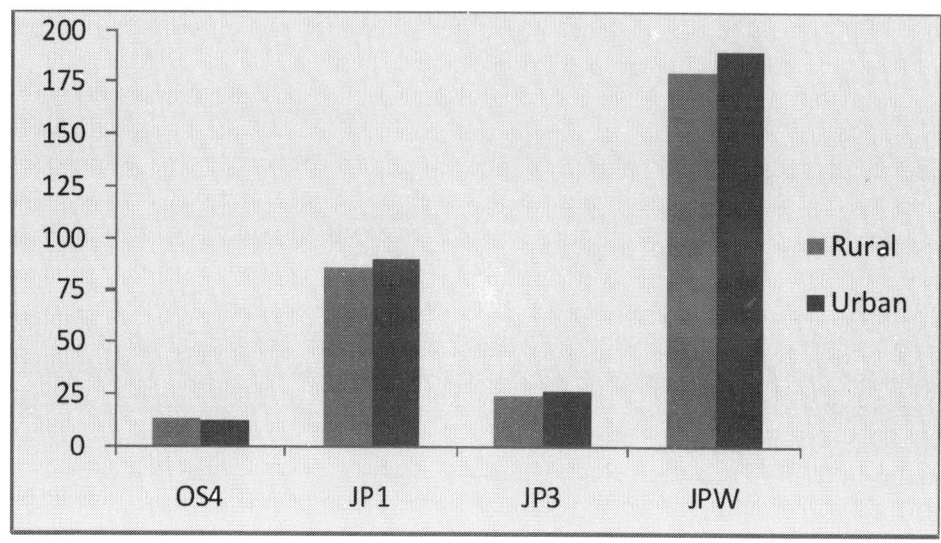

OS and JP Dimensions

Fig. 5.4: Mean Scores of the Dimensions of OS and JP of Higher Secondary Teachers with Respect to the Location of the School they are Working-in

than their counterparts; and job performance dimensions – task oriented behaviour, managerial capabilities and job performance as a whole with higher mean values for urban teachers than the rural teachers. Contradictory to this, the variable is not influencing the emotional intelligence dimensions – self-awareness, self-management, social awareness, social skills and emotional intelligence as a whole; occupational stress dimensions – organizational structure and climate, personal and professional efficiency, intra and interpersonal interactions, environmental factors and occupational stress as a whole; and job performance dimensions – interpersonally oriented behaviour, personal discipline and leadership qualities and job performance as a whole of higher secondary teachers.

Effect of 'Years of Experience' on the Emotional Intelligence, Occupational Stress and Job Performance of Higher Secondary Teachers

Table 5.12 clearly explains that the obtained t-values for self-awareness (1.21), self-management (1.40), social awareness (0.41), social skills (0.93) and emotional intelligence as a whole (1.17) are not significant at 0.05 level and hence the formulated hypothesis '*there exist significant difference in the emotional intelligence of higher secondary teachers due to variations in the years of experience*' is rejected. This implies that the variations in teachers' experience do not influence their emotional intelligence. Studies of Neelakandan (2007) on primary teachers, Rastegar and Memarpour (2009) on Iranian EFL teachers and Salami (2007) on secondary school teachers supported the present study findings; whereas, it is contradicted by the findings from the studies of Manoharan (2007) on high school.teachers, Mishra and Mohapatra

(2010) on corporate executives, Poornima (2010) on special education teachers, Puri (2011) on business executives, Rajkowa (2002) on IAS officers, Singh (2005) on managers and Ghanizadeh and Moafian (2009) on EFL teachers, who all claimed that experienced individuals are better in their emotional intelligence. Though the years of experience of teachers is not influencing the emotional intelligence of teachers, the interesting fact is that the mean scores of teachers having above 16 years experience are slightly higher than the mean scores of teachers below 15 years of experience with respect to self-awareness (41.32 and 40.55), self-management (47.24 and 46.22), social awareness (30.85 and 30.56), social skills (62.45 and 61.12) and emotional intelligence as a whole (181.87 and 176.46).

Table 5.12: Mean and SD of the EI, OS and JP Scores Higher Secondary Teachers with Respect to the Years of Experience and the Calculated t-values

Variables	Below 15 Years (N=179)		Above 16 Years (N=148)		Calculated t-values
	Mean	SD	Mean	SD	
Emotional Intelligence					
EI_1	40.55	5.92	41.32	5.54	1.21@
EI_2	46.22	6.31	47.24	6.66	1.40@
EI_3	30.56	6.53	30.85	6.08	0.41@
EI_4	61.12	12.91	62.45	12.80	0.93@
EIW	178.46	26.45	181.87	25.88	1.17@
Occupational Stress					
OS_1	37.09	7.95	37.04	8.81	0.05@
OS_2	30.53	7.38	30.44	7.90	0.09@
OS_3	29.44	8.09	30.47	8.50	1.12@
OS_4	13.78	5.16	12.85	5.10	1.63@
OS_5	31.68	8.91	31.36	9.27	0.31@
OSW	142.53	30.05	142.18	32.89	0.09@
Job Performance					
JP_1	87.28	17.04	89.21	15.77	1.06@
JP_2	43.75	10.60	43.24	9.97	0.45@
JP_3	25.49	6.54	25.89	7.31	0.50@
JP_4	28.19	6.71	27.65	8.17	0.64@
JPW	184.73	36.18	186.00	36.45	0.31@

Note: * Significant at 0.05 level; ** Significant at 0.01 level; @ Not Significant at 0.05 level

With regard to occupational stress, the formulated hypotheses '*there exist significant difference in the occupational stress of higher secondary teachers due to variations in their years of experience*' is rejected, as the calculated t-values for organizational structure and climate (0.05), personal and professional efficiency (0.09), intra and inter personal interactions (1.12), home-work interface (1.63), environmental factors (0.31) and occupational stress as a whole (0.09) are not significant at 0.05 level. This indicates the non influence of years of experience of higher secondary teachers on their occupational stress as a whole as well as its dimensions. These results are supported by the studies of Anbuchelvan (2010), Balaswamy (2011), and Al-Amir (2004) on primary and high school teachers, Naik (2011) on Anganwadi teachers, John (2007), Poornima (2010) and Ramkumar (2007) on special education teachers, Soyibo (1994) on Jamaican high school teachers, Yahaya *et. al.* (2010) on stress among technical teachers. Further, Majid (1998) and Yagil (1998) found that less experienced are more stressed; and stress increases with increase in experience was established from the studies of Chaturvedi and Purushothaman (2009) on female teachers, Chan *et. al.* (2010) on primary and secondary teachers in Hong Kong, Chaplain (1995) on English primary teachers, Poloskivokic and Bogdanic (2007) and Wang *et. al.* (2001) on coping strategies among primary and secondary teachers.

The same trend of insignificance continues with job performance and its dimensions. In this case, the mean scores of teachers with below 15 years and above 16 years of experience on the dimensions of task oriented behaviour (87.28 and 89.21), inter personally oriented behaviour (43.75 and 9.97) and managerial capabilities (24.49 and 28.89), personal discipline and leadership qualities (28.19 and 28.65) and job performance as a whole (184.73 and 186.00) do not significantly differ as the calculated t-values are not significant at 0.05 level and hence the formulated hypothesis '*there exist significant difference in the job performance of higher secondary teachers due to variations in their years of experience*' is rejected. This explains that the years of experience of higher secondary teachers do not play any significant role on their job performance. These findings are not in acceptance with the results of Kumaraswamy and Sivanandam (2004) and Hanif *et. al.* (2011), who found experience as a significant predictor of job performance among teachers.

From the above, it can be summed up that, the variable 'years of experience' is not significantly influencing the emotional intelligence dimensions – self-awareness, self-management, social awareness, social skills and emotional intelligence as a whole; occupational stress dimensions – organizational structure and climate, personal and professional efficiency, intra and interpersonal interactions, home-work interface, environmental factors and occupational stress as a whole; and job performance dimensions – task oriented behaviour, interpersonally oriented behaviour, managerial capabilities, personal discipline and leadership qualities and job performance as a whole of higher secondary teachers.

Effect of 'Age' on the Emotional Intelligence, Occupational Stress and Job Performance of Higher Secondary Teachers

Table 5.13 shows the mean and SD of the dimensions of emotional intelligence, occupational stress and job performance scores of higher secondary teachers with different age groups and the calculated F-values.

Table 5.13: Mean and SD Scores of the EI, OS and JP of Higher Secondary Teachers with Different Age Groups and the Calculated F-values

Variables	Up to 35 Years (N=114)		36 to 45 Years (N=129)		Above 46 Years (N=84)		Calculated F-Values
	Mean	SD	Mean	SD	Mean	SD	
EI							
EI_1	40.33	6.34	41.56	5.42	40.65	5.38	1.49@
EI_2	46.43	6.32	46.26	6.67	47.67	6.37	1.34@
EI_3	29.19	6.13	32.14	6.03	30.50	6.59	6.88**
EI_4	59.35	12.99	63.77	12.58	61.80	12.70	3.64**
EIW	175.31	26.57	183.75	25.54	180.64	26.05	3.21**
OS							
OS_1	36.90	7.75	37.08	8.61	37.27	8.76	0.04@
OS_2	30.19	6.83	31.13	8.50	29.91	7.17	0.78@
OS_3	30.59	8.20	29.65	8.79	29.38	7.60	0.62@
OS_4	14.19	5.59	13.30	4.85	12.32	4.82	3.25**
OS_5	33.12	8.44	30.42	9.38	31.09	9.17	2.84**
OSW	145.00	30.31	141.59	34.13	139.98	28.08	0.68@
JP							
JP_1	85.37	18.20	88.69	16.27	91.10	13.71	3.07**
JP_2	42.67	10.59	43.48	9.88	44.75	10.55	0.98@
JP_3	25.32	6.38	25.41	7.06	26.55	7.27	0.93@
JP_4	28.10	6.86	27.79	7.73	27.98	7.66	0.05@
JPW	181.48	37.28	185.37	36.38	190.40	34.39	1.46@

Note: @ Not Significant at 0.05 level; * Significant at 0.05 level; ** Significant at 0.01 level

From Table 5.13, it is clear that the obtained F-values with respect to the dimensions of emotional intelligence *i.e.,* social awareness (EI_3- 6.88), social skills (EI_4-3.64) and emotional intelligence as a whole (EIW-3.21) are significant at 0.01 level; whereas, the F-values with respect to self-awareness (EI_1-1.49) and self-management (EI_2-1.34) are not significant at 0.05 level. This result highlights the fact that the higher secondary teachers belonging to different age groups are similar in their self-awareness and self-management skills. At the same time, their social awareness, social skills, and emotional intelligence as a whole are significantly different. Hence, the formulated hypothesis '*there exist significant differences in the emotional intelligence of higher secondary teachers due to variations in their age*' is accepted only with respect to the dimensions – social awareness, social skills and emotional intelligence as a whole. The studies of Krishnaveni and Deepa (2009) found the impact of age on emotional intelligence; whereas, Bansibihari and Pathan (2004) and Poornima (2010) found that age is independent of emotional intelligence. Further, the mean values also indicate that the teachers with 36 to 45 years age group possess better social awareness (32.14), social skills (63.77) and emotional intelligence as a whole (183.75) followed by the teachers having above 46 years age group (EI_3-30.50; EI_4-61.80; and EIW-180.64) and teachers upto 35 years age group (EI_3-29.19; EI_4-59.35; and EIW-175.31). Punia (2005) found that teachers above 25 years and below 46 years possess better emotional intelligence; Puri (2011) found that 40 to 45 years business executives were higher in their emotional intelligence; and Rajkhowa (2002) established that 46 to 60 years IAS officers were high on emotional intelligence.

With regard to occupational stress, the F-values for the dimensions home-work interface (OS_4-3.25) and environmental factors (OS_5-2.84) are significant at 0.01 level. It means the variation in the age of higher secondary teachers has significant bearing on their stress due to home-work interface and environmental factors. The findings of Mathew (2005) also revealed that 'home-work interface' was one of the main sources of occupational stress among special teachers. Reddy (2011) found 'environmental factors' as one of the main sources of stress among university teachers. Further, the mean values also reveal that the teachers with upto 35 years age group (14.19) experience more stress with regard to home-work interface followed by their counterparts with 36 to 45 years age group (13.30) and above 46 years age group (12.32). This is strengthened by the findings of Chandraiah *et. al.* (2003) and Ling-Feng (2005) found that kindergarten teachers below 39 years had more stress than the teachers of 40 to 49 years age. In case of environmental factors, the teachers with 36 to 45 years age group possess low stress (30.42); whereas, teachers with upto 35 years have higher stress (33.12) followed by the teachers with above 46 years age group (31.09). The findings of Poornima (2010) on special teachers also found that the teachers with 30 years and below age group had higher stress followed by the teachers with above 46 years and 31 to 45 years age group.

On the otherhand, the F-values with respect to organizational structure and climate (OS_1-0.04), personal and professional efficiency (OS_2-0.78), intra and inter personal interactions (OS_3-0.62) and occupational stress as a whole (OSW-0.68) are not significant at 0.05 level, indicating the non-influence of the variable 'age' on the occupational stress of higher secondary teachers in the above said dimensions of occupational stress. Hence, the stated hypothesis '*there exist significant differences in the occupational stress of higher secondary teachers due to variations in their age*' is rejected with respect to organizational structure and climate, personal and professional efficiency, intra and inter-personal interactions and occupational stress as a whole only. Studies of Balaswamy (2011), John (2007), Naik (2011), Chona and Roxas (2009), Yahaya *et. al.* (2010) and Okoza *et. al.* (2010) supported the non impact of age on occupational stress. On the otherhand, Manoj Kumar (2006), Ramkumar (2007), Ravichandran and Rajenderan (2007), Yang *et. al.* (2009) and Sun *et. al.* (2011), found age as a significant predictor of stress among teachers and Reddy (2011) found 'organizational structure and climate' as the main source of stress among university teachers.

In case of the dimensions of job performance of higher secondary teachers belonging to various age groups, the calculated F-values with respect to the dimension task oriented behaviour (JP_1) is significant (3.07) at 0.01 level, indicating the influence of age variations on their job performance. With respect to this dimension, the job performance of teachers with higher age group is more (91.10) than their counterparts with 36 to 45 years age group (88.69) and upto 35 years age group (85.37). It means, higher the age group, better will be the job performance of teachers. On the otherhand, the F-values with respect to the dimensions – interpersonally oriented behaviour (JP_2-0.98), managerial capabilities (JP_3-0.93), personal discipline and leadership qualities (JP_4-0.05) and job performance as a whole (JPW-1.46) are not significant at 0.05 level, showing the non-impact of age variations on their job performance. Hence the formulated hypothesis '*there exist significant difference in the job performance of higher secondary teachers due to variations in their age*' is accepted with respect to task oriented behaviour only. Poropat (2011) and Kumaraswamy and Sivanandam (2004) also found that 'age' has its impact on the job performance of teachers. Figure 5.5 shows the significant mean scores of the dimensions of EI, OS and JP of higher secondary teachers with respect to their age.

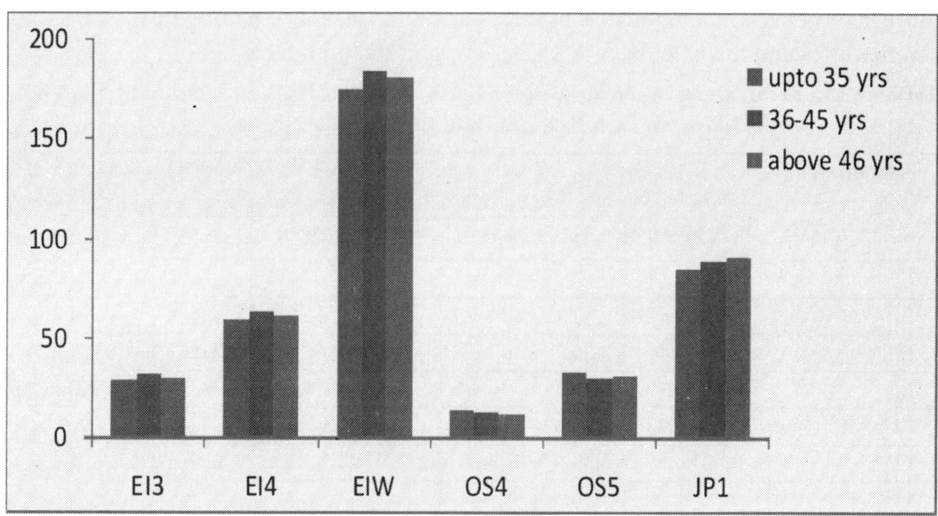

EI, OS and JP Dimensions

Fig. 5.5: Mean Scores of the Dimensions of EI, OS and JP of Higher Secondary Teachers with Respect to their Age

From the above discussion, it is concluded that the variable 'age' of the higher secondary teachers had significant bearing on their emotional intelligence dimensions – social awareness, social skills and emotional intelligence as a whole; occupational stress dimensions – home-work interface and environmental factors; and job performance dimension – task oriented behaviour. On the otherhand, the variable 'age' has not significantly influenced the higher secondary teachers' emotional intelligence dimensions – self-awareness, self-management; occupational stress dimensions – organizational structure and climate, personal and professional efficiency, intra and interpersonal interactions and occupational stress as a whole; and job performance dimensions – interpersonally oriented behaviour, managerial capabilities, personal discipline and leadership qualities and job performance as a whole. Further, the mean values indicate that the middle age group teachers possess better social awareness, social skills and emotional intelligence as a whole than their counterparts with above 46 years age group followed by upto 35 years age group. In occupational stress, the lower age group experience more stress due to home-work interface followed by their counterparts with 36 to 45 years and above 46 years age group teachers. Due to environmental factors, the teachers with upto 35 years age group experience more stress followed by the teachers having above 46 years age group and 36 to 45 years age group. In case of task oriented behaviour, the higher age group teachers' performance is better than their counterparts.

Effect of 'Community' on the Emotional Intelligence, Occupational Stress and Job Performance of Higher Secondary Teachers

The mean and SD scores of the emotional intelligence, occupational stress and job performance dimensions of higher secondary teachers belonging to different communities and the calculated F-values are presented in Table 5.14.

Table 5.14: Mean and SD Scores of the EI, OS and JP of Higher Secondary Teachers with Different Communities and the Calculated F-values

Variables	OC (N=44)		BC (N=201)		MBC, SC and ST (N=82)		Calculated F-Values
	Mean	SD	Mean	SD	Mean	SD	
EI							
EI_1	40.77	5.29	40.54	5.91	41.84	5.58	1.48@
EI_2	47.45	6.28	47.06	6.47	45.35	6.50	2.40*
EI_3	30.90	4.65	30.40	6.62	31.29	6.38	0.60@
EI_4	61.45	12.28	61.89	12.42	61.47	14.30	0.04@
EIW	180.59	23.56	179.90	26.08	179.96	28.11	0.01@
OS							
OS_1	37.06	7.92	36.44	8.72	38.60	7.42	2.99*
OS_2	30.56	8.84	30.05	7.46	31.52	7.24	1.08@
OS_3	30.86	9.58	29.61	8.67	30.13	6.39	0.45@
OS_4	14.22	6.15	12.91	5.11	14.00	4.54	2.63*
OS_5	32.68	10.28	30.79	9.50	32.74	6.92	1.75@
OSW	145.40	38.19	139.81	32.25	147.01	23.69	2.98*
JP							
JP_1	85.68	16.82	88.78	16.51	87.95	16.30	0.64@
JP_2	42.20	10.51	43.85	10.24	43.42	10.41	0.46@
JP_3	25.09	7.79	25.79	6.70	25.69	6.91	0.18@
JP_4	26.65	7.65	28.32	7.34	27.73	7.41	0.96@
JPW	179.63	37.96	186.76	35.95	184.80	36.21	0.70@

Note: @ Not Significant at 0.05 level; * Significant at 0.05 level; ** Significant at 0.01 level

The obtained F-values in Table 5.14 clearly shows that the self-management (EI_2-2.40) dimension of emotional intelligence is significant at 0.05 level; whereas, for other dimensions – self-awareness (EI_1-1.48), social awareness (EI_3-0.60), social skills (EI_4-0.04) and emotional intelligence as a whole (EIW-0.01) are not significant at 0.05 level. This implies that the variable 'community' is influencing the self-management skills of higher secondary teachers and hence, the stated hypothesis '*there exist significant difference in the emotional intelligence of higher secondary teachers due to variations in their community*' is accepted only for this dimension. Punia and Sangwan (2011) also found the influence of 'community' on emotional intelligence. Further, the mean values reveal that the teachers belonging to 'other communities' (OC-47.45) category are exhibiting higher self- management skills followed by the teachers of 'backward community' (BC-47.06) and 'most backward community, schedule cast and schedule tribes' (MBC, SC and ST - 45.35). These findings are contradicted to the findings of Poornima (2010) and Balaswamy (2011) who found that teachers of BC category have more stress followed by OC and MBC, SC and ST teachers.

With respect to occupational stress of higher secondary teachers, the formulated hypothesis '*there exist significant difference in the occupational stress of higher secondary teachers due to variations in their community*' is accepted for the dimensions-organizational structure and climate (OS_1-2.99), home-work interface (OS_4-2.63) and occupational stress as a whole (OSW-2.98), as the F-values are significant at 0.05 level. Further, the mean values show that the dimension-organizational structure and climate, and occupational stress as a whole are causing more stress for teachers coming under MBC, SC and ST (38.60) category followed by OC (37.06) and BC (36.44) categories which is also strengthened by Reddy (2011), who found that the university teachers belonging to MBC category are more stressed than their counterparts; and OC (14.22) teachers are highly stressed than the MBC, SC and ST (14.00) and BC (12.91) teachers due to the effect of home-work interface dimension of occupational stress which is supported by the Ramkumar (2007), who found that teachers belonging to OC category are more stressed than other category teachers. On the other hand, the F-values for personal and professional efficiency (OS_2-1.08), intra and interpersonal interactions (OS_3-0.45) signifies the non-influence of community on the occupational stress of teachers as their F-values are not significant at 0.05 level. Studies of Naik (2011), Poornima (2010), also found the non-impact of the variable 'community' on the occupational stress of teachers.

In case of job performance, the variable 'community' is not influencing the job performance of higher secondary teachers. The obtained F-values for the dimensions – task oriented behaviour (JP_1-0.64), interpersonally oriented behaviour (JP_2-0.46), managerial capabilities (JP_3-0.18), personal discipline and leadership qualities (JP_4-0.96) and job performance as a whole (JPW-0.70) are not significant at 0.05 level. Hence, the stated hypothesis '*there exist significant difference in the job performance of higher secondary teachers due to variations in their community*' is rejected for the above said dimensions and job performance as a whole. The significant mean scores of the dimensions of EI and OS of higher secondary teachers belonging to different communities are shown in Figure 5.6.

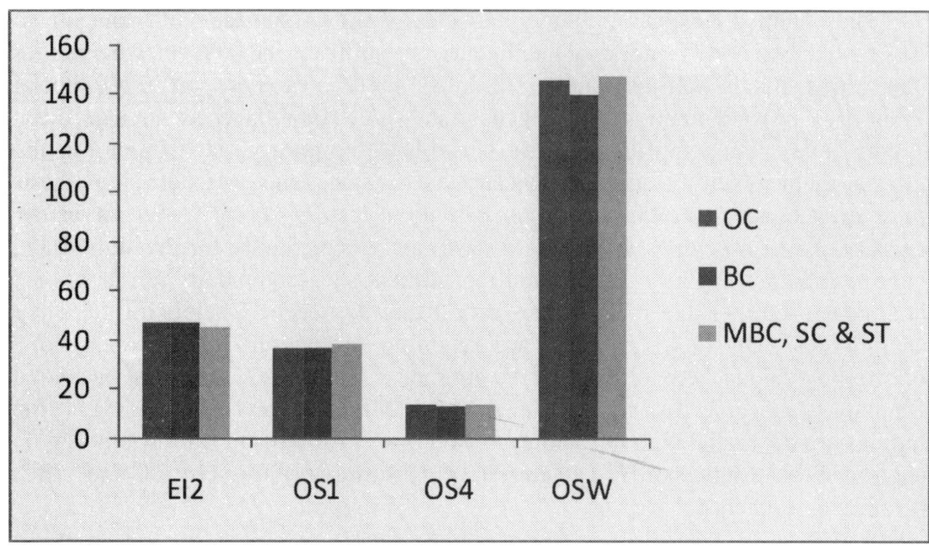

EI and OS Dimensions

Fig.5. 6: Mean Scores of the Dimensions of EI, OS and JP of Higher Secondary Teachers with Respect to their Community

On the whole, it is said that, the emotional intelligence dimension – self-management; and occupational stress dimensions – organizational structure and climate, home-work interface and occupational stress as a whole are influenced by the variable 'community' of higher secondary teachers. The mean values show that, the teachers of OC category are having more self-management skills than their counterparts with BC and MBC, SC and ST category respectively; MBC, SC and ST teachers are having higher occupational stress owing to the organizational structure and climate and occupational stress as a whole followed by OC and BC teachers, whereas, OC teachers are showing more stress due to home-work interface dimension than their counterparts belonging to MBC, SC and ST followed by BC teachers. On the otherhand, the variable 'community' has not significantly influenced the emotional intelligence dimensions – self-awareness, social awareness, social skills and emotional intelligence as a whole; occupational stress dimensions – personal and professional efficiency and intra and interpersonal interactions; and job performance dimensions – task oriented behaviour, interpersonally oriented behaviour, managerial capabilities, personal discipline and leadership qualities, and job performance as a whole.

Effect of 'Subjects Teaching' on the Emotional Intelligence, Occupational Stress and Job Performance of Higher Secondary Teachers

Table 5.15 shows the mean and SD scores of the dimensions of emotional intelligence, occupational stress and job performance of higher secondary teachers with respect to the subjects they are teaching and the calculated F-values.

Table 5.15: Mean and SD scores of the EI, OS and JP of Higher Secondary Teachers with Respect to the Different Subjects Teaching and the Calculated F-values

Variables	Languages (N=84)		Science (N=119)		Mathematics (N=67)		Commerce (N=57)		Calculated F-Values
	Mean	SD	Mean	SD	Mean	SD	Mean	SD	
EI									
EI_1	41.20	5.31	40.27	5.87	41.27	6.45	40.98	5.29	1.27@
EI_2	47.30	6.13	46.09	6.72	47.00	6.53	46.71	6.69	0.48@
EI_3	31.09	6.29	30.17	6.28	30.33	6.54	31.39	6.44	0.73@
EI_4	63.97	13.6	59.95	13.05	61.25	13.84	62.42	9.77	1.33@
EIW	183.5	26.1	176.5	26.61	179.86	28.89	181.51	22.29	1.13@
OS									
OS_1	36.12	9.05	36.21	7.43	39.75	8.50	37.14	8.44	2.49*
OS_2	28.97	6.45	30.75	7.24	32.12	9.84	30.37	6.92	1.66@
OS_3	28.24	7.933	29.22	6.99	32.34	11.36	30.76	6.41	2.80**
OS_4	12.45	5.02	12.73	4.73	15.77	6.50	13.23	3.57	4.95**
OS_5	30.81	9.39	32.58	7.56	34.39	10.67	32.92	8.39	4.04**
OSW	136.6	29.48	138.4	26.21	154.39	42.00	144.44	26.10	3.87**
JP									
JP_1	88.07	14.21	89.39	17.23	85.04	18.68	88.50	15.35	1.28@
JP_2	44.78	9.46	43.17	10.69	41.36	10.14	44.28	10.74	2.98**
JP_3	25.81	7.02	25.56	6.58	25.92	7.11	25.19	7.40	0.27@
JP_4	27.27	7.49	28.43	7.17	28.24	7.30	27.26	8.06	0.81@
JPW	185.9	33.35	186.5	36.72	180.57	38.92	185.25	37.13	0.93@

Note: @ Not Significant at 0.05 level; * Significant at 0.05 level; ** Significant at 0.01 level

The calculated F-values in Table 5.15 clearly shows that the emotional intelligence dimensions – self-awareness (EI_1-1.27), self-management (EI_2-0.48), social awareness (EI_3-0.73), social skills (EI_4-1.33) and emotional intelligence as a whole (EIW-1.13) are not significant at 0.05 level. It indicates that the variable 'subjects teaching' is not showing any impact on the emotional intelligence of higher secondary teachers and hence the formulated hypothesis '*there exist significant difference in the emotional intelligence of higher secondary teachers due to variations in their subjects teaching*' is rejected for the above said dimensions of emotional intelligence and emotional intelligence as a whole. This is contradicted in the studies of Jayanthi and Agarwal (2006) who claimed that science teachers are better in their emotional intelligence and

Subrmaniam and Cheong (2008) found that mathematics teachers are possessing high emotional intelligence than other subject teachers.

With regard to occupational stress, the stated hypothesis '*there exist significant difference in the occupational stress of higher secondary teachers due to variations in their subjects teaching'* is accepted for the dimensions – organizational structure and climate (OS_1-2.49), as the calculated F-value is significant at 0.05 level; and for other dimensions – intra and interpersonal interactions (OS_3-2.80), home-work interface (OS_4-4.95), environmental factors (OS_5-4.04) and occupational stress as a whole (OSW-3.87) are significantly different as their F-values are significant at 0.01 level. Further, the mean values also reflect that the teachers handling mathematics (OS_1-39.75; OS_3-32.34; OS_4-15.77; OS_5-34.39; and OSW-154.39) are showing higher stress followed by the teachers teaching commerce (OS_1-37.14; OS_3-30.76; OS_4-13.23; OS_5-32.92; and OSW-144.44), science (OS_1-36.21; OS_3-29.22; OS_4-12.73; OS_5-32.58; and OSW-138.40) and languages (OS_1-36.12; OS_3-28.24; OS_4-12.45; OS_5-30.81; and OSW-136.60) respectively owing to the organizational structure and climate, intra and interpersonal interactions, home-work interface, environmental factors and occupational stress as a whole. These findings are supported by Vijayalakshmi (2004), who established the impact of 'subjects teaching' on the stress of women lecturers; Hsiu-Ju Lin (2011), who revealed that language teachers are more stressed than other subject teachers; Bramaiah and Rao (2009) found that student teachers with science methodology are more stressed than their counterparts; and contradictory results were found from the studies of Soyibo (1994) and Aftab and Khatoon (2012), the non-impact of 'subjects teaching' on the stress of teachers. On the otherhand, the calculated F-value for the dimension – personal and professional efficiency (OS_2-1.66) is not significant at 0.05 level, showing that it is not influenced by the subject the teachers are handling.

In case of job performance of higher secondary teachers, the variable 'subjects teaching' has its bearing only on the dimension – interpersonally oriented behaviour (JP_2-2.98), as its F-value is significant at 0.01 level and hence, the stated hypothesis '*there exist significant difference in the job performance of higher secondary teachers due to variations in their subjects teaching,* is accepted only for this dimension. Further, the F-values for task oriented behaviour (JP_1-1.28), managerial capabilities (JP_3-0.27), personal discipline and leadership qualities (JP_4-0.81) and job performance as a whole (JPW-0.93) are not significant at 0.05 level showing its non-impact on the teachers' performance. On the otherhand, the mean values reflects that the teachers teaching languages (44.78) are ahead in their performance compared to the teachers handling commerce (44.28), science (43.17) and mathematics (41.36) owing to better interpersonally oriented behaviour. This is supported by the findings of Hsiu-Ju Lin (2011), that language teachers are better in their performance than other subject teachers. Figure 7 shows the significant mean scores of EI, OS and JP of higher secondary teachers with respect to the subjects they are handling.

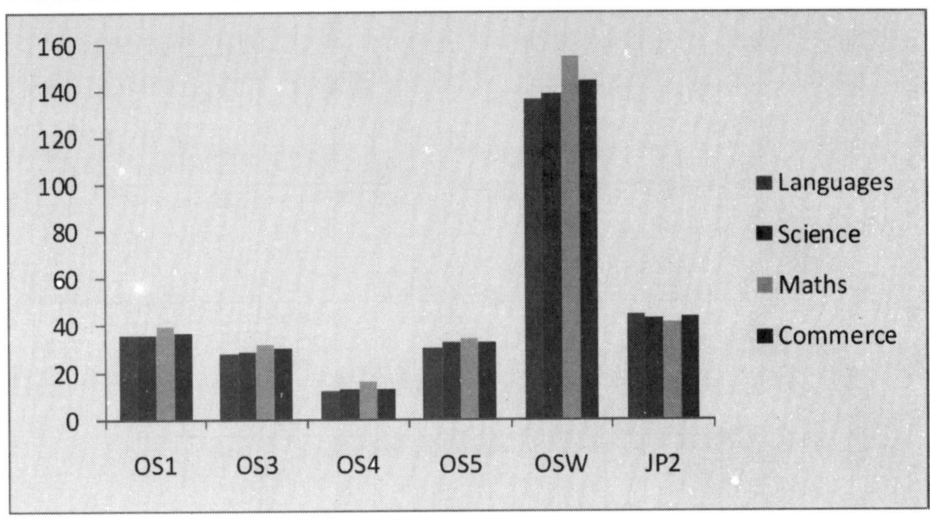

OS and JP Dimensions

Fig. 5.7: Mean Scores of the Dimensions of EI, OS and JP of Higher Secondary Teachers with Respect to the Subjects they are Teaching

On the whole, it can be said that, the variable 'subjects teaching' has significantly influenced the occupational stress dimensions – organizational structure and climate, intra and interpersonal interactions, home-work interface, environmental factors and occupational stress as a whole; and the job performance dimension – interpersonally oriented behaviour. On the otherhand, it has not shown any impact on the emotional intelligence dimensions – self-awareness, self-management, social awareness, social skills and emotional intelligence competency as a whole; occupational stress dimension – personal and professional efficiency; and job performance dimensions – task oriented behaviour, managerial capabilities, personal discipline and leadership qualities and job performance as a whole. Further, the mean values reflect that the teachers handling mathematics are having more stress due to organizational structure and climate, intra and interpersonal interactions, home-work interface, environmental factors and occupational stress as a whole followed by the teachers teaching commerce, science and languages; and teachers handling languages are showing better performance than their counterparts teaching commerce, science and mathematics respectively, owing to better interpersonal oriented behaviour of higher secondary teachers.

Effect of 'Salary Received' on the Emotional Intelligence, Occupational Stress and Job Performance of Higher Secondary Teachers

The mean and SD scores of emotional intelligence, occupational stress and job performance of higher secondary teachers with respect to the salary they receive per month and the calculated F-values are presented in Table 5.16.

Table 5.16: Mean and SD scores of the EI, OS and JP of Higher Secondary Teachers with respect to Salary Received by them and the Calculated F-values

Variables	Upto Rs.10,000 (N=91)		Rs.10,001 to Rs.15,000 (N=77)		Rs.15,001 to Rs.20,000 (N=88)		Above Rs.20,001 (N=71)		Calculated F-Values
	Mean	SD	Mean	SD	Mean	SD	Mean	SD	
EI									
EI_1	41.34	5.67	41.70	5.47	39.738	6.09	40.91	5.62	2.98**
EI_2	46.91	6.20	47.22	6.29	45.51	6.37	47.26	7.08	1.37@
EI_3	30.28	7.05	30.92	6.14	30.85	5.981	30.77	6.069	0.18@
EI_4	62.90	12.66	62.11	13.08	59.28	12.98	62.83	12.57	1.51@
EIW	181.4	26.52	181.9	25.50	175.38	26.17	181.78	26.46	1.25@
OS									
OS_1	37.20	8.59	36.11	8.07	36.97	7.28	38.04	9.50	0.66@
OS_2	29.09	6.44	29.36	7.61	32.01	8.02	31.61	8.08	3.33**
OS_3	28.83	8.07	28.19	7.86	30.06	8.11	32.95	8.53	4.99**
OS_4	13.71	5.04	12.41	4.60	13.85	5.32	13.32	5.587	1.27@
OS_5	31.30	9.42	29.20	8.14	32.06	8.38	33.70	9.89	3.23**
OSW	140.1	29.51	135.2	28.87	144.97	30.56	149.64	35.47	2.99**
JP									
JP_1	85.70	17.65	89.68	17.40	88.92	16.32	88.70	13.91	0.98@
JP_2	43.63	10.73	42.80	9.77	43.88	10.52	43.71	10.23	0.17@
JP_3	25.65	6.45	26.58	7.88	25.32	6.66	25.14	6.61	0.66@
JP_4	28.47	6.76	28.27	8.55	27.90	6.69	26.98	7.73	0.60@
JPW	183.4	36.71	187.3	38.48	186.04	35.79	184.54	34.33	0.18@

Note: @ Not Significant at 0.05 level; * Significant at 0.05 level; ** Significant at 0.01 level;

From Table 5.16, it can be clearly ascertained that the emotional intelligence dimension – self-awareness is significantly different among higher secondary teachers due to the variations in their monthly salary, as its F-value is significant at 0.01 level. Hence, the formulated hypothesis '*there exist significant difference in the emotional intelligence of higher secondary teachers due to variations in the salary they receive*' is accepted for this dimension alone. Further, the mean values with regard to self-awareness of teachers shows that the teachers receiving salary Rs. 10,001 to Rs. 15,000 and Rs. 15.001 to Rs. 20,000 are in the extreme high and low ends compared to the teachers receiving salary upto Rs. 10,000 and, above Rs. 20,001 being in the middle order respectively. It is contradicted by Poornima (2010) who found that teachers receiving higher salary are possessing high emotional intelligence. On the otherhand, the variable 'salary received' is not showing its impact on the self-management (EI_2-1.37), social awareness (EI_3-0.18), social skills (EI_4-1.51) dimensions and emotional intelligence as a whole (EIW-1.25), as their F-values are not significant at 0.05 level.

With respect to occupational stress of higher secondary teachers, the calculated F-values for the dimensions – personal and professional efficiency (OS_2-3.33), intra and interpersonal interactions (OS_3-4.99), environmental factors (OS_5-3.23) and occupational stress as a whole (OSW-2.99) are significant at 0.01 level. It means, the variable 'salary received' has its impact on the occupational stress of teachers due to the above mentioned dimensions and hence, the formulated hypothesis '*there exist significant difference in the occupational stress of higher secondary teachers due to variations in the salary they receive*'is accepted for these dimensions only. The findings of Litt and Turk (1985), Sun *et. al.* (2011), Yong (2011), Balaswamy (2011) and John (2007) also found the impact of 'salary received' on the stress of teachers. Further, the mean values shows that, the teachers receiving salary above Rs. 20,001 (OS_3-32.95; OS_5-33.70; OSW-149.64) are having more stress followed by the teachers receiving salary between Rs. 15,001 to Rs. 20.000 (OS_3-30.06; OS_5-32.06; OSW-144.97), upto Rs. 10,000 (OS_3-28.83; OS_5-31.30; OSW-140.10) and between Rs.10,001 to Rs. 15,000 (OS_3-28.19; OS_5-29.20; OSW-135.20), owing to intra and interpersonal interactions, environmental factors and occupational stress as a whole. On the otherhand, the dimensions – organizational structure and climate (OS_1-0.66) and home-work interface (OS_4-1.27) are not influenced by the salary the teachers receive, as their F-values are not significant at 0.05 level. The studies of Ramkumar (2007), Aftab and Khatoon (2012), Naik (2011) and Yahaya *et. al.* (2010) found the non impact of salary on the occupational stress of teachers.

With regard to job performance, the formulated hypothesis '*there exist significant difference in the job performance of higher secondary teachers due to variations in the salary they receive*' is rejected for the dimensions – task oriented behaviour (JP_1-0.98), interpersonally oriented behaviour (JP_2-0.17), managerial capabilities (JP_3-0.66), personal discipline and leadership qualities (JP_4-0.60) and job performance as a whole (JPW-0.18), as the calculated F-values are not significant at 0.05 level. It signifies that the job performance of higher secondary teachers is not influenced by the salary they receive. It is opposed by the findings of Kumaraswamy and Sivanandam (2004), who claimed that salary has it's impact on the job performance of teachers.

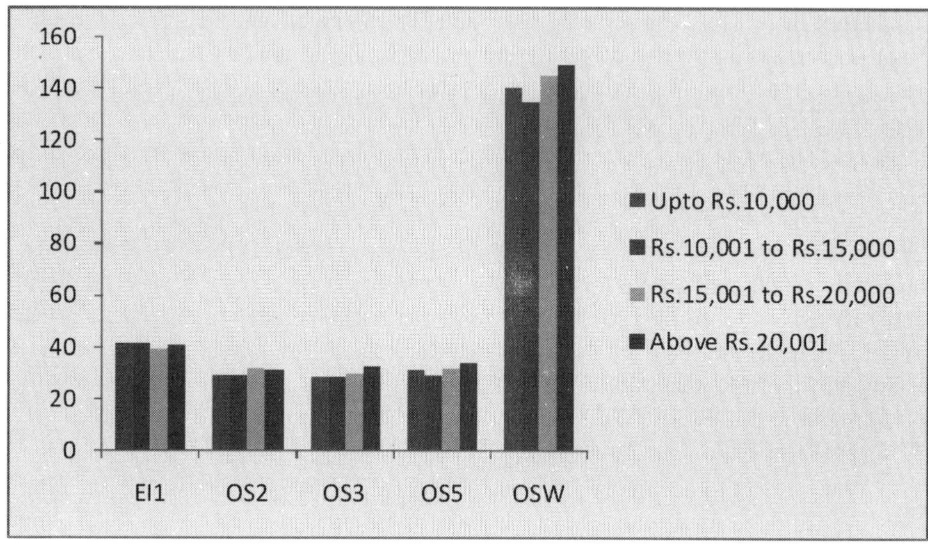

EI and OS Dimensions

Fig. 5.8: Mean Scores of the Dimensions of EI, and OS of Higher Secondary Teachers with Respect to the Salary they are Receiving

Form the above analysis, it can be concluded that, the variable 'salary received' has its significant bearing on the emotional intelligence dimension – self-awareness; occupational stress dimensions – personal and professional efficiency, intra and interpersonal interactions, environmental factors and occupational stress as a whole; whereas, it is not influencing the emotional intelligence dimensions – self-management, social awareness, social skills and emotional intelligence as a whole; occupational stress dimensions – organizational structure and climate, and home-work interface; and job performance dimensions – task oriented behaviour, interpersonally oriented behaviour, managerial capabilities, personal discipline and leadership qualities, and job performance as a whole. Further, the mean values indicate that the teachers receiving salary between Rs. 10,001 to Rs. 15,000 are having more self-awareness skills of emotional intelligence followed by the teachers receiving salary upto Rs. 10.000, Rs.20,001 and above, and between Rs. 15,001 to Rs. 20,000; whereas, teachers receiving salary above Rs.20,001 are more stressed followed by teachers receiving salary between Rs. 15,001 to Rs. 20,000; upto Rs. 10,000 and between Rs.10,001 to Rs. 15,000, owing to intra and interpersonal interactions, environmental factors and occupational stress as a whole.

CORRELATION STUDIES

One of the objectives of the study is to findout the relationship between the dimensions of emotional intelligence and occupational stress, dimensions of emotional intelligence and job performance, and dimensions of occupational stress and job performance of higher secondary teachers. To realize this objective, Karl Pearson's

Co-efficient of Correlation has been computed based on higher secondary school teachers' emotional intelligence, occupational stress and job performance.

Correlation between the Dimensions of Emotional Intelligence and Occupational Stress of Higher Secondary Teachers

Table 5.17 shows the relationship between the emotional intelligence dimensions and occupational stress dimensions of higher secondary teachers.

Table 5.17: Correlation between the Dimensions of Emotional Intelligence and Occupational Stress of Higher Secondary Teachers

EI / OS	OS_1	OS_2	OS_3	OS_4	OS_5	OSW
EI_1	0.053@	-0.120*	-0.128*	-0.177**	-0.094@	-0.105@
EI_2	0.019@	-0.180**	-0.142**	-0.126*	-0.096@	-0.125*
EI_3	0.026@	-0.090@	-0.076@	-0.119*	-0.029@	-0.063@
EI_4	0.026@	-0.121*	-0.123*	-0.156**	-0.114*	-0.114*
EIW	0.035@	-0.152**	-0.142*	-0.175**	-0.107@	-0.125*

Note: @ Not Significant at 0.05 level; ** Significant at 0.01 level; * Significant at 0.05 level

From Table 5.17, it is evinced that the dimension – self-management (EI_2) and emotional intelligence as a whole (EIW) have significant and negative relationship with OS_2 *i.e.*, personal and professional efficiency (-0.180 and -0.152), OS_3 *i.e.,* intra and interpersonal interactions (-0.142 and -0.142), OS_4 *i.e.,* home-work interface and OSW *i.e.,* occupational stress as a whole (-0.125 and -0.125). It means, higher the self-management skills and emotional intelligence competency as a whole, the lower will be the occupational stress owing to personal and professional efficiency, intra and interpersonal interactions, home-work interface and occupational stress as a whole. Similarly, the same trend is observed between self-awareness (EI_1) dimension and occupational stress dimensions – OS_2 *i.e.,* personal and professional efficiency (-0.120), OS_3 *i.e.,* intra and interpersonal interactions (-0.128) and OS_4 *i.e.,* home-work interface (-0.177). It indicates that higher the self-awareness of higher secondary teachers, the lower will be the occupational stress owing to personal and professional efficiency, intra and interpersonal interactions and home-work interface. Similarly, the social awareness (EI_3) has significant and negative relationship with the occupational stress dimension OS_4 *i.e.,* home-work interface (-0.119), showing higher the social awareness, the lower will be the occupational stress due to home-work interface. Similar results are found with regard to social skills (EI_4) dimension of emotional intelligence with OS_2 (-0.121), OS_3 (-0.123), OS_4 (-0.156), OS_5 (-0.114) and OSW (-0.114), showing higher the social skills in higher secondary teachers, lower will be the occupational stress owing to personal and professional efficiency, intra and interpersonal interactions, home-work interface, environmental factors and occupational stress as a whole. These findings are supported by Darolia and Darolia (2005), who found that emotionally intelligent people successfully deal with stressful events; Kauts and Saroj (2010), and Puri (2011) revealed that teachers with high emotional intelligence were having less occupational stress and more teacher effectiveness; Singh and Koteswari (2006) found that highly emotional intelligent people use more of coping resources of stress; whereas, Poornima (2010), Singh and Singh (2008) and Oginska-bulik (2005) found significant negative relationship between emotional intelligence and occupational stress through correlation studies.

Further, the table reveals that no significant relationship has been found between the emotional intelligence dimensions – self-awareness and OS_1 *i.e.,* organizational structure and climate (0.053), OS_5 *i.e.,* environmental factors (-0.094) and OSW *i.e.,* occupational stress as a whole (-0.105); self-management and OS_1 (0.019) and OS_5 (-0.096); social awareness and OS_1 (0.026), OS_2 (-0.090), OS_3 (-0.076), OS_5 (-0.029) and OSW (-0.063); social skills and OS_1 (0.026); and emotional intelligence as a whole and OS_1 (0.035) and OS_5 (-0.107), as their r-values are not significant at 0.05 level.

From the above, it is concluded that, the emotional intelligence dimension – self-management and emotional intelligence as a whole are negatively correlated with personal and professional efficiency, intra and interpersonal interactions, home-work interface and occupational stress as a whole. Likewise, the emotional intelligence dimension – self-awareness is also correlated negatively with personal and professional efficiency, intra and interpersonal interactions, home-work interface. Similarly, the emotional intelligence dimension – social skills has significant negative correlation with personal and professional efficiency, intra and interpersonal interactions, home-work interface, environmental factors and occupational stress as a whole; whereas, social awareness dimension of emotional intelligence is negatively correlated only with home-work interface. In contrast, the self-management and emotional intelligence as a whole has not significantly correlated with organizational structure and climate and environmental factors; self-awareness has not significantly correlated with organizational structure and climate, environmental factors and occupational stress as a whole; social awareness has not correlated to organizational structure and climate, personal and professional efficiency, intra and interpersonal interactions, environmental factors and occupational stress as a whole; and social skills is not significantly related to organizational structure and climate. It is also inferred that, higher the emotional intelligence, the lower will be the occupational stress of higher secondary teachers owing to personal and professional efficiency, intra and interpersonal interactions, home-work interface and occupational stress as a whole.

Correlation between the Dimensions of Emotional Intelligence and Job Performance Stress of Higher Secondary Teachers

Table 5.18 shows the relationship between the emotional intelligence dimensions and job performance dimensions of higher secondary teachers.

Table 5.18 clearly demonstrates that, the emotional intelligence dimension – social skills (EI_4) and emotional intelligence as a whole (EIW) have significant and positive relationship with the job performance dimensions – task oriented behaviour (JP_1: 0.14 and 0.17), interpersonally oriented behaviour (JP_2: 0.14 and 0.14), managerial capabilities (JP_3: 0.21 and 0.22), personal discipline and leadership qualities (JP_4: 0.17 and 0.19)

Table 5.18: Correlation between the Dimensions of Emotional Intelligence and Job Performance of Higher Secondary Teachers

EI / JP	JP_1	JP_2	JP_3	JP_4	JPW
EI_1	0.15**	0.11*	0.18**	0.12*	0.16**
EI_2	0.21**	0.12*	0.23**	0.23**	0.22**
EI_3	0.09@	0.08@	0.11*	0.11*	0.11*
EI_4	0.14**	0.14**	0.21**	0.17**	0.18**
EIW	0.17**	0.14**	0.22**	0.19**	0.20**

Note: @ Not Significant at 0.05 level; ** Significant at 0.01 level; * Significant at 0.05 level

and job performance as a whole (JPW: 0.18 and 0.20), as their r-values are significant at 0.01 level. It indicates that, higher the social skills and emotional intelligence competency as a whole, the better will be the job performance of higher secondary teachers owing to task oriented behaviour, interpersonally oriented behaviour, managerial capabilities, personal discipline and leadership qualities and job performance as a whole. The same trend is observed with regard to the dimensions – self-awareness and self-management with job performance dimensions – task oriented behaviour (JP_1: 0.15 and 0.21), interpersonally oriented behaviour (JP_2: 0.11 and 0.12), managerial capabilities (JP_3: 0.18 and 0.23), personal discipline and leadership qualities (JP_4 0.12 and 0.23) and job performance as a whole (JPW: 0.16 and 0.22), as their r-values are significant at 0.01 level except for interpersonally oriented behaviour and personal discipline and leadership qualities in self-awareness skills; and interpersonally oriented behaviour in self-management skills, as their r-values are significant at 0.05 level. From this, it can be estimated that, the teachers who are possessing high self-awareness and self-management skills are clearly exhibiting high level of performance due to task oriented behaviour, interpersonally oriented behaviour, managerial capabilities, personal discipline and leadership qualities and job performance as a whole. These outcomes are strengthened by the findings of Bansibihari and Surwade (2006), Puri (2011), Rathi and Rastogi (2009) and Sabu and Jangaiah (2005), who observed a positive relationship between emotional intelligence and organizational commitment and performance; Mishra and Mohapatra (2010) found that increased emotional intelligence scores were associated with increased performance among the executives working in various sectors; Bar-On, Handley, and Fund (2006) in their study on 1,171 Air Force recruiters, found that high performers had significantly higher emotional intelligence scores than the low performers; and Chang *et. al.*'s (2012) results based on 91 teams show that both average member emotional intelligence and leader emotional intelligence are positively associated with intra-team trust, which in turn positively relates to team performance.

On the otherhand, the emotional intelligence dimension – social awareness is having significant and positive relationship only with the job performance dimensions – managerial capabilities (0.21), personal discipline and leadership qualities (0.17) and job performance as a whole (0.18), as their r-values are significant at 0.01 level and;

it does not have any significant relationship with the other job performance dimensions – task oriented behaviour (0.09) and interpersonally oriented behaviour (0.08), as their r-values are not significant at 0.05 level, indicating that teachers with better social awareness skills are showing good performance due to managerial capabilities, personal discipline and leadership qualities and job performance as a whole. But, task oriented behaviour and interpersonally oriented behaviour aspects are not showing any impact on their performance.

On the whole, it can be concluded that, the teachers who are possessing higher self-awareness, self-management and social skills are showing better performance owing to task oriented behaviour, interpersonally oriented behaviour, managerial capabilities, personal discipline and leadership qualities and job performance as a whole; whereas, the social awareness skills is not showing it's impact on the job performance due to task oriented behaviour and interpersonally oriented behaviour aspects. Overall, it can be said that, higher the emotional intelligence competency as a whole, better will be the job performance as a whole of higher secondary teachers.

Correlation between the Dimensions of Occupational Stress and Job Performance of Higher Secondary Teachers

Table 5.19 shows the relationship between the occupational stress dimensions and job performance dimensions of higher secondary teachers.

Table 5.19: Correlation between the Dimensions of Occupational Stress and Job Performance of Higher Secondary Teachers

OS / JP	JP_1	JP_2	JP_3	JP_4	JPW
OS_1	-0.07@	-0.08@	-0.11*	-0.10@	-0.10@
OS_2	-0.25**	-0.15**	-0.25**	-0.21**	-0.24**
OS_3	-0.20**	-0.06@	-0.20**	-0.13*	-0.17**
OS_4	-0.19**	-0.06@	-0.15**	-0.11*	-0.15**
OS_5	-0.20**	-0.06@	-0.18**	-0.13*	-0.17**
OSW	-0.22**	-0.10@	-0.22**	-0.17**	-0.21**

Note: @ Not Significant at 0.05 level; ** Significant at 0.01 level; * Significant at 0.05 level

From Table 5.19 it is clear that, the occupational stress dimension – personal and professional efficiency (OS_2) is significantly and negatively correlated with all the job performance dimensions – task oriented behaviour (JP_1: -0.25), interpersonally oriented behaviour (JP_2: -0.15), managerial capabilities (JP_3: -0.25), personal discipline and leadership qualities (JP_4: -0.21) and job performance as a whole (JPW: -0.24), as their r-values are significant at 0.01 level. This indicates that higher the occupational stress due to personal and professional efficiency, lower will be the job performance owing to task oriented behaviour, interpersonally oriented behaviour, managerial capabilities, personal discipline and leadership qualities and job performance as a whole. Further, it is observed that the teachers who are reporting higher occupational stress due to intra and interpersonal interactions (OS_3), home-work interface (OS_4), environmental factors (OS_5) and occupational stress as a whole (OSW) are also showing lower job performance owing to the job performance dimensions – task oriented behaviour (OS_3: -0.20; OS_4: -0.19; OS_5: -0.20; and OSW: -0.22); managerial capabilities (OS_3: -0.20; OS_4: -0.15; OS_5: -0.18; and OSW: -0.22); personal discipline and leadership qualities (OSW: -0.17) and job performance as a whole (OS_3: -0.17; OS_4: -0.15; OS_5: -0.17; and OSW: -0.21), which are significantly and negatively correlated with the above said occupational stress dimensions, as their r-values are significant at 0.01 level, except for personal discipline and leadership qualities (OS_3 -0.13; OS_4 -0.11; OS_5 -0.13) which is significant at 0.05 level. This also strengthens the view that higher the occupational stress of teachers owing to intra and interpersonal interactions, home-work interface, environmental factors and occupational stress as a whole, lower will be the job performance due to: task oriented behaviour, managerial capabilities, personal discipline and leadership qualities and job performance as a whole. These findings are in tune with the findings of Akhlaq *et. al.* (2010), Akintayo (2010), Chen (2012), Giri and Kumar (2007), Hanif *et. al.* (2011), Ismail *et. al.* (2010), Khan *et. al.* (2012), and Siu (2003), who found negative and significant relationship between teachers stress and job performance; Kazmi *et. al.* (2008) found high job stress among the medical house officers, resulting in low job performance; and Manning *et. al.* (1986) studied the occupational stress: its causes and consequences for job performance among nurses and found that feelings of stress lead to depression, which, in turn, causes decrements in interpersonal and cognitive-motivational aspects of job performance.

Further, the job performance dimension – interpersonally oriented behaviour (JP_2) is not affected due to the high stress owing to OS_3 (-0.06), OS_4 (-0.06), OS_5 (-0.06) and OSW (-0.10), as their r-values are not significant at 0.05 level. This implies that the job performance dimension – interpersonally oriented behaviour of teachers is not affected by the occupational stress as a whole and all its dimensions except for personal and professional efficiency aspect. On the otherhand, occupational stress dimension – organizational structure and climate (OS_1) has significant and negative relationship only with job performance dimension – interpersonally oriented behaviour (JP_2 -0.11) signifying its impact on lower job performance owing to interpersonally oriented behaviour of teachers; whereas, it has non-significant influence on the other job performance dimensions – JP_1 (-0.07), JP_2 (-0.08), JP_4 (-0.10) and JPW (-0.10), as their r-values are not significant at 0.05 level.

From the above discussion, it can be concluded that, higher the occupational stress of higher secondary teachers owing to personal and professional efficiency, intra and interpersonal interactions, home-work interface, environmental factors and occupational stress as a whole, lower will be the job performance owing to task oriented behaviour, managerial capabilities, personal discipline and leadership qualities, and job performance as a whole, leaving alone interpersonally oriented behaviour of job performance which is affected by personal and professional efficiency aspect only. Further, the organizational structure and climate dimension of occupational stress has it's influence only on the managerial capabilities dimension of job performance.

STEPWISE MULTIPLE REGRESSION ANALYSIS

The task of scientific evaluation involves in establishing how much and how well a set of independent variables having logical bearing on the dependent variable. This can be accomplished by applying stepwise multiple regression analysis. The multiple regression analysis is carried out to predict the contribution of independent variable to the dependent variable. As one of the objectives of the study is to know how far and to what extent the independent variables (gender, age, community, marital status, educational qualification, nature of the subjects the teachers handling, salary they receive, type of school they are working-in, location of the school, and years of experience) predict the dependent variables (dimensions of EI, OS and JP) of teachers working at higher secondary level, stepwise multiple regression analysis has been carried out.

Further, to explore which of the specific dimensions of the independent variable (emotional intelligence) are the important predictors of the dimensions of occupational stress and job performance, stepwise multiple regression analysis is undertaken with occupational stress and job performance dimensions as the dependent variables. Further, to identify which of the dimensions of the independent variable (occupational stress) is the important predictor of the dependent variable (job performance), stepwise multiple regression analysis is carried out. The results of the analysis are presented in Tables 5.20 to 5.23.

Prediction of Independent Variables (Gender, Age,....) to the Dependent Variables (EI, OS and JP) of Higher Secondary Teachers

The percentage wise contribution of the independent variables (gender, age, community, marital status, educational qualification, nature of the subjects the teachers handling, salary they receive, type of school they are working-in, location of the school, and years of experience) to the dependent variables (emotional intelligence, occupational stress and job performance) of higher secondary teachers are presented in Table 5.20 along with the β co-efficient.

Table 5.20 shows that the independent variables – educational qualification, location, salary and experience are the only four variables that are accounting for the emotional intelligence of higher secondary teachers with 0.4 per cent, 0.1 per cent, 0.1 per cent and 0.3 per cent of variance respectively. In case of the occupational stress, the variable 'subjects teaching' is a significant predictor of occupational stress with 2 per cent variance, followed by 'salary' with 1.7 per cent, 'educational qualification' with 0.5 per cent, 'age' and 'marital status' with 0.4 per cent each, 'location' and 'community' with 0.2 per cent of variance each. With respect to job performance, out of ten independent variables, only three variables *i.e.,* 'location' with 1.9 per cent 'educational qualification' and 'age' with 0.9 per cent of variance each, are accounting for the occupational stress of higher secondary teachers. (*See table on next page*)

Table 5.20: Prediction of Independent Variables to EI, OS and JP of Higher Secondary Teachers

Dependent Variables	Independent Variables	Beta Co-efficients	Individual Contribution of Variable (R^2)	% Wise Contribution of Variable (R^2)
Emotional Intelligence	Qualification	-0.054	0.003	0.3
	Salary	-0.030	0.001	0.1
	Location	-0.024	0.001	0.1
	Experience	0.065	0.004	0.4
Occupational Stress	Age	-0.063	0.004	0.4
	Community	0.040	0.002	0.2
	Marital Status	0.061	0.004	0.4
	Qualification	-0.074	0.005	0.5
	Subject Teaching	0.147	0.022	2.0
	Salary	0.129	0.017	1.7
	Location	-0.039	0.002	0.2
Job Performance	Age	0.094	0.009	0.9
	Qualification	0.093	0.009	0.9
	Location	0.136	0.019	1.9

It can be concluded that 'location' and 'educational qualification' are the only independent variables that are significantly predicting all the three dependent variables *i.e.* EI, OS and JP. 'Salary' is accounting only for EI and OS, 'age' is predicting OS and JP, 'experience' is influencing the EI alone, and 'marital status', 'subjects teaching' and 'community' are accounting for OS of higher secondary teachers.

Prediction of Independent Variable (EI Dimension) to the Dependent Variable (OS Dimensions) of Higher Secondary Teachers

Table 5.21 illustrates the percentage-wise contribution of the dimensions of emotional intelligence to the dimensions of occupational stress of higher secondary teachers.

From Table 5.21, it is evident that, the emotional intelligence dimensions – self-awareness (EI_1), self-management (EI_2), social awareness (EI_3) and social skills (EI_4) emerged as the significant predicators of the dependent variable occupational stress dimensions – organizational structure and climate *i.e.* OS_1 (0.3%, nil, 0.1% and 0.1% of variance respectively); personal and professional efficiency *i.e.* OS_2 (1.4%, 3.2%, 0.8% and 1.5% of variance respectively); intra and interpersonal interactions *i.e.* OS_3 (1.6%, 2%, 0.6%, and 1.5% of variance respectively); home-work interface *i.e.* OS_4 (3.1%, 1.6%, 1.4% and 2.4% of variance respectively); and environmental factors *i.e.* OS_5 (0.9%, 0.9%, 0.1% and 1.3% of variance respectively).

Table 5.21: Prediction of Independent Variable (EI Dimensions) to Dependent Variable (OS Dimensions) of Higher Secondary Teachers

Independent Variable	Dependent Variable	Beta Co-efficients	Individual Contribution of the Variable (R^2)	% Wise Contribution of the Variable (R^2)
Self-awareness (EI_1)	OS_1	0.053	0.003	0.3
	OS_2	0.12	0.014	1.4
	OS_3	0.12	0.016	1.6
	OS_4	0.17	0.031	3.1
	OS_5	0.09	0.009	0.9
	OSW	0.10	0.011	1.1
Self-management (EI_2)	OS_1	0.019	0.00	0.00
	OS_2	0.18	0.032	3.2
	OS_3	0.14	0.020	2.0
	OS_4	0.12	0.016	1.6
	OS_5	0.09	0.009	0.9
	OSW	0.12	0.016	1.6
Social awareness (EI_3)	OS_1	0.026	0.001	0.1
	OS_2	0.09	0.008	0.8
	OS_3	0.076	0.006	0.6
	OS_4	0.11	0.014	1.4
	OS_5	0.029	0.001	0.1
	OSW	0.063	0.004	0.4
Social skills (EI_4)	OS_1	0.026	0.001	0.1
	OS_2	0.121	0.015	1.5
	OS_3	0.123	0.015	1.5
	OS_4	0.15	0.024	2.4
	OS_5	0.11	0.013	1.3
	OSW	0.11	0.013	1.3
Emotional Intelligence as a Whole (EIW)	OS_1	0.035	0.001	0.1
	OS_2	0.15	0.023	2.3
	OS_3	0.142	0.020	2.0
	OS_4	0.175	0.031	3.1
	OS_5	0.10	0.011	1.1
	OSW	0.12	0.016	1.6

A close look at the Table 5.21 also reveals that the contribution of self-awareness and Social skills dimensions are more to home work interface dimension of occupational stress *i.e.* OS_4 (3.1% and 2.4% respectively), self-management dimension is more for personal and professional efficiency *i.e.* OS_2 (3.2%), followed by intra and inter personal interactions *i.e.* OS_3 (2%). Further, it is found that emotional intelligence as a whole is a significant predictor contributing more for occupational stress dimensions – OS_4 (3.1%) followed by OS_2 (2.3%), OS_3 (2%), OSW (1.6%), OS_5 (1.1%) and least for OS_1 (0.1%).

Prediction of Independent Variable (EI Dimension) to the Dependent Variable (JP Dimensions) of Higher Secondary Teachers

Table 5.22 illustrates the percentage wise contribution of the dimensions of emotional intelligence to the dimensions of job performance of higher secondary teachers.

From Table 5.22 it is observed that, the emotional intelligence dimension – self-awareness is accounted more for the job performance dimension – managerial capabilities (JP_3) with 3.4 per cent, followed by job performance as a whole (JPW) with 2.6 per cent, task oriented behaviour (JP_1) with 2.3 per cent, personal discipline and leadership qualities (JP_4) with 1.5 per cent and interpersonally oriented behaviour (JP_2) with 1.2 per cent. When emotional intelligence dimension – self-management is considered, it is significantly predicting JP_4 with 5.4 per cent, closely followed by JP_3 with 5.3 per cent, JPW and JP_1 with 4.9 per cent and 4.4 per cent of variance, While, its contribution is least for JP_2 with 1.6 per cent of variance.

Similarly, the emotional intelligence dimension – social awareness is significantly predicting more for job performance dimension – JP_3 with 1.4 per cent and least for JP_2 with 0.8 per cent of variance. The remaining job performance dimensions are in the middle order with JPW having 1.3 per cent, JP_4 with 1.2 per cent and JP_1 with 0.9 per cent of variance. When social-skill dimension is taken into account, it's significant prediction is minimum for JP_1 with 2 per cent and maximum is for JP_3 with 4.4 per cent of variance followed by JPW with 3.3 per cent, JP_4 with 3.1 per cent and JP_2 with 2.2 per cent of variance. When emotional intelligence as a whole is considered, the dimension – JP_3 is being more influenced with 5.3 per cent of variance than JPW with 4.3 per cent, JP_4 with 3.9 per cent, JP_1 with 3.2 per cent and JP_2 with 2.2 per cent of variance. *(See table 5.22 on next page and 5.23 on 229 page)*

Prediction of Independent Variable (OS Dimensions) to the Dependent Variable (JP Dimensions) of Higher Secondary Teachers

Table 5.23 illustrates the percentage wise contribution of the dimensions of occupational stress to the dimensions of job performance of higher secondary teachers.

From Table 5.23, it is noted that the occupational stress dimensions emerged as the significant predictors for job performance dimensions with personal and professional efficiency (OS_2) accounting more for managerial capabilities (JP_3) with 6.5 per cent, task oriented behaviour (JP_1) with 6.3 per cent, job performance as a whole (JPW)

Table 5.22: Prediction of Independent Variable (EI Dimensions) to Dependent Variable (JP Dimensions) of Higher Secondary Teachers

Independent Variable	Dependent Variable	Beta Co-efficients	Individual Contribution of Variable (R^2)	% Wise Contribution of Variable (R^2)
Self-awareness (EI_1)	JP_1	0.15	0.023	2.3
	JP_2	0.11	0.012	1.2
	JP_3	0.18	0.034	3.4
	JP_4	0.12	0.015	1.5
	JPW	0.16	0.026	2.6
Self-management (EI_2)	JP_1	0.21	0.044	4.4
	JP_2	0.12	0.016	1.6
	JP_3	0.23	0.053	5.3
	JP_4	0.23	0.054	5.4
	JPW	0.22	0.049	4.9
Social awareness (EI_3)	JP_1	0.097	0.009	0.9
	JP_2	0.088	0.008	0.8
	JP_3	0.119	0.014	1.4
	JP_4	0.114	0.012	1.2
	JPW	0.11	0.013	1.3
Social skills (EI_4)	JP_1	0.14	0.020	2.0
	JP_2	0.14	0.022	2.2
	JP_3	0.21	0.044	4.4
	JP_4	0.17	0.031	3.1
	JPW	0.18	0.033	3.3
Emotional Intelligence as a Whole (EIW)	JP_1 JP_2	0.17 0.14	0.032 0.022	3.2 2.2
	JP_3	0.22	0.053	5.3
	JP_4	0.19	0.039	3.9
	JPW	0.20	0.043	4.3

Table 5.23: Prediction of Independent Variable (OS Dimensions) to Dependent Variable (JP Dimensions) of Higher Secondary Teachers

Independent Variable	Dependent Variable	Beta Co-efficients	Individual Contribution of the Variable (R^2)	% Wise Contribution of the Variable(R^2)
Organizational Structure and Climate (OS_1)	JP_1 JP_2	0.077 0.089	0.006 0.008	0.6 0.8
	JP_3	0.11	0.013	1.3
	JP_4	0.105	0.011	1.1
	JPW	0.103	0.011	1.1
Personal and Professional Efficiency (OS_2)	JP_1 JP_2	0.25 0.15	0.063 0.022	6.3 2.2
	JP_3	0.25	0.065	6.5
	JP_4	0.21	0.046	4.6
	JPW	0.24	0.062	6.2
Intra and Interpersonal Interactions (OS_3)	JP_1 JP_2	0.20 0.069	0.041 0.005	4.1 0.5
	JP_3	0.20	0.040	4.0
	JP_4	0.13	0.018	1.8
	JPW	0.17	0.031	3.1
Home-work Interface (OS_4)	JP_1 JP_2	0.19 0.061	0.037 0.004	3.7 0.4
	JP_3	0.15	0.023	2.3
	JP_4	0.10	0.012	1.2
	JPW	0.15	0.024	2.4
Environmental Factors (OS_5)	JP_1 JP_2	0.20 0.063	0.044 0.004	4.4 0.4
	JP_3	0.18	0.033	3.3
	JP_4	0.13	0.019	1.9
	JPW	0.10	0.011	1.1
Occupational Stress as a Whole (OSW)	JP_1 JP_2	0.22 0.10	0.052 0.011	5.2 1.1
	JP_3	0.22	0.050	5.0
	JP_4	0.17	0.030	3.0
	JPW	0.21	0.045	4.5

with 6.2 per cent, personal discipline and leadership qualities (JP_4) with 4.6 per cent and interpersonally oriented behaviour (JP_2) with 2.2 per cent of variance; followed by intra and interpersonal interactions (OS_3) contributing more for JP_1 with 4.1 per cent, JP_3 with 4 per cent, JPW with 3.1 per cent, JP_4 with 1.8 per cent and JP_2 with 0.5 per cent of variance; environmental factors (OS_5) predicting more for JP_1 with 4.4 per cent, JP_3 with 3.3 per cent, JP_4 with 1.9 per cent, JPW with 1.1 per cent and JP_2 with 0.4 per cent of variance; home-work interface (OS_4) is significantly influencing JP_1 with 3.7 per cent, JPW with 2.4 per cent, JP_3 with 2.3 per cent, JP_4 with 1.2 per cent and JP_2 with 0.4 per cent of variance; and organizational structure and climate (OS_1) predicting more for JP_3 with 1.3 per cent followed by JP_4 and JPW with 1.1 per cent each, JP_2 with 0.8 per cent and JP_1 with 0.6 per cent of variance. When occupational stress as a whole is considered, it is accounting more for JP_1 with 5.2 per cent and least for JP_2 with 1.1 per cent of variance. JP_3, JPW and JP_4 are in the middle order with 5 per cent, 4.5 per cent and 3 per cent of variance respectively.

The Summary and Suggestions of the present study are presented in Chapter 6.

6 SUMMARY AND SUGGESTIONS

INTRODUCTION

THE HIGHLY TURBULENT, dynamic, and competitive environment that has come to characterize the economic system at the dawn of the new millennium makes emotional intelligence (EI) more vital than ever before. Rapid technological change and an increasingly diverse workforce, contribute to a growing need for EI. Since education is viewed as an instrument to develop the cognitive understanding of people, it should prepare the younger generation to understand and face the realities of today's world. However, a teacher with innumerable degrees and high profile personality cannot necessarily be termed as a good teacher. The primary quality that makes a whole lot of difference is the classroom interaction and his/her teacher like behaviour. The teacher's behaviour not only as a person but also as a teacher is predominantly controlled by his emotional behaviour, which in turn depends upon the degree of emotional intelligence possessed by him/her. In the modern world it is not necessary to be just competent teachers, but teachers, who can question one's own actions and who are able to envisage new forms of professionalism. Emotional intelligence is a bridge between one's thoughts and feelings. It works in relation with cognitive intelligence to enable one to reach one's full potential. This quality develops over time, changes throughout life and grows with experience. One has to harmonize thought and feeling and not to separate them. Raising the levels of emotional intelligence at schools is not simply a manner of just teaching with the aim of changing the child. It is the duty of the teacher to develop and inculcate the emotional values among the students and also to be the role model for the children, particularly higher secondary students.

Higher secondary stage is the stage of education, which helps students to become matured members of the complex modern society. It is the most crucial and delicate period in the life of adolescents with lots of academic pressure and confusions over their future, which they can overcome only with the support and guidance from the teachers. It is the stage where, students find it difficult to decide on their own on many occasions as well as on many issues without proper advice and suggestions. It enables the adolescents to enter the real life as a knowledgeable, active-minded and sociable individual only when they are influenced and motivated by their teachers. For this, the teacher has to play many roles and produce value oriented citizens to the society.

Modern age of science and technology is marked by competition in every field. Surviving and progressing in such an unpredictable environment calls for the mutual functioning of the intellect, emotions and skills to manage stress and strain. Teaching has been identified as one of the most stressful occupation in many countries today. Occupational stress is an important issue in the teaching profession because of the health problems and reduction in work performance effectiveness that can result. Stress is not always bad, but it is a much-quoted ailment at work. The effects of stress are costly to both the employee as well as the organization if left unattended within a given time frame. These can lead to poorer teaching performance, lowered self-esteem, poor job satisfaction, increased absenteeism, poor decision-making and bad judgement (Quick and Quick, 1984). Much of the stress can be minimized through support, persistence, problem solving, active decision-making and planning, organizational adaptability and developing self-confidence and good human relations. Indeed, stress at work place is a barometer of the health of an organization. In this context, the present study aimed to identify the emotional intelligence, occupational stress and job performance of higher secondary teachers.

TITLE OF THE PROBLEM

"Emotional Intelligence, Occupational Stress and Job Performance of Teachers Working at Higher Secondary Level".

OPERATIONAL DEFINITION OF THE TERMS USED IN THE STUDY

The meaning and definition of the key terms used in the study along with the operational definitions are presented here under.

Emotional Intelligence

According to *The Oxford Dictionary* (2003), emotion is 'a strong mental or instinctive feeling' and emotional means 'relating to the emotions'; 'easily affected by or readily displaying emotion'; while the term intelligence refers to 'quickness of understanding'. *The Cambridge Advanced Learner's Dictionary and Thesaurus (2011)* defines emotional intelligence as 'the ability to understand the way people feel and react to use this skill to make good judgements and to avoid or solve problems'. *The Oxford On-Line Dictionary (2012)* defines emotional as 'arousing or characterized by intense feeling, having feeling that are easily excited and openly displayed, and intelligence means 'the ability to acquire and apply knowledge and skills'.

In this study, emotional intelligence of higher secondary teachers is used in terms of the ability of higher secondary teacher to understand one's own self and others in terms of his/her self-awareness, self-management, social awareness and social skills. Here Emotional Intelligence is a phrase that incorporates the intricate aspects of both emotion and intelligence.

Occupational Stress

The Cambridge Advanced Learner's Dictionary and Thesaurus (2011) defines occupation as 'a regular activity or hobby' and stress as 'a great worry caused by a difficult situation, or something which causes this condition'. According to *the Oxford On-Line Dictionary (2012),* occupational is 'relating to job or profession' and stress is 'a state of mental or emotional strain or tension resulting from adverse or demanding circumstances'.

Kyriacou and Sutcliffe (1978) defined teacher stress as 'a response to negative effect such as anger or depression of a teacher usually accompanied by psychological and biological changes resulting from aspects of teacher's job and medicated by the perception of the demands made upon the teacher which constitute a threat to his self-esteem'.

In this study, occupational stress of higher secondary teachers is defined in terms of ability of the teacher to face the challenges posed by the organizational structure and climate; personal and professional efficiency; intra and inter-personal interactions; home-work interface and; environmental factors.

Job Performance

According to *the Oxford Dictionary (2003)* the term job is referred as 'a piece of work'; 'a paid position of employment' and; performance means 'the execution or fulfillment of a duty'; 'the process of performing or carrying out'. Likewise, *The Longmans' Dictionary* (1998) defines job as 'the regular paid work that one does for an employer' and performance as 'the act of doing a piece of work, duty etc.'. *The Oxford On-Line Dictionary (2012)* has also defined job as 'a paid position of regular employment' and performance as 'a task or operation seen in terms of how successfully it is done'.

In this study, job performance of higher secondary teachers is defined as a multi-dimensional construct which refers to an individual's proficiency in task-oriented behaviour, inter-personally oriented behaviour, managerial capabilities and, the personal discipline and leadership qualities with which he/she performs goal relevant activities both directly and indirectly which contribute to the organization's as well as students overall development.

Higher Secondary Teachers

The Oxford Dictionary (2012) defines secondary education as 'relating to education for children from the age of eleven to sixteen years' and teachers as 'a person who teaches, especially in schools'.

In this study, the higher secondary teachers in the Indian context refers to 'the persons who teaches to the students in the age group of sixteen to eighteen years and are studying in 11th and 12th standard, *i.e.,* the students who are going to complete their school level education'.

OBJECTIVES OF THE STUDY

The following objectives have been framed for the present study:

1. To develop a tool to assess the level of Emotional Intelligence of teachers working at higher secondary level.
2. To develop a tool to assess the level of Occupational Stress of teachers working at higher secondary level.
3. To develop a tool to assess the level of Job Performance of teachers working at higher secondary level.
4. To develop a tool to assess the level of Job Performance of teachers working at higher secondary level as perceived by their respective Principal's/Headmaster's.
5. To find out the significant difference, if any, in the self-ratings of Job Performance of teachers working at the higher secondary level and the Job Performance rating by their respective school Principal's/Headmaster's.
6. To find out the significant difference, if any, in the Emotional Intelligence, Occupational Stress and Job Performance of teachers working at higher secondary level due to variations in their Gender (men/women); Age (up to 35 yrs / 36-45 yrs / 46 yrs and above); Community (OC / BC / MBC, SC and ST); Marital Status (married/unmarried); Educational Qualification (PG with B.Ed. and M.Ed. / PG with M.Ed. and M.Phil.); Nature of the Subject the Teachers Handling *i.e.* Languages (English, Tamil, Hindi, French) / Science (Physics, Chemistry, Botany, Zoology) / Mathematics / Commerce; Salary they Receive (up to Rs. 10,000/-, Rs. 10,001- Rs. 15,000/-, Rs. 15,001/- Rs. 20,000/-, Rs. 20,001/- and above); Type of School they are Working-in (government/private); Location of the School (rural/urban) and; Years of Experience (up to 15 yrs / 16 yrs and above).
7. To find out the relationship between the:
   - Emotional Intelligence and Occupational Stress,
   - Emotional Intelligence and Job Performance, and
   - Occupational stress and Job Performance.
8. To study how far and to what extent the independent variables (gender, age, community, marital status, educational qualification, nature of the subjects the teachers handling, salary they receive, type of school they are working-in, location of the school, and years of experience) influence the dependent variables (emotional intelligence, occupational stress and job performance).
9. To study how far and to what extent the independent variable (emotional intelligence dimensions) contribute to the dependent variables (occupational stress and job performance); independent variable (occupational stress dimensions) to the dependent variable (job performance).

ASSUMPTIONS

1. It is possible to develop tools to assess the Emotional Intelligence, Occupational Stress and Job Performance of teachers working at higher secondary level.

2. The Emotional Intelligence, Occupational Stress and Job Performance of teachers working at higher secondary level may vary.
3. It is possible to predict the contribution of independent variables (gender, age, community, marital status, educational qualification, nature of the subjects the teachers handling, salary they receive, type of school they are working-in, location of the school, and years of experience) to the dependent variables (Emotional Intelligence, Occupational Stress and Job Performance) of teachers working at higher secondary schools.
4. It is possible to predict the contribution of Emotional Intelligence dimensions to the Occupational Stress and Job Performance of teachers working at higher secondary level.

HYPOTHESES OF THE STUDY

1. There exists a significant difference in the emotional intelligence of higher secondary teachers due to variations in their gender, age, community, marital status, educational qualification, nature of the subjects the teachers handling, salary they receive, type of school the teachers are working-in, location of the school, and years of experience.
2. There exists a significant difference in the occupational stress of teachers working at higher secondary level due to variations in their gender, age, community, marital status, educational qualification, nature of the subjects the teachers handling, salary they receive, type of school the teachers are working-in, location of the school, and years of experience.
3. There exists a significant difference in the job performance of teachers working at higher secondary level due to variations in their gender, age, community, marital status, educational qualification, nature of the subjects the teachers handling, salary they receive, type of school the teachers are working-in, location of the school, and years of experience.
4. There is no significant difference in the assessment of job performance of teachers working at higher secondary level using their self rating scale and the assessment of job performance of the same teachers by their respective Principal's/Head Master's.
5. There is a positive significant correlation between the:
   - Emotional Intelligence and Occupational Stress of teachers working at higher secondary level,
   - Emotional Intelligence and Job Performance of teachers working at higher secondary level,
   - Occupational Stress and Job Performance of teachers working at higher secondary level.

SCOPE OF THE STUDY

The present study aims to identify the emotional intelligence, occupational stress and job performance of teachers working at higher secondary level. For this purpose, the Emotional Intelligence Rating Scale developed by Poornima (2010) for special education teachers based on certain emotional competencies of Goleman (2001) was adopted and modified by the investigator in accordance with the need of the present study. Similarly, the Occupational Stress Rating Scale developed by Reddy (2006), which was adopted and modified by Poornima (2010) for special education teachers has been re-modified and used for the present study. Further, the researcher has developed the Job Performance Rating Scale of teachers to assess the job performance at higher secondary level.

As the teachers self-rating scale alone may lead to biased results, the investigator also developed the Principal's/Head Master's Assessment of Teachers Job Performance Rating Scale to assess the job performance of higher secondary teachers. Here, the investigator has adopted the multi-methodology to assess the teachers' performance through the teachers self-rating as well as the assessment of the teachers by their respective principals to get an unbiased outcome. The study also intends to find out the significant differences, if any, in the emotional intelligence, occupational stress and job performance of higher secondary teachers due to variations in their gender, age, community, marital status, educational qualification, nature of the subjects the teachers handling, salary they receive, type of school they are working-in, nature of school the teachers are working-in, and years of experience.

Further, the study deliberated the relationship between emotional intelligence and occupational stress; emotional intelligence and job performance and; occupational stress and job performance of teachers working at the higher secondary level. The study also focused on how far and to what extent the personal variables such as, gender, age, community, marital status, educational qualification, nature of the subjects the teachers handling, salary they receive, type of school they are working-in, location of the school, and years of experience are contributing to the dependent variables, *i.e.,* emotional intelligence, occupational stress and job performance of higher secondary teachers. In addition, it also focuses its attention on the contribution of emotional intelligence dimensions to the dimensions of occupation stress and job performance and; occupational stress dimensions to the dimensions of job performance of higher secondary teachers.

NEED AND IMPORTANCE OF THE STUDY

Emotional intelligence has become a very popular concept in professional settings and is even analyzed in the academic domain. There is a growing consensus among the researchers, educationists and experts that in today's context, a world characterized by globalization, rapid technological change, work place diversity, and constant environmental turbulence, emotional intelligence is essential to effective individual and organizational performance. High level of emotional intelligence leads to less stress at occupational environment and positively related to organizational commitment and better performance. Numerous studies argue that personal qualities such as self-awareness, self-motivation, flexibility and integration, as well as interpersonal skills such as negotiation, listening, empathy, conflict management, and collaboration are critical ingredients for high performance (Spencer, McClelland, and Kelner, 1997;

Spencer and Spencer, 1993; Hall and Associates, 1996; Boyatzis, 1982). Individuals with greater emotional intelligence show higher levels of career, life and job satisfaction (Poornima, 2010) and become more resilient to occupational stress. The studies conducted in India and abroad on emotional intelligence of *teachers* (Amirtha and Kadiravan, 2006; Bansibihari and Pathan, 2004; David and Roy, 2010; Edannur, 2010; Lenka and Kant, 2012; Padhi and Verma, 2011; Poornima, 2010; Alfredo, 2012; Beach, 2010; Bracket *et. al.* 2010; Broli *et. al.* 2010; Hosotani and Imai-Matsumura, 2011; Karkus, 2012; Karim and weiz, 2011; Kinman *et. al.* 2011; Malik *et. al.* 2011; Nahid, 2012; Plastidou, 2011; Syed *et. al.* 2012; Trapp, 2010; Tseng, 2011; Tsouloupas *et. al.* 2010; Wong *et. al.* 2010 and so on); *students and student teachers* (Bai, 2009; Indu, 2009; Koneri, 2010; Mahajan, 2011; Nagpal, 2009; Panda, 2009; Panday, 2006; Punia and Sangwan, 2011; Shah and Thingujam, 2008; Shanwal, 2003; Shrivastava and Mukhopadhyay, 2009; Umadevi, 2009; Vijayalakshmi *et. al.* 2008; Bradshaw and Bell, 2008; Frederickson *et. al.* 2012; Han and Johnson, 2012; Lomas *et. al.* 2011; Rahim *et. al.* 2002; Ruiz-Aranda *et. al.* 2012 and so on); and *other professionals* (Faye *et. al.* 2011; Jadhav and Havalappanavar, 2009; Krishnaveni and Deepa, 2009; Prashanthi and Devi, 2009; Punia, 2005; Puri and Anju, 2011; Rajkhowa, 2002; Ramachandran *et. al.* 2011; Singh, 2005; Sinha and Jain, 2004; Goleman, Boyatzis and McKee, 2002; Jung-Hoon and Chihyung, 2012; Nelis *et. al.* 2009; Qin-Hu, 2011; Zeidner, 2004 and so on) also upholds the importance of emotional intelligence in any profession in general and teaching profession in particular.

On the other hand, there are many reasons for stress at workplace. The major sources of occupational stress are role ambiguity, loss of control, isolation, lack of administration support, emotional exhaustion, depersonalization, and lack of accomplishment in the job (Weiskopf, 1980; Maslach and Jackson, 1981; and Fimian, 1986). Occupational stress leads to the low occupational commitment and major effects on physical and psychological ill health (L. Jackson and S. Rothmann 2006; Wang Pei and Zhang Guoli 2007), absenteeism, turnover to other jobs and job dissatisfaction and low performance (Kobasaa 1982; Fimian and Santoro 1983; Siuoi-ling 2003; and Mokadad, 2005). Stress is often accepted as inescapable aspect of teaching. Teacher stress often affects the teacher's ability to function effectively (Blasé, 1986), sometimes to the extent of causing burnout (Seldman and Zager, 1998). The most serious implication of stress among teachers is the impact it has on the quality of teacher performance. Such stressed teachers cannot produce balanced and holistically developed students equipped to take on the challenges of the future. Ultimately it affects the quality of education in the country. Hence stress among teachers ought to be a matter of grave concern for one and all.

Teachers or any other employee's attitude towards their work can be best measured through their work performance, achievement, motivation and job satisfaction. In higher secondary educational institutions, teachers play an important role in development of motivation in students to strive for higher grades. Their guidance, suggestions and involvement in administrative activities help management of educational institutions to reach their goals of accomplishment. Teachers form the crux of the education system, preparing the young adolescents to build their nation with purpose and responsibility and confront the challenges of tomorrow. They are the social engineers and custodians of the future. The most pertinent question that arises in the present scenario is whether our teachers are indeed emotionally well equipped to handle the pressures and challenges of their vulnerable profession. The stressors operating in the lives of teachers is a critical issue with far reaching implications, influencing not only the quality of teachers but also the quality of the nation at large, thereby gaining prominence in academic circles.

It is a matter of great concern to all the teachers to improve the student's interest and performance in their subjects. Why do students show poor performance in any subject? Is it because of apathy, frustration, lack of motivation or aptitude, hostility, or is it because they do not understand due to lack of insight into the subject? Obviously different factors such as physiological, psychological, social, emotional and intellectual may cause aversion towards particular subject for a particular student. It is the duty of the teacher to identify and isolate these factors, especially for the students in higher secondary classes, as it is the crucial as well as transition period and a turning point in their life. The teacher has to mould and shape their ideas, expectations and ambitions into reality. For this, the teacher should have high level of emotional intelligence to understand the level of his/her pupils and help them to cope with their subjects. The teacher should also have optimum level of stress so that he/she can show good performance in his/her job there by promoting the better results of students. Many studies have supported these assumptions (Akhlaq *et. al.* 2010; Brand, 2007; Chughtai and Zafar, 2006; Gardner, 2005; Ismail *et. al.* 2009; and Kazmi *et. al.* 2008).

Studies conducted in India and abroad on stress of *teachers* (Aftab and Khatoon, 2012; Anbuchelvan, 2010; Balaswamy and Reddy, 2011; Chand and Monga, 2007; Chopra and Gartia, 2009; Naik and Reddy, 2011; Padmaja and Prabhakar, 2011; Poornima, 2010; Rao, 2010; Ravichandran and Rajenderan, 2007; Reddy, 2006; Reddy, 2011; Vijayalakshmi, 2004; Ahsan *et. al.* 2009; Borg and Riding, 1999; Chan *et. al.* 2010; Chona and Roxas, 2009; Cooper and Kelly, 1993; Crothers *et. al.* 2011; Hsiu-Julin, 2011; Leung *et. al.* 2011; McCormick and Barnett, 2011; Sprenger, 2011; Sun *et. al.* 2011, Yahaya *et. al.* 2010; Yong, 2011 and so on) have consistently concluded that teaching is a stressful occupation, and that a significant number of teachers are affected by work-related stress (Dunham, 1994; Kyriacou, 1987, 1998, 2001; Guglielmi and Tatrow, 1998). It is apparent that more research is needed into the complexities of teacher stress and its relationship to job performance, which may have some features unique to the profession in Indian context. All these research studies on emotional intelligence, occupational stress and job performance have been analyzed with varied applications in the western context. However, in Indian context, it is still relatively unclear what accounts for low levels of emotional intelligence, sources of occupational stress and the factors concerned with the job performance of higher secondary teachers.

Further, a critical view of the research studies reviewed in Chapter-II indicates the interdisciplinary studies conducted in relationship between *emotional intelligence and occupational stress* (Bajwa, 2007; Darolia and Darolia, 2005; Garg and Rastigi,

2009; Kauts and Saroj, 2010; Poornima and Reddy, 2011; Rathi and Rastogi, 2009; Singh and Koteswari, 2006; Singh and Singh, 2008; Adeyemo and Ogunyemi, 2007; Akintayo, 2010; Brand, 2007; Gardner, 2005; Jude, 2011; Mohammadyfar *et. al.* 2009; and Oginska-bulik, 2005); *emotional intelligence and job performance* (Mishra and Mohapatra, 2010; Bar-On, Handley and Fund, 2006; Chang *et al.* 2012; Farouk, 2011; Ghanizadeh and Moafian, 2009; Hulshegar *et. al.* 2010; and Nguyen, 2008); and *occupational stress and job performance* (Bhagat and Allie, 1989; Latha and Panchanatham, 2007; Akhlaq *et. al.* 2010; Chen, 2012; Chen and Cheng, 2012; Hanif *et. al.* 2011; Kazmi *et. al.* 2008; Khan *et. al.* 2012; Manning *et. al.* 1986; Siu, 2010; Sullivan and Bhagat, 1992; and Vergara *et. al.* 2010); but, the research on emotional intelligence, occupational stress and job performance of teachers working at higher secondary level are limited in both Indian and Western context.

As far as higher secondary education is concerned in India, the field is wide open to the researchers to explore the levels of teachers' emotional intelligence, occupational stress and job performance. Such studies facilitate to fill the research gaps in these aspects and further helps in identifying the factors contributing to the emotional intelligence, sources of occupational stress, which, in-turn helps the teacher to give better performance in his/her job. This helps to develop congenial and better working environment for the teachers, which will have positive implications for the students and quality education can be provided to the students. In fact, research in this area provide better insights to create effective organizational environment, healthy intra-personal relations, professional interactions, strengthening of the professional training and the ways and means to equip the teachers with personal and professional competencies to meet the needs of the global society (Reddy, 2011). Such studies explore the positive and negative factors associated with the levels of emotional intelligence, sources and consequences of stress on the teachers' profession. Similarly, the studies on job performance of teachers facilitate to know what factors are contributing the effective teaching and lower levels of teaching. Hence there is a need to study the emotional intelligence, occupational stress and job performance among the higher secondary teachers and the relationship between these variables. It may throw light on the teachers' level of emotional intelligence and their stress at work place which has an inverse effect on their performance. It enables the education facilitator and administrator to find the remedies and enhance the teachers' level of emotional intelligence and decrease their occupational stress which will have a positive impact on their job performance, thereby leading to a healthy and competitive school atmosphere.

METHODOLOGY USED IN THE STUDY

Method Survey Method is used in the Study

Tools Used in the Study

The objectives of the present study are to identify the emotional intelligence and occupational stress of higher secondary teachers and; the job performance of higher secondary teachers as assessed by teachers themselves and by their respective Principal's/Head Master's. To achieve the above stated objectives, the researcher developed and adopted the following rating scales.

1. Rating Scale to Assess the Emotional Intelligence of Teachers Working at Higher Secondary level (adopted and modified from Poornima, 2010).
2. Rating Scale to Assess the Occupational Stress of Teachers Working at Higher Secondary Level (developed by Reddy, 2006 and modified by Poornima, 2010 has been adopted and re-modified).
3. Rating Scale to Assess the Job Performance of Teachers Working at Higher Secondary Level - Self ratings (developed by the investigator).
4. Rating Scale to Assess the Job Performance of Teachers Working at Higher Secondary Level - ratings by their Principal's/H.M's (developed by the investigator).

The emotional intelligence rating scale was developed based on four dimensions *i.e.,* self-awareness, self-management, social awareness and social skills with 56 statements; the five dimensions used in the occupational stress rating scale were organizational structure and climate, personal and professional efficiency, intra and interpersonal interactions, home-work interface, and environmental factors consisting of 56 statements in total; the job performance rating scale of teachers consisting of 52 statements based on the dimensions – task oriented behaviour, interpersonally oriented behaviour, managerial capabilities, and personal discipline and leadership qualities; and the Principal's/H.M's rating scale was developed with the same dimensions as in job performance of teachers' rating scale under 20 sub dimensions in precise. The procedure adopted for developing the research tools with their reliability and validity were presented in detail in chapter-IV.

Locale and Sample of the Study

The higher secondar education of Vellore district is divided into two divisions *i.e.,* Vellore Educational District and Tirupattur Educational District with 10 blocks in each division. In each block, both government and private schools are functioning. For the purpose of the study, the investigator has selected 2 blocks in each division, considering the type of the school the teachers working-in (government/private) and location of the school (rural/urban), by using simple random sampling technique. The selected blocks are Vellore and Walaja in Vellore Educational District, and Gudiatham and Katpadi Blocks in Tirupattur Educational District.

In Vellore Block, there are 16 government and 8 private schools; Walaja Block, there are 10 government and 8 private schools; Gudiatham Block, there are 11 government and 3 private schools; and in Katpadi Block, 15 government and 10 private schools covering 52 government and 30 private schools in total, are functioning in both rural and urban areas. For the purpose of the study, the investigator has randomly selected 4 government and 4 private schools in each block taking the overall total to 16 government and 16 private schools in all the four blocks of both the Vellore and Tirupattur Educational districts, considering the location of the schools by using Simple Random Sampling Technique. All the teachers working in the selected government and private schools were the sample of the study *i.e.* 79 teachers from Vellore Block, 83 teachers from Walaja Block, 81 teachers from Gudiatham Block and 84 teachers from Katpadi Block, taking the total to 327 higher secondary teachers. The Principal's/ H.M's of the respective 32 schools are also the sample of the study to assess the job performance of the teachers working under their perview.

Data Collection

The developed tools were administered to the higher secondary teachers after establishing good rapport with the school heads and teachers. The teachers and Principal's/Head Master's were directed to go through the instructions before rating the statements in the respective tools.

Statistical Techniques Used in the Study

The collected data was analyzed by using appropriate statistical techniques such as number and percentage, mean, SD, t-test, F-test, correlations and stepwise multiple regression analysis with the help of SPSS package. To findout the number and percentage of higher secondary teachers coming under low, moderate and high levels of emotional intelligence (EI), Occupational Stress (OS) and Job Performance (JP), mean and standard deviation of EI, OS and JP scores have been computed for each teacher. By using mean ± 1SD, the number and percentage of teachers coming under low, moderate and high levels of EI, OS and JP was calculated. To identify the level of EI, OS and JP of higher secondary teachers, mean and SD of the EI, OS and JP scores have been computed for each statement. Mean ± 1 SD is used to categorize the statements into low, moderate and high levels of EI, OS and JP among higher secondary teachers. Further, to find out the significant difference, if any, in the EI, OS and JP due to variations in the independent variables (gender, age, community, marital status, educational qualification, nature of the subjects the teachers handling, salary they receive, type of school they are working-in, location of the school and years of experience) of higher secondary teachers; mean and standard deviation; t-test and F-test had been worked out. Whenever two groups are involved in a variable, t-test had been used. F-test was used when more than two groups are involved in a variable.

Correlations were computed to findout the relationship between emotional intelligence and occupational stress; emotional intelligence and job performance; and occupational stress and job performance of higher secondary teachers. To find out the contribution of the independent variables (gender, age.....) on the dependent variables (EI, OS and JP), stepwise multiple regression analysis was carried out. Also, the contribution of independent variable – EI dimensions to the dimensions of dependent variables – OS and JP; and independent variable – OS dimensions to the dimensions of dependent variable – JP has been worked out using stepwise multiple regression analysis.

FINDINGS OF THE STUDY

The results of the descriptive analysis in Part-I and differential analysis in Part-II are presented hereunder.

Part-I: Descriptive Analysis

1. More than 83 per cent of the teachers working in higher secondary schools possess moderate and low levels of emotional intelligence; whereas, 88 per cent of higher secondary teachers were experiencing moderate and high level of

occupational stress. Likewise, around 77 per cent of higher secondary teachers were showing moderate and high level of job performance (refer table 5.1).

2. The teachers working in higher secondary schools possess moderate level of EI in 7 aspects of *self-awareness* dimension *i.e.,* in defending themselves while receiving negative feedback, knowing their own feelings, acknowledging their own strengths and weaknesses, self-evaluating themselves to overcome difficult situations, feeling good about themselves, looking at their own positive and negative points and feeling confident in delivering their duty upto the expectations of the job. The same teachers are showing high level of emotional intelligence in identifying and distinguishing their own emotions, knowing their feelings and its impact on actions, knowing their priorities clearly, and in being happy with the way of looking at the things. Contrary to this, the teachers possess low level of self-awareness in only one aspect *i.e.,* continuing to act on their beliefs even under criticism.

In the dimension *self-management*, the higher secondary teachers possess moderate level of emotional intelligence in the aspects of having ability to change ideas and goals based on new information to fit into new situations, having presence of mind, feeling restless in accepting new ideas and information, ready to accept the mistakes when situation demands, impossible to do the entrusted duties with responsibility and commitment, ability to maintain the standards of honesty and integrity, ready to take calculated risks to reach the goals, initiating actions to create possibilities for the future, motivated by optimism to overcome any hurdles to go forward, and sometimes it is difficult to reach even the smallest goals. Further, the same teachers are exhibiting low levels of self-management in certain aspects such as: difficulty in controlling over their anger, ability to maintain patience on many occasions, capable of behaving calmly even in stressful situations, hesitate to take up new assignments , always acts on own values even at significant risks, and well organized in the work.

With regard to the dimension – *social awareness*, the higher secondary teachers are showing high level of social awareness by making themselves available to the students even after the school hours, if the students are in need. Contrary to this, the teachers are showing low level of self-management with respect to the interference in the feelings of others and helping them to overcome it, and ability to confront with the unethical actions of others. Further, the teachers are demonstrating moderate levels of social awareness on certain aspects such as; unable to see the people suffering, capable of handling teaching aids to cater to the needs of special children, sometimes finds it difficult to relate the curriculum to the diverse backgrounds of special children, able to understand the organizational values and unspelt rules in many situations, always work by understanding the organizational financial constraints and act accordingly, always works to meet the requirements of the job and not fully aware of the infrastructure available in the school.

Under the *social skills* dimension, the teachers exhibit low level of social skills only in two aspects such as; difficulty in seeking help from others when it is needed and not convinced by appealing to the students and parents interest. Their social skills are at high level in six aspects such as; appreciating others for their success, maintaining good relations and co-operating with the school personnel, having clear ideas to realize the vision of the school, quarrel with others when things are not in favour, adopt new teaching techniques to make learning more effective and establishing and maintaining close relationship with other professionals at work. Apart from this, the higher secondary teachers are demonstrating moderate level of social skills with regard to; encouraging colleagues to work even when things are not favourable, do not insist the students to learn what they are lacking, try to provide mentoring and coaching of colleagues, easy to make friends, not easy to get along with others in the work situations, ready to provide guidance and counseling to the students and their parents, can lead others by setting an example, trying to move away from the conflicting situations, like to be active partner in solving the conflicts in the school and believing that working with group leads to failure (refer table 5.2).

3. With respect to the OS dimension – *organizational structure and climate*, it is clear that, the long working hours and expectations to do more work, large class size with students of diverse needs and taking responsibilities for the activities of others are the major stressors causing high level of stress among the higher secondary teachers. Contrary to this, the teachers are having low level of occupational stress in certain aspects such as; carrying multiple responsibilities in a short span of time, lack of information in carrying out the professional responsibilities, working on assignments that are not necessary to the profession, inadequate trained human resources to carryout the work assigned and lack of time to pay individual attention to each special needs student. Further, the same teachers are showing moderate level of occupational stress in 6 aspects such as; lack of equipments and teaching learning materials, inadequate supportive staff in the school, lack of involvement in the decision-making process of the activities related to the teaching profession, lack of opportunities for promotion in the school, inadequate salary for the work done in the school and stringent rules and regulations in the school that hinders to act independently.

Certain aspects related to the *personal and professional efficiency*, such as; inadequate training to meet the demands of the profession, lack of commitment and interest to perform the job, difficulty in managing students in the classroom and difficulty in solving the problems that arise out of work are evoking low level of stress among teachers, whereas, the aspects such as; lack of opportunities for professional enhancements in the form of participation in professional meetings/seminars/ conferences, inadequate knowledge in using new aids and appliances, thrusting on development of curricular innovations and materials, over qualified to perform the job, problem in identification and assessment procedures, facing problems in decision-making process, unable to complete the task within a stipulate period of time and difficult to implement new policies and procedures in place of those already in practice are making the teachers experience moderate level of stress.

With regard to the dimension *intra and interpersonal interactions*, the higher secondary teachers exhibit moderate level of stress with regard to; difficulty in adjusting with the fellow teachers in the school, stressful interactions with parents and lack of parental support, lack of teamwork and professional collaboration to meet the diverse needs of children, being angry with the students for their continuous failure, difficulty in understanding the students behaviour, difficulty in satisfying the requirements of the management, misunderstanding the organizational values and goals, lack of pro-active communication with the management, poor quality of feedback and supervision that address the teachers' concern and difficult to discuss the failure of the students with their parents. On the other hand, the teachers are showing low level of stress in only two aspects *i.e.,* lack of healthy interactions between/among the teachers and inadequate knowledge to give guidance and counseling to students and parents.

Under the dimension *home-work interface*, the higher secondary teachers experience equal amount of low and moderate levels of stress with 3 aspects in each of them. The financial problems at home, difficulty in concentrating in the classroom due to tension with the spouse and priority for family needs are placing the teachers under low level stress category, whereas, health of their children, education of their children and insufficient salary are the sources of moderate level of stress.

With regard to the dimension *environmental factors*, the higher secondary teachers are showing high level of stress due to the seldom opportunities to utilise their abilities and experience independently. In the remaining aspects *i.e.,* bullying and frightening by the students inside and outside the school, complaints by the students, complaints by the staff members, problems with students indiscipline, lack of reward for the hard labour and efficient performance, problems of students with drug abuse, problems due to fraud and financial mismanagement within the school, polluted working environment, difficult to solve students disputes, problems with the theft and damage of the school property by the students, and lack of respect for teachers by the pupils, parents and society, the teachers are experiencing moderate level of stress (refer table 5.3).

4. The teachers working at higher secondary schools are exhibiting low level of job performance under the dimension – *task oriented behaviour* in 5 aspects *i.e.,* reviewing the prior lesson for student understanding and assess the knowledge acquired before starting the new lesson, using of appropriate audio-visual aids to make teaching more effective, do not make varying stimuli like movements, gestures, voice modulation, pausing etc. while teaching, do not resort to remedial teaching whenever necessary and do not require any orientation class, in-service training, workshop, short term bridge courses etc. to update the knowledge. The teachers' performance is moderately focused on the aspects such as; not planning the lesson to be taught in advance, writing being more legible and unambiguous, efficiency in handling any kind of teaching technology, following interactive and explorative way of teaching-learning in the class, pupils participation is appreciated with both verbal and non-verbal reinforces, assigning independent and group tasks to students to encourage their individuality, well informed about the contemporary or current events, memory is being fairly good, allowing the students to contact even after the class hours to clear their doubts and ready to acquire the required skills which are not present. The same teachers

are demonstrating high level of job performance with regard to; being confident and thoroughly prepare the content before taking the class, teaching is well organized according to the objectives, voice being audible to the student in the last bench, try to stimulate the intellectual curiosity of the students, conducting periodic tests after every unit, feedback is given to the students who fail in the final exams, refer other books relevant to the topic, enjoy the teaching to the full extent and satisfied with the teaching.

With regard to the dimension – *interpersonally oriented behaviour*, the higher secondary teachers' job performance is high in welcoming the suggestions of parents in the students' progress. With regard to; discussing the strengths and weaknesses of the students with their parents, generate awareness and understanding among the parents on different aspects of learning difficulties in children, parents and students will be given information about the courses offered and different avenues available after completing the higher secondary course, ignoring the view points of the students, importance of vocational education is highlighted to the students, to improve the writing skills of the students, more of written work will be given, to improve the oral communication, students are asked to give oral presentation, students creativity is being encouraged and curiosity is being stimulated to know the hidden truth behind the scientific facts, other colleagues are being involved in improving the weak students are being involved in improving the weak students, group studies among students is being encouraged and bright students are encouraged to help the students who are weak in their academics, the teachers job performance is at moderate level.

The higher secondary teachers have shown least performance under the dimension – *managerial capabilities* in 3 aspects *i.e.,* needs of special children is not being emphasized and brought to the notice of the administration, not involving in the schools decisions and difficulty to abide by the principles and priorities of the school. While the teachers are showing moderate level of job performance in the remaining 5 aspects such as; involving in the functions and programmes of the school, even though they are not related to the subject, concentration on developing self capabilities rather than on the position in the school, understanding the values and unspoken rules of the school, striving hard to maintain the identity of the school and teaching is being affected by the administrative policies of the school.

Under the dimension – *personal discipline and leadership qualities*, the higher secondary teachers' performance is high in their sense of duty and responsibility. Contrary to this, their performance is low in the aspects – difficulty to work effectively under the pressure of deadline and accepting the corporal punishment in the schools. In the remaining aspects, the teacher's exhibit moderate level of performance *i.e.,* being punctual and sticking to the school timings, habits being clean and inspiring, clarity and fluency in the language, gives the best in an unsupportive environment and being easily approachable (refer table 5.4).

5. The Principal's/H.M's rated the higher secondary teachers' performance moderately in all sub-dimensions except for 'punctuality' under the dimension – personal discipline and leadership qualities (PDLQ), where it is rated high. In

contrary, they rated 'contribution to progress of the school' under the dimension – managerial capabilities (MC), and 'fluency in language' and 'discipline' under the dimension – PDLQ, as low. On the otherhand, the teachers are high in their opinion about their 'written and oral skills', 'evaluation', and 'attitude and aptitude' under task oriented behaviour (TOB); developing good relationship 'with parents' under interpersonally oriented behaviour (IOB); and 'punctuality' under PDLQ. Further, the teachers placed themselves moderately in 3 sub-dimensions *i.e.,* 'content', 'methodology', 'knowledge enrichment', and TOB as a whole under the dimension TOB; 3 sub-dimension *i.e.,* 'relationship with students', 'colleagues', 'between students', and IOB as a whole under the dimension IOB; only one aspect *i.e.,* 'follows rules of the school' under the dimension MC; and 3 sub-dimensions under 'involves in school's activities', 'contributes to school's progress' and MC as a whole under MC; and 'fluency in language' and 'discipline' under PDLQ. On the whole, the Principal's/H.M's and the teachers rated moderately about the performance of higher secondary teachers (refer table 5.5).

6. When job performance as a whole is taken into account, the ratings of the higher secondary teachers and their Principal's/H.M's are same, except for the aspects *evaluation* and developing good relationship *with parents*. Overall, out of twenty job performance aspects, only in two aspects the teachers and Principal's/H.M's differ in their ratings about the job performance of higher secondary teachers. The dimension wise job performance of higher secondary teachers and job performance as a whole also indicate that the self-ratings of the teachers and the ratings of their Principal's/H.M's are going hand in hand and, hence, it can be said that the tool, used to assess the job performance of higher secondary teachers based on teachers self-ratings is valid (refer table 5.6).

Part – II: Differential Analysis

7. The variable *gender* has significant influence on the emotional intelligence dimensions – self-awareness, social skills and emotional intelligence as a whole; occupational stress dimensions – organization structure and climate, personal and professional efficiency, intra and interpersonal interactions, home-work interface, environmental factors and occupational stress as a whole. On the otherhand, the variable is not having significant bearing on the emotional intelligence dimensions – self-management and social awareness; and job performance dimensions – task oriented behaviour, interpersonally oriented behaviour, managerial capabilities, personal discipline and leadership qualities, and job performance as a whole. Further, the mean values indicate that women teachers are better in their self-awareness skills, social skills and emotional intelligence competency as a whole compared to their counterparts; and men teachers are possessing more occupational stress compared to women teachers owing to organizational structure and climate, personal and professional efficiency, intra and interpersonal interactions, home-work interface, environmental factors and occupational stress as a whole (refer table 5.7).

8. The variable *marital status* has its significant bearing on the occupational stress dimension – environmental factors alone and is not having any significant influence on the emotional intelligence dimensions – self-awareness, self-management, social awareness, social skills and emotional intelligence as a whole; occupational stress dimensions – organizational structure and climate, personal and professional efficiency, intra and interpersonal interactions, home-work interface and occupational stress as a whole; and job performance dimensions – task oriented behaviour, interpersonally oriented behaviour, managerial capabilities, personal discipline and leadership qualities, and job performance as a whole of higher secondary teachers (refer table 5.8).
9. The variable *educational qualification* is not significantly influencing any of the dimensions of emotional intelligence (self-awareness, self-management, social awareness, social skills and emotional intelligence as a whole), occupational stress (organizational structure and climate, personal and professional efficiency, intra and interpersonal interactions, home-work interface, environmental factors and occupational stress as a whole) and job performance (task oriented behaviour, interpersonally oriented behaviour, managerial capabilities, personal discipline and leadership qualities and job performance as a whole) of higher secondary teachers (refer table 5.9).
10. The occupational stress dimensions – personal and professional efficiency, intra and interpersonal interactions, environmental factors and occupational stress as a whole are significantly influenced by the variable *type of school the teachers are working-in*, indicating that the teachers working in the government higher secondary schools are more stressed than their counterparts. The insignificance of the variable is found with the emotional intelligence dimensions – self-awareness, self-management, social awareness, social skills and emotional intelligence as a whole; occupational stress dimensions – organizational structure and climate and home-work interface; and job performance dimensions – task oriented behaviour, interpersonally oriented behaviour, managerial capabilities, personal discipline and leadership qualities, and job performance as a whole (refer table 5.10).
11. The variable *location of the school* has its significant bearing on the occupational stress dimension – homework interface and the mean values indicating rural teachers having more stress due to this dimension than their counterparts; and job performance dimensions – task oriented behaviour, managerial capabilities and job performance as a whole with higher mean values for urban teachers than the rural teachers. Contradictory to this, the variable is not influencing the emotional intelligence dimensions – self-awareness, self-management, social awareness, social skills and emotional intelligence as a whole; occupational stress dimensions – organizational structure and climate, personal and professional efficiency, intra and interpersonal interactions, environmental factors and occupational stress as a whole; and job performance dimensions – interpersonally oriented behaviour, personal discipline and leadership qualities and, job performance as a whole of higher secondary teachers (refer table-11).

12. The variable *years of experience* is not significantly influencing the emotional intelligence dimensions – self-awareness, self-management, social awareness, social skills and emotional intelligence as a whole; occupational stress dimensions – organizational structure and climate, personal and professional efficiency, intra and interpersonal interactions, home-work interface, environmental factors and occupational stress as a whole; and job performance dimensions – task oriented behaviour, interpersonally oriented behaviour, managerial capabilities, personal discipline and leadership qualities, and job performance as a whole of higher secondary teachers (refer table 5.12).
13. The variable *age* of the higher secondary teachers had significant bearing on their emotional intelligence dimensions – social-awareness, social skills and emotional intelligence as a whole; occupational stress dimensions-home-work interface and environmental factors; and job performance dimension- task oriented behaviour. On the otherhand, the variable 'age' has not significantly influenced the higher secondary teachers' emotional intelligence dimensions – self-awareness, self-management; occupational stress dimensions – organizational structure and climate, personal and professional efficiency , intra and interpersonal interactions and occupational stress as a whole; and job performance dimensions – interpersonally oriented behaviour, managerial capabilities, personal discipline and leadership qualities, and job performance as a whole. Further, the mean values indicate that the middle age group teachers possess better social awareness, social skills and emotional intelligence as a whole than their counterparts with above 46 years age group followed by upto 35 years age group. In occupational stress, the lower age group experience more stress due to home-work interface followed by their counterparts with 36 to 45 years and above 46 years age group teachers. Due to environmental factors, the teachers with upto 35 years age group experience more stress followed by the teachers having above 46 years age group and 36 to 45 years age group. In case of task oriented behaviour, the higher age group teachers' performance is better than their counterparts (refer table 5.13).
14. The emotional intelligence dimension – self-management; and occupational stress dimensions – organizational structure and climate, home-work interface and occupational stress as a whole are influenced by the variable *community* of higher secondary teachers. The mean values show that, the teachers of OC category are having more self-management skills than their counterparts with BC and MBC, SC and ST category respectively; MBC, SC and ST teachers are having higher occupational stress owing to the organizational structure and climate and occupational stress as a whole followed by OC and BC teachers, whereas, OC teachers are showing more stress due to home-work interface dimension than their counterparts belonging to MBC, SC and ST followed by BC teachers. On the otherhand, the variable 'community' has not significantly influenced the emotional intelligence dimensions – self-awareness, social awareness, social skills and emotional intelligence as a whole; occupational stress dimensions – personal

and professional efficiency and intra and interpersonal interactions; and job performance dimensions – task oriented behaviour, interpersonally oriented behaviour, managerial capabilities, personal discipline and leadership qualities, and job performance as a whole (refer table 5.14).

15. The variable *subjects teaching* has significantly influenced the occupational stress dimensions – organizational structure and climate, intra and interpersonal interactions, home-work interface, environmental factors and occupational stress as a whole; and the job performance dimension – interpersonally oriented behaviour. On the otherhand, it has not shown any impact on the emotional intelligence dimensions – self-awareness, self-management, social awareness, social skills and emotional intelligence competency as a whole; occupational stress dimension – personal and professional efficiency; and job performance dimensions – task oriented behaviour, managerial capabilities, personal discipline and leadership qualities, and job performance as a whole. Further, the mean values reflect that the teachers handling mathematics are having more stress due to organizational structure and climate, intra and interpersonal interactions, home-work interface, environmental factors and occupational stress as a whole followed by the teachers teaching commerce, science and languages; and teachers handling languages are showing better performance than their counterparts teaching commerce, science and mathematics respectively, owing to better interpersonally oriented behaviour of higher secondary teachers (refer teble 5.15).

16. The variable *salary received* has its significant bearing on the emotional intelligence dimension – self-awareness; occupational stress dimensions – personal and professional efficiency, intra and interpersonal interactions, environmental factors and occupational stress as a whole; whereas, it is not influencing the emotional intelligence dimensions – self-management, social awareness, social skills and emotional intelligence as a whole; occupational stress dimensions – organizational structure and climate, and home-work interface; and job performance dimensions – task oriented behaviour, interpersonally oriented behaviour, managerial capabilities, personal discipline and leadership qualities, and job performance as a whole. Further, the mean values indicate that the teachers receiving salary between Rs. 10,001 to Rs. 15,000 are having more self-awareness skills of emotional intelligence followed by the teachers receiving salary upto Rs. 10.000, Rs. 20,001 and above, and between Rs. 15,001 to Rs. 20,000; whereas, teachers receiving salary above Rs. 20,001 are more stressed followed by teachers receiving salary between Rs. 15,001 to Rs. 20.000, upto Rs. 10,000 and between Rs. 10,001 to Rs. 15,000, owing to intra and interpersonal interactions, environmental factors and occupational stress as a whole (refer table 5.16).

Correlation Studies

17. The emotional intelligence dimension – self-management and emotional intelligence as a whole are negatively correlated with personal and professional efficiency, intra and interpersonal interactions, home-work interface and occupational stress as a whole. Likewise, the emotional intelligence dimension – self-awareness is

also correlated negatively with personal and professional efficiency, intra and interpersonal interactions, home-work interface. Similarly, the emotional intelligence dimension – social skills has significant negative correlation with personal and professional efficiency, intra and interpersonal interactions, home-work interface, environmental factors and occupational stress as a whole; whereas, social awareness dimension of emotional intelligence is negatively correlated only with home-work interface. In contrast, the self-management and emotional intelligence as a whole has not significantly correlated with organizational structure and climate and environmental factors; self-awareness has not significantly correlated with organizational structure and climate, environmental factors and occupational stress as a whole; social awareness has not correlated with organizational structure and climate, personal and professional efficiency, intra and interpersonal interactions, environmental factors and occupational stress as a whole; and social skills is not significantly related to organizational structure and climate. It is also inferred that higher the emotional intelligence, the lower will be the occupational stress of higher secondary teachers owing to personal and professional efficiency, intra and interpersonal interactions, home-work interface and occupational stress as a whole (refer table 5.17).

18. The teachers who are possessing higher self-awareness, self-management and social skills are showing better performance owing to task oriented behaviour, interpersonally oriented behaviour, managerial capabilities, personal discipline and leadership qualities, and job performance as a whole; whereas, the social awareness skills is not showing it's impact on the job performance due to task oriented behaviour and interpersonally oriented behaviour aspects. Overall, it can be said that, higher the emotional intelligence competency as a whole, better will be the job performance as a whole of higher secondary teachers (refer table 5.18).
19. Higher the occupational stress of higher secondary teachers due to personal and professional efficiency, intra and interpersonal interactions, home-work interface, environmental factors and occupational stress as a whole, lower will be the job performance owing to task oriented behaviour, managerial capabilities, personal discipline and leadership qualities, and job performance as a whole, leaving alone interpersonally oriented behaviour of job performance which is affected only by personal and professional efficiency aspect of occupational stress. Further, the organizational structure and climate dimension of occupational stress has it's influence only on the managerial capabilities dimension of job performance (refer table 5.19).

Step-wise Multiple Regression Analysis

20. The independent variables – *educational qualification, location, salary and experience* are the only four variables that are accounting for the emotional intelligence of higher secondary teachers with 0.4 per cent, 0.1 per cent, 0.1 per cent and 0.3 per cent of variance respectively. In case of the occupational stress, the variable *subjects teaching* is a significant predictor of occupational stress with 2 per cent variance, followed by *salary* with 1.7 per cent, *educational*

qualification with 0.5 per cent, *age* and *marital status* with 0.4 per cent each, *location* and *community* with 0.2 per cent of variance each. With respect to job performance, out of ten independent variables, only three variables *i.e., location* with 1.9 per cent *educational qualificat*ion and *age* with 0.9 per cent of variance each, are accounting for the occupational stress of higher secondary teachers (refer table 5.20).

21. The emotional intelligence dimensions – self-awareness (EI_1), self-management (EI_2), social awareness (EI_3) and social skills (EI_4) emerged as the significant predicators of the dependent variable occupational stress dimensions – organizational structure and climate *i.e.* OS_1 (0.3%, nil, 0.1% and 0.1% of variance respectively); personal and professional efficiency *i.e.* OS_2 (1.4%, 3.2%, 0.8% and 1.5% of variance respectively); intra and interpersonal interactions *i.e.* OS_3 (1.6%, 2%, 0.6%, and 1.5% of variance respectively); home-work interface *i.e.* OS_4 (3.1%, 1.6%, 1.4% and 2.4% of variance respectively); and environmental factors *i.e.* OS_5 (0.9%, 0.9%, 0.1% and 1.3% of variance respectively). The contribution of self-awareness and social skills dimensions are more to home work interface dimension of occupational stress *i.e.* OS_4 (3.1% and 2.4% respectively), self-management dimension is more for personal and professional efficiency *i.e.* OS_2 (3.2%), followed by intra and inter personal interactions *i.e.* OS_3 (2%). Further, it is found that emotional intelligence as a whole is a significant predictor contributing more for occupational stress dimensions – OS_4 (3.1%) followed by OS_2 (2.3%), OS_3 (2%), OSW (1.6%), OS_5 (1.1%) and least for OS_1 (0.1%) (refer table 5.21).

22. The emotional intelligence dimension – self-awareness is accounted more for the job performance dimension – managerial capabilities (JP_3) with 3.4 per cent, followed by job performance as a whole (JPW) with 2.6 per cent, task oriented behaviour (JP_1) with 2.3 per cent, personal discipline and leadership qualities (JP_4) with 1.5 per cent and interpersonally oriented behaviour (JP_2) with 1.2 per cent; self-management is significantly predicting JP_4 with 5.4 per cent, closely followed by JP_3 with 5.3 per cent, JPW and JP_1 with 4.9 per cent and 4.4 per cent of variance, While, its contribution is least for JP_2 with 1.6 per cent of variance; social-awareness is significantly predicting more for job performance dimension – JP_3 with 1.4 per cent, least for JP_2 with 0.8 per cent of variance, JPW having 1.3 per cent, JP_4 with 1.2 per cent and JP_1 with 0.9 per cent of variance; and When social-skill dimension is taken into account, it's significant prediction is minimum for JP_1 with 2 per cent and maximum is for JP_3 with 4.4 per cent of variance followed by JPW with 3.3 per cent, JP_4 with 3.1 per cent and JP_2 with 2.2 per cent of variance. When emotional intelligence as a whole is considered, the dimension – JP_3 is being more influenced with 5.3 per cent of variance followed by JPW with 4.3 per cent, JP_4 with 3.9 per cent, JP_1 with 3.2 per cent and JP_2 with 2.2 per cent of variance (refer table 5.22).

23. The occupational stress dimensions emerged as the significant predictors for job performance dimensions with personal and professional efficiency (OS_2)

accounting more for managerial capabilities (JP_3) with 6.5 per cent, task oriented behaviour (JP_1) with 6.3 per cent, job performance as a whole (JPW) with 6.2 per cent, personal discipline and leadership qualities (JP_4) with 4.6 per cent and interpersonally oriented behaviour (JP_2) with 2.2 per cent of variance; followed by intra and interpersonal interactions (OS_3) contributing more for JP_1 with 4.1 per cent, JP_3 with 4 per cent, JPW with 3.1 per cent, JP_4 with 1.8 per cent and JP_2 with 0.5 per cent of variance; environmental factors (OS_5) predicting more for JP_1 with 4.4 per cent, JP_3 with 3.3 per cent, JP_4 with 1.9 per cent, JPW with 1.1 per cent and JP_2 with 0.4 per cent of variance; home-work interface (OS_4) is significantly influencing JP_1 with 3.7 per cent, JPW with 2.4 per cent, JP_3 with 2.3 per cent, JP_4 with 1.2 per cent and JP_2 with 0.4 per cent of variance; and organizational structure and climate (OS_1) predicting more for JP_3 with 1.3 per cent followed by JP_4 and JPW with 1.1 per cent each, JP_2 with 0.8 per cent and JP_1 with 0.6 per cent of variance. When occupational stress as a whole is considered, it is accounting more for JP_1 with 5.2 per cent and least for JP_2 with 1.1 per cent of variance, whereas, JP_3, JPW and JP_4 are in the middle order with 5 per cent, 4.5 per cent and 3 per cent of variance respectively (refer table 5.23).

IMPLICATIONS OF THE STUDY

1. The study revealed that around 83 per cent of the higher secondary teachers possess moderate and low levels of emotional intelligence, and there is a need for enhancing and improving the emotional intelligence of teachers at in-service and pre-service levels. Researches indicate that social and emotional intelligence are associated with success in many areas of life, including effective teaching, student learning, quality relationships and academic performance. Integrated programmes should be introduced into schools that includes training on social and emotional skills for both teachers and students, and should receive backing from all levels of the authorities. Additionally, programmes should be field tested, evidence based, and focused on sound psychological or educational theory. EI training workshops for teachers should be organized to provide in-depth information about the EI skills which play an integral role in academic learning, decision-making, classroom management, stress management, interpersonal relationships, team building, and overall quality of teaching profession. Further, the educational institutions should appoint teachers based on their EI skills, train teachers on EI skills and concepts, create norms and values that encourage people to demonstrate EI skills, and put performance management system in place, such as specifying performance goals.
2. From the results it was found that, around 88 per cent of higher secondary teachers are experiencing moderate and high levels of occupational stress. This indicates the need for interventions in strengthening and reinforcing teacher's self-confidence and positive attitude, and weakening the stress creating factors. Stresses of job life can be conveniently managed, to a large extent, at different stages through various institutional interventions such as;
   - Prevention of stress through organizational interventions at the management level, like, selection of suitably qualified teachers, proper job designing and

training, adequate work conditions, effective supervision and incentive system, effective communication system, participative management, etc.

- Minimizing the frequency and intensity of stressful situations integral to the job at the organizational level.
- Moderating the intensity of integral job stressors and their consequent strains through the effect of other variables of positive values, such as high or extra salary, non-financial incentives, social support, generating team feeling, participative decision-making, etc.

3. As 77 per cent of the higher secondary teachers are showing moderate and high level of job performance, it is necessary to enhance and upkeep their performance level. For this, first and foremost, the teachers need to be aware of their abilities, emotions and accurately understand themselves; they also need to be adept in understanding their pupils concerns, needs, abilities, and feelings to relate well with them. To be effective in their teaching, the teachers need to be self-reliant and decisive in making realistic and effective performance as and when they handle the classes. This facilitates them to work effectively even under pressure and maintain positive approach. Also, the teachers should possess empathy, stress tolerance, high levels of emotional intelligence, self-regard, and flexibility. On the otherhand, it is essential to provide favourable working environment; improve planning and programming; provide modern teaching aids and technology; arrange for orientation classes, refresher courses, in-service training programmes, short term bridge courses, etc.
4. The level of job performance of higher secondary teachers as assessed from the teachers self-ratings and the ratings of their Principal's/H.M.'s, out of 20 sub-dimensions, the teachers rated high and low for 5 each and moderate for the remaining 10 sub-dimensions On the otherhand, the Principal's/H.M.'s rated moderately for all the sub-dimensions except for three and one sub-dimension which are rated as low and moderate. Overall, both the teachers and Principal's/H.M.'s rated job performance as a whole moderately.
5. Further, in the assessment of job performance of higher secondary teachers, the ratings of the Principal's/H.M's are in acceptance with the self-ratings of the teachers about their performance in all aspects except for 'evaluation' and 'relationship with parents'. The dimension wise job performance of higher secondary teachers and job performance as a whole also indicate that the self-ratings of the teachers and the ratings of their Principal's/H.M's are going hand in hand and hence, it can be said that the tool used to assess the job performance of higher secondary teachers based on teachers self-ratings is valid.
6. The study revealed that the EI of women teachers is better than their counterparts in terms of self-awareness and social skills; the social awareness, social skills and EI as a whole has more impact on the 'age' of higher secondary teachers with teachers belonging to 36 to 45 years age group than the teachers in the above 46 years and upto 35 years age group; the self-management has its bearing on the 'community' with teachers of OC category having more self-management skills

than their counterparts with BC and MBC, SC and ST category respectively; and 'salary' of the teachers is influenced by the self-awareness with teachers receiving salary between Rs. 10,001 to Rs. 15,000 having more self-awareness skills followed by the teachers receiving salary upto Rs. 10.000, Rs. 20,001 and above, and between Rs. 15,001 to Rs. 20,000. This trend indicates that while enhancing and giving EI training, these categories of teachers should be given due importance. More of soft skills training should be provided to men teachers, teachers in the above 46 years and upto 35 years age group, BC and MBC, SC and ST teachers, and teachers receiving salary upto Rs. 10.000, Rs. 20,001 and above, and between Rs. 15,001 to Rs. 20,000. They should be involved in group discussions and group meetings to understand the pupils and be more effective in teaching.

7. It is found that, men teachers are showing more occupational stress than the women teachers owing to occupational stress as a whole and its dimensions; the environmental factors of OS has influenced the 'marital status' with unmarried teachers being more affected by this; the OS dimensions – personal and professional efficiency (OS_2), intra and interpersonal interactions (OS_3), environmental factors (OS_5) and occupational stress as a whole (OSW) are significantly influenced by the 'type of school the teachers are working-in', indicating that the teachers working in the government higher secondary schools are more stressed than their counterparts; 'location of the school' has its significant bearing on the OS dimension – homework interface (OS_4) with rural teachers having more stress due to this dimension than their counterparts; 'age' has its impact on OS dimensions- OS_4 and OS_5 with lower age group being more stressed due to OS_4 followed by their counterparts with 36 to 45 years and above 46 years age group teachers, and teachers with upto 35 years age group experience more stress followed by the teachers having above 46 years age group and 36 to 45 years age group due to OS_5; OS dimensions – organizational structure and climate (OS_1), OS_4 and OSW are influenced by the variable 'community' of higher secondary teachers with MBC, SC and ST teachers having higher stress owing to the OS_1 and OSW followed by OC and BC teachers, whereas, OC teachers are showing more stress due to OS_4 dimension than their counterparts belonging to MBC, SC and ST followed by BC teachers; 'subjects teaching' has its impact on OS dimensions – OS_1, OS_3, OS_4, OS_5 and OSW with teachers handling mathematics showing more stress due to OS_1, OS_3, OS_4, OS_5 and OSW followed by the teachers teaching commerce, science and languages; and 'salary' has its impact on OS dimensions – OS_2, OS_3, OS_5 and OSW with teachers receiving salary above Rs. 20,001 are more stressed followed by teachers receiving salary between Rs. 15,001 to Rs. 20.000, upto Rs. 10,000 and between Rs. 10,001 to Rs. 15,000, owing to the above mentioned dimensions. Perhaps, the best way to reduce stress for teachers in the above mentioned categories is a problem solving approach, which involves identification of sources of stress in the particular working environment, so that adequate interventions can be planned as effectively as possible. Organizational support in the schools needs to be increased both quantitatively and qualitatively in terms of staffing levels, resources and time.

8. The study revealed that the JP of teachers due to 'location of the school' is better among urban teachers than their counterparts owing to JP dimensions – task oriented behaviour (JP_1), managerial capabilities (JP_3) and job performance as a whole (JPW); the higher 'age' group teachers' performance is better than their counterparts due to task oriented behaviour; and teachers handling languages are showing better performance than their counterparts teaching commerce, science and mathematics respectively, owing to better interpersonally oriented behaviour (JP_2). This implies that, steps must be taken to improve the quality and performance of rural schools, teachers of young and middle age groups, and teachers handling mathematics, science and commerce subjects , on par with their counterparts in terms of organizational support, infrastructural facilities, managerial involvement, developing better relationship among teachers, and perks and rewards to enhance their performance.
9. The correlation studies revealed that there is a significant negative correlation between EI and OS; OS and JP; and positive relationship between EI and JP. These results reinforce the need to enhance and inculcate EI among higher secondary teachers to reduce their OS and further improve their JP. Further, a reduction in stress may result in improved job performance provided stress is reduced by introducing healthy organizational conditions. Control at the individual level and correction at the institutional level of some work stress areas such as perceived career tension, heavy workload, supervisory evaluation, availability of information, and decision-making may considerably reduce the experienced job stress.
10. The results based on the stepwise multiple regression analysis revealed that all the dimensions of EI *i.e.,* self-awareness, self-management, social awareness and social skills have contributed for both occupational stress and job performance of higher secondary teachers. This further strengthens the need for developing more EI skills among the teachers to be included both in pre-service and in-service programmes to weaken their stress levels and upkeep their performance. In case of occupational stress, all its dimensions (organizational structure and climate, personal and professional efficiency, intra and interpersonal interactions, home-work interface, environmental factors and occupational stress as a whole) have significantly contributed to the job performance of higher secondary teachers indicating the need for improvement in the organizational structure and interpersonal relationships, efficiency of the teachers, and home-work environmental factors for better performance of teachers.

DELIMITATIONS OF THE STUDY

1. The study is confined to the Vellore District of Tamil Nadu state.
2. The study is limited only to the teachers working at the higher secondary level.
3. Rating Scale is the only tool used to assess the emotional intelligence, occupational stress and job performance of higher secondary teachers.
4. The emotional intelligence and occupational stress have been assessed only based on the self-ratings of the teachers.

5. Students' academic achievement results are not included to assess the job performance of the higher secondary teachers.
6. The effect of only a few personal variables such as gender, age, community, marital status, educational qualification, nature of the subjects the teachers handling, salary they receive, type of school they are working-in, location of the school, and years of experience on emotional intelligence, occupational stress and job performance has been studied.

SUGGESTIONS FOR FURTHER RESEARCH

1. Studies can be conducted to findout the emotional intelligence, occupational stress and job performance of higher secondary teachers in other districts of Tamil Nadu and other parts of India.
2. Studies can be conducted to identify the emotional intelligence, occupational stress and job performance of teachers working in primary, secondary and university levels.
3. Studies can be conducted to assess the emotional intelligence and occupational stress of teachers using multiple tools.
4. Studies can be attempted to assess the emotional intelligence, occupational stress and job performance of higher secondary teachers using multi methodologies for cross validation of the results.
5. Studies can be done to develop the tools to enhance or train the emotional intelligence of teachers at all levels.
6. Studies can be made to give special emphasis on emotional intelligence alone and develop standardized tool for higher secondary teachers in Indian context.
7. Studies can be carriedout to know/develop the coping strategies to reduce the occupational stress of higher secondary teachers.
8. Longitudinal studies can be made to know the stress patterns among the teachers.
9. Studies can be conducted to develop the performance enhancement packages for higher secondary teachers.
10. Studies can be conducted to findout the impact of other independent variables that are not included in the present study on the dependent variables *i.e.* EI, OS and JP of higher secondary teachers.

BIBLIOGRAPHY

Adams, J.S. (1963) 'Towards an Understanding of Inequity', *Journal of Abnormal and Social Psychology*, 67, pp. 422-436.

Adams, J.S. (1965) *Advances in Experimental Social Psychology*, in L. Berkowitz, Inequality in Social Exchange (2nd ed.), Academic Press: New York.

Adeyemo, D.A. and Ogunyemi, B. (2007) '*Emotional Intelligence and Self-efficacy as Predictors of Occupational Stress among Academic Staff in a Nigerian University*', Ph.D. Thesis, Department of Education, Olabisi Onabanj University, Ago-lwoye, Nigeria.

Adsul, R.K. and Kamble, V.S. (2009) 'Academic Stress, Achievement Motivation and Academic Achievement as Predictors of Adjustment among High School Students', *Asian Journal of Psychology and Education*, 42 (7-8), pp. 25-32.

Aftab, Maria. and Khatoon, Tahira. (2012) 'Demographic Differences and Occupational Stress of Secondary School Teachers', *European Scientific Journal,* 8 (5), pp. 159-175.

Ahsan, N., Abdullah, Z., Gunfie, D.Y. and Alam, S.S. (2009) 'A Study of Job Stress on Job Satisfaction among University Staff in Malaysia: An Empirical Study', *European Journal of Social Sciences*, 8 (1), pp. 121-131.

Akhlaq, M., Amjad, B.M., Mehamood, K., Hassan, Seed-ul. and Malik, S. (2010) 'An Evaluation of the Effects of Stress on the Job Performance of Secondary School Teachers', *Journal of Law and Psychology*, 43, pp. 136-144.

Akintayo, D.I. (2010) 'Managerial Effectiveness: Impact of Emotional Intelligence and work-family Role Conflict on Work Organizations in Nigeria', *Eastern African Social Science Review*, 26 (1), pp. 23-40.

Akram, M. J. (2010) '*Factors Affecting the Performance of Teachers at Higher Secondary Level in Punjab*', Ph.D Thesis, University Institute of Education and Research, Rawalpindi, Pakistan.

Akram, Muhammad.J., Raza, Syed.A., Khaleeq, Abdur.R. and Atika, Samrana. (2011) 'Principals' Perception Regarding Factors Affecting the Performance of Teachers', *Journal of International Education Research*, 7 (2), pp. 38-46.

Akrani, G. (2011) 'Relationship between Stress and Job Performance', *Industrial Psychology*, 9 (4), pp. 128-136.

Al-Amri, A.A. (2004) 'Job Stress among Teachers', *Journal of King Saud University-Arts,* 16 (2), pp. 36-42.

Alfredo, Fuentes. (2012) 'Closing the Mathematical Achievement Gap through the Heart to the Brain: *A Case Study of Urban High School Mathematics Teachers' Perceptions of How their Emotional Intelligence Facilitates Instruction and Learning in the Classroom*', Dissertation work, Department of Cognitive Psychology, University Of Hartford.

Alimi, Baba. Gana., Adda, Gana. Bukar. and Yabawa, Mohammed. Kadai. (2011) 'An Assessment of Teachers' Job Satisfaction and Job Performance in Three Selected Secondary Schools of Borno State in Nigeria', *Continental Journal of Education Research*, 4 (1), pp. 28-34.

Amirtha, A. and Kadhiravan, S. (2006) 'Influence of Personality on the Emotional Intelligence of Teachers', *EduTracks*, 5 (12), pp. 25-29.

Anbuchelvan, C. (2010) 'Occupational Stress of High School Teachers', *EduTracks*, 9 (9), pp. 31-33.

Anderson, J.G. (1991) 'Stress and Burnout among Nurses: A Social Network Approach', *Journal of Social Behaviour and Personality*, 6 (7), pp. 251-272.

Anderson, R.A. (1978) *Stress Power*, Human Services Press: New York.

Anjum, Ambreen., Yasmeen, Kausar. and Khan, Bashir. (2011) 'Performance Appraisal Systems in Public Sector Universities of Pakistan', *International Journal of Human Resource Studies*, 1 (1), pp. 41-51.

Antoniou, A.S., Polychroni, F. and Vlachakis, A.N. (2006) 'Gender and Age Differences in Occupational Stress and Professional Burnout between Primary and High School Teachers in Greece', *Journal of Managerial Psychology*', 21 (7), pp. 682-690.

Antoniou, A.S., Polychroni, F. and Walters, B. (2000) '*Sources of Stress and Professional Burnout of Teachers of Special Educational Needs in Greece*', Paper Presented at the International Special Education Congress held at University of Manchester from 24th to 28th July.

Anuradha, R.K. and Sreedevi, V. (2007) 'Job Competence and Job Performance of ICDS Supervisors', *Journal of Extension and Research,* 9 (1 and 2), pp. 18-22.

Anuradha, S. (1986) *Management and Job Performance,* Gyan Publications: New Delhi.

Appelbaum, S.A. (1973) 'Psychological Mindedness: Word, Concept, and Essence', *International Journal of Psycho-Analysis*, 54, pp. 35-46.

Argyris, C. (1964) *Integrating the Individual and Organization*, Wiley: New York.

Aryee, S. and Luk, V. (1996) 'Balancing Two Major Parts of Adult Life Experience: Work and Family Identity among Dual-Career Couple', *Human Relations*, 49, pp. 465-487.

Ashforth, B.E. and Humphrey, R.H. (1993) 'Emotional Labour in Service Roles: The Influence of Identity', *Academy of Management Review*, 18, pp. 88-115.

Ashforth, B.E. and Humphrey, R.H. (1995) 'Emotion in the Workplace: A Reappraisal', *Human Relations*, 48, pp. 97-124.

Azad, J.L. (2003) 'Teacher of the New Millennium', *International Educator*, 15 (2), pp. 9-14.

Bacharach, S.B., Bamberger, P. and Conley, S. (1990) 'Work Processes, Role Conflict, and Role Overload: The Case of Nurses and Engineers in the Public Sector', *Work and Occupations*, 17, pp. 199-228.

Bacharach, S.B., Bauer, S.C. and Conley, S. (1986) 'Organizational Analysis of Stress: The Case of Elementary and Secondary Schools', *Work and Occupations*, 13 (1), pp. 7-32.

Bachman, W. (1998) *Nice Guys Finish First: A Symlog Analysis of US Naval Commands,* in R.B. Polley, A.P. Hare, and P.J. Stone (eds.), The Symlog Practitioner: Applications of Small Group Research (pp. 133-153), Praeger: New York.

Bai, Saroja. (2011) 'Study of Anxiety Proneness and Emotional Intelligence in Relation to Academic Achievement of Pre-university Students', *International Referred Research Journal,* 2 (22), pp. 1-5.

Bajwa, S. (2007) 'Effect of Yoga Exercises on Emotional Stability and Academic Stress of High School Students', *Journal of Community Guidance and Research*, 24 (2), pp. 188-195.

Bakshi, R., Sudha, N. and Sandhu, P. (2008) 'Impact of Occupational Stress on Home Environment: An Analytical Study of Working Women of Ludhiana City', *Journal of Human Ecology*, 23 (3), pp. 231-235.

Balabaskar, K. (2010) 'Impact of Occupational Stress on Special Educators Working in Special Schools', *Disabilities and Impairments*, 24 (1), pp. 13-22.

Balaswamy, R.C. (2011) '*Occupational Stress of Primary School Teachers Working in Kuppam Mandal*', M.Phil. Dissertation, Dravidian University, Kuppam.

Bandura, A. (1997) *Self-efficacy: The Exercise of Control*, Freeman: New York.

Bansibihari, P. and Pathan, Y.G. (2004) 'Emotional Intelligence of Secondary Teachers in Relation to Gender and Age', *Asian Journal of Psychology and Education*, 39 (5-6), pp. 18-21.

Bansibihari, P. and Surwade, L. (2006) 'The Effect of Emotional Maturity on Teacher Effectiveness', *EduTracks*, 6 (1), pp. 37-38.

Barnard, C. (1938) *The Functions of the Executive,* Harvard University Press: Cambridge, MA.

Baron, A.R. and Byrne, D. (1997) *Social Psychology*, MA, Allyn and Bacon: Boston.

Bar-On, R. (1988) '*The Development of An Operational Concept of Psychological Well-being*', Ph.D. Thesis, Rhodes University, South Africa.

Bar-On, R. (1996, August) '*The Era of the EQ: Defining and Assessing Emotional Intelligence*', Poster Session Presented at the 104th Annual Convention of the American Psychological Association, Toronto, Canada.

Bar-On, R. (1997) *Bar-On Emotional Quotient Inventory: A Measure of Emotional Intelligence*, *Technical Manual (ed.)*, Multi-Health Systems: Toronto.

Bar-On, R. (1997a, August) '*Development of the Bar-On EQ-i: A Measure of Emotional and Social Intelligence*', Paper Presented at the 105th Annual Meeting of the American Psychological Association, Chicago.

Bar-On, R. (1997b) *The Emotional Quotient Inventory (EQ-i): Technical Manual*, Multi-Health Systems: Toronto, Canada.

Bar-On, R. (2000) Emotional *and Social Intelligence: Insights from the Emotional Quotient Inventory (EQ-i)*, in R. Bar-On and J.D.A. Parker (eds.), *Handbook of Emotional Intelligence*, Jossey-Bass: San Francisco.

Bar-On, R. (2003) 'How Important is it to Educate People to be Emotionally and Socially Intelligent, and it can be done?', *Perspectives in Education*, 21 (4), pp. 3-13.

Bar-On, R. (2004) *The Bar-On Emotional Quotient Inventory (EQ-i): Rationale, Description, and Summary of Psychometric Properties*, in G. Geher (ed.), Measuring Emotional Intelligence: Common Ground and Controversy (pp. 111-142), Hauppauge, Nova Science Publishers: New York.

Bar-On, R. (2006) 'The Bar-On Model of Emotional-Social Intelligence (ESI)', *Psicothema, 18*, Supl., pp. 13-25.

Bar-On, R. and Handley, R. (2003a) *The Bar-On EQ-360,* Multi-Health Systems: Toronto, Canada.

Bar-On, R. and Handley, R. (2003b) *The Bar -On EQ-360: Technical Manual*, Multi-Health Systems: Toronto, Canada.

Bar-On, R. and Parker, J. D. A. (Eds.) (2000) *The Handbook of Emotional Intelligence: Theory, Development, Assessment, and Application at Home, School, and in the Workplace*, Jossey-Bass: San Francisco.

Bar-On, R., Handley, P. and Fund, S. (2006) *The Impact of Emotional Intelligence on Performance*, in V.U. Druskat, F.A. Sala, and G. Mount (eds.), Linking Emotional Intelligence at work: Current Research Evidence with Individuals and Groups, Mahwah, New Jersey: Erlbaum.

Barrick, M.R. and Mount, M.K. (1991) 'The Big Five Personality Dimensions and Job Performance: A Meta-analysis', *Personal Psychology*, 44, pp. 1-26.

Barrick, M.R. and Mount, M.K. (1993) 'Conscientiousness and Performance of the Sales Representatives: Test of the Mediating Effects of Goal Setting', *Journal of Applied Psychology*', 78, pp. 715-722.

Barsade, S.G. and Gibson, D.E. (1998) *Group Emotion; A View from Top and Bottom*, in D.H. Gruenfeld, B. Mannix and M. Neale (eds.), Research on Managing Groups and Teams; Composition (Vol. 1, pp. 81-102), JAI Press: Greenwich, CT.

Basowitz, H., Persky, H., Korchin, S.J. and Grinker, R.R. (1958) 'Anxiety in a Life Stresses', *Journal of Psychology,* 38, pp. 503-510.

Basu, J., Mitra, S.K. and Bhattacharya, P. (2004) 'Mothering the Mentally Challenged Child: A Qualitative Explanation of the Stress and Strengths', *Journal of Community Guidance and Research*, 21 (3), pp. 282-292.

Basu, Sarah. (2009) 'Stress among Teacher Educators', *University News*, 47 (49), pp. 22-24.

Bateman, T.S. and Organ, D.W. (1983) 'Job Satisfaction and the Good Soldier: The Relationship between Affect and Employee Citizenship', *Academy of Management Journal*, 26, pp. 587-595.

Beach, Kyong. C. (2010) '*Emotional Intelligence among Elementary Learners, Parents, and Teachers in Korean English Language Institutes*', Dissertation, Bilingual Education, Foreign language institution, North-Central University, Korea.

Beehr, T.A. (1976) 'Perceived Situational Moderators of the Relationship between Subjective Role Ambiguity and Role Strain', *Journal of Applied Psychology*, 61, pp. 35-40.

Beehr, T.A. (1985) *The Role of Social Support in Coping with Organizational Stress*, in T.A. Beehr and R.S. Bhagat (eds.), Human Stress and Cognition in Organizations (pp. 375-398), John Wiley: New York.

Beehr, T.A. (1985a) *Organizational Stress and Employee Effectiveness: A Job Characteristics Approach*, in T.A. Beehr and R.S. Bhagat (eds.), Human Stress and Cognition in Organizations, John Wiley: New York.

Beehr, T.A. (1995) *Psychological Stress in the Workplace*, Routledge and Kegan Paul: London.

Beehr, T.A. and Newman, J.E. (1978) 'Job Stress, Employee Health, and Organizational Effectiveness: A Facet Analysis, Model and Literature Review', *Personnel Psychology*, 31, pp. 665-669.

Beer, J. and Beer, J. (1992) 'Burnout and Stress, Depression and Self-esteem of Teachers', *Psychological Reports,* 71 (3), pp. 1331-1336.

Begley, D. (1982) '*Burnout among Special Education Administrators*', Paper Presented at the Summer Convention of the Council for Exceptional Children, Houston, Texas.

Behere, Shashank. P., Yadav, Richa. and Behere, Prakash. B. (2011) 'A Comparative Study of Stress among Students of Medicine, Engineering, and Nursing', *Indian Journal of Psychological Medicine,* 33 (2), pp. 145-148.

Ben-Bakr, K.A., Al-Shammari, I.S. and Jefri, O.A. (1995) 'Occupational Stress in Different Organizations: A Saudi Arabian survey', *Journal of Management Psychology*, 10 (5), pp. 24-28.

Best, J.W. (1989) *Research in Education*, Prentice Hall of India Pvt. Ltd., New Delhi.

Bhagat, R.S. and Allie, S.M. (1989) 'Organizational Stress, Personal Life Stress, and Symptoms of Life Strains: An Examination of the Moderating Role of Sense of Competence', *Journal of Vocational Behaviour,* 35 (3), pp. 231-253.

Biswas, A., Kapur, M. and Kaliaperumal, V.G. (1995) 'Stressful Life Events and Adjustment Pattern of Psychologically Disturbed and Non-disturbed Children of the Middle Childhood Period', *Indian Journal of Clinical Psychology*', 22 (10), pp. 7-13.

Biswas, S., Giri, V.N. and Srivastava, K.B.L. (2007) 'Assessing the Impact of Organizational Culture and Communication on Employee Performance and Organizational Effectiveness', *National Academy of Psychology, India,* 52 (1), pp. 20-28.

Blasé, J.J. (1982) 'A Social-psychological Grounded Theory of Teacher Stress and Burnout', *Educational Administration Quarterly*, 18 (4), pp. 93-113.

Blasé, J.J. (1986) 'A Qualitative Analysis of Sources of Teacher Stress: Consequences for Performance', *American Educational Research Journal*, 23, pp. 13-40.

Blix, A.G., Cruise, R.J., Mitchell, B.M. and Blix, G.G. (1994) 'Occupational Stress among University Teachers', *Educational Research*, 36 (2), pp. 157-69.

Bobko, P., Roth, P.L. and Potosky, D. (1999) 'Derivation and Implications of a Meta-Analytic Matrix Incorporating Cognitive Ability, Alternative Predictors, and Job Performance', *Personnel Psychology*, 52, pp. 561-589.

Bokti, N.L.M. and Talib, M.A. (2009) 'A Preliminary Study on Occupational Stress and Job Satisfaction among Male Navy Personnel at a Naval Base in Lumut, Malaysia', *Journal of International Social Research*, 2 (9), pp. 1-9.

Borg, M. (1990) 'Occupational Stress in British Educational Settings: A Review', *Educational Psychology*, 10, pp. 103-126.

Borg, M.G. and Riding, R.J. (1991) 'Occupational Stress and Satisfaction in Teaching', *British Educational Research Journal*, 17 (3), pp. 263-281.

Borman, W.C. and Brush, D.H. (1993) 'More Progress towards Taxonomy of Managerial Performance Requirements', *Human Performance*, 6(1), pp. 1-21.

Borman, W.C. and Motowidlo, S.J, (1997) 'Task Performance and Contextual Performance: The Meaning for Personnel Selection Research' *Human Performance*, 10 (2) pp. 99-109.

Borman, W.C. and Motowidlo, S.J. (1993) *Expanding the Criterion Domain to Include Elements of Contextual Performance*, in N. Schmitt and W.C. Borman (eds.), Personnel Selection in Organizations (pp. 71-98), Jossey-Bass: San Francisco, CA.

Borman, W.C., Motowidlo, S.J., Rose, S.R. and Hansen, L.M. (1985) *Development of A Model of Soldier Effectiveness,* Personnel Decisions Research Institute: Minneapolis, MN.

Bowling, N.A. (2007) 'Is the Job Satisfaction – Job Performance Relationship Spurious? A Meta-analytic Examination,' *Journal of Vocational Behaviour,* 71 (2), pp. 167-185.

Boyatzis, R.E. (1982) *The Competent Manager; A Model for Effective Performance*, Wiley: New York.

Boyatzis, R.E. and Burrus, J.A. (1995) *The Heart of Human Resource Development: Counseling Competencies*, Consortium for Research on Emotional Intelligence in Organizations, (www.eiconsortium.org).

Boyatzis, R.E., Goleman, D. and Hay Group (2001) *The Emotional Competence Inventory (ECI)*, Hay Group: Boston.

Boyatzis, R.E., Goleman, D. and Rhee, K. (2000) *Clustering Competence in Emotional Intelligence: Insights from the Emotional Competence Inventory (ECI)*, in R. Bar-On and J.D.A. Parker (eds.), The Handbook of Emotional Intelligence: Theory, Development, Assessment and Application at Home, School and in the Workplace (pp. 343-362), Jossey-Bass: San-Francisco.

Boyle, G.J., Borg, M.G., Fazlon, J.M. and Baglioni, A.J. (1995) 'A Structural Model of the Dimensions of Teacher Stress', *British Journal of Educational Psychology*, 65, pp. 49-67.

Brackett, M.A., Palimera, Raquel., Mojsa-Kaja, J., Reyes, M.R. and Salovey, P. (2010) 'Emotion-regulation Ability, Burnout, and Job Satisfaction among British Secondary-school Teachers', *Psychology in the Schools*, 47 (4), pp. 406-417.

Bradley, J. and Eachus, P. (1995) 'Occupational Stress within a UK Higher Education Institution', *International Journal of Stress Management*, 2 (3), pp. 145-158.

Bradshaw, Felicia Bell. (2008) '*Exploring the Relationship between Emotional Intelligence and Academic Achievement in African American Female College Students'*, Ph.D. Thesis, College of Notre Dame of Maryland.

Brahmaiah, T. and Rao, D.B. (2009) *Stress of Student Teachers*, Discovery Publishing House: New Delhi.

Brand, T. (2007) '*Exploration of the Relationship between Burnout, Occupational Stress and Emotional Intelligence in the Nursing Industry*', M.A. Dissertation Work, Department of Industrial Psychology, University of Stellenbosch, Western Cape, South Africa.

Brayfield, A. (1995) 'Juggling Jobs and Kids: The Impact of Employment Schedules on Fathers Caring for Children', *Journal of Marriage and the Family*, 57, pp. 321-332.

Brett, J.M. (1980) *The Effect of Job Transfer on Employees and Their Families*, in C.L. Cooper and R. Payne (eds), Current Concerns in Occupational Stress, John Wiley: New York.

Brief, A.P. and Motowidlo, S.J. (1986) 'Pro-social Organizational Behaviour', *Academy of Management Review*, 11, pp. 710-725.

Brogden, H. and Taylor, E.K. (1950) 'The Dollar Criterion: Applying the Cost Accounting Concept to Criterion Construction', *Personnel Psychology*, 3, pp. 133-154.

Broli, Luisa., Berrone, Carlo., Renati, Roberta., and Zanetti, Maria-Assunta. (2011) 'Emotional Intelligence as a Protective Factor in Times of Educational Reforms: First Steps of An Investigation on Italian high-school Teachers', *Literacy Information and Computer Education Journal (LICEJ),* 2 (1), pp. 285-289.

Brown, M. and Ralph, S. (1992) 'Towards the Identification of Stress in Teachers', *Research in Education*, 48, pp. 103-110.

Bruce, C. (1994) *Supervising Literature Reviews*, in O. Zuber-Skerritt, and Y. Ryan, (eds), Quality in Post-graduate Education, Kogan Page: London.

Bruce, C. S. (1994) 'Research Student's Early Experiences of the Dissertation Literature Review' *Studies in Higher Education*, 19 (2), pp. 217-229.

Bunker, K.A. (1997) 'The Power of Vulnerability in Contemporary Leadership', *Consulting Psychology Journal*, 49 (2), pp. 122-136.

Burke, R. (1988) 'Type A Behaviour, Occupational and Life Demands, Satisfaction and Well-being', *Psychological Reports*, 63, pp. 451-458.

Burke, R.J., Greenglass, E.R. and Schwarzer, R. (2007) 'Predicting Teacher Burnout Over Time: Effects of Work Stress, Social Support, and Self-doubts on Burnout and its Consequences', *Anxiety, Stress and Coping*, 9 (3), pp. 261-275.

Byrne, B.M. (1994) 'Burnout: Testing for the Validity, Replication, and Invariance of Causal Structure Across Elementary, Intermediate, and Secondary Teachers', *American Educational Research Journal*, 31 (3), pp. 645-673.

Cambridge Advanced Learner's Dictionary and Thesaurus (2011) *dictionary.cambridge.org/dictionary/british/*

Cameron, A. (2004) *Work Profile Questionnaire: Emotional Intelligence*, in B.S. Blake, J.C. Impara, and R.A. Spies (eds.), The Fifth Mental Measurements Year Book, Buros Institute of Mental Measurements: Lincoln, NE.

Campbell, J. P. (2005) *Learning from History*, in L.L. Hoppes (Ed.), *The Science and Practice of Industrial and Organizational Psychology: Historical Aspects from the First Hundred Years,* Erlbaum: Mahwah, New Jersey.

Campbell, J.P. (1990) *Modeling the Performance Prediction Problem in Industrial and Organizational Psychology*, in M.D. Dunnette and L.M. Hough (eds.), Handbook of Industrial and Organizational Psychology (2nd ed., pp. 687-732), Consulting Psychologists Press: Palo Alto, CA.

Campbell, J.P. (1990b) 'An Overview of the Army Selection and Classification Project', *Personnel Psychology, 43,* pp. 231-239.

Campbell, J.P. (1990c) *The Role of Theory in Industrial and Organizational Psychology*, in M. D. Dunnette and L. M. Hough (eds.), Handbook of Industrial and Organizational Psychology (2nd ed., Vol. 1, pp. 39-73), Consulting Psychologists Press: Palo Alto, CA.

Campbell, J.P. and Knapp, D. (2001) *Project A: Exploring the Limits of Performance Improvement through Personnel Selection and Classification,* Erlbaum: Hillsdale, New Jersey.

Campbell, J.P., Dunnette, M.D., Lawler, E.E.III. and Weick, K.E. (1970) *Managerial Behaviour, Performance and Effectiveness,* McGraw-Hill: New York.

Campbell, J.P., Gasser, M.B. and Oswald, F.L. (1996) *The Substantive Nature of Job Performance Variability*, in K.R. Murphy (ed.), Individual Differences and Behaviour in Organizations (pp. 258-299), Jossey-Bass: San Francisco.

Campbell, J.P., McCloy, R.A., Oppler, S.H. and Sager, C.E. (1993) *A Theory of Performance*, in N. Schmitt and W.C. Borman (eds.), Personnel Selection in Organizations (pp. 35-70), Jossey-Bass: San Francisco, CA.

Cannon, W. (1914) 'The Interrelations of Emotions as Suggested by Recent Physiological Researches', *American Journal of Psychology*, 25, pp. 256-282.

Capel, S.A. (1987) 'The Incidence of and Influences on Stress and Burnout in Secondary Teachers', *British Journal of Educational Psychology*, 57, pp. 279-288.

Capel, S.A. (1997) 'Changes in Students' Anxieties and Concerns After their First and Second Teaching Practices', *Educational Research*, 39, pp. 211-228.

Caplan, R.D., Cobb, S. and French, J.R.P. (1975) 'Relationships of Cessation of Smoking with Job Stress, Personality, and Social Support', *Journal of Applied Psychology*, 60, pp. 211-219.

Carmeli, A., Yitzhak-Halevy, M. and Weisberg, J. (2009) 'The Relationship between Emotional Intelligence and Psychological Well-being', *Journal of Managerial Psychology*, Vol. 24, pp. 66-78.

Chadha, N. K. and Singh, D.(2001) *How to Measure your EQ*, in Dalip Singh, Emotional Intelligence at work: A Professional Guide, Response Books: New Delhi.

Chan, A.H.S., Chen, K. and Chong, Y.L. (2010) '*Work Stress of Teachers from Primary and Secondary Schools in Hong Kong'*, Paper Presented at the International Multi Conference of Engineers and Computer Scientists held at Hong Kong from March 17-19.

Chan, D.W. (1998) 'Stress, Coping Strategies and Psychological Distress among Secondary School Teachers in Hong Kong', *American Educational Research Journal*, 35 (1), pp. 145-163.

Chan, D.W. (2008) 'Emotional Intelligence, Self-efficacy, and Coping among Chinese Prospective and in-service Teachers in Hong Kong', *Educational Psychology*, 28 (4), pp. 397-408.

Chan, D.W. and Hui, E.K.P. (1995) 'Burnout and Coping among Chinese Secondary School Teachers in Hong Kong', *British Journal of Educational Psychology*, 65, pp. 15-25.

Chand, P. and Monga, O.P. (2007) 'Correlates of Job Stress and Burnout', *Journal of Community Guidance and Research*, 24 (3), pp. 243-252.

Chandraiah, K., Agarwal, S.C., Marimuthu, P. and Manoharan, N. (2003) 'Occupational Stress and Job Satisfaction among Managers', *Indian Journal of Occupational and Environmental Medicine*, 7 (2), pp. 6-8.

Chang, Jin Wook., Sy, Thomas. and Choi, Jin Nam. (2012) 'Team Emotional Intelligence and Performance; Interactive Dynamics between Leaders and Members', *Small Group Research,* 43 (1), pp. 75-104.

Chapin, F. S. (1942) 'Preliminary Standardization of a Social Impact Scale', *American Sociological Review,* 7, pp. 214-225.

Chaplain, R. (1995) 'Stress and Job Satisfaction: A Study of English Primary School Teachers', *Educational Psychology*, 15 (4), pp. 473-489.

Chaturvedi, M. and Purushothaman, T. (2009) 'Coping Behaviour of Female Teachers: Demographic Determinants', *Indian Psychiatry Journal*, 18 (1), pp. 36-38.

Chayya, M.P. (2001) *Effective Teacher-Effective Strategies of Teaching*, Alpha Publications: New Delhi.

Chen, Ping. (2012) '*The Relationship between Principal's Organizational Citizenship Behaviour and Teacher's Organizational Citizenship Behaviour on Tainan City's Public Elementary School: Teacher's Organizational Commitment and Teacher's Job Stress as Mediators'*, M.A. Project Work Department of Graduate Institute of Education Entrepreneurship and Management,

Chen, Yigean. and Cheng, Joanan. (2012) 'Leadership Behaviour and Job Performance of Teachers in Public and Private Kindergartens: The Perspectives of Institutionalization, Reason, and Feeling', *School Effectiveness and School Improvement: An International Journal of Research, Policy and Practice*, 23 (1), pp. 1-19.

Cherniss, C. and Goleman, D. (eds.) (2001) *The Emotionally Intelligent Workplace: How to Select, Measure, and Improve Emotional Intelligence in Individuals, Groups and Organizations*, Jossey-Bass: New York.

Cherns, A. (1976) 'The Principles of Socio-Technical Design', *Human Relations*, 29, pp. 783-792.

Chona, C. and Roxas, M.A. (2009) 'Stress among Public Elementary School Teachers', *University of Cordilleras Research Journal*, 1 (4), pp. 86-108.

Chopra, R. and Gartia, R. (2009) 'Accountability of Secondary School Teachers in Relation to their Occupational Stress', *EduTracks*, 8 (7), pp. 41-43.

Chughtai, Aamir. Ali. and Zafar, Sohail (2006) 'Antecedents and consequences of Organizational Commitment among Pakistani University Teachers', *Applied H.R.M. Research*, 11 (1), pp. 39-64.

Ciarrochi, J. and Mayer, J.D. (2007) *Applying Emotional Intelligence: A Practitioner's Guide*, Psychology Group, Taylor and Francis Group: New York and Hove.

Clegg, C. (2000) 'Socio-technical Principles for System Design', *Applied Ergonomics*, 31, pp. 463-477.

Cockburn, A.D. (1996) 'Primary Teachers Knowledge and Acquisition of Stress Relieving Strategies', *British Journal of Educational Psychology*, 66, pp. 399-410.

Cohen, Aaron. and Liu, Ying. (2011) 'Relationships between in-role Performance and Individual Values, Commitment, and Organizational Citizenship Behaviour among Israeli Teachers', *International Journal of Psychology*, 46 (4), pp. 271-287.

Colarelli, S.M., Dean, R.A. and Konstans, C. (1987) 'Comparative Effects of Personal and Situational Influences on Job Outcomes of New Professionals', *Journal of Applied Psychology*, 72, pp. 558-566.

Collins, J. M. (1996) '*A Narrative and Empirical Evaluation of the Socialization Trait as a Predominant Predictor of Productive and Counterproductive Work Behaviour*', Symposium Presentation at the 11th Annual Conference of the Society for Industrial and Organizational Psychology (SIOP), San Diego, CA.

Collins, V.L. (2001) '*Emotional Intelligence and Leadership Success'*, Doctoral Dissertation, University of Nebraska, NE.

Comish, R. and Swindle, B. (1994) 'Managing Stress in the Workplace', *National Public Accountant*, 39 (2), pp. 24-28.

Conway, J.M. (1999) 'Distinguishing Contextual Performance from Task Performance for Managerial Jobs', *Journal of Applied Psychology*, 84, pp. 3-13.

Cooper, C.L. (1981) *The Stress Check*, Prentice Hall: Englewood Cliffs, NJ.

Cooper, C.L. and Kelly, M. (1993) 'Occupational Stress of Head Teachers: A National UK Study', *British Journal of Educational Psychology*, 73 (1), pp. 130-143.

Cooper, C.L. and Lewis, S. (1998) *Balancing Career, Family and Life*, Kogan Page: London.

Cooper, C.L. and Marshall, J. (1976) 'Occupational Sources of Stress: A Review of the Literature Relating to Coronary Heart Disease and Mental ill Health', *Journal of Occupational Psychology*, 49 (1), p. 12.

Cooper, C.L. and Payne, R. (eds.) (1990) *Causes, Coping and Consequences of Stress at Work*, Wiley: Chichester, New York.

Cooper, C.L. and Roden, J. (1985) 'Mental Health and Satisfaction among Tax Officers', *Social Science Medicine*, 21 (17), pp. 747-751.

Cooper, C.L., Dewe, P.J. and O'Driscoll, M.P. (2001) *Organizational Stress: A Review and Critique of Theory, Research, and Applications*', A Sage Publications Series: Thousand Oaks, California.

Cooper, C.L., Sloan, S.J. and Williams, S. (1988) *Occupational Stress Indicator Management Guide*, NFER-Nelson: Windsor.

Cooper, C.L., Cooper, R.D. and Eaker, L.H. (1988a) *Living with Stress*, Penguin Health: London.

Cooper-Hakim, Amy. and Viswesvaran, Chockalingam. (2005) 'The Construct of Work Commitment: Testing an Integrative Framework', *Psychological Bulletin*, 131 (2), pp. 241-259.

Cotton, P. and Hart, P.M. (2003) 'Occupational Well-being and Performance: A Review of Organizational Health Research', *Australian Psychologist*, 32 (2), pp. 143-156.

Cox, A. (2000). The Importance of Employee Participation in Determining Pay System Effectiveness, *International Journal of Management Reviews*, 2 (4), pp. 357-375.

Cox, T. (1978) *Stress*, McMillan: London.

Cox, T., Griffiths, A.J., Barlow, C. Randall, R., Thomson, T. and Real Gonzalez, E. (2000) *Organizational Interventions for Work Stress: A Risk Management Approach*, HSE Books: Sudbury.

Cox, T.H., Lobel, S.A. and Mcleod, P.L. (1991) 'Effects of Ethnic Group Cultural Differences on Cooperative and Competitive Behaviour on a Group Task', *Academy of Management Journal*, 34, pp. 827-847.

Crandall, R. and Perrewe, P.L. (eds.) (1995) *Occupational Stress: A Handbook*, Taylor and Francis: Washington, DC.

Crant, J.M. (1995) 'The Proactive Personality Scale and Objective Job Performance among Real Estate Agents', *Journal of Applied Psychology*, 80, pp. 532-537.

Crothers, L.M., Kanyongo, G.Y., Kolbert, J.B., Lipinski, J., Kachmar, S.P. and Koch, G.D. (2011) 'Job Stress and Locus of Control in Teachers: Comparisons between Samples from the United States and Zimbabwe', *International Review of Education,* 56 (5-6), pp. 651-669.

Daley, M.R. (1979) 'Burnout: Smouldering Problems in Protective Services', *Social Work*, 24 (5), pp. 375-379.

Darmody, M. and Smyth, E. (2011) '*Job Satisfaction and Occupational Stress among Primary School Teachers and School Principals in Ireland*', A Report Compiled by the Economic and Social Research Institute-ESRI on behalf of the Teaching Council, Dublin.

Darmody, M., Smyth, E. and Doherty, C. (2010) '*Designing Primary Schools for the Future*', ESRI Research series No. 16, ESRI: Dublin.

Darolia, C.R. and Darolia, Shashi (2005) '*The Punjab Heritage*', Vol. 20.

Darwin, C. (1872 /1965) '*The Expression of the Emotions in Man and Animals*' University of Chicago Press, Chicago.

Dash, Neena. (2005) 'Changing Role of the Teacher', *EduTracks,* 4 (7), pp. 22-23.

David, R.S. and Roy, R. (2010) 'Relationship between Emotional Intelligence and Teachers Competency', *Journal of Community Guidance and Research*, 27 (2), pp. 191-201.

Davidson, R.J., Jackson, D.C. and Kalin, N.H. (2000) 'Emotion, Plasticity, Context and Regulation: Perspectives from Affective Neuroscience', *Psychological Bulletin*, 126 (6), pp. 890-909.

DeNobile, J.J. and McCormick, J. (2007) '*Occupational Stress of Catholic Primary School Staff: Investigating Biographical Differences*', A Paper Presented at the

Annual Conference of the Australian Association for Research in Education, Fremantle, Held between November 25-29.

Doll, E.A. (1935) 'A Generic Scale of Social Maturity', *American Journal of Orthopsychiatry, 5*, pp. 180-188.

Dominguez-Cruz, G. (2003) '*Relationship of Leadership Orientations to Emotional Intelligence of Public Elementary, Intermediate and High School Principals in Puerto Rico*', Ph.D. Thesis, Dowling College, Puerto Rica.

Doyle, C. and Hind, P. (1998) 'Occupational Stress, Burnout and Job Status in Female Academics', *Gender, Work and Organization*, 5, pp. 67-82.

Druskat, V.U., Sala, F. and Mount, G. (2005) *Linking Emotional Intelligence and Performance at work: Current Research Evidence with Individuals and Groups*, Lawrence Erlbaum Associations: New Jersey.

Dua, J. (1994) 'Job Stressors and their Effects on Physical Health, Emotional Health and Job Satisfaction in a University', *Journal of Educational Administration*, 32 (1), pp. 59-79.

Dulewicz, V. and Higgs, M. (1999) 'Emotional Intelligence: Can it be Measured Reliably and Validly using Competency data?', *Competency*, 6 (1), pp. 28-37.

Dunbar, H.F. (1947) *Mind and Body*, Random House: New York.

Dunbar, P. (1954) *The Practice of Management,* Harper and Row: New York.

Dunham, J. (1976a) *Stress Situations and Responses*, in NAS / UWT (1976), Stress in Schools, Hemel Hempstead: London.

Dunham, J. (1992) *Stress in Teachers*, Routledge: New York.

Dunham, J. (1994) *Developing Effective School Management*, Routledge: London.

Dunham, J. and Varma, V. (2003) *Stress in Teachers: Past, Present and Future*, Whurr Publishers: London.

Edannur, Sreekala. (2010) 'Emotional Intelligence of Teacher Educators', *International Journal of Educational Science,* 2(2), pp. 115-121.

Elstad, Eyvind., Christophersen, Knut Andreas. and Turmo, Are. (2011) 'Social Exchange Theory as an Explanation of Organizational Citizenship Behaviour among Teachers', *International Journal of Leadership in Education: Theory and Practice*, 14 (4), pp. 405-421.

Encyclopedia of Applied Psychology (2006) Academic Press, New York.

Enueme, C.P. and Egwunyenga, E.J. (2008) 'Principal's Instructional Leadership Roles and Effect on Teachers' Job Performance: A Case Study of Secondary Schools in Asaba Metropolis, Delta State, Nigeria', *Journal of Social Science*, 16 (1), pp. 13-17.

Ericsson, K.A. Smith, J. (1991) *Prospects and Limits of the Empirical Study of Expertise: An Introduction*, in K.A. Ericsson and J. Smith (eds.), Toward a General Theory of Expertise: Prospects and Limits (pp. 1-38), Cambridge University Press: Cambridge.

Ericsson, K.A. and Lehmann, A.C. (1996) 'Expert and Exceptional Performance: Evidence of Maximal Adaptation to Task Constraints', *Annual Review of Psychology*, 47, pp. 273-305.

Erkutlu, H.V. and Chafra, J. (2006) 'Relationship between Leadership Power Bases and Job Stress of Subordinates: Example from Boutique Hotels', *Management Research News*, 29 (5), pp. 285-297.

Farooq, A. (2003) '*Effect of Emotional Intelligence on Academic Performance*', Research Paper Submitted to the Department of Clinical Psychology, University of Karachi, Pakistan.

Farouk, Shameem A. (2011) 'Investigating the Relationship between Emotional Intelligence and High Managerial Performance in Selected Corporations in Belgium and Malaysia, *African Journal of Business Management,* 5 (34), pp. 322-329.

Fay, D. and Sonnentag, S. (2000) '*Stressors and Personal Initiative: A Study on Organizational Behaviour*', Manuscript Submitted for Publication.

Faye, Abhijeet., Swamy, Rajeev., Shukla, Aniket., Subramanyam, Alka. and Kamath, Ravindra. (2011) 'Study of Emotional Intelligence and Empathy in Medical Post-graduates', *Indian Journal of Psychiatry*, 53(2), pp. 140-144.

Fernandez, Susan. (2011) '*The Relationship between Teachers' Emotional Intelligence and Sense of Humor, and Student Achievement*', Ph.D. Thesis, Union Institute and University, Florida.

Ferries, G.R. *et. al.* (1988) 'Personal Characteristics, Job Performance and Absenteeism of Public School Teachers', *Journal of Applied Social Psychology,* 50 (2), pp. 165-174.

Fielding, M. (1982) '*Personality and Situational Correlates of Teacher Stress and Burnout*', Dissertation Abstracts International, 43/02 A.

Fimian, M.J. (1986) 'Social Support and Occupational Stress in Special Education', *Exceptional Children*, 52, pp. 436-442.

Fimian, M.J. and Santoro, T.M. (1981) 'Correlates of Occupational Stress as Reported by Full-time Special Education Teachers, I. Sources of Stress, II. Manifestations of Stress', *Educational Information Research Centre,* 1, pp. 219-543.

Fimian, M.J., and Santoro, T.M. (1983) 'Sources and Manifestations of Occupational Stress as Reported by Full-time Special Education Teachers', *Exceptional Children*, 49 (6), pp. 540-543.

Finlay-Jones, R. (1986) 'Factors in the Teaching Environment Associated with Severe Psychological Distress among Teachers', *Australian and New Zealand Journal of Psychiatry',* 20, pp. 304-313.

Fisher, C.D. and Gitleson, R. (1983) 'A Meta-analysis of the Correlations of Role Conflict and Ambiguity', *Journal of Applied Psychology*, 68, pp. 320-333.

Fletcher, B. and Payne, R.L. (1982) 'Levels of Reported Stressors and Strain amongst School Teachers: Some UK data', *Educational Research*, 34, pp. 267-278.

Folkman, S. (1984) 'Personal Control and Stress and Coping Process: A Theoretical Analysis', *Journal of Personality and Social Psychology*, 46, pp. 839-852.

Fotinatos-Vintouratos, R. and Cooper, C. (2005) 'The Role of Gender and Social Class in Work Stress', *Journal of Managerial Psychology*, 20 (1), pp. 14-23.

Frederickson, Norah., Petrides, and Simmonds, Elizabeth. (2012) 'Trait Emotional Intelligence as a Predictor of Socio-emotional Outcomes in Early Adolescence', *Personality and Individual Differences,* 52 (3), pp. 323-328.

Freedman, J., Jenson, A., Rideout, M. and Freedman, P. (1998) *Handle with Care: Emotional Intelligence Activity Book*, Six Seconds Publications: California.

French, J.R.P. and Caplan, R.D. (1973) *Organizational Stress and Individual Strain*, in A.J. Marrow (ed.), The Failure of Success, John-Wiley: New York.

Frese, M. and Sonnentag, S. (2000) '*High Performance: An Action Theory Approach*', Working Paper, University of Giessen and University of Konstanz.

Frese, M. and Zapf, D. (1994) *Action as the Core of Work Psychology: A German Approach,* in H. C. Triandis, M. D. Dunnette, and L. M. Hough (eds.), Handbook of Industrial and Organizational Psychology (2nd ed., Vol. 4, pp. 271-340), Consulting Psychologists Press: Palo Alto, CA.

Frese, M., Fay, D., Hilburger, T., Leng, K. and Tag, A. (1997) 'The Concept of Personal Initiative: Operationalization, Reliability and Validity in two German Samples', *Journal of Occupational and Organizational Psychology*, 70, pp. 139-161.

Frese, M., Kring, W., Soose, A. and Zempel, J. (1996) 'Personal Initiative at Work: Differences between East and West Germany', *Academy of Management Journal*, 39, pp. 37-63.

Frese, M., Teng, E., and Wijnen, C.J.D. (1999) 'Helping to Improve Suggestion Systems: Predictors of Making Suggestions in Companies', *Journal of Organizational Behaviour*, 20, pp. 1139-1155.

Fried, Y. (1991) 'Meta-analytic Comparison of the Job Diagnostic Survey and Job Characteristics Inventory as Correlates of Work Satisfaction and Performance', *Journal of Applied Psychology*, 76, pp. 690-697.

Fried, Y. and Ferries, G.R. (1987) 'The Validity of the Job Characteristics Model: A Review and Meta-analysis', *Personnel Psychology*, 40, pp. 287-322.

Friedman, H. and DiMatteo, R. (1982) *Interpersonal Issues in Health Care*, Academic Press: New York.

Frone, M.R. (2003) *Work Family Balance*, in J.C. Quick and L.E. Tetrick (eds.), Handbook of Health Psychology (pp. 143-162), American Psychological Association: Washington DC.

Frone, M.R., Russel, M. and Cooper, M. (1992) 'Prevalence of Work-family Conflict: Are Work and Family Boundaries Asymmetrically Permeable?', *Journal of Organizational Behaviour*, 13, pp. 723-729.

Furnham, Adrian., Dissou, Georgia., Sloan, Peter. and Chamorro-Premuzic, Tomas. (2007) 'Personality and Intelligence in Business People: A Study of Two Personality and Two Intelligence Measures', *Journal of Business and Psychology,* 22 (1), pp. 99-109.

Galloway, D., Panckhurst, F., Boswell, K., Boswell, C. and Green, K. (1982b) 'Sources of Stress for Class Teachers', *National Education*, 64, pp. 166-169.

Ganster, D.C. and Schaubroeck, J. (1991a) 'Role Stress and Worker Health: An Extension of the Plasticity Hypothesis', *Journal of Social Behaviour and Personality*, 6, pp. 349-360.

Ganster, D.C. and Schaubroeck, J. (1991b) 'Work Stress and Employee Health', *Journal of Management*, 17, pp. 235-271.

Gardner, H. (1983) '*Frame of Mind: The Theory of Multiple Intelligence*', Basic Books: New York.

Gardner, L. (2005) '*Emotional Intelligence and Occupational Stress',* Ph.D. Thesis, Swinburne University, Melbourne, Australia.

Garg, P. and Rastogi, R. (2009) 'Emotional Intelligence and Stress Resiliency: A Relationship Study', *International Journal of Educational Administration*, 1 (1), pp. 1-16.

Garg, Pooja. and Rastogi, Renu. (2006) 'Climate profile and OCBs of Teachers in Public and Private Schools of India', *International Journal of Educational Management,* 20 (7), pp. 529-541.

Garrett, E.H. (1966) *Statistics in Psychology and Education*, David McKey Company, Inc. and Longman Group Ltd: London.

Garrett, E.H. and Woodsworth, R.S. (1981) *Statistics in Psychology and Education*, Vakkils, Feffer and Simons Ltd: Bombay.

George, J.M. and Bettenhausen, K. (1990) 'Understanding Pro-social Behaviour, Sales Performance and Turnover: A Group level Analysis', *Journal of Applied Psychology*, 75, pp. 698-709.

George, J.M. and Brief, A.P. (1992) 'Feeling Good-doing Good: A Conceptual Analysis of the Mood at Work Organizational Spontaneity Relationship', *Psychological Bulletin*, *112*, pp. 310-329.

Ghanizadeh, A. and Moafian, F. (2009) 'The Role of EFL Teachers' Emotional Intelligence in their Success', *ELT Journal*, 64 (3), p. 84.

Gibbs, N. (1995, October) 'The EQ Factor', *Time Magazine*, 146, pp. 60-68.

Gillespie, N., Walsh, M., Winefield, A., Dua, J. and Stouch, C. (2001) 'Occupational Stress in Universities: Staff Perceptions of the Causes, Consequences and Moderators of Stress', *Work and Stress*, 15 (1), pp. 53-72.

Giri, V.N. and Kumar, P.B. (2007) 'Impact of Organizational Climate on Job Satisfaction and Job Performance', *National Academy of Psychology-India,* 52 (2), pp. 131-133.

Gold, Y. and Roth, ra. (1993) *Teachers Managing Stress and Preventing Burnout: The Professional Health Solution*, Falmer Press: London.

Goleman, D. (1995) *Emotional Intelligence*, Bantam Books: New York.

Goleman, D. (1995a) Emotional intelligence: Why It Matters More than IQ, Bantam Books: New York.

Goleman, D. (1998) *Working with Emotional Intelligence*, Bantam Books: New York.

Goleman, D. (2001) *An EI Based Theory of Performance*, in C. Cherniss and D. Goleman (eds.), The Emotionally Intelligence Workplace, Jossey-Bass, San Francisco.

Goleman, D., Boyatzis, R. and McKee, A. (2002) *Primal Leadership: Realizing the Power of Emotional Intelligence*, Harvard Business School Press: Boston, MA.

Greenberg, J. (1990) 'Organizational Justice: Yesterday, Today, and Tomorrow', *Journal of Management*, 16, pp. 399-432.

Greenhaus, J. and Parasuraman, S. (1994) *Work-family Conflict, Social Support and Well-being*, in M. Davidson and R. Burke (eds.), Women in Management: Current Research Issues, Paul Chapman: London.

Gregory, A. (1990) 'Are Women Different and Why are Women thought to be Different?: Theoretical and Methodological Perspectives', *Journal of Business Ethics*, 9 (4 and 5), pp. 257-266.

Greiner, B.A. and Leitner, K. (1989) *Assessment of Job Stress: The RHIA-Instrument*, in K. Landau and W. Rohmert (eds.), Recent Developments in Work Analysis (pp. 53-66), Taylor and Francis: London.

Griffin, R.W. (1991) 'Effects of Work Redesign on Employee Perceptions, Attitudes and Behaviours: A Long-term Investigation', *Academy of Management Journal*, 34, pp. 425-435.

Groves, K.S. and Vance, C.M. (2009) 'Examining Managerial Thinking Styles, EQ, and Organizational Commitment', *Journal of Managerial Issues*, 21, pp. 344-366.

Guglielmi, R. and Tatrow, K. (1998) 'Occupational Stress, Burnout and Health in Teachers: A Methodological and Theoretical Analysis', *Review of Educational Research*, 68 (1), pp. 61-99.

Gupta, A. and Chandwani, R. (2011) 'Job Stress and Performance', Organizational Behaviour and Human Resource Management at IIM Bangalore, *tejas@iimb, an IIMB Management Review Initiative.*

Gupta, B. and Mishra, S. (2011) 'Effect of Emotional Labour on Emotional Exhaustion: A Study of Retail Sector in India', *International Journal of Indian Culture and Business Management*, 4 (1), pp. 73-87.

Gupta, N. and Jenkins, D.G. (1985) *Dual Career Couples: Stress, Stressors, Strains and Strategies*, in T.A. Beehr and R.S. Bhagat (eds.), Human Stress and Cognition in Organizations (pp. 141-176), John Wiley: New York.

Gupta, V. and Singh, S. (2011) 'Developing a Scale for Measuring Ability-Based Emotional Intelligence in Indian context', *International Journal of Indian Culture and Business Management,* 4 (2), pp. 28-32.

Guzzo, R.A., Jette, R.D. and Katzell, R.A. (1985) 'The Effects of Psychologically Based Intervention Programmes on Worker Productivity: A Meta-analysis', *Personnel Psychology*, 38, pp. 275-291.

Hacker, W. (1973) 'General Work and Engineering Psychology: Mental Atigkeiten Structure and Regulation of Arbeitst, VEB German Academic Publishers: Berlin.

Hacker, W. (1998) 'General Work Psychology: Mental Atigkeiten Regulation of Arbeitst, Huber: Bern.

Hackman, J.R. and Oldham, G.R. (1976) 'Development of the Job Diagnostic Survey', *Journal of Applied Psychology*, 60, pp. 159-170.

Hackman, J.R. and Oldham, G.R. (1976a) 'Motivation through the Design of Work: Test of a Theory', *Organizational Behaviour and Human Performance*, 16, pp. 250-279.

Hall, D.T. and Associates (1996) *The career is Dead: Long Live the Career*, Jossey-Bass: San Francisco.

Han, Heeyoung. and Johnson, Scott. D. (2012) 'Relationship between Students' Emotional Intelligence, Social Bond, and Interactions in Online Learning', *Educational Technology and Society, 15* (1), pp.78-89.

Hanif, Rubina., Tariq, Sadaf. and Nadeem, Masood. (2011) 'Personal and Job Related Predictors of Teacher Stress and Job Performance among School Teachers', *Pakistan Journal of Commerce and Social Science* 5 (2), pp. 319-329.

Hargreaves, D. (1978) 'What Teaching Does to Teachers', *New Society*, (43), pp. 540-543.

Hart, P.M., Wearin, A.J. and Conn, M. (1995) 'Conventional Wisdom is a Poor Predictor of the Relationship between Discipline Policy, Student Misbehaviour and Teacher Stress', *British Journal of Educational Psychology,* 65, pp. 27-48.

Harvey, D.F. and Brown, D.R. (1984) *OD Interpersonal Interventions*, in D.F. Harvey and D.R. Brown (eds.), An Experiential Approach to Organizational Development (3rd Edition), Prentice Hall International: Englewood Cliffs, New Jersey.

Hasket, R.A. (2003) '*Emotional Intelligence and Teaching Success in Higher Education*', Ed.D. Degree, Indiana University.

Hassan, T. and Hassan, M. (1998) '*Development and Validation of Occupational Stress Scale',* Unpublished Monograph, Department of Educational Foundation and Management, Olabisi Onabanjo University, Ago-Iwoye, Nigeria.

Hassan, T. and Hassan, M.I. (1998) 'Cross Validation of Some MMPI Clinical Scales in an Africa Culture', *Journal of Research in Counselling Psychology*, 6, pp. 121-124.

Hattrup, K., O'Connell, M.S. and Wingate, P.H. (1998) 'Prediction of Multidimensional Criteria: Distinguishing Task and Contextual Performance', *Human Performance*, 11, pp. 305-319.

Health Education Authority (1988) '*Stress in the Public Sector: Nurses, Police, Social Workers and Teachers*', Health Education Authority: London.

Hesketh, B. and Neal, A. (1999) *Technology and Performance*, in D.R. Ilgen and E.D. Pulakos (eds.), The Changing Nature of Performance: Implications for Staffing, Motivation, and Development (pp. 21-55), Jossey-Bass: San Francisco, CA.

Hill, E., Miller, B., Weiner, S. and Colihan, J. (1998) 'Influences of the Virtual Office of Aspects of Work and Work/Life Balance', *Personnel Psychology*, 51, pp. 667-684.

Hochschild, A.R. (1983) *The Managed Heart: Commercialization of Human Feelings*, University of California Press: Berkley.

Hosotani, Rika. and Imai-Matsumura, Kyoko (2011) 'Emotional Experience, Expression, and Regulation of High-quality Japanese Elementary School Teachers', *Teaching and Teacher Education,* 27 (6), pp. 1039-1048.

House, R.J. (1988) *Charismatic and Non-Charismatic Leaders: Differences in Behaviour and Effectiveness*, in J.A. Conger, R.N. Kanungo and Associates, Charismatic leadership: The Elusive Factor in Organizational Effectiveness, Jossey-Bass: San Francisco.

Hsiu-Ju Lin (2011) '*The Study of the Relationships among Job Stress, Emotional Management and Job Satisfaction of Elementary School Teachers in Kaohsiung City*', Master's Thesis, Department of Instructional Supervision, University of Malaysia.

Hülsheger, Ute R., Lang, Jonas W. B. and Maier, Günter W (2010) 'Emotional Labour, Strain, and Performance: Testing Reciprocal Relationships in a Longitudinal Panel study', *Journal of Occupational Health Psychology*, 15(4), pp. 505-521.

Hunter, J.E. (1983) '*Test Validation for 12,000 Jobs: An Application of Job Classification and Validity Generalization to General Aptitude Test Battery* (USES Test Research Report No. 45), United States Department of Labour, Washington, DC.

Hunter, J.E. and Hunter, R.F. (1984) 'Validity and Utility of Alternative Predictors of Job Performance', *Psychological Bulletin*, 96, pp. 72-98.

Hurrel, J.J., Jr, Nelson, D.L. and Simmons , B.L. (1993) 'Measuring Job Stressors and Strains: Where We have been, Where we are, and Where we Need to Go', *Journal od Occupational Health Psychology*, 3, pp. 368-389.

Huy, Q.N. (1999) 'Emotional Capability, Emotional Intelligence and Radical Change', *Academy of Management Review*, 24 (2), pp. 325-345.

Hyde, A., Pathe, S. and Dhar, U. (2002) *Manual for Emotional Intelligence Scale*, Vedant Publications: Lucknow.

Ilgen, D.R., Fisher, C.D. and Tayler, M.S. (1979) 'Consequences of Individual Feedback on Behaviour in Organizations', *Journal of Applied Psychology*', 64, pp. 349-371.

ILO Report (1981) '*Employment and Conditions of Work of Teachers*', International Labour Organization, Geneva.

Indu, H. (2009) 'Emotional Intelligence of Secondary Teacher Trainees', *EduTracks*, 8 (9), pp. 34-36.

Isenberg, D.J. (1986) 'Thinking and managing: A Verbal Protocol Analysis of Managerial Problem Solving', *Academy of Management Journal*, 29, pp. 775-788.

Ismail, A. Yao, A., Yeo, E., Lai-Kuan, K. and Soon-Yew, J. (2010) 'Occupational Stress, Emotional Intelligence and Job Performance: An Empirical Study in Private Institutions of Higher Learning', *Journal of Management Science*, 17 (6), pp. 7-13.

Ivancevich, J.M. and Matteson, M.T. (1980) *Stress and Work: A Managerial Perspective*, Scott Foresman: Glenview, IL.

Jackson, Leon. And Rothmann, Sebastiaan (2006) 'Occupational Stress, Organizational Commitment and Ll-health of Educators in the North West Province', *South African Journal of Education,* 26 (1), pp. 75-95.

Jackson, S.E. and Schuler, R.S. (1985) 'A Meta-analysis and Conceptual Critique of Research on Role Ambiguity and Role Conflict in Work Settings', *Organizational Behaviour and Human Decision Processes*, 36, pp. 16-78.

Jadhav, S.G. and Havalappanavar, N.B. (2009) 'Emotional Intelligence and Self-efficacy of Police Constable Trainees', *Indian Psychological Review*, 73, Special issue, pp. 307-314.

Jamal, M. and Baba, V.V. (2009) 'Type-A Behaviour, Job Performance and Well-being in College Teachers', *International Journal of Stress Management*, 8 (3), pp. 231-240.

Jayamma, H.R., Suhas and Nagaraj, T. (2007) '*Prevalence of Occupational Stress of Primary School Teachers in Relation to their Personality Factors*', Paper Presented in the International Conference on Educational Research in the Era of Globalization held at the Department of Education, Periyar University, Salem from 28th to 30th November.

Jayanthi and Agarwal, R. (2006) 'A Study of the Socio-emotional Climate of the Classroom in Respect of Teaching Experience, Total Income, Age, Teaching Subject and Sex of the Secondary School Teachers', *Asian Journal of Psychology and Education*, 39 (7), pp. 2-11.

Jayasree, P.G. (2008) '*Influence of Emotional Intelligence, Locus of Control and Rigidity on Mathematics Achievement of Students at Degree Level*', Ph.D. Thesis, School of Pedagogical Sciences, Mahatma Gandhi University, Kottayam, Kerala.

Jex, S.M. (1998) *Stress and Job Performance: Theory, Research and Implications for Managerial Practice*, Sage Publications: Thousand Oaks, CA.

John, Aesha., (2012) 'Stress among Mothers of Children with Intellectual Disabilities in Urban India: Role of Gender and Maternal Coping', *Journal of Applied Research in Intellectual Disabilities*, 3 (1), pp. 78-92.

John, B. (2007) '*Occupational Stress of Teachers Working in the Schools for Visually Impaired Children in the Malabar Region of Kerala*', M.Phil. Dissertation, Department of Education, Alagappa University, Karaikudi.

Jose-Maria, Augusto Landa, E., Lopez-Zafra, R., Antonana, M.D. and Pulido, M. (2006) 'Perceived Emotional Intelligence and Life Satisfaction among University Teachers', *Psicothema*, 18, Supl. pp. 152-157.

Jude, A.M. (2011) 'Emotional Intelligence and Occupational Stress among Secondary School Teachers in Ondo State, Nigeria', *Pakistan Journal of Social Sciences*, 8 (4), pp. 159-165.

JungHoon, Lee. and Chihyung, O.K. (2012) 'Reducing Burnout and Enhancing Job Satisfaction: Critical Role of Hotel Employees' Emotional Intelligence and Emotional Labour', *International Journal of Hospitality Management,* 1 (6), pp. 1101-1112.

Jyotsna, C. (2002) *Kick Out Your Stress*, Pustak Mahal: New Delhi.

Kafetsios, K. and Zampetakis. L.A. (2008) 'Emotional Intelligence and Job Satisfaction: Testing the Mediatory Role of Positive and Negative Affect at Work', *Personality Individual Differences*, 44, pp. 712-722.

Kahn, R. (1980) *Conflict, Ambiguity and Overload: Three Elements in Job Stress*, in D. Katz, R. Kahn, J. Adams (eds.), The Study of Organizations (pp. 418-28), Jossey-Bass: San Francisco, CA.

Kahn, R., Wolffe, D., Quinn, R. and Snoek, J. (1964) *Organizational Stress: Studies in Role Conflict and Ambiguity* (eds.), John Wiley: New York.

Kahn, R.L. and Byosiere, P. (1990) *Stress in Organizations*, in M.D. Dunnette and L.M. Hough (eds.), Handbook of Industrial and Organizational Psychology (2nd ed., pp. 571-650), Consulting Psychologists Press: Palo Alto, CA.

Kanfer, R. and Heggestad, E. D. (1997) Motivational Traits and Skills: *A Person-centered Approach to Work Motivation*, in L.L. Cummings and B.M. Staw (eds.), Research in Organizational Behaviour (Vol. 19, pp. 1-56), JAI Press: Greenwich, CT.

Karakus, Mehmet. (2012) 'Emotional Intelligence and Negative Feelings: A Gender Specific Moderated Mediation Model', *Educational Studies, (*DOI 10.1080/03055698.2012.671514)

Karasek, R.A. (1979) 'Job Demands, Job Decision Latitude, and Mental Strain: Implications for Job Redesign', *Administrative Science Quarterly*, 24, pp. 285-306.

Karasek, R.A. and Theorell, T. (1990) *Healthy Work,* Basic Book: New York.

Karasek, R.A., Baker, D., Marxer, F., Ahlbom, A. and Theorell, T. (1981) 'Job Decision Latitude, Job Demands, Cardiovascular Disease: A Prospective Study of Swedish men', *American Journal of Public Health*, 71, pp. 694-705.

Karim, Jahanvash. and Weisz, Robert. (2007) 'Emotional Intelligence as a Moderator of Affectivity/Emotional Labour and Emotional Labour/Psychological Distress Relationships', *Psychological Studies*, 56 (4), pp. 348-359.

Kashdan, Ferssizidis., Collins, and Muraven. (2010) 'Procedure to Measure Emotional Differentiation', *Psychological Sciences*, 21(9), 1341-1347.

Kashyap, S. and Sidhu, R. (2005) 'Difference in Stress and Coping Mechanism used by Adolescents of Science and Commerce Streams', *Journal of Community Guidance and Research*, 22 (1), pp. 81-89.

Katyal, S., Jain, M. and Dhanda, B. (2011) 'A Comparative Study of Job Stress and Type of Personality of Employees Working in Nationalized and Non-nationalized Banks', *Journal of Psychology*, 2 (2), pp. 115-118.

Katz, D. (1964) 'The Motivational Basis of Organizational Behaviour', *Behavioural Science*, 9, pp. 131-146.

Katz, D. and Kahn, R.L. (1978) *The Social Psychology of Organizations* (2nd ed.), John Wiley: New York.

Kaur, M. and Kaur, S. (2007) 'Occupational Stress and Burnout among Women Police', *Journal of Community Guidance and Research*, 24 (3), pp. 262-265.

Kaur, S. (2008) 'Occupational Stress in Relation to Teacher Effectiveness among Secondary School Teachers', *EduTracks*, 7 (10), pp. 27-29.

Kauts, Amit. and Saroj, Richa. (2010) 'Study of Teacher Effectiveness and Occupational Stress in Relation to Emotional Intelligence among Teachers at Secondary Stage', *Journal of History and Social Sciences*, 2 (1), July.

Kazmi, R., Amjad, S. and Khan, H. (2008) 'Occupational Stress and its Effect on Job Performance', Retrieved from *http:// www.ayubmed, edu.PK/JAM/PAST/20-3/ Rubina.Pdf.*

Kemery, E.R. (1991) *Affective Disposition, Role Stress and Job withdrawal*, in P.L. Perrewe (ed.), Handbook of Job Stress, Special Issue, *Journal of Behaviour and Personality*, 6, pp. 183-195.

Ketz de Vries, M.F.R. (1984) *Organizational Stress Management Audit*, in A.S. Sethi and R.S. Schuler (eds.), Handbook of Organizational Stress Coping Strategies, Ballinger: Cambridge, MA.

Khan, Anwar., Shah, Ishak.M., Khan, Sadaf. and Gul, Shafiq. (2012) 'Teachers' Stress, Performance and Resources: The Moderating Effects of Resources on Stress and Performance', *International Review of Social Sciences and Humanities*, 2 (2), pp. 21-29.

Khan, M.A. and Kumar, A. (2008) 'Relationship between Emotional Intelligence and Achievement Motivation among Women Teachers of Secondary Schools of Delhi', *Journal of Teacher Education and Research*, 3 (1), pp. 15-18.

Kinman, G., Wray, S. and Strange, S. (2011) 'Emotional Labour, Burnout and Job Satisfaction in UK Teachers: The Role of Workplace Social Support', *Educational Psychology*, 31 (7), pp. 843-856.

Kirkaldy , B. and Martin, T. (2000) 'Job Stress and Satisfaction among Nurses: Individual Differences', *Stress Medicine*, 16, pp. 77-89.

Kluger, A.N. and DeNisi, A. (1996) 'The Effects of Feedback Interventions on Performance: A Historical Review, A Meta-analysis, and a Preliminary Feedback Intervention Theory', *Psychological Bulletin*, 119, pp. 254-284.

Kobasa, S.C. (1982) The Hardy Personality; *Toward a Social Psychology of Stress and Health*, in J. Suls and G.S. Sanders (eds), The Social Psychology of Health and Illness, Erlbaum: Hillsdale, New Jersey.

Kokkinos, C. M. (2007) 'Job Stressors, Personality and Burnout in Primary School Teachers', *British Journal of Educational Psychology*, 77, pp. 229-243.

Kokkinos, C.M., Panayiotou, G. and Davazoglous, A.M. (2005) 'Correlates of Teacher Appraisals of Student Behaviour', *Psychology in the Schools*, 42, pp. 79-89.

Koplan, F. (2003) 'Educating the Emotions: *Emotional Intelligence Training for Early Childhood Teachers and Caregivers*', Ph.D. Thesis, Cardinal Stretch University.

Koneri, R.R. (2010) '*A Study of Emotional Intelligence in Relation to Parental Involvement and Self-concept of Adolescents*', Ph.D. Thesis, Karnatak University, Dharwad.

Kornhauser, a. (1965) *The Mental Health of the Industrial Worker,* Wiley: New York.

Kothari, C.R. (1995) *Research Methodology: Methods and Techniques*, Second Edition, Wishwa Prakashan: New Delhi.

Koubek, R.J. and Salvendy, G. (1991) 'Cognitive Performance of Super-experts on Computer Programme Modification Tasks', *Ergonomics*, 34, pp. 1095-1112.

Kram, K.E. and Cherniss, C. (2001) *Implementing Emotional Intelligence Programmes in Organizations*, in C. Cherniss and D. Goleman (eds.), The Emotionally Intelligent Workplace: How to Select, Measure, and Improve Emotional Intelligence in Individuals, Groups and Organizations (pp. 286-304), Jossey-Bass, San Francisco.

Krishnaveni, R. and Deepa, R. (2008) '*Diagnosing Employees' Emotional Intelligence in the IT/ITES Sector of South India*', Research Supported by All India Council for Technical Education (AICTE) Grant 8023/BOR/RID/RPS-212/2008-09.

Kuhl, J. (1985) *Volitional Mediators of Cognition-Behaviour Consistency: Self-Regulatory Processes and Action vs. State Orientation*, in J. Kuhl and J. Beckmann (eds.), Action Control: From Cognition to Behaviour (pp. 101-128), Springer: New York.

Kulsum, Umme. (2000) *Teacher Effectiveness Scale*, Psycho-Educational Testing Centre: Janakpuri, New Delhi.

Kumar, J. (2003) 'Sources of Stress among Adolescents', *Journal of Community Guidance and Research*, 22 (1), pp. 28-34.

Kumar, N. (2007) '*Influence of Certain Psycho-sociological Factors on the Occupational Stress among the Public and Private School Teachers of Orissa*', Ph.D. Thesis, Utkal University.

Kumaran, D. (2003) 'Organizational Health and Academic Performance', *Perspectives in Education*', 19 (4), pp. 221-234.

Kumaraswamy, T. and Sivanandam, L. (2004) 'Performance of Primary School Teachers', *International Educator,* 16 (2), pp. 14-19.

Kushmir, T. and Melamed, S. (1991) 'Workload, Perceived Control and Psychological Distress in Type A/B Industrial Workers', *Journal of Organizational Behaviour*, 12, pp. 155-168.

Kwong, J.Y.Y. and Cheung, F.M. (2003) 'Prediction of Performance Facets using Specific Personality Traits in the Chinese context', *Journal of Vocational Behaviour*, 63 (1), pp. 99-110.

Kyriacou, C. (1987) 'Teacher Stress and burnout: An International Review', *Educational Research,* 29 (2), pp. 146-152.

Kyriacou, C. (1997) *Effective Teaching in Schools* (2nd edition), Stanley Thorne: Cheltenham.

Kyriacou, C. (2001) 'Teacher Stress: Direction for Future Research', *Educational Review*, 53 (1), pp. 27-35.

Kyriacou, C. and Chien, P.Y. (2004) 'Teacher Stress in Taiwanese Primary Schools', *Journal of Educational Enquiry*, 5 (2), pp. 86-103.

Kyriacou, C. and Sutcilff, J. (1978) 'A Model of Teacher Stress', *Educational Studies*, 4, pp. 1-6.

Kyriacou, C. and Sutcliff, J. (1979a) 'Teacher Stress and Satisfaction', *Educational Research*', 21 (2), pp. 89-96.

Landsbergis, P. A. (1988) 'Occupational Stress among Health-care Workers: A Test of the Job Demands-Control Model'. *Journal of Organizational Behaviour*, 9, pp. 217-239.

Lanre Olaitan, O., Oyerinde, O.O., Obeyemi, O. and Kayode, O.O. (2010) 'Prevalence of Job Stress among Primary School Teachers in South-West Nigeria', *African Journal of Microbiology Research*, 4 (5), pp. 339-342.

Latack, J.C. (1986) 'Coping with Job Stress: Measures and Future Directions for Scale Development', *Journal of Applied Psychology*, 71, pp. 377-385.

Latha, A., Sangeetha, R. and Anantha Sayanam, R. (2005) 'Study of Emotional Intelligence and its Effects on Teacher Effectiveness among School Teachers', *Journal of Educational Research and Extension*, 42 (3), pp. 20-29.

Latha, G. and Panchanatham, N. (2007) 'Job Stress Related Problems and Coping Strategies', *Journal of Community Guidance and Research*, 24 (3), pp. 235-242.

Latha, G. and Panchanatham, N. (2010) 'Call Center Employees: Is Work Life Stress a Challenge?', *Sabaragamuwa University Journal*, 9 (1), pp. 1-9.

Lazarus, R.S. (1966) *Psychological Stress and the Coping Process*, McGraw-Hill: New York.

Lazarus, R.S. (1990) 'Theory Based Stress Management', *Psychological Inquiry*, 1, pp. 3-13.

Lazarus, R.S. (1991) 'Psychological Stress in the Workplace', *Journal of Social Behaviour and Personality*, 6, pp. 1-13.

Lazarus, R.S. (1999) *Stress and Emotion: A New Synthesis*, Springer Publishing Company: New York.

Lazarus, R.S. and Folkman, S. (1984) *Stress, Appraisal and Coping*, Springer: New York.

Lee, F.K., Sheldon, K.M. and Turban, D.B. (2003) 'Personality and the Goal Striving Process: The Influence of Achievement Goal Patterns, Goal Level, and Mental Focus on Performance and Enjoyment', *Journal of Applied Psychology*, 88, pp. 256-265.

Lee, F.M. (2003) '*Conflict Management Styles and Emotional Intelligence of Faculty and Staff At A Selected College in Southern Taiwan (China)*', Ed.D. Degree, University of Florida.

Lenka, Samir. K. and Kant, Ravi. (2012) 'Emotional Intelligence of Secondary School Teachers in Relation to their Professional Development', *Asian Journal of Management Sciences and Education,* Leena and Luna International, Oyama, Japan.

Leung, S.S.K., Mak, Y.W., Chui, Y.Y., Chiang, V.C.L. and Lee, A.C.K. (2009) 'Occupational Stress, Mental Health Status and Stress Management Behaviours among Secondary School Teachers in Hong Kong', *Journal of Health Education*, 68 (4), pp. 328-343.

Leung, Sharron.S.K., Chiang, Vico.C.L., Chui, Ying-Yu., Lee, Angel.C.K. and Mak, Yim-Wah. (2011) 'Feasibility and Potentials of Online Support for Stress Management among Secondary School Teachers', *Stress and Health*, 53 (4), pp. 280-286.

Ling-feng, W. (2005) 'Stress and Mental Health of the Kindergarten Teachers in Huzhou', *Chinese Journal of School Health*, Retrieved from http://en.cnki.com.cn/Article-en/CJFDTOTAL-XIWS200511011.htm.

Litt, D.M. and Turk, C.M. (1985) 'Sources of Stress and Dissatisfaction in Experienced High School Teachers', *The Journal of Educational Research*, 78 (3), pp. 178-185.

Liu, Y. and Zhu, B. (2009) '*Numerical Analysis and Comparison on Stress between Male and Female Academic Faculty in Chinese Universities*', Paper Presented at the 2nd International Conference on Information and Computing Science, Held at Manchester, UK, on May 21-22.

Locke E.A. and Lotham, G.P. (1990) *A Theory of Goal Setting and Task Performance*, Prentice-Hall: Upper Saddle River, NJ.

Locke, E.A. and Lotham, G.P. (1984) 'Goal Setting: *A Motivational Technique that Works*', Prentice-Hall, Englewood Cliffs, NJ.

Lomas, Justine., Stough, Con., Hansen, Karen. and Downey, Luke. A. (2011) *'Emotional Intelligence, Victimization and Bullying in Adolescents'*, Brief Report Submitted to the Brain Sciences Institute, Swinburne University, Melbourne, Australia.

Longman Dictionary of Contemporary English (1998) *Complete Guide to Written and Spoken English* (1st Indian Ed.), Thompson Press: India.

Lordanoglou, D. (2007) 'Teacher as Leader: the Relationship between Emotional Intelligence, Leadership Effectiveness, Commitment and Satisfaction', *Journal of Leadership Studies*, 1 (3), pp. 57-66.

Louise, M.R. (1980) 'Surprise and Sense Making: What New Comers Experience in Entering Unfamiliar Organizational Settings', *Administrative Science Quarterly*, 25 (2), pp. 226-251.

Lowenstein, L.F. (1991) 'Teacher Stress Leading to Burnout: Its Prevention and Cure', *Education Today*, 41 (2), pp. 12-16.

Luthans, F. and Kreitner, R. (1975) *Organizational Behaviour Modification*, Scott, Glenview, IL.

Mahajan (2011) 'Academic Achievement in Relation to Emotional Intelligence and Spiritual Intelligence', *EduTracks*, 10 (9), pp. 32-36.

Majid, I.B.A. (1998) '*Occupational Stress and Teachers' Job Satisfaction: Implications to the Human Relations Management Approach*', Research Paper Submitted to the Department of Human Sciences, International Islamic University, Malaysia.

Male, D.B. and May, D. (1997) 'Stress, Burnout and Workload in Teachers of Children with Special Educational Needs', *British Journal of Special Education*, 24 (3), pp. 133-140.

Malik, Allah Bakhsh., Khatoon, Sufiana. and Khurshid, Fauzia., (2011) 'Perceived Learning Environment and Emotional Intelligence among Prospective Teachers', *British Journal of Humanities and Social Sciences*, 2 (2), pp. 1-9.

Mancini, V., Wuest, D., Clark, E. and Ridosh, N. (1982) '*A Comparison of the Interaction Patterns and Academic Learning time of Low-Burnout and High-Burnout Physical Educators*', Paper Presented at Big Ten Symposium on Research on Teaching, Lafayette, Indiana.

Mancini, V., Wuest, D., Vantine, K. and Clark, E. (1984) 'Use of Instruction and Supervision in Interaction Analysis on Burnedout Teachers: Its Effects on Teaching Behaviours, Level of Burnout and Academic Learning Time', *Journal of Teachers in Physical Education*, 3 (2), pp. 29-46.

Mangal, S.K. (2002) *Statics in Psychology and Education* (2nd ed.), PHI Learning Private Limited: New Delhi.

Manning, Michael, R., Motowidlo, Stephan, J., Packard and John, S. (1986) 'Performance: Physicians, Medical Professions, Nurses, Organizational Effectiveness', *Journal of Applied Psychology*, 71(4), pp. 618-629.

Manoharan, B. (2007) '*Emotional Intelligence and Personality Characteristics among High School Teachers: A Correlational Analysis*', Paper Presented in the International Conference on Educational Research in the Era of Globalization held at the Department of Education, Periyar University, Salem from 28th to 30th November.

Manoj Kumar, K. (2006) '*Occupational Stress and Coping Styles of High School Teachers in Nellore District*', M.Phil. Dissertation, Madurai Kamaraj University.

Manthei, R., Gilmore, A., Tuck, B. and Adair, V. (1996) 'Teacher Stress in Intermediate School', *Educational Research*, 38, pp. 3-19.

Margolis, B. L., Kores, W. H. and Quinn, R. P. (1974) 'Job Stress: An Unlisted Occupational Hazard', *Journal of Occupational Medicine*, 16, pp. 654-661.

Mark, George. and Smith, Andrew.P. (2012) 'Effects of Occupational Stress, Job Characteristics, Coping, and Attribution Style on the Mental Health and Job Satisfaction of University Employees', *Anxiety, Stress and Coping: An International Journal*, 25 (1), pp. 63-78.

Mary and Samuel (2010) 'Influence of Emotional Intelligence on Attitude towards Teaching of Student Teachers', *EduTracks*, 9 (12), pp. 27-32.

Maslach, C. (1982) 'Understanding Burnout: Definitional Issues in Analyzing a Complex Phenomenon', in W.S. Paine (ed.), Job stress and Burnout (pp. 29-40), Sage: Baverly Hills

Maslach, C. and Jackson, S.E. (1981) 'The Measurement of Experienced Burnout', *Journal of Occupational Behaviour*, 2, pp. 99-113.

Mathew, L. (2005) '*Sources, Effects and the Coping Strategies of Occupational Stress among Special Education Teachers in India'*, Ph.D. Thesis, Department of Psychology, Calicut University.

Mathews, S.A. (2005) 'Occupational Stress of Teachers', *Journal of Community Guidance and Research*, 22 (2), pp. 121-126.

Mayer, J. (2009) 'Emotional Intelligence Information', Retrieved from http://www.unh.edu/emotional_intelligence/ on October 5, 2011.

Mayer, J.D. (1999) 'Emotional Intelligence: Popular or Scientific Psychology', *Monitor*, American Psychological Association, 30 (50).

Mayer, J.D. and Salovey, P. (1993) 'The Intelligence of Emotional Intelligence', *Intelligence*, 17, pp. 433-442.

Mayer, J.D. and Salovey, P. (1997) What is Emotional intelligence?, in P. Salovey and D. Sluyter (eds.), Emotional Development and Emotional Intelligence: Implications for Educators (pp. 3-31), Basic Books: New York.

Mayer, J.D., Caruso, D.R. and Salovey, P. (1999) 'Emotional Intelligence Meets Traditional Standards of Intelligence', *Intelligence*, 27, pp. 267-299.

Mayer, J.D., Salovey, P. and Caruso, D. (2002) *MSCEIT Technical Manual*, Multi-Health System: Toronto, Canada.

Mayer, J.D., Salovey, P. and Caruso, D.R. (2008) 'Emotional Intelligence: New Ability or Eclectic Traits', *American Psychologist*, 63, pp. 503-517.

Mayer, J.D., Salovey, P. Caruso. D. and Sitarenios, G. (2003) 'Measuring Emotional Intelligence with the MSCEIT V2.0, *Emotion*, 3, pp. 97-105.

Mazzola, Joseph.J., Schonfeld, Irvin.S. and Spector, Paul.E. (2011) 'What Qualitative Research has Taught us about Occupational Stress', *Stress and Health*, 27 (2), pp. 93-110.

McCann, C. and Roberts, R.D. (2008) 'Consensus Scoring and Empirical Option Weighing of Performance-based Emotional Intelligence Tests' *Personality and Individual Differences*, 36, pp. 645-662.

McCormick, J. (1997) 'An Attribution Model of Teachers' Occupational Stress and Job Satisfaction in A Large Educational System', *Work and Stress*, 11 (1), pp. 17-32.

McCormick, John. and Barnett, Kerry. (2011) 'Teachers' Attributions for Stress and their Relationships with Burnout', *International Journal of Educational Management*, 25 (3), pp. 278-293.

McCrae, R.R. and Costa, P.T. (1996) *Toward A New Generation of Personality Theories: Theoretical Contexts for the Five Factor Model*, in J.S. Wiggins (ed.), The Five Factor Model of Personality (pp. 51-87), Guilford: New York.

McGrath, J.E. (1976) *Stress and Behaviour in Organizations*, in M.D. Dunnette (ed.), 1976 Handbook of Industrial and Organizational Psychology, Consulting Psychologists Press: Palo Alto, CA.

McGrath, J.E. (1984) *Groups: Interaction and Performance*, Upper Saddle River, Prentice Hall: New Jersey.

Mearns,M. and Cain, J.E. (2003) 'Relationships between Teachers' Occupational Stress and their Burnout and Distress: Roles of Coping and Negative Mood Regulation Expectancies', *Anxiety, Stress and Coping* , 16 (1), pp. 71-82.

Milstein, M.M. and Golaszewski, T.J. (1985) 'Effects of Organizationally-based and Individually-based Stress Management Efforts in Elementary School Settings', *Urban Education*, 19 (4), pp. 389-409.

Miner, J.B. and Brewer, J.F. (1976) *Management of Ineffective Performance*, in M.D. Dunette (ed.), Handbook of Industrial and Organizational Psychology, Rand McNally: Chicago.

Mishra, Badrinarayan., Mehta, S.C., Sinha, N.D., Shukla, S.K., Ahmed, Nadeem. and Kawatra, Abhishek. (2011) 'Evaluation of Work Place Stress in Health University Workers: A Study from Rural India', *Indian Journal of Community Medicine,* 36 (1), pp. 39-44.

Mishra, P.S. and Mohapatra, A.K.D. (2010) 'Relevance of Emotional Tntelligence for Effective Job Performance: An Empirical Study', *Vikalpa*, 35 (1), pp. 53-61.

Mitchell, T.R. (1997) *Matching Motivational Strategies with Organizational Contexts*, in L.L. Cummings and B.M. Staw (eds.), Research in Organizational Behaviour (Vol. 19, pp. 57-149), JAI Press: Greenwich, CT.

Mitchell, T.R., Hopper, H., Daniels, D. and George-Falvy, J. (1994) 'Predicting Self-Efficacy and Performance during Skill Acquisition', *Journal of Applied Psychology*, 79, pp. 506-517.

Mogojo, Thandi. and Williams, Annelieze. C. (2010) '*Occupational Stress and Work Engagement among Special Needs Educators in the Umlazi District of KwaZulu-Natal*', M.A. Project Work, Department of Psychology, University of KwaZulu-Natal, Durban.

Mohammad, Ali. Mohammadyfar., Mahmmod, S. Khan. and Bahman, Kord. Tamini. (2009) 'The Effect of Emotional Intelligence and Job Burnout on Mental and Physical Health', *Journal of the Indian Academy of Applied Psychology*, 35 (2), pp. 219-226.

Mokdad, M. (2005) 'Occupational Stress among Algerian Teachers', *African Newsletter on Occupational Health and Safety*, 15, pp. 46-47.

Moracco, J.C., D'Arienzo, R.V. and Danford, D. (1983) 'Comparison of Perceived Occupational Stress between Teachers who are Contented and Discontented in their Career Choices', *The Vocational Guidance Quarterly*, 11 (2), pp. 44-51.

Moreno, J.M.T., Bordas, C.S., Lopez, M.O.L., Peracho, C.V., Lopez, A.C.L., Miguel, E.E.D. and Vazquez, L.B. (2010) 'Descriptive Study of Stress and Satisfaction at Work in the Saragossa University Services and Administration Staff', *International Journal of Mental Health Systems*, 4 (7).

Morrison, E.W. and Phelps, C.C. (1999) 'Taking Charge at Work: Extra Role Efforts to Initiate Workplace Change', *Academy of Management Journal*, 42, pp. 403-419.

Moss, F.A. and Hunt, T. (1927) 'Are You Socially Intelligent?', *Scientific American*, 137, pp. 108-110.

Moss, F.A., Hunt, T., Omwake, K.T. and Woodward, L.G. (1927) *Manual for the George Washington University Series Social Intelligence Test,* Centre for Psychological Services: DC.

Moss, L. (1981) *Management Stress*, Addison-Wesley: Reading, Mass.

Motowidlo, S.J. and Schmit, M.J. (1999) *Performance Assessment in Unique Jobs*, in D.R. Ilgen and E.D. Pulakos (eds.), The Changing Nature of Job Performance: Implications for Staffing, Motivation, and Development (pp. 56-86), Jossey-Bass: San Francisco, CA.

Motowidlo, S.J. and Van Scotter, J.R. (1994) 'Evidence that Task Performance Should be Distinguished from Contextual Performance', *Journal of Applied Psychology*, 79, pp. 475-480.

Motowidlo, S.J., Borman, W.C. and Schmit, M.J. (1997) 'A Theory of Individual Differences in Task and Contextual Performance', *Human Performance*, 10, pp. 71-83.

Motowidlo, S.J., Packard, J.S. and Manning, M.R. (1986) 'Occupational Stress: Its Causes and Consequences for Job Performance', *Journal of Applied Psychology*, 71, pp. 618-629.

Moulay, G.J. (1964) *The Science of Educational Researce*, American Book Company: New York.

Muchinsky, P.M. (1993) *Psychology Applied to Work* (4th ed.), Brooks/Cole: Pacific Grove, CA.

Mukhopadhyay, L. (1999) 'Stress in the Lives of Working Women and Coping Mechanisms', *Social Welfare*, 46 (4), pp. 26-29.

Munaf and Seema (2009) 'Motivation, Performance and Satisfaction among University Teachers: Comparing Public and Private Sectors in Pakistan and Malaysia', *South Asian Journal of Management*, Oct-Dec.

Muralidharan, Karthik. and Sundararaman, Venkatesh. (2011) 'Teacher Opinions on Performance Pay: Evidence from India', *Economics of Education Review*, 30 (3), pp. 394-403.

Murphy, K. (1994) *Towards Broader Conception of Jobs and Job Performance: Impact of Changes in the Military Environment on the Structure, Assessment, and Prediction of Job Performance* in M. Rumsey, C. Walker and J. Harris (Eds.), Personnel Selection and classification (pp. 85-102), Hillsdale, NJ: Erlbaum.

Murphy, K.R. (1989) *Dimensions of Job Performance*, in R. Dillon and J.W. Pellegrino (eds), Testing: Theoretical and Applied Perspectives (pp. 218-247), Praeger: New York.

Murphy, K.R. (1995) 'Is the Relationship between Cognitive Ability and Job Performance Stable Over Time?', *Human Performance*, 2, pp. 183-200.

Murphy, L.R. (1984) 'Occupational Stress Management; A Review and Appraisal', *Journal of Occupational Psychology*, 57, pp. 1-15.

Murphy, L.R. (1985) *Individual Coping Strategies*, in C.L. Cooper and M.J. Smith (eds), Job Stress and Blue Collar Work, John Wiley: New York.

Murphy, L.R. (1987) *Workplace Interventions for Stress Reduction and Prevention*, in C.L. Cooper and R. Payne (eds.), Causes, Coping and Consequences of Stress at work, Wiley: Chichester.

Murphy, L.R. and Hurrel, J.J. (1987) 'Stress Management in the Process of Occupational Stress Reduction', *Journal of Managerial Psychology*, 2, pp. 18-23.

Murphy, L.R. and Hurrel, J.J. (1987a) *Stress Measurement and Management in Organizations: Development and Current Status*, in A.W. Riley and S.J. Zaccaro (eds.), Occupational Stress and Organizational Effectiveness, (pp. 29-51), Praeger: New York.

Murray, M. (2009, September 22) 'Minimizing the Fallout from Burnout', Retrieved from The Irish Times: http://www.lexisnexis.com/us/lnacademic /results/docview/docview. do?docLinkInd=trueandrisb=2 on November 1, 2011.

Muto, S., Muto, T., Seo, A., Yoshida, T., Taoda, K. and Watanabe, M. (2007) 'Job Stressors and Job Stress among Teachers Engaged in Nursing Activity', *Industrial Health*, 45 (1), pp. 44-48.

Nagpal, Chirag. (2009) 'Emotional Intelligence and Self-concept among Prospective Teachers', *International Research Journal*, 1 (2).

Nahid, N. A. (2012) 'Teachers: Emotional Intelligence, Job Satisfaction, and Organizational Commitment', *Journal of Workplace Learning*, 24 (4), pp. 256-269.

Naik, B.K. (2011) '*Occupational Stress of Anganwadi Teachers Working in Kuppam Mandal*', M.Ed. Dissertation, Dravidian University, Kuppam.

Narayanan, l., Menon, S. and Spector, P. (1999) 'Stress in the Workplace: A Comparison of Gender and Occupation', *Journal of Organizational Behaviour*, 20, pp. 63-74.

NAS/UWT (1976) *Stress in Schools*, National Association of Schoolmasters/Union of Women Teachers: UK.

National Institute for Occupational Safety and Health-NIOSH (1999) *Stress at Work*, Cincinnati, OH: Publication No. 99-101, US Department of Health and Human Services.

Near, J.P. (1983) *Predictive and Explanatory Models of Work and Non-work*, in M.D. Lee and R.N. Kanungo (eds.), Management of Work and Personal Life, Praeger Scientific: New York.

Needle, R.H., Griffin, T., Svendsen, R. and Berney, C. (1980) 'Teacher Stress: Sources and Consequences', *Journal of School Health*', 50 (2), pp. 96-99.

Neelakandan ,R. and Rajendran, K. (2007) 'Job Satisfaction of Public Sector Employees', *Journal of Community Guidance and Research*, 22 (1), pp. 76-80.

Nelis, D., Quoidbach, J., Mikolajczak, M. and Hansenne, M. (2009) 'Increasing Emotional Intelligence: (How) is it Possible?', *Personality and Individual Differences,* 47 (1), pp. 36-41.

Neubert, M.J. (1998) 'The Value of Feedback and Goal Setting Over Goal Setting Alone and Potential Moderators of this Effect: A Meta-analysis', *Human Performance*, 11, pp. 321-335.

Newman, D.A., Joseph, D.L. and McCann, C. (2010) 'Emotional Intelligence and Job Performance: The Importance of Emotion Regulation and Emotional Labour Context', *Industrial and Organizational Psychology*, 3, pp. 159-164.

Ng, T.W.H., Sorensen, K.L. and Yim, F.H.K. (2009) 'Does the Job Satisfaction-Job Performance Relationship vary Across Cultures?', *Journal of Cross-cultural Psychology,* 40 (5), pp. 761-796.

Nguyen, T.T.V. (2008) '*The Relationship between Emotional Intelligence and Instructor Performance in Ho Chi Minh City University of Foreign Languages and Information Technology (HUILIT), Vietnam*', Research Thesis, Graduate School of Education, University of Thailand.

Nhundu, T. J. (1992) 'Job Performance, Role Clarity, and Satisfaction among Teacher Interns in the Edmonton Public School System', *Alberta Journal of Educational Research, 38,* pp. 335-354.

Nikolaou, I. and Tsaousis, I. (2002) 'Emotional Intelligence in the Workplace: Exploring its Effects on Occupational Stress and Organizational Commitment', *International Journal of Organizational Analysis,* Special Issue on Emotional Intelligence, 10 (4), pp. 327-342.

Nowack, K.M. (1990) 'Initial Development of An Inventory to Assess any Health Risk' *American Journal of Health Promotion*, 4, pp. 173-180.

Nowack, K.M. and Hanson, A.L. (1983, November) 'The Relationship between Stress, Job Performance, and Burnout in College Student Resident Assistants', *Journal of College Student Personnel*, pp. 545-550.

NPE (1986) '*National Policy on Education*', Ministry of Human Resource Development, Government of India, New Delhi.

Nygren, D.J. and Ukeritis, M.D. (1993) *The Future of Religious Orders in the United States*, Praeger: New York.

O' Driscoll, M.P. and Beehr, T.A. (1994) 'Supervisor Behaviours, Role Stressors and Uncertainity As Predictors of Personal Outcomes for Subordinates', *Journal of Organizational Behaviour*, 15, pp. 145-155.

O'Boyle, E.H., Humphrey, R.H., Pollack, J.M., Hawver, T.H. and Story, P.A. (2010) 'The Relation between Emotional Intelligence and Job Performance: A Meta-analysis', *Journal of Organizational Behaviour*, 32, pp. 788-818.

O'Driscoll, M. (1996) 'The Interface between Job and off- Job Roles: Enhancement and Conflict', *International Review of Industrial and Organizational Psychology*, 11, pp. 279-306.

O'Driscoll, M., Ilgen, D. and Hildreth, k. (1992) 'Time Devoted to Job and off- Job Activities, Inter Role Conflict and Affective Experiences'; *Journal of Applied Psychology*, 77, pp. 272-279.

O'Reilly, C.A. and Chatman, J.A. (1986) 'Organizational Commitment and Psychological Attachment: The Effects of Compliance, Identification and Internalization on Pro-social Bahaviour', *Journal of Applied Psychology*, 71, pp. 492-499.

O'Reilly, C.A. and Chatman, J.A. (1994) 'Working Smarter and Harder: A Longitudinal Study of Managerial Success', *Administrative Science Quarterly*, 39, pp. 603-627.

Oginska-Bulik, N. (2005) 'Emotional Intelligence in the Work place: Exploring its Effect on Occupational Stress and Health Outcomes in Human Service Workers', *International Journal of Occupational Medicine and Environmental Health*, 18 (2), pp. 167-175.

Ohja, S. and Rani, U. (2004) 'A Comparative Study of the Level of Life Stress and Various Dimensions of Mental Health among Working and Non-working Indian women', *Journal of Community Guidance and Research*, 21 (3), pp. 293-296.

Okebukola, P.A. and Jegede, O.F. (1989) 'Determinants of Occupational Stress among Teachers in Nigeria', *Educational Studies*, 15 (1), pp. 23-36.

Okorie, A.N. (1997) 'Signals, Sources and Management of Stress among Educators and School Administrators in Nigeria', *International Journal of Educational Management,* 2 (1), pp. 1-8.

Okoza, J., Imhonde, H.O. and Aluede, O. (2010) 'The Jailor or the Jailed: Stress and Prison Workers in Nigeria', *Research Journal of Social Sciences*, 2 (2), pp. 65-68.

Ololube, N.P. (2006) 'Teachers Job Satisfaction and Motivation for School Effectiveness: An Assessment', *Essays in Education*, 18 (9), Fall.

Ones, D.S. and Viswesvaran, C. (1996) A General Theory of Conscientiousness at Work: *Theoretical Underpinnings and Empirical Findings*, in J.M. Collins (Chair), Personality Predictors of Job Performance: Controversial Issues, Symposium Conducted at the XIth Annual Meeting of the Society for Industrial and Organizational Psychology, San Diego: CA, April.

Ones, D.S., Viswesvaran, C. and Schmidt, F.L. (1993) 'Comprehensive Meta-analysis of Integrity Test Validities: Findings and Implications for Personnel Selection and Theories of Job Performance', *Journal of Applied Psychology*, 78, pp. 679-703.

Organ, D.W. (1988) *Organizational Citizenship Behaviour*, D.C. Heath: Lexington, MA.

Organ, D.W. (1994) *Organizational Citizenship Behaviour and the Good Soldier*, in M.G. Rumsey, C.B. Walker and J.H. Harris (eds.), Personnel Selection and Classification (pp. 53-67), Lawrence Erlbaum: Hillsdale, NJ.

Organ, D.W. and Ryan, K. (1995) 'A Meta-analytical Review of Attitudinal and Dispositional Predictors of Organizational Citizenship Behaviour', *Personnel Psychology*, 48, pp. 775-802.

Orly, Shapira-Lishchinsky. (2012) 'Teachers' withdrawal Behaviours: Integrating Theory and Findings', *Journal of Educational Administration*, 50 (3), pp. 307-326.

Osipow, S.H. (1998) *Occupational Stress Inventory; Revised Edition (OSI-R): Professional Manual*, Psychological Assessment Resources, Odessa, Florida.

Osipow, S.J. (1981) *Occupational Stress Inventory Manual Research Version*, Psychological Assessment Resources: Odessa, FL.

Otto, R. (1986) Teachers under Stress: *Health Hazards in a Work Role and Modes of Response*, Hill of Content: Melbourne.

Oxford Dictionary (2003) '*Oxford Dictionary of English*', Oxford University Press, USA.

Oxford Online Dictionary (2012) oxforddictionaries.com/words/what-s-new.

Padhi, K.S. and Verma, J. (2011) 'Effectiveness of Secondary School Teachers in Relation to Emotional Intelligence and Life Satisfaction', *EduTracks,* 11 (2), pp. 20-25.

Padmaja, P. and Prabhakar, K. (2011) 'Stress of Assistant Professors in Angrau, Rajendranagar, Hyderabad', *Journal of Research ANGRAU,* 39 (1/2), pp. 79-81.

Padmaja, P. and Prabhakar, K. (2011) 'Stress of Professors in Angrau, Rajendranagar, Hyderabad', *Journal of Research ANGRAU,* 39 (1/2), pp. 72-73.

Palmer, B. and Stough, C. (2001) Workplace SUEIT: *Swinburne University Emotional Intelligence Test-Interim Technical Manual*, Organizational Psychology Research Unit: Swinburne University, Australia.

Panda, S.K. (2009) 'Emotional Intelligence and Personality Traits of Pupils and Teachers', *Journal of Community Guidance and Research*, 26 (2), pp. 122-136.

Panday, K. (2006) 'Deprivation among Emotionally Intelligent Girls', *Journal of Educational Studies*, 4 (1 and 2), pp. 9-16.

Parameswaran, E.G. (2001) 'Evolving Role of School Teacher: A Historical Perspective', *EduTracks*, 1 (3), pp. 6-17.

Pareek, U. (1983a) *Organizational Role Stress*, in L.D. Goodstein and J.W. Pfeiffer (eds.), The 1983 Annual for Facilitators, Trainers and Consultants (pp. 115-118), University Associates: san Diego, California.

Pareek, U. (1983c) Role Stress Scale: *ORS Booklet, Answer Sheet and Manual*, Navin Publications: Ahmedabad.

Patricia, Devlin. (2011) 'Enhancing Job Performance', *Intellectual and Developmental Disabilities*, 49 (4), pp. 221-232.

Payne, R. (1980) *Organizational Stress and Support*, in C.L. Cooper and R. Payne (eds.), Current Concers in Occupational Stress, John Wiley: New York.

Payne, R. (1985) 'Job Stress and Burnout: Research Theory and Intervention Perspectives', *Journal of Occupational Psychology,* 57, pp. 175-176.

Pearce, J. (1981) 'Bringing Some Clarity to Role Ambiguity Research', *Academy of Management Review*, 6, pp. 665-674.

Penrose, A., Perry, C. and Ball, I. (2007) 'Emotional Intelligence and Teacher Self-efficacy: The Contribution of Teacher Status and Length of Experience', *Issues in Educational Research*, 17, pp. 107-126.

Peterson, C., Maiser, S. and Seligman, M.E.P. (1993) *Learned helplessness*, Oxford University Press: New York.

Peterson, M.F., Smith, P.B. Akande, A., Ayestaran, S., Bochner, S. and Callan, V. (1995) 'Role Conflict, Ambiguity and Overload: A 21 Nation Study', *Academy of Management Journal*, 38, pp. 429-452.

Pethe, S., Chaudhari, S. and Dhar, U. (2001) *Manual for Organizational Climate Scale*, National Psychological Corporation: Agra.

Petrides, K. V. (2009) *Technical Manual for the Trait Emotional Intelligence Questionnaires* (TEIQue), London Psychometric Laboratory: London.

Petrides, K.V. and Furnham, A. (2006) 'The Role of Trait Emotional Intelligence in a Gender-Specific Model of Organizational Variables', *Journal of Applied Social Psychology*, 36 (2), pp. 552-569.

Phin, D. A. (2009) 'Emotional Intelligence and Employment Practices Liability Part I: The Nature and Importance of Emotional Intelligence'. Retrieved from Zero Risk HR: http://www.zeroriskhr.com/articles/eplic1.aspx, On November 20, 2011.

Piero, J.M., Gonzalez Romo, V., Tordera, N. and Manas, M.A. (2001) 'Does Role Stress Predict Burnout Overtime among Health-care Professional?', *Psychology and Health,* 16 (5), pp. 511-525.

Pines, A. (1982a) *Helpers Motivation and Burnout Syndrome*, in T.A. Wills (ed.), Basic Processes in Helping Relationships, Academic Press: London and san Diego.

Pines, A., Aronson, E. and Kafry, D. (1981) *Burnout: From Tedium to Personal Growth*, The Free Press: New York.

Pithers, R. T. and Fogarty, G. J. (1995) 'Occupational Stress among Vocational Teachers', *British Journal of Educational Psychology*, 65, pp. 3-14.

Pithers, R.T. (1995) 'Teacher Stress Research: Problems and Progress', *British Journal of Educational Psychology,* 65, pp. 387-392.

Platsidou, M. (2010) 'Trait Emotional Intelligence of Greek Special Education Teachers in Relation to Burnout and Job Satisfaction', *School Psychology International February,* 31 (1), pp. 60-76.

Poloskivokic, N. and Bogdanic, A. (2007) 'Individual Differences and Occupational Stress Perceived: *A Croatian Survey*', Working Paper Series Submitted to the Faculty of Economics and Business, University of Zagreb, Croatia.

Poornima, R. (2010) '*Emotional Intelligence, Occupational Stress and Job Satisfaction of Special Education Teachers*', Ph.D. Thesis, Department of Education, Dravidian University, Kuppam.

Poornima, R. and Reddy, G. L. (2011) 'Emotional Intelligence and Occupational Stress of Special Education Teachers Working in the Schools for Hearing-impaired Children' *EduTracks,* 10 (12), pp. 27-33.

Poropat, A.E. (2011) 'The Eysenckian Personality Factors and their Correlations with Academic Performance', *British Journal of Educational Psychology,* 81 (1), pp. 41-58.

Prakke, B., Peet, A.V. and Wolf, K.V. (2007) 'Challenging Parents, Teachers Occupational Stress and Health in Dutch Primary Schools', *International Journal about Parents in Education*, 1 (1), pp. 36-44.

Prashanthi, S. M. and Sharada Devi (2009) 'Relationship between Emotional Competence and Family Variables', *Journal of Educational Psychology*, 66 (3), pp. 14-20.

Pratt, J. (1978) 'Perceived Stress among Teachers: The Effect of Age and Background of Children Taught', *Educational Review,* 30, pp. 3-14.

Punia, B.K. (2005) 'Impact of Demographic Variables on Emotional Intelligence and Leadership Behaviour of Corporate Executives', *Journal of Organizational Behaviour*, 4 (2), pp. 7-22.

Punia, Shakuntala. and Sangwa, Santosh. (2011) 'Emotional Intelligence and Social Adaptation of School Children', *Journal of Psychology*, 2(2), pp. 83-87.

Puri, Anju (2011) '*The Emotional Intelligence of Business Executives in the Indian Corporate Sector*', Ph.D. Thesis, School of Management Studies, University of Punjab, Patiala.

Qin. Hu, Chen. Yunzhe, and Meng, Hui. (2011) '*The Relationship between Emotional Labor, Emotional Intelligence and Job Burnout*', Ph.D. Thesis, Department of Applied Psychology, East China Normal University, Shanghai.

Quick, J.C. and Quick, J.D. (1984) *Organizational Stress and Preventive Management*, McGraw-Hill: New York.

Quick, J.C., Sekade, L. and Eakin, M.E. (1986) 'Thinking Styles and Job Stress', *Personnel*, 40, pp. 44-48.

Quinnones, M.A., Ford, J.K. and Teachout, M.S. (1995) 'The Relationship between Work Experience and Job Performance: A Contextual and Meta-analytical Review', *Personnel Psychology*, 48, pp. 887-910.

Rahim, M. Afzalur., Psenicka, Clement., Polychronlou, Panagiotis. and Zhao, Jing-Mua. (2002) 'A Model of Emotional Intelligence and Conflict Management Strategies: A Study in Seven Countries', *International Journal of Organizational Analysis*, 10 (4), pp. 302-326.

Rahim, M.A. and Miners, N.R. (2003) 'Confirmatory factor Analysis of the Styles of Handling Interpersonal Conflict: First Order Factor Model and its Invariance Across Groups', *Journal of Applied Psychology*, 80, pp. 122-132.

Rahim, M.A. and Psenicka, C. (1996) 'A Structural Equations Model of Stress, Locus of Control, Social Support, Psychiatric Symptoms and Propensity to Leave a Job', *Journal of Social Psychology*, 136, pp. 69-84.

Rajkhowa, Roopsmita. (2002) '*Emotional Intelligence of IAS Officers*', Unpublished Work Carried out in the Department of Psychology, University of Delhi, India.

Rajput, J.S. and Walia, K. (2010) 'Reforms in Teacher Education in India', *Journal of Educational Change*, 2 (3), pp. 239-256.

Raju, Mohan. P. and Srivastava, R.C. (1994) 'Factors Contributing to Commitment to the Teaching Profession', *International Journal of Educational Management*, 8 (5), pp. 7-13.

Ramachandran, Yashotha., Jordan, Peter.J., Troth, Ashlea.C. and Lawrence, Sandra. A. (2011) 'Emotional Intelligence, Emotional Labour and Organizational Citizenship Behaviour in Service Environments', *International Journal of Work Organization and Emotion,* 4 (2), pp. 136-157.

Ramkrishnaiah, D. and Bhaskar Rao, D. (1998) *Job Satisfaction of College Teachers,* Discovery Publishing House: New Delhi.

Ramkumar (2007) '*Occupational Stress of Special Education Teachers Working in Schools for Mentally Retarded Children in Malabar Region of Kerala*', M.Phil. Dissertation, Alagappa University, Karaikudi.

Rao, K.P. (2010) '*Occupational Stress of Teachers Working in Dravidian University*', M.Ed. Dissertation, Dravidian University, Kuppam.

Rao, K.V. (2008) 'Academic Stress of College Students in Relation to their Study Habits and Mental Health', *Journal of Pedagogics*, 7 (1), pp. 98-102.

Rastegar, M. and Memarpour, S. (2009) 'The Relationship between Emotional Intelligence and Self-efficacy among Iranian EFL Teachers', *Science Direct*, 37 (4), pp. 700-707.

Rathi, N. and Rastogi, R. (2009) 'Assessing the Relationship between Emotional Intelligence, Occupational Self-efficacy and Organizational Commitment', *Journal of Indian Academy of Applied Psychology*, 35, Special Issue, pp. 93-102.

Ravegad and Zilberman (1998) *The Indian College and University Staff Evaluation Programme*, School and Society: New York.

Ravichandran, R. and Rajendran, R. (2007) 'Perceived Sources of Stress among the Teachers', *Journal of the Indian Academy of Applied Psychology*, 33 (1), pp. 133-136.

Reddy, G.L. (1992) 'Discrepancy between Ideology and Practice of Instructor-Role Performance as Perceived by the National Adult Education Programme instructors', *International Educator*, 7 (1), pp. 29-35.

Reddy, G.L. (2006) '*Occupational Stress, Professional Burnout and Job Satisfaction among Special Education Teachers in South India'*, Major Research Project Report Submitted to the Ministry of Social Justice and Empowerment, Government of India, New Delhi.

Reddy, G.L. (2011) *Occupational Stress, Professional Burnout and Job Satisfaction of University Teachers in South India,* UGC Major Research Project, Department of Education, Dravidian University, Kuppam.

Reddy, G.L. and Poornima, R. (2007) '*A Study on Occupational Stress of Teachers Working in the Special Schools for Visually Impaired Children',* Paper Presented at the International Conference on Educational Research in the Era of Globalization Held at the Department of Education, Periyar University, Salem from 28th to 30th November.

Reddy, P.V. and Reddy, V.S. (2004) 'Stress and Coping Strategies in Children', *EduTracks*, 3 (10), pp. 30-32.

Reddy, V.R. (2007) '*Classroom Performance of Teacher Trainees in Colleges of Education'*, Ph.D. Thesis, Department of Education, Sri Venkateshwara University, Tirupati.

Reddy, V.S., Koteswari, V.B. and Rao, T.T. (2005) 'Sources of Stress among Adolescents', *Journal of Community Guidance and Research*, 22 (2), pp. 127-138.

Rees, K. (1997) 'Journey of Discovery: *A Longitudinal Study of Learning During A Graduate Professional Programme*', Ph.D. Thesis, Case Western Reserve University, Cleveland.

Reglin, G. and Reitzammer, R.A. (1997) 'Dealing with the Stress of Teachers', *Education,* 118 (4), pp. 590-597.

Rahman (2006) 'Attitude of Malaysian Teachers toward a Performance-Appraisal System', *Essays in Education*, 19, pp. 33-42.

Rizzo, J.R. House, R.J. and Lirtzman, S.I. (1970) 'Role Conflict and Ambiguity in Complex Organizations', *Administrative Science Quarterly*, 15, pp. 150-163.

Robbins, S.P. and Judge, T.A. (2009) *Essentials of Organizational Behaviour* (10th Edition), Upper Saddle River, Prentice Hall: NJ.

Robertson, I.T., Cooper, C.L. and Williams, J. (1990) 'The Validity of the Occupational Stress Indicator', *Work and Stress*, 4, pp. 29-39.

Roe, R.A. (1999) Work Performance: *A Multiple Regulation Perspective*, in C.L. Cooper and I.T. Robertson (eds.), International Review of Industrial and Organizational Psychology (Vol. 14, pp. 231-335), Wiley: Chichester.

Roethlisberger, F. and Dickson, W. (1939) *Management and the Worker*, Harvard University Press: Cambridge.

Roger, D. and *Najarian, B. (1989) Emotional Control Questionnaire, Reteived from* http: //www. scribd.com/doc /53076993/5/Emotion-Control-Questionnaire-ECQ2.

Rose, Raduan. C., Kumar, Naresh. and Pak, Ong.G. (2009) 'The Effect of Organizational Learning on Organizational Commitment, Job Satisfaction and Work Performance', *International Journal of Educational Management*, 25 (6), pp 45-58.

Rosier, R.H. (Ed) (1996) *The Competency Model Handbook,* Vol. 3, Linkage: Boston.

Ross Azura, Z. and Normah, C.D. (2008) 'Teacher Stress: *An Examination of Factors Influencing Teaching Performance in the Rural Elementary Schools*', Paper Presented at the Simposium Held at Sains Kesihatan Kebangsaan Ke 7, Hotel Legend, Koula Lumpur on 18th-19th of June.

Ross, R.R. and Altmair, E.M. (1994) *Interventions in Occupational Stress*, Sage Publications: New York.

Roth, D.L. and Holmes, D.S. (1987) 'Influence of Aerobic Exercise Training and Relaxation Training on Physical and Psychological Health following Stressful Life Events', *Psychosomatic Medicine*, 49, pp. 355-365.

Roth, P.L., BeVier, C.A., Switzer, F.S., and Schippmann, J. S. (1996) 'Meta-analyzing the Relationship between Grades and Job Performance', *Journal of Applied Psychology,* 81. pp. 548-556.

Roth, Philip. L., Purvis, Kristen. L. and Bobko, Philip. (2011) 'A Meta-Analysis of Gender Group Differences for Measures of Job Performance in Field Studies' Research Report Submitted to the Department of Management, Clemson University, Clemson, USA.

Rotundo, M. and Sackett, P.R. (2002) 'The Relative Importance of Task, Citizenship, and Counter Productive Performance to Global Ratings of Job Performance: A Policy-capturing Approach', *Journal of Applied Psychology*, 87, pp. 66-80.

Ruiz-Aranda, Desiree., Castillo, Ruth., Salguero, Jose-Martin and Cabello, Rosario. (2012) 'Short and Midterm Effects of Emotional Intelligence Training on Adolescent Mental Health', *Journal of Adolescent Health,* 2 (3), in Press.

Rupashree, K. (2008) *Know Your Stress–Manage Your Stress,* Neelkamal Publications: Hyderabad.

Russel, D.W., Altmaier, E. and Dawn, V.V. (1987) 'Job-Related Stress, Social Support, and Burnout among Classroom Teachers', *Journal of Applied Psychology*, 72 (2), pp. 269-274.

Sabu, S. and Jangaiah, C. (2005) 'Stress and Teaching Competence', *International Educator,* 17 (1), pp. 19-21.

Sackett, P.R., Zedeck, S. and Fogli, L. (1988) 'Relations between Measures of Typical and Maximum Job Performance', *Journal of Applied Psychology, 73*, pp. 482-486.

Sahaya Mary, R. and Manorama Samuel (2010) 'Influence of Emotional Intelligence on Attitude towards Teaching of Student-teachers', *EduTracks,* 9 (12), pp. 42-46.

Saks, A.M. (1995) 'Longitudinal field Investigation of the Moderating and Mediating Effects of Self-efficacy on the Relationship between Training and Newcomer Adjustment', *Journal of Applied Psychology*, 80, pp. 211-225.

Salami, S.O. (2007) 'Relationship of Emotional Intelligence and Self-efficacy to Work Attitude among Secondary School Teachers in South Western Nigeria', *Essays in Education*, 20, pp. 43-56, Spring.

Salami, S.O. (2008) 'Impact of Job Satisfaction and Organizational Commitment on Organizational Citizenship Bahaviour: The Moderating Role of Group Cohesiveness', *Perspectives in Education*, 24 (1), pp. 40-50.

Salovey, P. and Mayer, J. (1990) 'Emotional Intelligence', *Imagination, Cognition and Personality,* 9, pp. 185-211.

Salovey, P. and Mayer, J. (1997) 'EI Meets Traditional Standards for An Intelligence', *Intelligence*, 27, pp. 267-298.

Salovey, P. and Sluyter, D.J. (eds.) (1997) *Emotional Development and Emotional Intelligence; Implications for Educators*, Basic Books: New York.

Saranya, R. and Velayudham, A. (2008) 'Analyzing Pro-social Behaviour and Emotional Intelligence among University Students', *Psycho lingua*, 38 (2), pp. 126-132.

Satapathy, S. (2003) 'Stress and Behavioural Problems among Visually Impaired Adolescents: Grade and Gender Differences', *Disabilities and Impairment: An Interdisciplinary Research Journal*, 17 (2), pp. 77-85.

Schaubroeck, J., Cotton, J. and Jennings, K. (1989) 'Antecedents and Consequences of Role Stress: A Covariance Structure Analyses, *Journal of Organizational Behaviour*, 10, pp. 35-58.

Schmidt, F.L. and Hunter, J.E. (1989) 'Inter-rater Reliability Co-efficients Cannot be Computed when only one Stimulus is Rated', *Journal of Applied Psychology, 74*, pp. 368-370.

Schmidt, F.L. and Hunter, J.E. (1998) 'The Validity and Utility of Selection Methods in Personnel Psychology: Practical and Theoretical Implications of 85 Years of Research Findings', *Psychological Bulletin*, 124, pp. 262-274.

Schmidt, F.L., Hunter, J.E. and Outerbridge, A.N. (1986) 'Impact of Job Experience and Ability on Job Knowledge, Work Sample Performance, and Supervisory Ratings of Job Performance', *Journal of Applied Psychology*, 71, pp. 432-439.

Schmidt, F.L., Hunter, J.E., Outerbride, A.N. and Goff, S. (1988) 'Joint Relation of Experience and Ability with Job Performance: Test of Three Hypotheses', *Journal of Applied Psychology*, 73, pp. 46-57.

Schmidt, F.L., Viswesvaran, C. and Ones, D.S. (2000) 'Reliability is not Validity and Validity is not Reliability', *Personnel Psychology*, 53, pp. 901-912.

Schuler, R.S. (1980) 'Definition and Conceptualization of Stress in Organizations', *Organizational Behaviour and Human Performance,* 25, pp. 184-215.

Schuler, R.S. (1984) Organizational Stress and Coping: *A Model and Review*, in A.S. Sethi and R.S. Schuler (eds.), Handbook of Organizational Stress Coping Strategies, Ballinger: Cambridge, MA.

Schulman, P. (1995) *Explanatory Style and Achievement in School and Work*, in G. Buchanan and M. Seligman (eds.), Explanatory Style (pp. 159-171), Erlbaum: Mahwah, New Jersey.

Schutte N. S., Malouff, J. M., Hall, L. E., Haggerty, D. J., Cooper, J. T., Golden, C. J. and Dornheim, L. (1998) 'Development and Validation of a Measure of Emotional Intelligence', *Personality and Individual Differences,* 25, pp. 167-177.

Schwab, R.L. (1981) '*The Relationship of Role Conflict, Role Ambiguity, Teacher Background Variables and Perceived Burnout among Teachers',* Dissertation Abstract International, 41 (09-A), (2): 3823-a.

Seldman, S. and Zager, J. (1998) 'The Teacher Burnout Scale', *Educational Research Quarterly,* 11(1), pp. 26-33.

Seligman, M.E.P. and Csikszentmihalyi, M. (2000) 'Positive Psychology: An Introduction', *American Psychologist*, 55, pp. 5-14.

Seyle, Hans (1956) *The Stress of Life,* McGraw-Hill: New York.

Shaft, T.M. and Vessey, I. (1998) 'The Relevance of Application Domain Knowledge: Characterizing the Computer Programme Comprehension Process', *Journal of Management Information Systems*, 15, pp. 51-78.

Shah, Mukti. and Thingujam, Nutankumar. S. (2008) 'Perceived Emotional Intelligence and Ways of Coping among Students', *Journal of the Indian Academy of Applied Psychology*, 34 (1), pp. 83-91.

Shanwal, V.K. (2003) 'A Study of Correlates and Nurturance of Emotional Intelligence in Primary School Children', Retrieved from *http:// www.jmi.nic.in / Research / ab 2003-edn-vinodkumar shanwal.htm*

Sharma, H.C. and Bharadwaj, R. 1995, *Manual for the Scale of Emotional Competencies*, Mapan Bal Nivas: Agra.

Sharpley, C.F., Reynolds, R., Acosta, A. and Dua, J.K. (1996) 'The Presence, Nature and Effects of Job Stress on Physical and Psychological Health at a Large Australian University', *Journal of Educational Administration*, 34 (4), pp. 73-86.

Sheena, Johnson., Cooper, C., Cartwright, S., Ian, D.P.T., and Millet ,C. (2005) 'The Experience of Work-related Stress Across Occupations', *Journal of Managerial Psychology*, 20 (2), pp. 178-187.

Shephard, R. (1999) 'Age and Physical Work Capacity', *Experimental Aging Research*, 25, pp. 331-343.

Shirom, A. (1989) *Burnout in work Organizations*, in C.L. Cooper and I. Robertson (eds.), International Review of Organizational Psychology (pp. 25-48), Wiley: London.

Shirom, A. (2003) Job Related Burnout: *A Review*, in J.C. Quick and I.E. Tetrick (eds.), Handbook of Health Psychology (pp. 245-264), American Psychological Association: Washington DC.

Shrivastava, Anupama. and Mukhopadhyay, Anjana. (2009) 'Alienation and Emotional Intelligence of Adolescents with Internalizing Symptoms', *Journal of the Indian Academy of Applied Psychology,* 35 (1), pp. 99-105.

Shukran, Abdul. Rahman. (2006) 'Attitudes of Malaysian Teachers toward a Performance-Appraisal System', *Journal of Applied Social Psychology,* 36 (12), pp. 331-342.

Siegrist J. (1998) Adverse Health Effects of Effort-Imbalance At Work: *Theory, Empirical Support and Implications for Prevention*, in C.L. Cooper (ed.), Theories of Organizational Stress (pp. 190-204), Oxford University Press: Oxford.

Siegrist, J. (1996) 'Adverse Health Effects of High Effort-low Reward Conditions at Work', *Journal of Occupational Health Psychology*, 1, pp. 27-43.

Sifneos, P.E. (1967) 'Clinical Observations on Some Patients Suffering from a Variety of Psychosomatic Diseases', *Acta Medicina Psychosomatica*, 7, pp. 1-10.

Sifneos, P.E. (1973) 'The Prevalence of Alexithymic Characteristics in Psychosomatic Patients', *Psychotherapy and Psychosomatics*, 22, pp. 255-262.

Sifneos, P.E. (1975) 'Problems of Psychotherapy of Patients with Alexithymic Characteristics and Physical Disease', *Psychotherapy and Psychosomatics*, 26, pp. 65-70.

Singh, D. (2003) *Emotional Intelligence at Work: A Professional Guide*, 2nd ed., Sage Publications: New Delhi.

Singh, D. (2005) '*EQ and Managerial Effectiveness: An International Study'*, D. Litt. Thesis, Bundelkhand University, Jhansi, India.

Singh, D. (2006) *Emotional Intelligence at Work: A Professional Guide*-3rd Edition, Response Books: A Division of Sage Publications, New Delhi.

Singh, S. and Koteswari, V.B. (2006) 'Emotional Intelligence and Coping Resources of Stress among Project Managers', *EduTracks,* 5 (12), pp. 33-36.

Singh, S.K. (2009) 'Leveraging Emotional Intelligence for Managing Executive's Job Stress: A Framework', *Indian Journal of Industrial Relations*, 45 (2), pp. 255-264.

Singh, S.K. and Singh, S. (2008) 'Managing Role Stress through Emotional Intelligence: A Study of Indian Medico Professionals', *International Journal of Indian Culture and Business Management*, 5 (4), pp. 377-396.

Sinha, A.K. and Jain, A.K. (2004) 'Emotional Intelligence: Imperative for the Organizationally Relevant Outcome', *Psychological Studies*, 49 (2), pp. 81-96.

Sinha, Tanuka. Roy., Chatterjee, Debmallya. and Iskanius, Paivi. (2011) 'Measuring Stress among Hospital Nurses: An Empirical Study using Fuzzy Evaluation', *International Journal of Logistics Economics and Globalization,* 3 (2-3), pp. 142-154.

Siu, Oi-ling. (2003) 'Job Stress and Job Performance among Employees in Hong Kong: The Role of Chinese Work Values and Organizational Commitment', *International Journal of Psychology,* 38 (6). , pp. 337-347.

Siu, Oi-ling. (2009) 'A Study of Resiliency among Chinese Health-care Workers: Capacity to Cope with Workplace Stress', *Journal of Research in Personality*, 43, pp. 770-776.

Sjöberg, L. (2008) *Emotional Intelligence and Life Adjustment*, in J.C. Cassady and M.A. Eissa (eds.), Emotional Intelligence: Perspectives on Educational and Positive Psychology (pp. 169-184), Peter Lang Publishing: New York, NY.

Slaski, M. and Cartwright, S. (2003) 'EI Training and Its Implications for Stress, Health and Performance', *Stress and Health*, 19 (4), pp. 233-239.

Slavin, R.E. (1987) *Small Group Methods*, in M.J. Dunkin (ed.), The International Encyclopedia of Teaching and Teacher Education (pp. 237-243), Pergman: Oxford.

Smith, A., Brice, C., Collins, A., Mathews, V. and McNamara, R. (2000) '*The Scale of Occupational Stress: A Further Analysis of the Impact of Demographic Factors and Type of Job*', Research Report Prepared for Centre for Occupational and Health Psychology, School of Psychology, Cardiff University, Retrieved from *http:// www.isma.org.uk/Pdf/publications/crr00311.Pdf.*

Smith, B.L. (1989) '*The Effect of Situational Constraints on the Job Satisfaction/Job Performance Relationship: Is there a choice?* Ph.D. Thesis, University of Washington, Seattle.

Smith, C. A., Organ, D.W. and Near, J. P. (1983) 'Organizational Citizenship Behaviour: Its Nature and Antecedents', *Journal of Applied Psychology*, 68, pp. 653-663.

Smith, M. K. (2002) 'Howard Gardner and Multiple Intelligences' Retrieved from http://www.infed.org/thinkers/gardner.htm, on November 15, 2011.

Smith, T .W. (1992) 'Hostility and Health: Current Status of a Psychosomatic Hypotheses', *Health Psychology*, 11(3), pp. 139-150.

Sobha, B.C. (2006) 'Emotional Intelligence and Frustration Tolerance of Adolescents', *International Educator*, 18 (2), pp. 39-41.

Sofer, C. (1970) *Men in Mid Career,* Cambridge University Press: London.

Sonnentag, S. (2000) *Expertise at Work: Experience and Excellent Performance*, in C. L. Cooper and I.T. Robertson (eds.), International Review of Industrial and Organizational Psychology (pp. 223-264), Wiley: Chichester.

Soyibo, K. (1994) 'Occupational Stress Factors and Coping Strategies among Jamaican High School Science Teachers', *Research in Science and Technology Education*, 12 (2), pp. 187-192.

Speier, C. and Frese, M. (1997) 'Self-efficacy As A Mediator between Resources At Work and Personal Initiative: A Longitudinal Field Study in East Germany', *Human Performance*, 10, pp. 171-192.

Spencer, L. and Spencer, S. (1993) *Competence at Work: Models of Superior Performance*, Wiley: New York.

Spencer, L.M., McClelland, D.C. and Kelner, S. (1997) '*Competency Assessment Method: History and State of the Art*', Paper Presented at a Meeting of the Consortium for Social and Emotional Competency in the Workplace, Boston, October.

Spielberger, C. (ed.) (2004) *Encyclopedia of Applied Psychology,* Academic Press: New York.

Spielberger, C.D. and Vagg, P.R. (1999) *Job Stress Survey: Professional Manual*, Psychological Assessment Resources: Lutz, Florida.

Sprenger, Jeff. (2011) '*Stress and Coping Behaviours among Primary School Teachers*', Master's Thesis, Department of Health Education, East Carolina University.

Srivastava, A.K. (1999) *Management of Occupational Stress: Theories and Practice*, Gyan Publishing House: New Delhi.

Srivastava, A.K. and Krishna, A. (1991) 'Development of a Functional Role Stress Scale', *Advances in Psychology*, 6, pp. 11-17.

Srivastava, A.K. and Singh, A.P. (1984) 'Construction and Standardization of an Occupational Stress Index: A Pilot Study', *Indian Journal of Clinical Psychology*, 8, pp. 8-12.

Srivastava, S., Hagtvet, K.A. and Sen, A.K. (1994) 'A Study of Role Stress and Job Anxiety among Three Groups of Employees in a Private Sector Organization', *Social Science International*, 10 (1-2), pp. 25-30.

Stajkovic, A.D. and Luthans, F. (1997) 'A Meta-analysis of the Effects of Organizational Behaviour Modification on Task Performance', *Academy of Management Journal*, 40, pp. 1122-1149.

Stajkovic, A.D. and Luthans, F. (1998) 'Self-efficacy and Work-related Performance: A Meta-analysis', *Psychological Bulletin*, 124, pp. 240-261.

Staw, B.M. (1975) 'Attribution of the Causes of Performance: A New Alternative Interpretation of Cross Sectional Research on Organizations', *Organizational Behaviour and Human Performance*, 13, pp. 414-432.

Staw, B.M. and Barsade, S.G. (1993) 'Affect and Managerial Performance: A Test of the Sadder-but-wiser *vs.* Happier-and-smarter Hypotheses', *Administrative Science Quarterly,* 38, pp. 304-331.

Staw, B.M., Sutton, R.I. and Pelled, L.H. (1994) 'Employee Positive Emotion and Favorable Outcomes at the Workplace', *Organization Science,* 5, pp. 51-71.

Steel, R.P. and Lloyd, R.F. (1988) 'Cognitive, Affective, and Behavioural Outcomes of Participation in Quality Circles: Conceptual and Empirical Findings', *Journal of Applied Behavioural Science, 24,* pp. 1-17.

Steele, C.M. (1997) 'A Threat in the Air: How Stereotypes Shape Intellectual Identity and Performance', *American Psychologist*, 52, pp. 613-629.

Subramaniam, S.R. and Cheong, L.S. (2008) 'Emotional Intelligence of Science and Mathematics Teachers: A Malaysian Experience', *Journal of Science and Mathematics Education in Southeast Asia*, 31 (2), pp. 132-163.

Sukirno, Sununta. Siengthai, (2011) 'Does Participative Decision-making Affect Lecturer Performance in Higher Education?', *International Journal of Educational Management*, 25 (5), pp. 486-494.

Sullivan, S.E. and Bhaget, R.S. (1992) 'Organizational Stress, Job Satisfaction and Job Performance: Where do we go from here?', *Journal of Management,* 18 (2), pp. 353-374.

Sun, Wei., Wu, Hui. And Wang, Lie. (2011) 'Occupational Stress and Its Related Factors among University Teachers in China', *Journal of Occupational Health*, 53 (4), pp. 280-286.

Sushila, S. (2004) *Stress in Education: Indian Experience*, Rawat Publications: New Delhi.

Sweeney, P. (1999, February 14) 'Teaching New Hires to Feel at Home', *New York Times*, p. C4.

Syed, S. S.S., Rohany, Nasir., Mohammad, A. S., Mohamed, A. and Muhammad, B. M. (2012) 'The Role of Emotional Intelligence on Job Satisfaction among School Teachers', *The Social Sciences,* 7 (1), pp. 125-129.

Taj, Haseen. (1991) '*Social, Psychological and Situational Correlates of Administrative Behaviour of Secondary School Heads*', Ph.D. Thesis, Department of Education, Bangalore University, Bangalore.

Taj, Haseen. (2004) *Teachers Participation in School Administration Scale*, Rakhi Prakashan: Agra.

Taylor, F.W. (1911) *Principles of Scientific Management*, Harper and Row: New York.

Taylor, G.J. (2001) *Low Emotional Intelligence and Mental Illness*, in J. Ciarrochi and J.P. Forgas (eds.), Emotional Intelligence in Everyday Life: A Scientific Inquiry (pp. 67-81), Psychology Press/Taylor and Francis: Philadelphia.

Tellenbeck, S., Brenner, S.O. and Lofgren, H. (1983) 'Teacher Stress: Explanatory Model Building', *Journal of Occupational Psychology*, 56, pp. 19-33.

Terborg, J.R. (1985) *Working Women and Stress*, in T.A. Beehr and R.S. Bhagat (eds.), Human Stress and Cognition in Organizations, John Wiley: New York.

Tett, R. P., Jackson, D. N. and Rothstein, M. (1991) 'Personality Measures as Predictors of Job Performance: A Meta-analytic Review', *Personnel Psychology*, 44, pp. 703-742.

Thondike, E.L. (1920) 'Intelligence and Its Uses', *Harper's*, 140, pp. 227-235.

Tiwary, P.S.N. and Srivastava, N. (2004) 'Schooling and Development of Emotional Intelligence', *Journal of the National Academy of Psychology*, 49 (2 and 3), pp. 151-154.

Torres, R.M., Lambert, M.D. and Lawver, R.G. (2009) '*Job Stress among Secondary Agriculture Teachers: An Explanatory Study*', Conference Proceedings of American Association for Agricultural Education Research, held from May 20-22, Louisville, KY, pp. 587-97.

Totterdell, P., Kellett, S., Teuchmann, K. and Briener, R.B. (1998) 'Evidence of Mood Linkage in Workgroup', *Journal of Personality and Social Psychology*, 74, pp. 1504-1515.

Trapp, Caryn S. (2010) '*The Association among Emotional Intelligence, Resilience, and Academic Performance of Pre-service Teachers*', Project Work, Department of Educational Psychology, University of Phoenix.

Traverse, C.J. and Cooper, C.L. (1993) 'Mental Health, Job Satisfaction and Occupational Stress among UK Teachers', *Work and Stress*, 7 (3), pp. 203-219.

Traverse, C.J. and Cooper, C.L. (1996) *Teachers Under Pressure: Stress in the Teaching Profession*, Routledge: London.

Trist, E.L. and Bamforth, K.W. (1951) 'Some Social and Psychological Consequences of the Long-wall Method of Coal-getting', *Human Relations*, 4, pp. 3-38.

Tsai, E., Fung, L. and Chow, L. (2006) 'Sources and Manifestations of Stress in Female Kindergarten Teachers', *International Educational Journal*, 7 (3), pp. 364-370.

Tseng, Hsiu-yueh. (2011) '*Influence of Emotional Intelligence and Burnout on Public Elementary School Teachers' Quality of Life*', Master's Dissertation, Department of Graduates International Business, University of Taipei, Taiwan.

Tsouloupas, C.N., Carson, R.L., Matthews, R., Grawitch, M.J. and Barber, L.K. (2010) 'Exploring the Association between Teachers' Perceived Student Misbehaviour and Emotional Exhaustion: The Importance of Teacher Efficacy Beliefs and Emotion Regulation', *Educational Psychology*, 30 (2), pp. 173-189.

Tubbs, T.C. and Collins, J.M. (2000) 'A Meta-analysis of the Relationships between Role Ambiguity, Role Conflict, and Job Performance', *Journal of Management*, 26, pp. 155-169.

Tyagi, S. K. (2004) 'Emotional Intelligence of Secondary Teachers in Relation to Gender and Age', *Journal of Educational Research and Extension*, 41 (3), pp. 39-45.

Umadevi, M.R. (2009) 'Relationship between Emotional Intelligence, Achievement Motivation and Academic Achievement', *EduTracks*, 8 (12), pp. 31-35.

Upadhyaya, P. (2006) 'Personality of Emotionally Intelligent Student', *Journal of Educational Studies*, 4 (1 and 2), pp. 37-41.

Upadhyaya, P. (2008) *Emotional Intelligence in Teacher Education*, Anubhav Publishing House: Allahabad.

Upton, G. and Varma, V. (eds.) (1996) *Stress in Special Education Needs Teachers*, Aldershot: Arena.

Uris, A. (1972) 'How Managers Ease Job Pressures', *International Management*, 27, pp. 45-46.

Usha Rao. (2008) 'Emotional Maturity and Role of the Teacher', *EduTracks*, 7 (8), p. 12

Ushasree, S. and Jamuna, D. (1990) '*Role Conflict and Job Stress among Special and General School Teachers*', Paper Presented at the 27th Annual Conference of IAAP, Aligarh Muslim University, Aligarh.

Ushasri, V. (2007) '*An Analysis of Occupational Stress of Special Education Teachers of Salem District'*, Paper Presented in the International Conference on Educational Research in the Era of Globalization held at the Department of Education, Periyar University, Salem from 28th to 30th November.

Uzole, T. (….) '*Professional Stress among Latvian Teachers'*, Research Paper Submitted to the Daugavpils University, Daugavpils, Latvia.

Vagg, P.R. and Spielberger, C.D. (1998) 'Occupational Stress: Measuring Job Pressure and Organizational Support in the Workplace', *Journal of Occupational Health Psychology*, 3(4), pp. 294-305.

Vaijayanthi, R. and Sunny, J. (2010) 'Stress among Student Teachers in Coimbatore City', *Research Highlights*, 20 (1), pp. 51-57.

Van Dyne, L. and LePine, J.A. (1998) 'Helping and Voice Extra-role Behaviours: Evidence of Construct and Predictive Validity', *Academy of Management Journal*, 41, pp. 108-119.

Van Rooy, D.L. and Viswesvaran, C. (2004) 'Emotional Intelligence: A Meta-analytic Investigation of Predictive Validity and Logical Net', *Journal of Vocational Behaviour*, Vol. 65, pp. 71-95.

Van Scotter, J.R. and Motowidlo, S.J. (1996) 'Interpersonal Facilitation and Job Dedication as Separate Facets of Contextual Performance', *Journal of Applied Psychology*, 81, pp. 525-531.

Vance, B., Miller, S., Humphreys, S. and Reynolds, F. (1989) 'Sources and Manifestation of Occupational Stress as Reported by Full Time Teachers Working in a BIA School', *Journal of American Indian Education*, 28 (2).

Vanessa, D., Fabio, S. and Gerald, M. (2006) *Linking Emotional Intelligence and Performance at Work: Current Research Evidence with Individuals and Groups*, Lawrence Erlbaum Associates Publishers: London.

Vashishtha, A. and Mishra, P.C. (2005) 'Occupational Stress and Social Support as Predictors of Affective Commitment', *Journal of Community Guidance and Research*, 22 (1), pp. 76-80.

Vergara, Maria. Belen., Smith, Norris. and Keele, Bruce. (2010) 'Emotional Intelligence, Coping Responses, and Length of Stay as Correlates of Acculturative Stress among International University Students in Thailand', *Procedia-Social and Behavioural Sciences*, 5, pp. 1498-1504.

Verma, S. and Choudhary, O.P. (2009) 'Stress in Farmers: An Exploration', *Asian Journal of Psychology and Education*, 42 (1-2), pp. 23-26.

Vijayalakshmi, A., Aminabhavi, Shamuth. and Kamble, V. (2004) 'A Study of Work Motivation and Stress Coping Behaviour of Technical Personnel at a Railway Workshop', *Journal of Community Guidance and Research*, 21 (3), pp. 227-232.

Vijayalakshmi, G. (2004) 'Stress among Women Lecturers Working in Colleges in Relation to Some Variables', *EduTracks*, 4 (4), pp. 29-30.

Vijayalakshmi, V., Bhattacharyya, Sanghamitra., Bhartia, Abha. and Muthuvel, R. (2008) 'Emotional Intelligence and Social Reticence of Post-graduate Female Students', *Journal of the Indian Academy of Applied Psychology,* 34 (1), pp. 93-100.

Vinchur, A.J., Schippmann, J.S., Switzer, F.S. and Roth, P.L. (1998) 'A Meta-analytic Review of Predictors of Job Performance for Sales People', *Journal of Applied Psychology*, 83, pp. 586-597.

Viswesvaran, C. (1993) '*Modeling Job Performance: Is There a General Factor?*' Ph.D. Thesis, University of Iowa, Iowa City, IA.

Viswesvaran, C. and Ones, D.S. (1995) 'Theory Testing: Combining Psychometric Meta-analysis and Structural Equations Modeling', *Personnel Psychology*, 48, pp. 865-885.

Viswesvaran, C. and Ones, D.S. (2000) 'Perspectives on Models of Job Performance', *International Journal of Selection and Assessment*, 8, pp. 216-226.

Viswesvaran, C., Ones, D.S. and Schmidt, F.L. (1996) 'Comparative Analysis of the Reliability of Performance Ratings', *Journal of Applied Psychology*, 81, pp. 557-574.

Viswesvaran, C., Sanchez, J.I. and Fisher, J. (1999) 'The Role of Social Support in the Process of Work Stress: A Meta-analysis', *Journal of Vocational Behaviour*, 54 (2), pp. 314-334.

Vroom, V.H. (1964) *Work and Motivation*, Wiley: New York.

Waldman, D.A. (1994) 'Contributions of total Quality Management to the Theory of Work Performance', *Academy of Management Review*, 19, pp. 510-536.

Waldman, D.A. and Spangler, W.D. (1989) Putting Together the Pieces: A Closer look at the Determinants of Job Performance, *Human Performance,* 2(1), pp. 29-59.

Wall, T. D. and Davids, K. (1992) *Shop Floor Work Organization and Advanced Manufacturing Technology*, in C. L. Cooper and I. R. Robertson (eds.), International Review of Industrial and Organizational Psychology (pp. 363-398), Wiley: Chichester.

Wall, T. D., Jackson, P. R. and Davids, K. (1992) 'Operator Work Design and Robotics System Performance: A Serendipitous Field Study, *Journal of Applied Psychology*, 77, pp. 353-362.

Wall, T.D. and Clegg, C.W. (1981) 'A Longitudinal Field Study of Group Work Redesign', *Journal of Occupational Behaviour*, 2, pp. 31-49.

Wall, T.D. and Jackson, P.R. (1995) *New Manufacturing Initiatives and Shop Floor Job Design*, in A. Howard (ed.), The Changing Nature of work (pp. 139-174), Jossey-Bass: San Francisco, CA.

Wall,T.D., Corbett, M., Martin, R., Clegg, C.W. and Jackson, P.R. (1990) 'Advanced Manufacturing Technology, Work Design, and Performance: A Change Study', *Journal of Applied Psychology*, 75, pp. 691-697.

Wang, Pei. And Zhang, Gouli. (2007) 'Survey of Occupational Stress of Secondary and Elementary School Teachers and the Lessons Learned', *Chinese Education and Society*, 40 (5), pp. 32-39.

Wang, Z., Lan, Y., Li, J. and Wang, m. (2001) 'Appraisal of Occupational Stress and Strain in Primary and Secondary School Teachers', *Journal of West China University of medical Sciences*, 33 (3), pp. 392-395.

Webster's New Universal Unabridged Dictionary (1996) Barnes Noble: New York.

Wechler, D. (1940) 'Non Intellective Factors in General Intelligence', *Psychological Bulletin*, 37, pp. 444-445.

Wechsler, D. (1939) *The Measurement of Adult Intelligence,* Williams and Wilkins: Baltimore.

Wechsler, D. (1943) 'Non-intellective Factors in General Intelligence', *Journal of Abnormal Social Psychology*, 38, pp. 100-104.

Wechsler, D. (1944) *The Measurement of Adult Intelligence (3rd ed.),* Williams and Wilkins: Baltimore.

Weisinger, H. (1998) *Emotional Intelligence At Work*, Jossey-Bass: San Francisco.

Weiskopf, P.E. (1980) 'Burnout among Teachers of Exceptional Children', *Exceptional Children*, 47, pp. 18-23.

Westerhouse, M.A. (1979) '*The Effect of Tenure, Role Conflict and Role Conflict Resolution on the Work Orientation and Burnout of Teachers'*, Dissertation Abstract International, 41 (01A), 8014928, 174.

Westman, M. and Eden, D. (1992) 'Exclusive Role Demand and Subsequent Performance', *Journal of Organizational Behaviour*', 13, pp. 519-529.

Williams, H.W. (2008) 'Characteristics that Distinguish Outstanding Urban Principals' Emotional Intelligence, Social Intelligence and Environmental Adaptation', *Journal of Management Development*, 27 (1), pp. 36-54.

Williams, K. and Alliger, G. (1994) 'Role Stressors, Mood Spillover, and Perceptions of Work-family Conflict in Employed Parents', *Academy of Management Journal*, 37, pp. 837-868.

Williams, L.J. and Anderson, S.E. (1991) 'Job Satisfaction and Organizational Commitment as Predictors of Organizational Citizenship and in-role Behaviours', *Journal of Management*, 17, pp. 601-617.

Williams, S. and Cooper, C. L. (1998) 'Measuring Occupational Stress: Development of the Pressure Management Indicator' *Journal of Occupational Health Psychology*, 3 (4), pp. 306-321.

Wisniewski, L. and Gargiulo, R.M. (1997) 'Occupational Stress and Burnout among Special Educators: A Review of the Literature', *Journal of Special Education,* 31 (3), pp. 325-346.

Woitaszewski, S.A. and Aalsma, M.C. (2004) 'The Contribution of Emotional Intelligence to the Social and Academic Success of Gifted Adolescents as Measured by the Multifactor Emotional Intelligence Scale-Adolescent Version', *Roper Review,* 27 (1), p. 25.

Wolff, H. G. (1950) '*Life Stress and Bodily Disease - A Formulation in Life Stress and Bodily Diseases*', Proceedings of Association for Research in Nervous and Mental Disorder, 2-3 of December, Williams and Wilkins, Baltimore, New York.

Wong, Chi-Sum., Wong, Ping-Man. And Peng, K.Z. (2010) 'Effect of Middle-Level Leader and Teacher Emotional Intelligence on School Teachers' Job Satisfaction', *Educational Management, Administration and Leadership,* 38 (1), pp. 59-70.

Wong, C-S. and Law, K.S. (2002) 'The Effects of Leader and Follower Emotional Intelligence on Performance and Attitude: an Exploratory Study', *Leadership Quarterly*, 13, pp. 243-274.

Wong, C-S., Law, K.S. and Wong, P-M. (2004) 'Development and Validation of a Forced Choice Emotional Intelligence Measure for Chinese Respondents in Hong Kong', *Asia Pacific Journal of Management*, 21, pp. 535-559.

Wong, C-S., Wong, P-M. and Law, K.S. (2007) 'Evidence of the Practical Utility of Wong's Emotional Intelligence Scale in Hong Kong and Mainland China', *Asia Pacific Journal of Management*, 24, pp. 43-60.

Wu, Hui., Sun, Wei. and Wang, Lie. *(2011)* 'Factors Associated with Occupational Stress among Chinese Female Emergency Nurses', Ph.D. Thesis, Department of Social Medicine, School of Public Health, China Medical University, Shenyang, Liaoning, PR China.

Wu, S., Li, J., Wang, Z. and Li, H. (2006) 'Intervention on Occupational Stress among Teachers in the Middle Schools in China', *Stress and Health*, 22 (5), pp. 329-336.

Yagil, D. (1998) 'Occupational Stress among Inexperienced Teachers', *International Journal of Stress Management*, 5 (3), pp. 179-188.

Yahaya, A., Hashim, S. and Kim, T.S. (2010) 'Occupational Stress among Technical Teachers in Technical School in Johore, Melacca and Negeri Sembilan', Reteived from http:// eprints.utm.my/10613/.

Yahaya, N., Yahaya, A., Tamyes, F.A., Ismail, J. and Jaalam, S. (2010) 'The Effect of Various Modes of Occupational Stress, Job Satisfaction, Intention to Leave and Absenteism on Companies Commission of Malaysia', *Australian Journal of Basic and Applied Sciences*, 4 (7), pp. 1676-1684.

Yang, X., Ge, C., Hu, B., Chi, T. and Wang, L. (2009) 'Relationship between Quality of Life and Occupational stress among Teachers', *Public Health*, 12 (11), pp. 750-755.

Yang, X.W., Wang, Z.M., Lan, Y.J. and Wang, M.Z. (2004) 'Comparing the Occupational Stress and Work Ability among the Police Officers, Doctors and Teachers', *Journal of Sichuan University, Medical Science Edition,* 35 (2), pp. 251-254.

Yerks, R. and Dodson, J.D. (1908) 'The Relationship of Stimulus to Rapidity of Habit Formation', *Journal of Comparative Neurological Psychology*, 18, pp. 459-72.

Yong, and Wang. (2011) '*Research on the Sources of Occupational Stress of College Teachers'*, Research Paper Presented in the International Conference on Human Health and Biomedical Engineering (HHBE), held at the College of Arts, Changchun University of Technology, Changchun, China, from 19-22 August.

Zeidner, M., Matthews, G. and Roberts, R. D. (2004) 'Emotional Intelligence in the Workplace: A Critical Review', *Applied Psychology*, 53, pp. 371-399.

Zeidner, M., Matthews, G. and Roberts, R.D. (2009) *What we know about Emotional Intelligence: How it Affects Learning, Work, and our Mental Health*, MIT Press: Cambridge, MA.

Zipkin, A. (2000, May 31) 'The Wisdom of Thought Fulness', *New York Times*, pp. C1, C10.

INDEX

A

Absence of fairness, 30

Analysis of EI, OS and JP of higher secondary teachers, 169-

Assumptions, 234

B

Bar-On, 12

Breakdown of community, 30

Burnout, 32

C

Campbell, 35

Clinton, Bill, 53

Commitment, 29

Components of EI, 7

- self-awareness, 8
- self-regulation, 8
- serf-motivation, 8
- social awareness, 8
- social skill, 8

Concept, 3

Construction of research tools, 147

Correlation studies, 218-223

D

Definition, 3

Description of rating scale, 148-154

Design of the study, 146-147

Development of the research tools, 148

Differential analysis, 191-218

E

EISA, 61

Emotion, 4

Emotional assimilation, 11

Emotional dissonance, 53

Emotional Intelligence, 3, 5, 61, 232

Emotional perception, 11

Environmental factors, 155

F

Findings, 241

Four branch ability of emotional intelligence, 10

G

Goleman, Daniel, 5, 13, 16

Goleman's mixed model of EI, 13-16

- motivation, 15
- self awareness, 14
- self regulation, 14
- social skills, 15

H

Higher secondary teachers, 233

Home work interface, 154

HRM, 45

Hypothesis of the study, 235

I

Importance of EI, 16

Inspiration, 1

Insufficient reward, 29

Interpersonally oriented behaviour, 157, 159, 185, 186, 187

Intra-sender role conflict, 24

Introduction, 1-3

IQ, 4

J

Job dissatisfaction, 33

Job performance, 34, 233

- concept, 34-36
- definitions, 34-36
- determinants, 36-37
- meaning, 34-36
- perspectives, 37-51
  - individual differences, 38-39
  - performance regulation perspective, 40-42
  - relationship among various perspectives, 42-43
  - situational perspective, 39-40
- theories of Borman and Motowidlo's theory of conceptual performance, 47-48
- theories of Campbell's taxonomy of job performance, 46-47
- theories of job performance, 45
- theories of Murphy's theory of job performance, 49-51
- theories of Viswesvaran's theory of Job performance, 48-49.
- types of performance, 43
  - contextual performance, 44
  - relationship between task and contextual performance, 44
  - task performance, 43-44

Job performance of higher secondary teachers assessed by teachers self-ratings and principal's ratings, 189-191

Job tenure, 29

K

Knowledgement, 1

L

Lack of control, 29

Leadership qualities, 158, 159

Level of EI of highcr sccondary teachers, 171

Level pf JP of higher secondary teachers, 180-184

- and accordance with teachers self-ratings and head master's ratings, 185-189

Locale and sample of the study, 163, 240

M

Managerial capabilities, 158, 159, 185

Mayer and Salovey's conception, 10

Meaning, 3

Mental ill health, 32

Mixed model of EI of Bar-On, 12-13

Motivation, 1

N

Natioanl Policy on Education, 1, 2

Need for EI for bhigher secondary teachers, 1718

Need of the study, 236-239

O

Objectives of the study, 234

Occupational stress, 18-34, 233

- burnout theory, 29
- concept of occupational stress, 18-19
- consequences of, 31
  - physiological diseases, 31
  - psychological diseases, 31
  - unwanted feelings and behaviours, 31
- definition of occupational stress, 18-19
- demand-control/support model, 28-29
- environment specific stressors, 26
- individual related stressors, 26-28
- international theories, 25
- inter-role conflict, 24
- job related stressors, 21
- meaning of occupational stress, 18-19

nature and sources of stress, 21
organization specific stressors, 23
person role conflict, 24
role ambiguity, 23
role conflict, 24
symptoms, 20-21
transactional theories, 30
cognitive phenomenological theory, 30
effort-reward imbalance model, 30
work stress theories/models, 25
Organizational structure and climate, 154
Overwiew of the research reviewed, 130-131

P

PDLQ, 187
Performance, 29
Personal and professional efficiency, 154
Personal discipline, 158, 159

R

Relationship between EI, occupational stress and job performance, 51
EI and Occupational stress, 51-52
OC and JP, 52-53
EI and JP, 53-54Cooper, 55
Relationship between EQ and IQ, 6-7
Relationship management, 14
Relationship studies EI, OS and JP (India), 85-88
Bajwa, 85
Bhagat, 86
Darolia, 86
Garg, 86
Kauts, 86
Latha, 87
Mishra, 87
Poornima, 87
Rathi, 88
Singh, 88
Relationship studies on EI, OS and job performance, 123-129
Reliability of research tools, 160-162
Roosevelt, Franklin, 53

S

Salovey and Mayer, 15
SCAT, 61
Scope of the study, 235
Self awareness, 13, 173
Self management, 13, 174
Singh, Dalip, 5
Skills, 11
Social awareness 174
Social skilss, 174
Sources and level of OS of higher secondary teachers, 175-180
Statement of the problem, 132-145
assumption, 135
higher secondary teachers, 134
hypothesis, 136
introduction, 132
job performance, 134
need of the study, 137-145
objectives, 134-135
occupational stress, 133
scope of study, 136
Statistical techniques used in study, 166
Stepwise multiple regression analysis, 224-230
Studies on EI of other professionals (abroad), 98-99
Studies on EI of other professionals (India), 64-67
Faye, 64
Jadhav, 65
Krishnaveni, 65
Prashanthi, 65
Punia, 65
Puri, Anju, 65
Rajkhowa, 66
Ramachandran, 67
Singh, 67

Sinha, 67
Studies on EI of students (abroad), 96-98
Studies on EI of students and student teachers (India), 60-64
Bai, 60
Indu, 61
Koneri, 61
Mahajan, 61
Nagpal, 61
Panda, 62
Panday, 62
Punia, 62
Saranya, 62
Shah, 62
Shanwal, 63
Shrivastava, 63
Sobha, 63
Tiwary, 63
Umadevi, 63
Upadhyaya, 64
Vijayalakshmi, 64
Studies on EI of teachers (abroad), 88-96
Alfredo, 88-89
Augustolanda, J.M., 91
Beach, 89
Brackett, 89
Broli, 89
Chan, 90
Dominguez-Cruz, 90
Fernandez, 90
Hasket, 90
Kafetsios, 91
Kaplan, 91
Karakus, 91
Karim, 92
Kimman, 92
Lee, 92
Lordanoglou, 93
Malik, 93
Nahid, 93
Platsidou, 94
Rastegar, 94
Salami, 94
Syed, 95
Trapp, 95
Tseng, 95
Tsouloupas, 95
Wong, 95
Studies on EI of teachers (India), 56-60
Amirtha, 57
Bansibihari, 57
Edannur, 57
Jayanthi, 57
Latha, 58
Lenka, 58
Manoharan, 58
Neelakandan, 58
Padhi, 59
Poornima, 59
Subrmaniam, 60
Tyagi, 60
Williams, 60
Khan, 58
Studies on JP of teachers (abroad), 116-123
Studies on JP of teachers and other professionals (India), 82-85
Anuradha, 82
Bansibihari, 82
Biswas, 83
Giri, 83
Kumaran, 83
Kumaraswamy, 83
Muralidharan, 84
Raju, 84
Reddy, 84, 85
Studies on occupational stress of higher education teachers (abroad), 110-113
Studies on occupational stress of other professionals (abroad), 113-116
Studies on occupational stress of other professionals (India), 78-82

Bakshi, 78
Basu, 78
Chandraiah, 78
John, 79
Katyal, 79
Kaur, 79
Latha, 80
Mishra, 80
Mukhopadhyay, 80
Ojha, 80
Sinha, 81
Vashishtha, 81
Verma, 81
Vijalakshmi, 81
Viswesvaran, 82

Studies on occupational stress of school teachers (abroad), 99-110

Studies on occupational stress of teachers (India), 67-75
Aftab, 68
Anbuchelvan, 68
Balaswamy, 68
Chand, 68
Chopra, 69
Chturvedi, 69
Jayamma, 74
John, 69
Kaur, 69
Kumar, 70
Kumar, Manoj, 70
Mathew, 70
Naik, 70
Padmaja, 71
Poornima, 71
Ramkumar, 72
Rao, 72
Ravichandran, 72
Reddy, 73
Sabu, 74
Ushasree, 74
Ushasri, 74
Vijayalaskmi, 75

Studies on stress of students and student teachers (India), 75-78
Adsul, 75
Behere, 76
Kashyap, 76
Rao, 76
Reddy, 77
Satapathy, 77
Vijayanthi, 77

Suggestions, 256

T

Task oriented behaviour, 157, 159, 185
Teacher's personality and burnout, 33
Theories/moels of EI, 9-10
Thorndike, Edward, 3

U

Utility.35

V

Validity of the research tools content validity, 162
Validity of the research tools, 162
criterion validity, 162
face validity, 162
intrinsic validity, 162
Value conflict, 30

W

Wechsler, David, 3
Work overload, 29
Written and oral skilss, 185

Z

Zafer, 238
Zeidner, 150